A Study Companion to
Introduction to the Hebrew Bible

RYAN P. BONFIGLIO

Fortress Press

Minneapolis

A STUDY COMPANION TO INTRODUCTION TO THE HEBREW BIBLE
Second Edition

Cover design: Tory Herman
Cover image © Erich Lessing / Art Resource, NY

Library of Congress Cataloging-in-Publication Data
Print ISBN: 978-1-4514-8361-1
eBook ISBN: 978-1-4514-8423-6

The paper used in this publication meets the minimum requirements of American National Standard for Information Sciences — Permanence of Paper for Printed Library Materials, ANSI Z329.48-1984.

Manufactured in the U.S.A.

CONTENTS

FOR THE STUDENTS:
HOW TO USE THIS GUIDE

This study guide is intended to help you get the most out of *Introduction to the Hebrew Bible*—to further your understanding of the biblical narrative and to spark your critical thinking about the personalities, themes, and genres of writing in the Bible, and the various ways of interpreting these. Each section of the guide corresponds to a chapter in the book and includes key terms, key figures, primary sources, a summary of the key points of each chapter, and additional readings with close reading tips and questions for discussion and reflection.

Before you begin reading the text, or after reading a chapter to ensure you understood the main ideas, read the *Key Points*. These offer a basic overview of each chapter's major themes and issues.

Also before you read each part, it might be useful to note the *Key Terms* and *Key Personalities* listed in the corresponding section of this guide. These are the headings for a selected list of terms (concepts particular to a biblical book or period, names of important geographical locations, terms important for exegesis or interpretation, etc.) and one of significant individuals. You will want to be at least familiar with these by the time you have finished reading the section. Many of the key terms are listed in the glossary of the textbook as well.

Excerpts from primary sources are included as often as possible, including biblical and extra-biblical sources. The primary source readings in this study companion were selected with the goal of introducing you, by way of the texts themselves, to the important themes in biblical interpretation. They were selected with the hope that through them you will get even a brief glimpse of the richness and complexity of the ancient world. Please consider them an invitation to go further in your explorations of biblical studies.

The *Study Companion* ends with a guide to writing exegetical research papers. In this last chapter you will find a helpful step by step guide, beginning with selecting your text, and ending with polishing your final draft. You will be introduced to a number of methods of text analysis, including: literary criticism, source criticism, form criticism, socio-historical interpretation, and history of interpretation. The guide also includes bibliographies of reference works, commentaries, online resources, and periodical literature, which will all be helpful supplements to your own reading of the text.

Introduction

What Are the Hebrew Bible and Old Testament?

Key Points

Christianity and Judaism are often described as "religions of the book" due to the central role the Bible plays in both traditions. As a result, it is important to ask what *type* of book the Hebrew Bible or the Christian Old Testament is? How is it arranged? When were its texts written, translated, and accepted as a fixed collection? What sort of literature does it include? How do we attend to its interpretation? Thus understanding the Hebrew Bible involves not only knowing more about its content, but also about its history and development as a collection of books.

The Hebrew Bible is actually more like a library than an individual book. In the Jewish tradition, it consists of twenty-four books arranged in three divisions (the Law, the Prophets, and the Writings). These books were written over a long period of time and reflect diverse theological perspectives. This "library" also includes various types of literature: historical narratives, poetry, law, prophecy, and wisdom literature. In light of its complexity, scholars have traditionally analyzed the Hebrew Bible using multiple interpretive methods, such as source, form, and redaction criticism. More recently, scholars have begun to utilize insights from other fields, including ancient Near Eastern studies, sociology, and art history, to shed new light on the meaning and background of biblical literature.

The books of the Hebrew Bible were originally written and preserved on individual scrolls. However, we do not have access to these original texts today. Modern English translations are based on complete manuscripts of the Hebrew Bible from the tenth and eleventh centuries CE. The form of the Hebrew Bible in these manuscripts was established by ancient scribes known as the Masoretes. Much earlier evidence of biblical books is found among the Dead Sea Scrolls (third century BCE–first century CE), but these texts are mostly preserved in small fragments. Though written predominantly in Hebrew, biblical scrolls were translated into Greek by the second century BCE. The list of books we have in the Hebrew Bible today was first accepted as "canonical" in the first century CE. Early Christianity recognized the content of the Hebrew Bible as part of its Scriptures, but slightly different canons are used in Protestant, Roman Catholic, Greek Orthodox, and other Eastern churches.

Key Terms

Canon   The term canon, meaning "rule" or "measuring stick," refers to the corpus of biblical books viewed as sacred Scripture. The canon of the Hebrew Bible, which consists of twenty-four books, emerged gradually over time and attained its final form in the first century CE. The Christian Old Testament includes the same content, but in a slightly different arrangement.

Septuagint (LXX)   The Septuagint is the Greek translation of the Old Testament. Its name comes from the legendary *Letter of Aristeas*, which claims that the Torah was first translated into Greek by seventy-two Jewish elders (Septuagint means "seventy") at the request of an Egyptian king. Eventually, the term Septuagint was applied to the whole collection of Greek Scriptures, which included a variety of books not found in the Hebrew Bible.

Masoretes/Masoretic text (MT)   The Masoretes were ancient scribes responsible for transmitting the Hebrew Bible. They established the form of the Hebrew Bible, known as the Masoretic text (MT), that modern English translations are based on. This text is preserved in the most important ancient manuscripts of the Hebrew Bible, including the Aleppo Codex from the early tenth century CE.

Dead Sea Scrolls   The Dead Sea Scrolls are a large collection of texts found in caves near Qumran (south of Jericho) and dating from as early as the third century BCE. This collection includes about two hundred small fragments of biblical scrolls as well as the whole book of Isaiah. These texts correspond closely to the Masoretic text, but in some cases they reflect a form closer to what is presupposed by the Septuagint.

Apocrypha/Deuterocanonical books   In Protestant terminology, Apocrypha (literally, "hidden away") refers to books in the Greek Orthodox and Roman Catholic canons that are not found in the Hebrew Bible. These same books are often called deuteronocanonical (or "secondarily canonical") by Catholics. Examples include Tobit, Judith, Wisdom of Solomon, Ecclesiasticus, Baruch, and 1–2 Maccabees.

Key Personalities

Julius Wellhausen

Julius Wellhausen (1844–1918) was a German biblical scholar most well known for his work in the area of source criticism. This method of biblical interpretation, which in the nineteenth century was known as "literary criticism," attempts to come to terms with the composite character of a literary text by separating and describing its underlying sources. While this method can by applied to both biblical and non-biblical texts, Wellhausen primarily used source criticism in his work on the Pentateuch. Wellhausen's "Documentary Hypothesis" which will be discussed in more detail in chapter two, made an enormous contribution to the scholarly understanding of the origins of the Pentateuch.

Hermann Gunkel

Hermann Gunkel (1862–1932), another prominent German biblical scholar, is regarded as the founder of form criticism. While not denying the validity of source criticism, Gunkel shifted focus toward the literary form or genre of smaller textual units. Gunkel also emphasized the importance of the social location (the *Sitz im Leben*) of the text for understanding its meaning. Gunkel's form critical approach drew heavily upon newly discovered ancient Near Eastern literature, which offered new possibilities for comparison with biblical stories, themes, and imagery.

Questions for Study and Discussion

1. The chapter claims that the Hebrew Bible is problematic as a source for history. What are some of the arguments used in support of this claim? Do you agree with them? Why or why not?

2. For many religious people, the Hebrew Bible continues to have an authoritative status. Do the arguments presented in this chapter discredit or call into question the Hebrew Bible's status in religious communities? Why or why not?

3. What are some of the major methodological changes and archaeological discoveries that have shaped biblical studies over the last several hundred years? What sorts of problems and possibilities do they bring to light?

4. Why are the Dead Sea Scrolls important for understanding the Hebrew Bible?

1

The Near Eastern Context

Key Points

The ancient Near East produced some of the world's earliest cultures of writing and literature. Canaan, where Israel would carve out its territory, lay in between two major regional societies. Mesopotamia (Assyria and Babylonia) to the northeast and Egypt to the south were vibrant and enduring civilizations with far-reaching impact in antiquity. A historical understanding of the Hebrew Bible requires an appreciation of these influential cultures, religions, and literatures.

The Mesopotamian myths share robust features with biblical stories, but they deserve attention in their own right. They present the creation of the world, the council of the gods, and primordial humans, to name a few comparative topics. *Atrahasis*, a text named for its flood hero, recounts the creation of humanity and the polytheistic drama of a divine flood. The *Enuma Elish* describes the supernatural conflicts that established the divine council of Babylonian gods. After creating order out of watery chaos, the high god creates the earth and humans. The *Epic of Gilgamesh* recounts escapades of a legendary hero. He journeys to the end of the world to receive wisdom from the Sumerian flood hero, who tells him a flood story.

Our sources of Canaanite myths come from a number of fourteenth-century BCE tablets discovered at Ugarit, an ancient port city in what is now northern Syria. The *Baal Cycle* features a divine pantheon of familiar biblical names, including El (which means "god" in Hebrew) and Baal. The myths reflect fertility and seasonal changes.

Egyptian creation myths offer weaker parallels with the Bible than Mesopotamian and Canaanite literature. However, Egyptian literature, art, and religion provide an important conceptual background for understanding certain aspects of the Hebrew Bible. For instance, the history of Egyptian religion furnishes a striking comparative case in the development of monotheism with the reign and religious reforms of Akhenaten.

One marked distinction between ancient Near Eastern myth and the Hebrew Bible is the presence of goddesses. They frequently appear as creator deities and play a large role in polytheistic plots. With the exception of Ishtar, the second millennium saw the decline of goddesses into smaller roles, being supplanted or replaced by male deities.

Key Terms

Atrahasis   *Atrahasis* is an Old Babylonian myth of creation and flood (c. 1700 BCE). Anthropomorphic deities represent spheres of the natural world and meet in council to achieve balance. Conflicts arise because of labor and population. Enki helps Atrahasis, the flood hero, avoid multiple divine destructions.

Enuma Elish   *Enuma Elish* was popular at a high point of the Babylonian kingdom (c. 1100 BCE). It recounts the ascendency of Marduk as king of the divine council after defeating Tiamat (watery chaos). Marduk then creates the world, humans, and receives a temple in Babylon.

Epic of Gilgamesh   The *Epic of Gilgamesh* (c. 2000–800 BCE) comprises legends of an ancient Sumerian king focusing on the human condition. One-third mortal, two-thirds divine, Gilgamesh goes on adventures with Enkidu, a primordial man. In grief after the death of his friend, Gilgamesh journeys to the ends of the earth to consult the flood hero, Utnapishtim, about eternal life.

Canaanite mythology   Best represented by the texts from Ugarit, Canaanite mythology features gods also mentioned in the Hebrew Bible, especially El, Baal, and Asherah. The famous *Baal Cycle* sees the divine warrior's leadership challenged by Yamm (sea) and Mot (death).

The myths reflect seasonal changes and various threats to the survival of life.

Akhenaten   An Egyptian Pharaoh (reign c. 1353–1336 BCE), Akhenaten is often called the first monotheist. He asserted the sole worship of Aten, the solar disc, over the other gods, especially Amun. His religious reform involved political moves, changing the capital city, and socially marginalizing competing priests. His son and successor, Tutankhamun, reversed Akhenaten's reforms.

Key Personalities

Marduk

A divine warrior and leader of the Babylonian pantheon, Marduk's rise to power is recounted in the *Enuma Elish*. As god of the national state, he became the creator and ruler of the universe. He defeated Tiamat and created a world of order with his artful works and supreme decrees.

Baal

Baal ("lord" or "owner" in Hebrew) was the son of El and a powerful Canaanite deity. He is known as a storm god, "rider on the clouds." His battles with Mot (death) reflect cycles of fertility and drought. His battles with Yamm (sea) reflect more general threats of chaos over heaven. In both cases, Baal must defend his reign, sometimes aided by the warrior goddess Anat.

Questions for Study and Discussion

1. Many biblical stories borrow themes, motifs, and even character types from other ancient Near Eastern texts. What might this indicate about how biblical literature was written?
2. Goddess worship is very important in most ancient Near Eastern religions. Within the Hebrew Bible, however, goddess worship is given very little attention, and in some cases it is flatly condemned. What might have brought about this rejection of the goddesses?
3. How is the creation account in Genesis 1:1—2:3 similar to *Enuma Elish*? The *Baal Cycle*? How do you explain both the similarities and the differences?
4. In the *Baal Cycle*, Baal's death and resurrection are closely tied in to agricultural and fertility motifs. What does this suggest about how ancient Near Eastern people understood the relationship between the "natural world" and the "divine world"? Do you see a similar understanding in the Hebrew Bible?
5. This chapter provides a definition of myth that is quite different from its normal definition in everyday language. Myth refers to "sacred stories, or traditional stories deemed to have religious import." Based on that definition and your own knowledge of the Hebrew Bible, do you think that the Hebrew Bible contains "myths"?

Primary Texts

Enuma Elish

Source: excerpted from Pritchard, *Ancient Near Eastern Texts Relating to the Old Testament,* 3rd edition (Princeton University Press: 1969).

CLOSE READING TIPS

- Note the character of Marduk and the marks of his power, especially in IV:1-30.
- Tiamat is introduced in IV:31. She is part of the original primordial couple who gave birth to all the gods (theogony) and signifies the watery beginnings of the world (cosmogony). Her name is cognate with the Hebrew word *tehom,* which means "the deep" (Gen. 1:2). Earlier in the story, the gods kill their father, Tiamat's husband, and then plot to kill Tiamat because she is enraged and poised for battle.
- Note the images used to describe Marduk's preparations for battle against Tiamat (especially in IV:35-64)?
- Kingu is introduced in IV:66. He plays a role in both the battle and post-battle drama.
- Note the accusations Marduk levies against Tiamat (IV:77-86).
- Note the Tablets of Fate in IV:121.
- After Marduk's post-battle actions, he creates the world starting in IV:135.

> ▸ Marduk and Ea (primordial god of the deep waters) plan out how to create humans in VI:1-34.
> ▸ The high gods decide how to honor Marduk in VI:49-58.
> ▸ The *Enuma Elish* was read annually during the New Year's Festival in Babylon to celebrate spring (April).

TABLET IV

They erected for him a princely throne.
Facing his fathers, he sat down, presiding.
"Thou art the most honored of the great gods,
Thy decree is unrivaled, thy command is Anu.
Thou, Marduk, art the most honored of the
    great gods,
Thy decree is unrivaled, thy word is Anu.
From this day unchangeable shall be thy
    pronouncement.
To raise or bring low—these shall be (in) thy
    hand.
Thy utterance shall be true, thy command shall
    be impeachable.
No one among the gods shall transgress they
    bounds! (10)
Adornment being wanted for the seats of the
    gods,
Let the place of their shrines ever be in thy
    place.
O Marduk, thou art indeed our avenger.
We have granted thee kingship over the uni-
    verse entire.
When in Assembly thou sittest, thy word shall
    be supreme.
Thy weapons shall not fail; they shall smash thy
    foes!
O lord, spare the life of him who trusts thee,
But pour out the life of the god who seized
    evil."

Having placed in their midst a piece of cloth,

They addressed themselves to Marduk, their
    first-born: (20)

"Lord, truly thy decree is first among gods.
Say but to wreck or create; it shall be.
Open thy mouth: the cloth will vanish!
Speak again, and the cloth shall be whole!"

At the word of his mouth the cloth vanished.
He spoke again, and the cloth was restored.
When the gods, his fathers, saw the fruit of his
    word,
Joyfully they did homage: "Marduk is king!"
The conferred on him scepter, throne, and
    vestment;
They gave him matchless weapons that ward
    off the foes: (30)

"Go and cut off the life of Tiamat.
May the winds bear her blood to places
    undisclosed."

Bel's destiny thus fixed, the gods, his fathers,
Caused him to go the way of success and
    attainment.
He constructed a bow, marked it as his weapon,
Attached thereto the arrow, fixed its bow-cord.
He raised the mace, made his right hand grasp
    it;
Bow and quiver he hung at his side.
In front of him he set the lightening,
With a blazing flame he filled his body. (40)
He then made a net to enfold Tiamat therein.

The four winds he stationed that nothing of her
might escape,
The South Wind, the North Wind, the East
Wind, the West Wind.
Close to his side he held the net, the gift of his
father, Anu.
He brought forth Imhullu "the Evil Wind," the
Whirlwind, the Hurricane,
The Fourfold Wind, the Sevenfold Wind, the
Cyclone, the Matchless Wind;
Then he sent forth the winds he had brought
forth, the seven of them.
To stir up the inside of Tiamat they rose up
behind him.
Then the lord raised up the flood-storm, his
mighty weapon.
He mounted the storm-chariot irresistible
[and] terrifying. (50)
He harnessed (and) yoked to it a team-of-four,
The Killer, the Relentless, the Trampler, the
Swift.
Sharp were their teeth, bearing poison.
There were versed in ravage, in destruction
skilled.
On his right he posted the *Smiter*, fearsome in
battle,
On the left the Combat, which repels all the
zealous.
For a cloak he was wrapped in an armor of
terror;
With his fearsome halo his head was turbaned.
The lord went forth and followed his course,
Towards the raging Tiamat he set his face. (60)
In his lips he held a spell;
A plant to put out poison was grasped in his
hand.
Then they milled about him, the gods milled
about him,

The gods, his fathers, milled about him, the
gods milled about him.
The lord approached to scan the inside of
Tiamat,
(And) of Kingu, her consort, the scheme to
perceive.
As he looks on, his course becomes upset,
His will is distracted and his doings are
confused.
And when the gods, his helpers, who marched
at his side,
Saw the valiant hero, blurred became their
vision. (70)
Tiamat emitted [a cry], without turning her
neck,
Framing savage defiance in her lips:

"Too [imp]ortant art thou [for] the lord of the
gods to rise up against thee!
Is it in their place that they have gathered, (or)
in thy place?"

Thereupon the lord, having [raised] the flood-
storm, his mighty weapon,
[To] enraged [Tiamat] he sent word as follows:

"*Why* are thou risen, art haughtily exalted,
Thou hast charged thine own heart to stir up
conflict,
. . . sons reject their own fathers,
Whilst thou, who hast born them, hast fore-
sworn love! (80)
Thou hast appointed Kingu as they consort,
Conferring upon him the rank of Anu, not
rightfully his.
Against Anshar, king of the gods, those seekest
evil;
[Against] the gods, my fathers, thou hast confirmed thy wickedness.

[Though] drawn up be thy forces, girded on
    thy weapons,
Stand thou up, that I and thou meet in single
    combat!"

When Tiamat heard this,
She was like one possessed; she took leave of
    her senses.
In fury Tiamat cried aloud.
To the roots her legs shook both together. (90)
She recites a charm, keeps casting her spell,
While the gods of battle sharpen their
    weapons.
Then joined issue Tiamat and Marduk, wisest
    of gods.
They strove in single combat, locked in battle.
The lord spread out his net to enfold her,
The Evil Wind, which followed behind, he let
    loose in her face.
When Tiamat opened her mouth to consume
    him,
He drove in the Evil Wind that she close not
    her lips.
As the fierce winds charged her belly,
Her body was distended and her mouth was
    wide open. (100)
He released the arrow, it tore her belly,
It cut through her insides, splitting the heart.
Having thus subdued her, he extinguished her
    life.
He cast down her carcass to stand upon it.
After he had slain Tiamat, the leader,
Her band was shattered, her troupe broken up;
And the gods, her helpers who marched at her
    side,
Trembling with terror, turned their backs
    about,
In order to save and preserve their lives.
Tightly encircled, they could not escape. (110)

He made them captives and he smashed their
    weapons.
Thrown into the net, they found themselves
    ensnared;
Placed in cells, they were filled with wailing;
Bearing his wrath, they were held imprisoned.
And the eleven creatures which she has
    charged with awe,
The band of demons that marched [. . .]
    before her,
He cast into fetters, their hands [. . .].
For all their resistance, he trampled (them)
    underfoot.
And Kingu, who had been made chief among
    them,
He bound and accounted him to Uggae. (120)
He took from him the Tablets of Fate, not
    rightfully his.
Sealed (them) with a seal and fastened (them)
    on is breast.
When he has vanquished and subdued his
    adversaries,
Had . . . the vainglorious foe,
Had wholly established Anshar's triumph over
    the foe,
Nudimmud's desire had achieved, valiant
    Marduk
Strengthened his hold on the vanquished gods,
And turned back to Tiamat whom he had
    bound.
The lord trod on the legs of Tiamat,
With his unsparing mace he crushed her skull.
    (130)
When the arteries of her blood he had severed,
The North Wind bore (it) to places
    undisclosed.
On seeing this, his fathers were joyful and
    jubilant,

They brought gifts of homage, they to him.

Then the lord paused to view her dead body,

That he might divide the monster and do artful works.

He split her like a shellfish into two parts:

Half of her he set up and ceiled it as sky,

Pulled down the bar and posted guards.

He bade them to allow not her waters to escape. (140)

He crossed the heavens and surveyed the regions.

He squared Apsu's quarter, the abode of Nudimmud,

As the lord measured the dimensions of Apsu.

The Great Abode, its likeness, he fixed Esharra,

The Great Abode, Esharra, which he made as the firmament.

Anu, Enlil, and Ea he made occupy their places.

TABLET V

He constructed stations for the great gods,

Fixing their astral likenesses as constellations.

He determined the year by designating the zones:

He set up three constellations for each of the twelve months.

After defining the days of the year [by means] of (heavenly) figures,

He founded the station of Nebiru to determine their (heavenly) bands,

That none might transgress or fall short.

Alongside it he set up the stations of Enlil and Ea.

Having opened up the gates on both sides,

He strengthened the locks to the left and the right. (10)

In her belly he established the zenith.

The Moon he caused to shine, the night (to him) entrusting.

He appointed him a creature of the night to signify the days:

"Monthly, without cease, form designs with a crown.

At the month's very start, rising over the land,

Thou shalt have luminous horns to signify six days,

On the seventh day reaching a [half]-crown.

At full moon stand in opposition in mid-month.

When the sun [overtakes] thee at the base of heaven,

Diminish [thy crown] and retrogress in light. (20)

[At the time of disappearance] approach thou the course of the sun,

And [on the twenty-ninth] though shalt again stand in opposition to the sun."

[The remainder of this tablet is broken away or too fragmentary for translation.]

TABLET VI

When Marduk hears the words of the gods,

His heart prompts (him) to fashion artful works.

Opening his mouth, he addresses Ea

To impart the plan he had conceived in his heart:

"Blood I will mass and cause bones to be.

I will establish a savage, 'man' shall be his name.

Verily, savage-man I will create.

He shall be charged with the service of the gods

That they might be at ease!

The ways of the gods I will artfully alter.

Though alike revered, into two (groups) they
　　shall be divided." (10)

Ea answered him, speaking a word to him,
Giving him another plan for the relief of the
　　gods:

"Let but one of their brothers be handed over;
He alone shall perish that mankind may be
　　fashioned.
Let the great gods be here in Assembly,
Let the guilty be handed over that they may
　　endure."

Marduk summoned the great gods to
　　Assembly;
Presiding graciously, he issues instructions.
To his utterance the gods pay heed.
The king addresses a word to the Anunnaki:
　　(20)

"If your former statement was true,
Do (now) the truth on oath by me declare!
Who was it that contrived the uprising,
And made Tiamat rebel, and joined battle?
Let him be handed over who contrived the
　　uprising.
His guilt I will make him bear. You shall dwell
　　in peace!"

The Igigi, the great gods, replied to him,
To Lugaldimmerankia, counselor of the gods,
　　their lord:

"It was Kingu who contrived the uprising,
And made Tiamat rebel, and joined battle."
　　(30)

They bound him, holding him before Ea.
They imposed on him his guilt and severed his
　　blood (vessels).
Out of his blood they fashioned mankind.

He imposed the service and let free the gods.
After Ea, the wise, had created mankind,
Had imposed upon it the service and let free
　　the gods.
That work was beyond comprehension;
As artfully planned by Marduk, did Nudim-
　　mud create it—
Marduk, the king of the gods divided
All the Anunnaki above and below. (40)
He assigned (them) to Anu to guard his
　　instructions.
Three hundred in the heavens he stationed as
　　a guard.
In like manner the ways of the earth he
　　defined.
In heaven and on earth six hundred (thus) he
　　settled.
After he had ordered all the instructions,
To the Anunnaki of heaven and earth had
　　allotted their portions,
The Anunnaki opened their mouths
And said to Marduk, their lord:

"Now, O lord, thou who hast caused our
　　deliverance,
What shall be our homage to thee? (50)
Let us build a shrine whose name shall be
　　called
'Lo, a chamber for our nightly rest'; let us
　　repose in it!
Let us build a throne, a recess for his abode!
On the day that we arrive we shall repose in it."
When Marduk heard this,
Brightly glowed his features, like the day:

"Like that of *lofty* Babylon, whose building you
　　have requested,
Let its brickwork be fashioned. You shall name
　　it 'The Sanctuary.' "

DISCUSSION QUESTIONS

1. What similarities do you note between the creation of the world in the *Enuma Elish* and the Priestly creation in Genesis 1?
2. The *Enuma Elish* recounts how Marduk became the high god of the Babylonian pantheon. How do his character and his actions justify his status among the divine council?
3. The *Enuma Elish's* conflict in heaven showcases Marduk as divine warrior. While the Genesis creation does not recount a similar conflict, where do we see the biblical God characterized as a warrior?
4. Focusing on Tiamat and Marduk, how does gender function in the *Enuma Elish*? How does this compare to the gender of God in the Hebrew Bible?
5. Knowing the *Enuma Elish* was read during the New Year's festival, what aspects of the myth seem to refer to ritual?

2

The Nature of Pentateuchal Narrative

Key Points

The Pentateuch or the Torah contains the first five books of the Hebrew Bible: Genesis, Exodus, Leviticus, Numbers, and Deuteronomy. It tells the story of the prehistory of Israel, including the narratives of creation, the flood, the ancestors, the liberation from Egypt and the giving of the Sinai law, the wandering in the desert, and the farewell speech of Moses.

The Pentateuch is traditionally associated with Moses. However, scholars have long recognized that the Pentateuch shows signs of being a composite work that was written by multiple authors. By the end of the 1800s, centuries of inquiry culminated in Julius Wellhausen's Documentary Hypothesis. According to this hypothesis, the Pentateuch is the result of the combination of four separate and earlier sources of literature, known as J, E, D, and P. Each of these sources is distinguished by a consistent profile of literary characteristics, such as variation in divine names or interest in certain themes. While scholars like Rendtorff and Blum challenge the theory, all agree that the Pentateuch contains various traditional materials from different eras and points of view. The process of composition cannot have ended sooner than the postexilic period.

Because the Documentary Hypothesis continues to have many adherents, it represents the best way to understand the complex composition of the Pentateuch. The two earliest sources, J and E, are difficult to distinguish. The Yahwist (J) includes many of the well-known tales of Genesis and Exodus, including the story of Adam and Eve and a version of the flood. While J probably reflects stories of southern Judah, the Elohist (E) is associated with the northern tribes of Israel. The Deuteronomist (D) is almost exclusively limited to the book by the same name. It is connected with the seventh-century reforms of King Josiah in Judah. The Priestly source (P) is an exilic or postexilic composition largely concerned with issues of ritual practice and covenant. It contains a distinct legal source called the Holiness Code (H) in Leviticus 17–26. The source P is easily identified by its formulaic style and attention to detail.

Key Terms

Torah   Also called the Pentateuch or the five books of Moses, the Torah consists of Genesis, Exodus, Leviticus, Numbers, and Deuteronomy. While the Hebrew word *torah* is often translated as "law," this term has can refer more broadly to teaching or instruction. The Torah combines the revelation of law on Mt Sinai with foundational Israelite narratives.

Multiple authorship   A complex process of authorship produced the Pentateuch, which shows signs of composite layers from different periods of Israelite history. Pre-modern thinkers already challenged the traditional notion that Moses wrote the entire Pentateuch. Today, scholars use the source theory along with redaction, tradition, and form criticisms to study the Pentateuch's multiple layers.

Documentary Hypothesis   According to the Documentary Hypothesis, four originally separate sources were brought together to form the Pentateuch. Julius Wellhausen, responsible for its classic formulation, named them JEPD. D (Deuteronomy) and P (Priestly) are the latest sources. Earlier and more difficult to distinguish, J (Yahwist) and E (Elohist) use different names for God, usually translated LORD and God, respectively.

Yahwist source   The J source is associated with Judah in the south (c. ninth century BCE) and contains colorful stories. YHWH is described in anthropomorphic terms and is sometimes represented by an angel. In the story of Adam and Even (Gen. 2–3), YHWH forms humans from clay, walks in the garden, and talks to them. The theme of promise and fulfillment is accomplished through YHWH's trial and error.

Priestly source   The P source can be identified by a concern for priestly matters: the tabernacle in Exodus, the Sabbath in Genesis 1, and Leviticus are quintessential examples. The narratives are formulaic and include dates and "technical" details, connecting events with genealogies. Covenants with ancestors figure prominently: Noah, Abraham, and Moses.

Key Personalities

YHWH in J flood

The J flood showcases YHWH's anthropomorphic qualities: he experiences grief and regret (Gen. 6:6-7), closes the door to the ark (Gen. 7:16), and smells Noah's sacrifice (Gen. 8:21) which induces his decision to never flood the earth again. The theme of trial and error carries over from earlier J texts as YHWH uses the flood to start over with humanity.

God in P flood

The Priestly account sets God's decision to flood the earth in the context of his first covenant with humanity. God provides Noah with detailed directions and measurements for the boat, and Noah's righteousness is reflected in his obedience to commands. The symmetry of God's cosmos in the Priestly creation (Gen. 1) can be found in the repeated reference to pairs of animals, the waters above and below, and the command to be fruitful and multiply. God in the P flood concludes with the first laws for all humanity and the rainbow as a sign of the covenant.

Questions for Study and Discussion

1. How would you react to the following statement: The Bible makes it clear that Moses is the sole author of the Pentateuch. To what evidence would you appeal in your response?
2. What evidence has led scholars to conclude that the Pentateuch, far from being the work of a single author, is in fact the world of many scribes over centuries?
3. P and D are the easiest sources to recognize in the Pentateuch. What are some features of both? Where in the Pentateuch does one find these two sources?
4. The classical formulation of the Documentary Hypothesis—in which J and E are the earliest sources and D and P the latest—has come under fire on several fronts. What are some of the alternative models that have been proposed? What are some of the problems with the JEDP hypothesis?

Primary Texts

Genesis 6–9 in Yahwistic Version

CLOSE READING TIPS

▶ Note the anthropomorphic qualities of YHWH in Genesis 6:6-7.
▶ The J account lacks instructions to build an ark.
▶ Note who boards the ark (Gen. 7:1).
▶ How many animals of each kind join Noah on the ark? (Gen. 7:2).
▶ Note the repetition of "40 days and 40 nights" in chapter 7.
▶ YHWH shuts Noah into the ark (Gen. 7:16).
▶ Note the narrative of the birds in Genesis 8:8-12.
▶ The narrative of the sacrifice at the end of chapter 8 highlights the anthropomorphic character of YHWH.

---

6 5 The LORD saw that the wickedness of humankind was great in the earth, and that every inclination of the thoughts of their hearts was only evil continually. 6 And the LORD was sorry that he had made humankind on the earth, and it grieved him to his heart. 7 So the LORD said, "I will blot out from the earth the human beings I have created—people together with animals and creeping things and birds of the air, for I am sorry that I have made them." 8 But Noah found favor in the sight of the LORD.

9b Noah was a righteous man, blameless in his generation;

7 1 Then the LORD said to Noah, "Go into the ark, you and all your household, for I have seen that you alone are righteous before me in this generation. 2 Take with you seven pairs of all clean animals, the male and its mate; and a pair of the animals that are not clean, the male and its mate; 3 and seven pairs

of the birds of the air also, male and female, to keep their kind alive on the face of all the earth. ⁴ For in seven days I will send rain on the earth for forty days and forty nights; and every living thing that I have made I will blot out from the face of the ground." ⁵ And Noah did all that the LORD had commanded him.

⁸ Of clean animals, and of animals that are not clean, and of birds [went into the ark with Noah.] ¹⁰ And after seven days the waters of the flood came on the earth. ¹² The rain fell on the earth forty days and forty nights. ¹⁶ᵇ And the LORD shut him in. ¹⁷ The flood continued forty days on the earth. ²³ He blotted out every living thing that was on the face of the ground, human beings and animals and creeping things and birds of the air; they were blotted out from the earth. Only Noah was left, and those that were with him in the ark

8 ²ᵇ The rain from the heavens was restrained, ³ and the waters gradually receded from the earth.

⁶ At the end of forty days Noah opened the window of the ark that he had made. ⁸ Then he sent out the dove from him, to see if the waters had subsided from the face of the ground; ⁹ but the dove found no place to set its foot, and it returned to him to the ark, for the waters were still on the face of the whole earth. So he put out his hand and took it and brought it into the ark with him. ¹⁰ He waited another seven days, and again he sent out the dove from the ark; ¹¹ and the dove came back to him in the evening, and there in its beak was a freshly plucked olive leaf; so Noah knew that the waters had subsided from the earth. ¹² Then he waited another seven days, and sent out the dove; and it did not return to him any more. ¹³ᵇ And Noah removed the covering of the ark, and looked, and saw that the face of the ground was drying. In the second month, on the twenty-seventh day of the month, the earth was dry.

²⁰ Then Noah built an altar to the LORD, and took of every clean animal and of every clean bird, and offered burnt offerings on the altar. ²¹ And when the LORD smelled the pleasing odor, the LORD said in his heart, "I will never again curse the ground because of humankind, for the inclination of the human heart is evil from youth; nor will I ever again destroy every living creature as I have done.

> ²² As long as the earth endures,
> seedtime and harvest, cold and heat,
> summer and winter, day and night,
> shall not cease

DISCUSSION QUESTIONS

1. How well does the J flood story hold together?
2. How does the anthropomorphic character of YHWH affect your interpretation of the J flood?
3. Do you detect the theme of YHWH's trial and error in the J flood?
4. How does the J flood compare with the *Atrahasis* or *Gilgamesh* flood stories?

Genesis 6–9 in Priestly Version

CLOSE READING TIPS

▶ Note the genealogical introduction in Genesis 6:9-10.

▶ Who are Ham, Shem, and Japheth (Gen. 6:10 and 7:13)?

▶ Note the detailed instructions for building an ark (Gen. 6:14-16).

▶ Note the covenant in Genesis 6:18.

▶ How many animals of each kind join Noah on the ark? (Gen. 7:19)

▶ Notice how many specific numbers and dates are included (Gen. 7:6, also 7:11, 20, 24; 8:4, 5, 13, 14).

▶ Compare the fountains of the great deep and floodgates of the sky (Gen. 7:11; 8:2) with Genesis 1:6-7.

▶ Compare the report about the days of water in Genesis 7:24 (P) with Genesis 7:17 (J).

▶ Note the short report of the bird in Genesis 8:7.

▶ Compare "be fertile and increase, and fill the earth" in Genesis 9:1 with Genesis 1:28.

▶ Note the laws of the Noahic covenant in Genesis 9:3-7.

▶ Compare the "image of God" in Genesis 9:6 with Genesis 1:26-27.

▶ With whom does God make the covenant in Genesis 9:9-10?

▶ What is the sign of the covenant in Genesis 9:12-13?

▶ What happens when God brings clouds over the earth in Genesis 9:14?

6 ⁹ These are the descendants of Noah. Noah was a righteous man, blameless in his generation; Noah walked with God. ¹⁰ And Noah had three sons, Shem, Ham, and Japheth.

¹¹ Now the earth was corrupt in God's sight, and the earth was filled with violence. ¹² And God saw that the earth was corrupt; for all flesh had corrupted its ways upon the earth. ¹³ And God said to Noah, "I have determined to make an end of all flesh, for the earth is filled with violence because of them; now I am going to destroy them along with the earth. ¹⁴ Make yourself an ark of cypress wood; make rooms in the ark, and cover it inside and out with pitch. ¹⁵ This is how you are to make it: the length of the ark three hundred cubits, its width fifty cubits, and its height thirty cubits. ¹⁶ Make a roof for the ark, and finish it to a cubit above; and put the door of the ark in its side; make it with lower, second, and third decks. ¹⁷ For my part, I am going to bring a flood of waters on the earth, to destroy from under heaven all flesh in which is the breath of life; everything that is on the earth shall die. ¹⁸ But I will establish my covenant with you; and you shall come into the ark, you, your sons, your wife, and your sons' wives with you. ¹⁹ And of every living thing, of all flesh, you shall bring two of every kind into the ark, to keep them alive with you; they shall be male and female. ²⁰ Of the birds according to their kinds, and of the animals according to their kinds, of every creeping thing of the ground according to its kind, two of every kind

shall come in to you, to keep them alive. [21] Also take with you every kind of food that is eaten, and store it up; and it shall serve as food for you and for them." [22] Noah did this; he did all that God commanded him

7 [6] Noah was six hundred years old when the flood of waters came on the earth. [7] And Noah with his sons and his wife and his sons' wives went into the ark to escape the waters of the flood. [8b] And of everything that creeps on the ground, [9] two and two, male and female, went into the ark with Noah, as God had commanded Noah.

[11] In the six hundredth year of Noah's life, in the second month, on the seventeenth day of the month, on that day all the fountains of the great deep burst forth, and the windows of the heavens were opened. [13] On the very same day Noah with his sons, Shem and Ham and Japheth, and Noah's wife and the three wives of his sons entered the ark, [14] they and every wild animal of every kind, and all domestic animals of every kind, and every creeping thing that creeps on the earth, and every bird of every kind—every bird, every winged creature. [15] They went into the ark with Noah, two and two of all flesh in which there was the breath of life. [16] And those that entered, male and female of all flesh, went in as God had commanded him.

[17b] And the waters increased, and bore up the ark, and it rose high above the earth. [18] The waters swelled and increased greatly on the earth; and the ark floated on the face of the waters. [19] The waters swelled so mightily on the earth that all the high mountains under the whole heaven were covered; [20] the waters swelled above the mountains, covering them fifteen cubits deep. [21] And all flesh died that moved on the earth, birds, domestic animals, wild animals, all swarming creatures that swarm on the earth, and all human beings; [22] everything on dry land in whose nostrils was the breath of life died. [24]

And the waters swelled on the earth for one hundred fifty days.

8 [1] But God remembered Noah and all the wild animals and all the domestic animals that were with him in the ark. And God made a wind blow over the earth, and the waters subsided; [2] the fountains of the deep and the windows of the heavens were closed. [3b] At the end of one hundred fifty days the waters had abated; [4] and in the seventh month, on the seventeenth day of the month, the ark came to rest on the mountains of Ararat. [5] The waters continued to abate until the tenth month; in the tenth month, on the first day of the month, the tops of the mountains appeared.

[7] And [Noah] sent out the raven; and it went to and fro until the waters were dried up from the earth.

[13] In the six hundred first year, in the first month, on the first day of the month, the waters were dried up from the earth. [14] In the second month, on the twenty-seventh day of the month, the earth was dry. [15] Then God said to Noah, [16] "Go out of the ark, you and your wife, and your sons and your sons' wives with you. [17] Bring out with you every living thing that is with you of all flesh—birds and animals and every creeping thing that creeps on the earth—so that they may abound on the earth, and be fruitful and multiply on the earth." [18] So Noah went out with his sons and his wife and his sons' wives. [19] And every animal, every creeping thing, and every bird, everything that moves on the earth, went out of the ark by families.

9 [1] God blessed Noah and his sons, and said to them, "Be fruitful and multiply, and fill the earth. [2] The fear and dread of you shall rest on every animal of the earth, and on every bird of the air, on everything that creeps on the ground, and on all the fish of the sea; into your hand they are delivered. [3] Every

moving thing that lives shall be food for you; and just as I gave you the green plants, I give you everything. ⁴ Only, you shall not eat flesh with its life, that is, its blood. ⁵ For your own lifeblood I will surely require a reckoning: from every animal I will require it and from human beings, each one for the blood of another, I will require a reckoning for human life.

⁶ Whoever sheds the blood of a human,
by a human shall that person's blood be shed;
for in his own image
God made humankind.

⁷ And you, be fruitful and multiply, abound on the earth and multiply in it."

⁸ Then God said to Noah and to his sons with him, ⁹ "As for me, I am establishing my covenant with you and your descendants after you, ¹⁰ and with every living creature that is with you, the birds, the domestic animals, and every animal of the earth with you, as many as came out of the ark. ¹¹ I establish my covenant with you, that never again shall all flesh be cut off by the waters of a flood, and never again shall there be a flood to destroy the earth." ¹² God said, "This is the sign of the covenant that I make between me and you and every living creature that is with you, for all future generations: ¹³ I have set my bow in the clouds, and it shall be a sign of the covenant between me and the earth. ¹⁴ When I bring clouds over the earth and the bow is seen in the clouds, ¹⁵ I will remember my covenant that is between me and you and every living creature of all flesh; and the waters shall never again become a flood to destroy all flesh. ¹⁶ When the bow is in the clouds, I will see it and remember the everlasting covenant between God and every living creature of all flesh that is on the earth." ¹⁷ God said to Noah, "This is the sign of the covenant that I have established between me and all flesh that is on the earth

DISCUSSION QUESTIONS

1. What elements of the Priestly flood cohere with the Priestly version of creation in Genesis 1?
2. What typical features of the Priestly source appear in this version?
3. When compared with the *Enuma Elish*, the Priestly creation (Gen. 1) and flood share the concept of water as cosmic chaos. How does the Priestly author use water and chaos in its flood story?
4. How does the Priestly covenant with Noah impact its version of the flood story?

3

The Primeval History

Key Points

Genesis 1–11 comprise the Primeval History. An account of primordial beginnings, it contains creation and flood stories as well as foundational descriptions of families and society.

Genesis 2–3, a parade example of the J source, provides one of the most well-known biblical stories. It describes YHWH's creation of Adam and Eve as well as the collective disobedience that led to their expulsion from the garden of Eden. This story also introduces the serpent. Although it tempts Adam and Eve to eat from the tree of the knowledge of good evil, it is only in later tradition that the serpent is identified as Satan. Genesis 2–3 shares several features with other ancient Near Eastern creation stories. For example, when Adam and Eve eat the fruit, they transition to a state of self-consciousness and awareness of death. The *Epic of Gilgamesh* contains similar elements, especially Enkidu's coming of age and Gilgamesh's loss of the plant of eternal life by the stealth of a snake.

The P source also provides a creation story in Genesis 1:1—2:4a. This story supplements the J account with an orderly and comprehensive story of the Israelite cosmos. Famous for its seven-day structure, Genesis 1 gives a prominent position to humans, both male and female, and culminates in the Sabbath ritual. It anticipates the Priestly version of the flood story with its attention to details, repeated phrases, and cosmic scope. Typical of the Priestly source, its flood story ends with the covenant with Noah, which provides a set of laws applicable to all humanity.

The Priestly source links the Primeval History to the story of Abraham (Gen. 12). It uses genealogies to integrate the family story of Cain and Abel (J) and table of nations in the Tower of Babel (J). The episode in Genesis 6:1-4 on the sons of God, which is difficult to assign to a source, is probably a fragment of a polytheistic myth used to explain the Nephilim.

Key Terms

Yahwistic Creation (Genesis 2–3) The Yahwistic creation story is a negative coming of age tale. YHWH makes a human (Adam) to keep the garden of Eden, but he is alone. Adam names the animals, finally recognizing Eve as his partner, although their actions lead to their removal from the garden. The Yahwistic creation shares qualities with *Atrahasis* and *Gilgamesh*.

Knowledge of good and evil At the center of Eden is a special tree of the knowledge of good and evil (Gen. 2:17). Adam and Eve, desiring divine wisdom, disobediently eat from the tree. Their subsequent opened eyes, need for clothes, and pronouncement of death highlight the themes of mortality and self-consciousness that are shared in the story of Gilgamesh.

The fall Christian tradition reads Adam and Eve's disobedience and subjection to death as an original sin. Unlike the positive depiction of the transition from primordial to civilized man in Gilgamesh, the Yahwist portrays this transition negatively. Through a series of misleading communiqués and the transgression of YHWH's command, the snake, the woman, and the man are cursed (Gen. 3:14-19).

Priestly creation (Genesis 1) Poetically and structurally formulaic, Genesis 1 is paradigmatically Priestly. It recounts the creation of the cosmos in seven days. With some parallels to the *Enuma Elish*, creation by divine word brings order to chaos. Humans, the culmination of creative work, are made as a pair in the image of God in striking contrast to the Yahwistic account.

Etiology Etiologies are stories or myths that explain the origin of culture or religion. The Primeval History contains numerous etiological explanations. For example, the curses in Genesis 3 explain why snakes don't have legs or women experience pain in childbirth. Genesis 1 ends on a day of rest, explaining the liturgical observance of Sabbath.

Key Personalities

Adam

Adam, the generic word for human, is the primordial first human in the J creation story. Fashioned out of the soil by YHWH, he is made to do agricultural work in the garden, similar to the humans in *Atrahasis*. Adam's isolation prompts the creation of potential partners starting with animals and ending with Eve. After eating forbidden fruit, he is expelled and cursed with difficult labor and mortality.

Eve

Eve, the mother of all life (Gen. 3:20), is the primordial first woman in the J creation story. Fashioned from Adam's rib, she is Adam's partner with a close bond. Eve converses with a crafty snake about a command from YHWH she did not hear first-hand. After eating forbidden fruit, she is expelled and cursed to experience pain in childbirth and to be ruled by her husband.

Enkidu

Enkidu is wild man who comes of age as a human companion of Gilgamesh. His sexual awakening gives him wisdom like the gods and accompanies civilized lessons in eating, drinking, and wearing clothes. His story is a positive version of a primordial transition, with similarities to Genesis 2–3.

Questions for Study and Discussion

1. In the popular imagination, Eve is often depicted as a seductress who tempted Adam and drew him away from God and toward evil. The image of the woman, in other words, is often fused with the image of the serpent, and humanity's woes are her responsibility. How does this popular image of Eve compare with the actual depiction of Eve in Genesis 2–3?

2. People often debate about the historicity of the events in Genesis 1–11. Within the United States, advocates and legislators argue about whether the creation and flood accounts in Genesis 1–11 are meant to be interpreted as scientific accounts. Based on what you have learned in this chapter, how do you respond to the claim that Genesis 1–11 is made up of several scientifically accurate accounts of the world's origins and early history?

3. There are many echoes of non-biblical ancient Near Eastern literature in the Primeval History (Genesis 1–11). How do these echoes change or affect your understanding of these chapters?

4. How would you respond to the following claim: The serpent in Genesis 3 is clearly the devil—Satan himself—who came to derail humanity from the very beginning?

Primary Texts

The P creation account (Genesis 1:1–2:4a)

CLOSE READING TIPS

▸ Verse 1 could be translated either as an independent sentence that summarizes what follows ("In the beginning, God created. . .") or as a temporal clause that describes the situation when God started creating ("When God began to create . . . the earth was a formless void").

▸ Note that verse 2 does not describe creation "out of nothing" (*ex nihilo*). Rather, it emphasizes that God creates order from the primordial chaos.

▸ It is possible that the word for "deep" (Heb. *tehom*) in verse 2 is related to the Babylonian goddess Tiamat, a chaos monster, who was defeated by Marduk in the *Enuma Elish*.

▸ There is a correspondence between days 1–3 and 4–6. In the first set of three days, God creates three spheres (day/night, sky/waters, land/plants) and in the second set of three days God creates entities to rule or fill those spheres (greater/lesser lights, birds/fish, animals/humans).

▸ The "us" and "our" in verse 26 likely refers to God's heavenly council, which consists of multiple divine beings.

▸ The "image of God" in verse 27 has been interpreted as referring to a spiritual likeness between God and humanity, though it is also possible that this language draws on the common ancient Near Eastern notion that rulers physically resembled the deity who authorized their power.

---

1 [1] In the beginning when God created the heavens and the earth, [2] the earth was a formless void and darkness covered the face of the deep, while a wind from God swept over the face of the waters. [3] Then God said, "Let there be light"; and there was light. [4] And God saw that the light was good; and God separated the light from the darkness. [5] God called the light Day, and the darkness he called Night. And there was evening and there was morning, the first day.

[6] And God said, "Let there be a dome in the midst of the waters, and let it separate the waters from the waters." [7] So God made the dome and separated the waters that were under the dome from the waters that were above the dome. And it was so. [8] God called the dome Sky. And there was evening and there was morning, the second day.

[9] And God said, "Let the waters under the sky be gathered together into one place, and let the dry land appear." And it was so. [10] God called the dry land Earth, and the waters that were gathered together he called Seas. And God saw that it was good. [11] Then God said, "Let the earth put forth vegetation: plants yielding seed, and fruit trees of every kind on earth that bear fruit with the seed in it." And it was so. [12] The earth brought forth vegetation: plants yielding seed of every kind, and trees of every kind bearing fruit with the seed in it. [13] And God saw that it was good. And there was evening and there was morning, the third day.

[14] And God said, "Let there be lights in the dome of the sky to separate the day from the night; and let them be for signs and for seasons and for days and years, [15] and let them be lights in the dome of the sky to give light upon the earth." And it was so. [16] God made the two great lights—the greater light to rule the day and the lesser light to rule the night—and the stars. [17] God set them in the dome of the sky to give light upon the earth, [18] to rule over the day and over the night, and to separate the light from the darkness. And God saw that it was good. [19] And there was evening and there was morning, the fourth day.

[20] And God said, "Let the waters bring forth swarms of living creatures, and let birds fly above the earth across the dome of the sky." [21] So God created the great sea monsters and every living creature that moves, of every kind, with which the waters swarm, and every winged bird of every kind. And God saw that it was good. [22] God blessed them, saying, "Be fruitful and multiply and fill the waters in the seas, and let birds multiply on the earth." [23] And there was evening and there was morning, the fifth day.

[24] And God said, "Let the earth bring forth living creatures of every kind: cattle and creeping things and wild animals of the earth of every kind." And it was so. [25] God made the wild animals of the earth of every kind, and the cattle of every kind, and everything that creeps upon the ground of every kind. And God saw that it was good.

[26] Then God said, "Let us make humankind in our image, according to our likeness; and let them have dominion over the fish of the sea, and over the birds of the air, and over the cattle, and over all the wild animals of the earth, and over every creeping thing that creeps upon the earth."

[27] So God created humankind in his image,
in the image of God he created them;
male and female he created them.

[28] God blessed them, and God said to them, "Be fruitful and multiply, and fill the earth and subdue it; and have dominion over the fish of the sea and over the birds of the air and over every living thing that moves upon the earth." [29] God said, "See, I have given you every plant yielding seed that is upon the face of all the earth, and every tree with seed in its

fruit; you shall have them for food. [30] And to every beast of the earth, and to every bird of the air, and to everything that creeps on the earth, everything that has the breath of life, I have given every green plant for food." And it was so. [31] God saw everything that he had made, and indeed, it was very good. And there was evening and there was morning, the sixth day.

2 [1] Thus the heavens and the earth were finished, and all their multitude. [2] And on the seventh day God finished the work that he had done, and he rested on the seventh day from all the work that he had done. [3] So God blessed the seventh day and hallowed it, because on it God rested from all the work that he had done in creation.

[4] These are the generations of the heavens and the earth when they were created

Discussion questions

1. Where do you see characteristic concerns of the P source in Gen 1:1—2:4a?
2. How would you characterize the relationship between humanity and the rest of creation in the P account?
3. What is different about the concluding words of the sixth day from all the other days? What does this indicate about God's intention for creation?

The J creation account (Gen 2:4b-9; 2:15—3:7; 3:22-24)

Close reading tips

▶ Note that Genesis 2:4b-6 presents a very different starting point than Genesis 1:1-2. Descriptions of pre-creation are often found in ancient Near Eastern creation myths.

▶ The Hebrew word for "man" (*'adam*) and "ground" (*'adamah*) in verse 7 is a wordplay that emphasizes the connectedness of humanity and the soil.

▶ Note that in Genesis 2:18-19, animals are created after the human (contrast with Gen. 1:24-25).

▶ In Hebrew, the verb "cling" in verse 24 implies a special connection, but it does not necessarily imply marriage in any modern sense of the term.

▶ While the serpent is described as "crafty" (Gen. 3:1) it is only in later theological traditions that it is identified with the devil.

▶ Note that the humans are expelled from the garden because god fears that they will eat from the tree of life and become immortal (Gen. 3:22).

▶ In the ancient Near East, cherubim were hybrid creatures, half human and half lion, often with wings. Cherubim statues were often placed at the entrance of temples or palaces as guardians. A similar situation seems to be implied by the placement of the cherubim in Genesis 3:24.

2 [4b] In the day that the LORD God made the earth and the heavens, [5] when no plant of the field was yet in the earth and no herb of the field had yet sprung up—for the LORD God had not caused it to rain upon the earth, and there was no one to till the ground; [6] but a stream would rise from the earth, and water the whole face of the ground— [7] then the LORD God formed man from the dust of the ground, and breathed into his nostrils the breath of life; and the man became a living being. [8] And the LORD God planted a garden in Eden, in the east; and there he put the man whom he had formed. [9] Out of the ground the LORD God made to grow every tree that is pleasant to the sight and good for food, the tree of life also in the midst of the garden, and the tree of the knowledge of good and evil.

[15] The LORD God took the man and put him in the garden of Eden to till it and keep it. [16] And the LORD God commanded the man, "You may freely eat of every tree of the garden; [17] but of the tree of the knowledge of good and evil you shall not eat, for in the day that you eat of it you shall die."

[18] Then the LORD God said, "It is not good that the man should be alone; I will make him a helper as his partner." [19] So out of the ground the LORD God formed every animal of the field and every bird of the air, and brought them to the man to see what he would call them; and whatever the man called every living creature, that was its name. [20] The man gave names to all cattle, and to the birds of the air, and to every animal of the field; but for the man there was not found a helper as his partner.

[21] So the LORD God caused a deep sleep to fall upon the man, and he slept; then he took one of his ribs and closed up its place with flesh. [22] And the rib that the LORD God had taken from the man he made into a woman and brought her to the man.

[23] Then the man said,

"This at last is bone of my bones
      and flesh of my flesh;
this one shall be called Woman,
      for out of Man this one was taken."

[24] Therefore a man leaves his father and his mother and clings to his wife, and they become one flesh. [25] And the man and his wife were both naked, and were not ashamed.

3 [1] Now the serpent was more crafty than any other wild animal that the LORD God had made. He said to the woman, "Did God say, 'You shall not eat from any tree in the garden'?" [2] The woman said to the serpent, "We may eat of the fruit of the trees in the garden; [3] but God said, 'You shall not eat of the fruit of the tree that is in the middle of the garden, nor shall you touch it, or you shall die.'" [4] But the serpent said to the woman, "You will not die; [5] for God knows that when you eat of it your eyes will be opened, and you will be like God, knowing good and evil." [6] So when the woman saw that the tree was good for food, and that it was a delight to the eyes, and that the tree was to be desired to make one wise, she took of its fruit and ate; and she also gave some to her husband, who was with her, and he ate. [7] Then the eyes of both were opened, and they knew that they were naked; and they sewed fig leaves together and made loincloths for themselves.

[22] Then the Lord God said, "See, the man has become like one of us, knowing good and evil; and now, he might reach out his hand and take also from the tree of life, and eat, and live forever"— [23] therefore the Lord God sent him forth from the garden of Eden, to till the ground from which he was taken. [24] He drove out the man; and at the east of the garden of Eden he placed the cherubim, and a sword flaming and turning to guard the way to the tree of life.

DISCUSSION QUESTIONS

1. Where do you see characteristic elements of the J source in this account?
2. What differences and similarities do you see between how the J and P creation accounts portray the relationship between man and woman?
3. Despite their differences, do you think the P and J creation stories are still compatible? In what ways might they complement each other?

Excerpt from *Atrahasis*

Source: *Context of Scripture* 1.130, selections (from Dalley, *Myths from Mesopotamia*)

CLOSE READING TIPS

▶ The "Igigi" were lesser gods who were made to carry out hard manual labor for the greater gods
▶ As the god of earth, Enlil (or Ellil) is described as the counselor of the gods. The Igigi rise up against him in rebellion.
▶ The solution to the Igigi's rebellion was the creation of a "mortal man" who could carry out the labor of the gods in their place.
▶ Note that the god Mami, also known as Belet-ili, uses clay in the creation of humans not unlike Genesis 2:7. However, the flesh and blood of a slaughtered god is also required for creation in this account.

When the gods instead of man
Did the work, bore the loads,
The gods' load was too great,
The work too hard, the trouble too much,
The great Anunnaki made the Igigi
Carry the workload sevenfold.
[. . .]
The gods had to dig out canals,
Had to clear channels, the lifelines of the land.
The gods dug out the Tigris river
And then dug out the Euphrates.
. . . in the deep
. . . they set up
. . . the Apsu
. . . of the land
. . . inside it

. . . raised its top
. . . of all the mountains
They were counting the years of loads
. . . the great marsh,

They were counting the years of loads.
For 3,600 years they bore the excess,
Hard work, night and day.
They groaned and blamed each other,
Grumbled over the masses of excavated soil:

> Let us confront our Chamberlain
> And get him to relieve us of our hard
>   work!
> Come, let us carry the Lord
> The counselor of the gods, the warrior
>   from his dwelling.

[. . .]

When they reached the gate of warrior Ellil's
    dwelling,
It was night, the middle watch,
The house was surrounded, the god had not
    realized.
When they reached the gate of warrior Ellil's
    dwelling,
It was night, the middle watch,
Ekur was surrounded, Ellil had not realized.

Yet Kalkal was attentive, and had it closed,
He held the lock and watched the gate.
Kalkal roused Nusku.
They listened to the noise of the Igigi.
Then Nusku roused his master,
Made him get out of bed:

> My lord, your house is surrounded,
> A rabble is running around your door!
> Ellil, your house is surrounded,

[. . .]

Anu made his voice heard and spoke to Nusku

> Nusku, open your door, take up your
>   weapons,
> Bow in the assembly of the great gods,
>   then stand
> And tell them. . .
> Your father Anu, your counselor warrior
>   Ellil,
> Your chamberlain Ninurta and your canal
>   controller Ennugi
> Have sent me to say
> Who is in charge of the rabble? Who will
>   be in charge of battle?
> Which god started the war?
> A rabble was running around my door!

When Nusku heard this,
He took up his weapons,
Bowed in the assembly of the great gods, then
    stood
And told them

> Your father Anu, your counselor warrior
>   Ellil,
> Have sent me to say,
> Who is in charge of the rabble? Who is in
>   charge of the fighting?
> Which god started the war? A rabble was
>   running around Ellil's door!

Ea made his voice heard
And spoke to the gods his brothers,

> Why are we blaming them?
> Their work was too hard, their trouble was
>   too much.
> Every day the earth resounded.
> The warning signal was loud enough, we
>   kept hearing the noise.
> There is. . .
> Belet-ili the womb goddess is present
> Let her create a mortal man
> So that he may bear the yoke. . .
> So that he may bear the yoke, the work of
>   Ellil,
> Let man bear the load of the gods!
> . . .
> Belet-ili the womb goddess is present,
> Let the womb goddess create offspring,
> And let them bear the load of the gods!

They called up the goddess, asked
The midwife of the gods, wise Mami,

> You are the womb-goddess, to be the cre-
>   ator of Mankind!

Create a mortal, that he may bear the
    yoke!
Let him bear the yoke, the work of Ellil
Let him bear the load of the gods!

Nintu made her voice heard
And spoke to the great gods,

> On the first, seventh, and fifteenth of the
>   month
> I shall make a purification by washing.
> Then one god should be slaughtered.
> And the gods can be purified by
>   immersion.
> Nintu shall mix the clay
> With his flesh and blood.
> Then a god and a man
> Will be mixed together in clay.

[. . .]

After she had mixed that clay,
She called up the Anunnaki, the great gods.
The Igigi, the great gods,
Spat spittle upon the clay
Mami made her voice heard
And spoke to the great gods,

> I have carried out perfectly
> The work that you ordered of me.
> You have slaughtered a god together with
>   his intelligence.
> I have relieved you of your hard work,
> I have imposed your load on man.
> You have bestowed noise on man,
> You have bestowed noise on mankind.
> I have undone the fetter and granted
>   freedom.

They listened to the speech of hers,
And were freed from anxiety, and kissed her
    feet.

DISCUSSION QUESTIONS

1. What motivations lie behind the creation of humanity in the P account, the J account, and *Atrahasis*?
2. What do these differences suggest about the character of God or the deities in each account?

4

The Patriarchs

Key Points

In Genesis 11–50 we transition from primeval history (chapters 1–10) to a cycle of stories about Israel's earliest ancestors. These chapters contain some of the most well-known material in all of the Hebrew Bible: the tower of Babel (chapter 11), the call of Abraham (chapter 12), the binding of Isaac (chapter 22), Jacob's "wrestling match" with God (chapter 32), and the Joseph novella (chapters 37–50). The lasting power of these stories owes much to the fact that they address enduring themes, including sibling rivalry, the desire for an heir, survival in a foreign land, trickery, and the wise courtier.

The patriarchal stories are notoriously difficult to study in historical terms. They offer no reference to publically verifiably events and it is likely that they were written nearly a thousand years after the date implied by their internal chronology. As a result, it is best to follow Gunkel in treaty this material as a series of legends. Legends may preserve historical memories but unlike historiography they primarily aim to explain the cause or origins of phenomena, people, names, and rituals. Many scholars study Genesis 11–50 in an effort to describe the function and setting in life of these legends (form criticism) or to trace the history of oral traditions that lie behind them (tradition history). It is also possible to study these stories as literature, analyzing prominent motifs, plot development, characterization, narrative structure, irony, and so forth.

The religion of the patriarchs is quite different than that which is espoused by Deuteronomy or the Priestly source. They set up altars at various places and worship God as different manifestations of El. These practices likely reflect a form of popular, family religion that flourished prior to the late monarchic period. Even though this form of religion was opposed by the Deuteronomists, the patriarchal stories touch upon themes that continue to be relevant to the Israelites into the postexilic period, such as covenant, divine promise, sacrifice, the transition from captivity to power, rituals, and genealogical lists. Thus, while the material in Genesis 11–50 is entertaining in its own right, it is also meant to teach and inspire readers as a religious narrative.

Key Terms

Legends   Legends are stories of oral tradition, characterized by folk belief, interest in personal and private matters, a desire to inspire and please rather than report "what actually happened." Hermann Gunkel's seminal work sought to identify not only why legends were told (that is, their function as a story) but also the setting in life in which they originally emerged (their *Sitz im Leben*). For example, Israelites developed legends about the temple at Bethel (Gen. 28) or pillars of salt at the Dead Sea (Gen. 19).

Patriarchal religion   The personal relationship with "the God of the fathers" evokes a religious society of migratory clans or tribes. Features like tithes and shrines reflect a settled population. Genesis presents all divine manifestations as the same deity, despite varying names (YHWH, God, El Shaddai, and so on). Patriarchal stories reflect elements of pre-Deuteronomistic religion such as altars and worship of Canaanite El.

Abraham covenant   God's promises to the patriarchs are formalized in the covenant with Abraham as father of a chosen people in a designated land. The J version (Gen. 15) takes place over a ritual with animals in which God unconditionally promises land and children on a grand scale. Circumcision is a requirement and a sign of the covenant in the P version (Gen. 17).

Binding of Isaac   In Genesis 22, Abraham offers up Isaac as a sacrifice. Offspring are a prominent theme in the promises to the patriarchs: Abraham, Sarah, and Hagar struggle to produce one heir. Abraham's willingness to kill Isaac is praised in this story though elsewhere in the Hebrew Bible (especially in Deuteronomy and Jeremiah) the practice of child sacrifice is condemned.

Trickster   Tricksters are underdogs or outsiders who achieve success through deception. Abraham and Isaac pass off their wives as sisters to fool powerful men. The trickster motif is most evident in the Jacob cycle. For instance, the younger twin, Jacob, steals Esau's birth-right and blessing, Laban tricks Jacob, Jacob's sons trick the men of Shechem, and Tamar tricks Judah to admit publically his injustice towards her.

Key Personalities

Jacob

The son of Isaac and Rebecca, Jacob is the father of the twelve tribes of Israel. A plucky trickster, Jacob achieves the inheritance of the patriarchs by deceiving his twin Esau and his father Isaac. Two divine manifestations in Genesis 28 and 32 associate Jacob with the important shrine at Bethel and the new name "Israel." Despite morally ambiguous aspects of his career, Jacob retains the promises of God.

Joseph

The final patriarch of Genesis, Joseph stars in the novella of Genesis 37–50. Similar to the longer prose narratives of Ruth, Esther, and Daniel, Joseph's story traces his rise to international prominence. From his childhood of grandiose dreams and paternal favoritism to the authority gained as a dream interpreter in Egypt, Joseph's brushes with personal adversity illustrate the theme of providence. His narrative serves as a bridge between the patriarchs in Genesis and the oppression of the Israelites in Egypt.

El

El is the common Hebrew word meaning "god," but it is also the personal name of the high god in Canaanite myths from Ugarit. The patriarchs worshiped El under different names and in different manifestations, including El Elyon (God Most High) and El Shaddai (God Almighty). In a dream Jacob see angels of God going up and down a ladder to heaven and he calls the place Beth-el (house of God) and later he names the place where he wrestled with God Peniel or Penuel (face of God). Most likely, El and Yahweh were originally separate deities but are eventually recognized as one and the same God in biblical religion.

Questions for Study and Discussion

1. Many attempts have been made to date the patriarchal stories. Why has this task proven to be difficult?
2. Divine promises are at the center of the patriarchal stories. In these stories, what is the relationship between divine promise and human initiative, human cunning and divine power? Do the promises come about entirely without human effort? Or do humans have something to contribute to the fulfillment of divine promise?
3. It is clear that the ancestral stories assume a patriarchal society—that is a society in which male authority dominates. This does not mean, however, that women are powerless in Hebrew narrative. How do women exercise power and their will in the patriarchal stories?
4. How would you describe the religion of the patriarchs? Provide evidence from the texts themselves.
5. Abraham nearly sacrificed his son at God's command. The author of the New Testament book of Hebrews saw this as an action of great faith (Heb. 11:17-19). Other Second Temple Jewish sources lifted up Isaac as a courageous martyr. In our current world, which is highly sensitive to child abuse, how do you respond to Abraham's willingness to go through with such an act? Is Abraham truly an example of faith?

Primary Texts

Genesis 16:1-16 (J version of Hagar)

CLOSE READING TIPS

- ▶ LORD (YHWH), J's divine name, appears eight times in verses 2, 5, 7, 9, 10, 11, 13.
- ▶ Note the theme of children and heirs in verse 2.
- ▶ Note the agency of Sarai in verses 2-6.
- ▶ The text refers to the land as Canaan (verse 3).
- ▶ The angel is a typical manifestation of YHWH in J (verses 7, 9, 10, 11).
- ▶ Note the inner-household dynamics of patriarchal families in verse 6.
- ▶ Note the promise to Hagar in verse 10 while she is still pregnant.

▶ Ishmael means "El hears" or "God hears" in verse 11.

▶ Note the association of Ishmael with a desert people group in verse 12.

▶ Hagar names YHWH "El Roi" in verse 13 which means "God who sees."

▶ Beer-lahai-roi means "Well of the Living One who sees" in verse 14. Note the association of this story with a specific place name.

▶ Ishamel is Abram's first biological son in verse 15.

1 Now Sarai, Abram's wife, bore him no children. She had an Egyptian slave-girl whose name was Hagar, 2 and Sarai said to Abram, "You see that the LORD has prevented me from bearing children; go in to my slave-girl; it may be that I shall obtain children by her." And Abram listened to the voice of Sarai. 3 So, after Abram had lived ten years in the land of Canaan, Sarai, Abram's wife, took Hagar the Egyptian, her slave-girl, and gave her to her husband Abram as a wife. 4 He went in to Hagar, and she conceived; and when she saw that she had conceived, she looked with contempt on her mistress. 5 Then Sarai said to Abram, "May the wrong done to me be on you! I gave my slave-girl to your embrace, and when she saw that she had conceived, she looked on me with contempt. May the LORD judge between you and me!" 6 But Abram said to Sarai, "Your slave-girl is in your power; do to her as you please." Then Sarai dealt harshly with her, and she ran away from her.

7 The angel of the LORD found her by a spring of water in the wilderness, the spring on the way to Shur. 8 And he said, "Hagar, slave-girl of Sarai, where have you come from and where are you going?" She said, "I am running away from my mistress Sarai." 9 The angel of the LORD said to her, "Return to your mistress, and submit to her." 10 The angel of the LORD also said to her, "I will so greatly multiply your offspring that they cannot be counted for multitude."

11 And the angel of the LORD said to her,

"Now you have conceived and shall bear a son;
    you shall call him Ishmael,
        for the LORD has given heed to your
            affliction.
12 He shall be a wild ass of a man,
with his hand against everyone,
    and everyone's hand against him;
and he shall live at odds with all his kin."

13 So she named the Lord who spoke to her, "You are El-roi"; for she said, "Have I really seen God and remained alive after seeing him?" 14 Therefore the well was called Beer-lahai-roi; it lies between Kadesh and Bered.

15 Hagar bore Abram a son; and Abram named his son, whom Hagar bore, Ishmael. 16 Abram was eighty-six years old when Hagar bore him Ishmael.

DISCUSSION QUESTIONS

1. What are the family dynamics among Sarai, Abram, and Hagar?

2. How does this story reflect "Patriarchal Religion?"

3. What legendary or etiological features occur in Genesis 16?

4. Consider Genesis 12–16, especially chapter 15 which formalizes the promise of offspring in the J covenant with Abram. How does the story of Hagar in chapter 16 advance the plot of children, offspring, and heirs in the Abraham cycle?

Genesis 21:8-21 (E version of Hagar)

CLOSE READING TIPS

▶ Isaac is likely between the ages of 2–3 when he is weaned (verse 8).

▶ Ishmael is 14 years older than Isaac (verse 9).

▶ Note the reasons Sarah casts Hagar and Ishmael out of the household (verses 9-10).

▶ Note God's affirmation of Sarah's will (verse 12).

▶ Note the dual promises in verses 12-13.

▶ Note the double abandonment of Ishmael in verses 14-15.

▶ Note the basic issues of subsistence, especially water (verses 14, 15, 19).

[8] The child grew, and was weaned; and Abraham made a great feast on the day that Isaac was weaned. [9] But Sarah saw the son of Hagar the Egyptian, whom she had borne to Abraham, playing with her son Isaac. [10] So she said to Abraham, "Cast out this slave woman with her son; for the son of this slave woman shall not inherit along with my son Isaac." [11] The matter was very distressing to Abraham on account of his son. [12] But God said to Abraham, "Do not be distressed because of the boy and because of your slave woman; whatever Sarah says to you, do as she tells you, for it is through Isaac that offspring shall be named for you. [13] As for the son of the slave woman, I will make a nation of him also, because he is your offspring." [14] So Abraham rose early in the morning, and took bread and a skin of water, and gave it to Hagar, putting it on her shoulder, along with the child, and sent her away. And she departed, and wandered about in the wilderness of Beer-sheba.

[15] When the water in the skin was gone, she cast the child under one of the bushes. [16] Then she went and sat down opposite him a good way off, about the distance of a bowshot; for she said, "Do not let me look on the death of the child." And as she sat opposite him, she lifted up her voice and wept. [17] And God heard the voice of the boy; and the angel of God called to Hagar from heaven, and said to her, "What troubles you, Hagar? Do not be afraid; for God has heard the voice of the boy where he is. [18] Come, lift up the boy and hold him fast with your hand, for I will make a great nation of him." [19] Then God opened her eyes and she saw a well of water. She went, and filled the skin with water, and gave the boy a drink.

[20] God was with the boy, and he grew up; he lived in the wilderness, and became an expert with the bow. [21] He lived in the wilderness of Paran; and his mother got a wife for him from the land of Egypt.

DISCUSSION QUESTIONS

1. How does the E version compare with the J version in Genesis 16:1-16?
2. What are the family dynamics among Abraham, Sarah, and Hagar?
3. Consider Genesis 12–25, especially chapter 22 in which Abraham binds Isaac for a sacrifice. How does the story of Hagar in chapter 21 advance the plot of children, offspring, and heirs in the Abraham cycle?
4. According to Muslim tradition, Abraham binds Ishmael to be sacrificed (compare with chapter 22), Hagar and Ishmael settle in Mecca near a well, and the patriarchal line continues through him instead of Isaac. How do the Hagar stories in chapters 16 and 21 relate to this tradition?

Genesis 25:21-34 (Jacob and Esau)

CLOSE READING TIPS

▶ Note that barrenness also drives the plot in the Abraham cycle (see Gen. 11:30).
▶ In verse 26, the name Jacob is understood to be related to the word for heel (Heb. *ăqōb*).
▶ The birthright refers to the leadership role and extra inheritance that is owed to the eldest son.
▶ The success of a younger brother is a common motif in ancient folklore.

[21] Isaac prayed to the LORD for his wife, because she was barren; and the LORD granted his prayer, and his wife Rebekah conceived. [22] The children struggled together within her; and she said, "If it is to be this way, why do I live?" So she went to inquire of the LORD.

[23] And the LORD said to her,

"Two nations are in your womb,
    and two peoples born of you shall be
        divided;
the one shall be stronger than the other,
    the elder shall serve the younger."

[24] When her time to give birth was at hand, there were twins in her womb. [25] The first came out red, all his body like a hairy mantle; so they named him Esau. [26] Afterward his brother came out, with his hand gripping Esau's heel; so he was named Jacob. Isaac was sixty years old when she bore them.

[27] When the boys grew up, Esau was a skillful hunter, a man of the field, while Jacob was a quiet man, living in tents. [28] Isaac loved Esau, because he was fond of game; but Rebekah loved Jacob.

[29] Once when Jacob was cooking a stew, Esau came in from the field, and he was famished. [30] Esau said to Jacob, "Let me eat some of that red stuff, for I am famished!" (Therefore he was called Edom.) [31] Jacob said, "First sell me your birthright." [32] Esau said, "I am about to die; of what use is a birthright to me?" [33] Jacob said, "Swear to me first." So he swore to him, and sold his birthright to Jacob. [34] Then Jacob gave Esau bread and lentil stew, and he ate and drank, and rose and went his way. Thus Esau despised his birthright.

DISCUSSION QUESTIONS

1. In what ways does the struggle in Rebekah's womb (verse 22) anticipate the plot as a whole in the Jacob cycle?
2. Can you think of another story in Genesis that features a tension between a hunter and a shepherd?
3. How is Esau characterized in this story?

Genesis 32:3-32

CLOSE READING TIPS

▶ Though pursuing reconciliation with his brother, Jacob still prioritizes self-preservation when he divides his flock (verses 6-8).

▶ Note that Jacob's bases his prayer on what God had already promised to him in Genesis 28:10-22.

▶ Note that Jacob does not realize who he is wrestling with prior to verse 29.

▶ Receiving a new name indicates a pivotal transition in life. The patriarch was once named Jacob ("supplanter") but is now called Israel, which means "the one who strives with God."

▶ Peniel/Penuel, which means "face of El," is one of the first capitals of the Northern Kingdom (1 Kings12:25), thus suggesting the E source

▶ Despite the reference in verse 32, a specific prohibition against eating the thigh muscle of an animal does not appear in the Hebrew Bible.

³ Jacob sent messengers before him to his brother Esau in the land of Seir, the country of Edom, ⁴ instructing them, "Thus you shall say to my lord Esau: Thus says your servant Jacob, 'I have lived with Laban as an alien, and stayed until now; ⁵ and I have oxen, donkeys, flocks, male and female slaves; and I have sent to tell my lord, in order that I may find favor in your sight.' "

⁶ The messengers returned to Jacob, saying, "We came to your brother Esau, and he is coming to meet you, and four hundred men are with him." ⁷ Then Jacob was greatly afraid and distressed; and he divided the people that were with him, and the flocks and herds and camels, into two companies, ⁸ thinking, "If Esau comes to the one company and destroys it, then the company that is left will escape."

⁹ And Jacob said, "O God of my father Abraham and God of my father Isaac, O LORD who said to me, 'Return to your country and to your kindred, and I will do you good,' ¹⁰ I am not worthy of the least of all the steadfast love and all the faithfulness that you have shown to your servant, for with only my staff I crossed this Jordan; and now I have become two companies. ¹¹ Deliver me, please, from the hand of my brother, from the hand of Esau, for I am afraid of him; he may come and kill us all, the mothers with the children. ¹² Yet you have said, 'I will surely do you good, and make your offspring as the sand of the sea, which cannot be counted because of their number.' "

¹³ So he spent that night there, and from what he had with him he took a present for his brother Esau, ¹⁴ two hundred female goats and twenty male

goats, two hundred ewes and twenty rams, [15] thirty milch camels and their colts, forty cows and ten bulls, twenty female donkeys and ten male donkeys. [16] These he delivered into the hand of his servants, every drove by itself, and said to his servants, "Pass on ahead of me, and put a space between drove and drove." [17] He instructed the foremost, "When Esau my brother meets you, and asks you, 'To whom do you belong? Where are you going? And whose are these ahead of you? ' [18] then you shall say, 'They belong to your servant Jacob; they are a present sent to my lord Esau; and moreover he is behind us. ' " [19] He likewise instructed the second and the third and all who followed the droves, "You shall say the same thing to Esau when you meet him, [20] and you shall say, 'Moreover your servant Jacob is behind us. ' " For he thought, "I may appease him with the present that goes ahead of me, and afterwards I shall see his face; perhaps he will accept me." [21] So the present passed on ahead of him; and he himself spent that night in the camp.

[22] The same night he got up and took his two wives, his two maids, and his eleven children, and crossed the ford of the Jabbok. [23] He took them and sent them across the stream, and likewise everything that he had. Jacob was left alone; and a man wrestled with him until daybreak. [25] When the man saw that he did not prevail against Jacob, he struck him on the hip socket; and Jacob's hip was put out of joint as he wrestled with him. [26] Then he said, "Let me go, for the day is breaking." But Jacob said, "I will not let you go, unless you bless me." [27] So he said to him, "What is your name?" And he said, "Jacob." [28] Then the man said, "You shall no longer be called Jacob, but Israel, for you have striven with God and with humans, and have prevailed." [29] Then Jacob asked him, "Please tell me your name." But he said, "Why is it that you ask my name?" And there he blessed him. [30] So Jacob called the place Peniel, saying, "For I have seen God face to face, and yet my life is preserved." [31] The sun rose upon him as he passed Penuel, limping because of his hip. [32] Therefore to this day the Israelites do not eat the thigh muscle that is on the hip socket, because he struck Jacob on the hip socket at the thigh muscle.

DISCUSSION QUESTIONS

1. What sort of strategies does Jacob use to appease his brother?
2. Where else have we seen name changes in the patriarchal stories?
3. Gunkel identifies several different types of legends. Based on verse 32, what type of legend is this?
4. In what sense do you think Jacob's struggle was internal, that is, with his own conscience? Is there any evidence in the text to suggest that this was the case?

Genesis 22:1-19 (The Binding of Isaac)

CLOSE READING TIPS

▶ Genesis 22 is one of the most frequently discussed texts of the patriarchal narratives in later rabbinic and Christian traditions.

▶ Note that verse 1 informs the reader of something Abraham himself does not know—that what follows will be a test.

▶ The syntax of verse 2 ("your son, your only son Isaac, whom you love") emphasizes how difficult the test will be.

▶ This story is often understood as a form of child sacrifice but the text itself never specifies Isaac's age.

▶ In verse 5, Abraham's promise that he and his son will return may suggest faith that God would provide an alternative means of sacrifice.

▶ Some later Jewish traditions claim that Abraham actually sacrificed Isaac, making Isaac a model of a faithful Jewish martyr.

▶ Abraham names the place "The LORD will provide," which reflects his earlier hope that God would provide a lamb for the sacrifice (verse 8).

▶ Verses 15-18 are likely a later editorial addition

---

¹ After these things God tested Abraham. He said to him, "Abraham!" And he said, "Here I am." ² He said, "Take your son, your only son Isaac, whom you love, and go to the land of Moriah, and offer him there as a burnt offering on one of the mountains that I shall show you." ³ So Abraham rose early in the morning, saddled his donkey, and took two of his young men with him, and his son Isaac; he cut the wood for the burnt offering, and set out and went to the place in the distance that God had shown him. ⁴ On the third day Abraham looked up and saw the place far away. ⁵ Then Abraham said to his young men, "Stay here with the donkey; the boy and I will go over there; we will worship, and then we will come back to you." ⁶ Abraham took the wood of the burnt offering and laid it on his son Isaac, and he himself carried the fire and the knife. So the two of them walked on together. ⁷ Isaac said to his father Abraham, "Father!" And he said, "Here I am, my son." He said, "The fire and the wood are here, but where is the lamb for a burnt offering?" ⁸ Abraham said, "God himself will provide the lamb for a burnt offering, my son." So the two of them walked on together.

⁹ When they came to the place that God had shown him, Abraham built an altar there and laid the wood in order. He bound his son Isaac, and laid him on the altar, on top of the wood. ¹⁰ Then Abraham reached out his hand and took the knife to kill his son. ¹¹ But the angel of the LORD called to him from heaven, and said, "Abraham, Abraham!" And he said, "Here I am." ¹² He said, "Do not lay your hand on the boy or do anything to him; for now I know that you fear God, since you have not withheld your son, your only son, from me." ¹³ And Abraham

looked up and saw a ram, caught in a thicket by its horns. Abraham went and took the ram and offered it up as a burnt offering instead of his son. [14] So Abraham called that place "The LORD will provide"; as it is said to this day, "On the mount of the LORD it shall be provided."

[15] The angel of the LORD called to Abraham a second time from heaven, and said, "By myself I have sworn, says the LORD: Because you have done this, and have not withheld your son, your only son, [17] I will indeed bless you, and I will make your off-spring as numerous as the stars of heaven and as the sand that is on the seashore. And your offspring shall possess the gate of their enemies, [18] and by your off-spring shall all the nations of the earth gain blessing for themselves, because you have obeyed my voice." [19] So Abraham returned to his young men, and they arose and went together to Beer-sheba; and Abraham lived at Beer-sheba.

Discussion questions

1. How does this "test" put in jeopardy God's earlier promises to Abraham?
2. Why do you think Abraham is praised for his willingness to carry out this sacrifice? In your opinion, is this ethically problematic or is there a way to resolve this issue?
3. In what ways do verses 15-18 integrate this story with the larger theme of divine promise in the Abraham cycle?

5

The Exodus from Egypt

Key Points

The Exodus story, which is told primarily in the first half of the book, covers two major themes: the revelation of YHWH and the liberation of Israel from slavery. When YHWH reveals himself to Moses, he charges him to participate in the divine initiative to end Israelite suffering and oppression.

Although the J and P layers are difficult to distinguish, theses chapters do show ample evidence of composite composition. They contain different genres, exhibit inconsistent plot elements, and reference variant traditions. For example, the old poetry in Exodus 15 is mythological and poetic. With no mention of enslavement, plagues, or even the Israelites crossing on dry ground, this hymn to YHWH only celebrates an amazing victory over Egyptian armies in the sea. This tradition was later supplemented by the prose narrative in Exodus 14.

No archaeological or extra-biblical evidence supports a straightforward reading of the exodus and these chapters should not be understood as a work of historiography. Instead, numerous loose comparative connections to culture and history can be discerned. Moses' birth story resembles a legend about Sargon. The Hebrew slaves evoke the Habiru immigrant laborers in Egypt. The story of Moses and the burning bush (sineh) parallels other traditions about Sinai, such as Mosaic revelation in Exodus 19 and the abode of YHWH as divine warrior in other Hebrew compositions. These composite tales and poems possibly spring from some historical memory of people enslaved in Egypt, but they reflect numerous and disparate Israelite traditions.

The exodus story in its current form connects the departure from Egyptian slavery, observance of the first Passover festival, crossing the Sea of Reeds, and the journey to Mt. Sinai to receive the Mosaic law. The late Priestly story of the Passover illustrates how the exodus came to be celebrated as a national charter narrative. Originally a festival celebrated in the home, the Passover and the exodus came to represent a central story and national ritual for Israel. Perhaps first important in the northern kingdom, the exodus came to be a central tradition in later Judaism.

Key Terms

Passover During YHWH's final plague, the slaughter of the first-born, the Israelites eat a meal as YHWH "passes over" blood-marked homes. Originally a spring-time family festival, Passover developed into a national pilgrimage. The priestly author honors Passover as a celebration of the exodus, the most important event in Israelite history.

Hyksos and Habiru Two historical Semitic and west Asian groups are loosely connected to the exodus story. The Syrian Hyksos ruled Egypt (c. 1530 BCE) from a capital city that was later occupied by Ramesses II. Habiru, a class of Semitic fugitives and marauders, helped build Ramesses II's capital city.

Divine name Exodus 6:2 (P) indicates that Moses is the first to be introduced to God's divine name. Possibly a verbal causative form of "to be," YHWH plays on his own name in Exodus 3:14 when he answers Moses, "I am who I am." The revelation of YHWH's name is associated with his mission to relieve the suffering of Israel.

Charter myth A charter myth authorizes and empowers present social life in terms of origins. Like American Thanksgiving, the exodus became a foundational story in Israelite society expressing social values. Evidence of its importance in the Northern monarchy suggests that Israelites abhorred practices of forced labor.

Sea imagery Exodus's crossing of "the Sea of Reeds" (Yam Sûp) participates in a widespread poetic use of sea imagery in Israelite religion. The exodus hymn in chapter 15 celebrates how YHWH cast Egyptian armies into the sea.

"Depths of the sea" served as a metaphor for distress. Ugaritic and Hebrew Psalmic literature invoke the theme of divine combat and triumph over the sea.

Key Personalities

Moses

The most important character in the Pentateuch, Moses' story takes place in Egypt and the wilderness. His birth (chapter 2), crime (Exod. 2:11-15), and flight to Midian (Exod. 2:16—3:1) lead to the story of the burning bush where he meets YHWH and receives his liberating mission. Joined by his brother Aaron, Moses and Pharaoh exchange demonstrations of power in the ten plagues. Moses then leads the Israelite departure from Egypt and parting of the Sea of Reeds, bringing the Israelites to Mt. Sinai to receive instruction.

YHWH

YHWH's old poetic association with Mt. Sinai emphasizes the divine warrior motif. In the burning bush, YHWH observes the misery of a people and vows to liberate them from service to Egypt. Exodus highlights the secrecy of YHWH's name: "I am who I am" suggests an unwillingness to divulge the divine name (Exod. 3:13) and "by my name I did not make myself known" exhibits the Priestly tradition of the Genesis patriarchs in which YHWH was not used (Exod. 6:2).

Pharaoh

Pharaoh, a title used for the king of Egypt, enslaves the Israelites at the outset of the exodus story. Although he is never named, it is possible that this pharaoh was Ramesses II (1304–1237 BCE).

Exodus 7–11 depicts a struggle between YHWH and Moses on the one hand and the pharaoh on the other. YHWH hardens the pharaoh's heart so that he refuses to let Israel go free, but ultimately the Israelites are liberated when the pharaoh and his army are cast into the depths of the sea in Exodus 15. No longer bound to serve the pharaoh, the Israelites are free to serve YHWH instead.

Questions for Study and Discussion

1. Exodus is an ancient story of liberation from slavery that has been revered by many people for millennia. What are some of the problems and possibilities of using such a story in the contemporary world as a paradigm for liberation? How does the book of Exodus compare to other narratives of liberation that you are aware of?

2. Who are the "insiders" and "outsiders" in the book of Exodus? What kind of power does their station in life afford them?

3. The chapter claims that the exodus is, at least in part, nationalistic and vengeful. Do you agree with this evaluation?

4. The book of Exodus depicts God as a powerful and decisive agent. How would you evaluate and characterize the God of Exodus? Do you find the deity's actions commendable? Problematic?

5. The chapter claims that the Book of Exodus, while containing some historical kernel, is not a "history" in the modern sense of the word. What evidence lends support to this viewpoint? Do you agree with this argument?

6. According to chapter 5, YHWH's revelation and liberation from slavery are the two dominant themes in the account of Israel's exodus from Egypt. What are some other important themes you noticed?

Primary Texts

Burning Bush in Exodus 3:1-14

CLOSE READING TIPS

▶ Note the setting on Mt. Horeb.
▶ The Hebrew word for bush is *sineh* (compare with Sinai).
▶ Note E and J names for divine: God and LORD.
▶ Compare Exodus 3:6 with Exodus 6:2.
▶ Note the identity of God in terms of both past and future.

¹ Moses was keeping the flock of his father-in-law Jethro, the priest of Midian; he led his flock beyond the wilderness, and came to Horeb, the mountain of God. ² There the angel of the LORD appeared to him in a flame of fire out of a bush; he looked, and the bush was blazing, yet it was not consumed. ³ Then Moses said, "I must turn aside and look at this great sight, and see why the bush is not burned up." ⁴ When the LORD saw that he had turned aside to see, God called to him out of the bush, "Moses, Moses!" And he said, "Here I am." ⁵ Then he said, "Come no closer! Remove the sandals from your feet, for the place on which you are standing is holy ground." ⁶ He said further, "I am the God of your father, the God of Abraham, the God of Isaac, and the God of Jacob." And Moses hid his face, for he was afraid to look at God.

⁷ Then the Lord said, "I have observed the misery of my people who are in Egypt; I have heard their cry on account of their taskmasters. Indeed, I know their sufferings, ⁸ and I have come down to deliver them from the Egyptians, and to bring them up out of that land to a good and broad land, a land flowing with milk and honey, to the country of the Canaanites, the Hittites, the Amorites, the Perizzites, the Hivites, and the Jebusites. ⁹ The cry of the Israelites has now come to me; I have also seen how the Egyptians oppress them. ¹⁰ So come, I will send you to Pharaoh to bring my people, the Israelites, out of Egypt." ¹¹ But Moses said to God, "Who am I that I should go to Pharaoh, and bring the Israelites out of Egypt?" ¹² He said, "I will be with you; and this shall be the sign for you that it is I who sent you; when you have brought the people out of Egypt, you shall worship God on this mountain."

¹³ But Moses said to God, "If I come to the Israelites and say to them, 'The God of your ancestors has sent me to you,' and they ask me, 'What is his name?' what shall I say to them?" ¹⁴ God said to Moses, "I AM WHO I AM." He said further, "Thus you shall say to the Israelites, 'I AM has sent me to you.' "

DISCUSSION QUESTIONS

1. In Exodus 3:11, Moses, the proto-typical Israelite prophet, asks, "Who am I that I should go?" How many times in the larger Exodus narrative does Moses convey his resistance and how does YHWH respond each time?
2. Why is Moses in Midian and what significant life events occur there?
3. What is YHWH's identity in this passage?
4. How does this passage compare with the Sinai tradition (especially in Exod. 19)?

J Account of Exodus 14

CLOSE READING TIPS

▸ Note that the Israelites do not cross the sea themselves in this account.

▸ Note the imagery of God as a pillar of fire and cloud.

⁵ᵇ The minds of Pharaoh and his officials were changed toward the people, and they said, "What have we done, letting Israel leave our service?" ⁶ So he had his chariot made ready, and took his army with him. ⁹ The Egyptians pursued them.

¹⁰ The Israelites looked back, and there were the Egyptians advancing on them, [and they were] in great fear. ¹³ But Moses said to the people, "Do not be afraid, stand firm, and see the deliverance that the LORD will accomplish for you today; for the Egyptians whom you see today you shall never see again. ¹⁴ The LORD will fight for you, and you have only to keep still."

¹⁹ᵇ And the pillar of cloud moved from in front of them and took its place behind them. ²⁰ It came between the army of Egypt and the army of Israel. And so the cloud was there with the darkness, and it lit up the night; one did not come near the other all night.

²¹ᵇ The LORD drove the sea back by a strong east wind all night, and turned the sea into dry land. ²⁴ At the morning watch the LORD in the pillar of fire and cloud looked down upon the Egyptian army, and threw the Egyptian army into panic. ²⁵ᵇ The Egyptians said, "Let us flee from the Israelites, for the LORD is fighting for them against Egypt."

²⁷ᵇ And at dawn the sea returned to its normal depth. As the Egyptians fled before it, the LORD tossed the Egyptians into the sea.

³⁰ Thus the LORD saved Israel that day from the Egyptians; and Israel saw the Egyptians dead on the seashore. ³¹ Israel saw the great work that the LORD did against the Egyptians. So the people feared the LORD and believed in the LORD and in his servant Moses.

Discussion questions

1. What kind of attributes can be associated with God in this story?
2. How does the dark and light imagery in verse 20 impact your reading of the text?

Songs of Moses and Miriam in Exodus 15:1-20

Close reading tips

► Compare Miriam's words (verse 21) with Moses' opening line (verse 1).
► Note "sea of reeds" in verse 4.
► Note the shift in focus to a march into the promised land in verses 13-17.
► Note the words "on dry ground" in verse 19.

[1] Then Moses and the Israelites sang this song to the LORD:

"I will sing to the LORD, for he has triumphed gloriously;
> horse and rider he has thrown into the sea.

[2] The LORD is my strength and my might,
> and he has become my salvation;
this is my God, and I will praise him,
> my father's God, and I will exalt him.

[3] The LORD is a warrior;
> the LORD is his name.

[4] "Pharaoh's chariots and his army he cast into the sea;
> his picked officers were sunk in the Red Sea.

[5] The floods covered them;
> they went down into the depths like a stone.

[6] Your right hand, O LORD, glorious in power—
> your right hand, O LORD, shattered the enemy.

[7] In the greatness of your majesty you overthrew your adversaries;
> you sent out your fury, it consumed them like stubble.

[8] At the blast of your nostrils the waters piled up,
> the floods stood up in a heap;
> the deeps congealed in the heart of the sea.

[9] The enemy said, 'I will pursue, I will overtake,
> I will divide the spoil, my desire shall have its fill of them.
> I will draw my sword, my hand shall destroy them.'

[10] You blew with your wind, the sea covered them;
> they sank like lead in the mighty waters.

[11] "Who is like you, O LORD, among the gods?
> Who is like you, majestic in holiness,
> awesome in splendor, doing wonders?

[12] You stretched out your right hand,
> the earth swallowed them.

[13] "In your steadfast love you led the people whom you redeemed;
> you guided them by your strength to your holy abode.

[14] The peoples heard, they trembled;
> pangs seized the inhabitants of Philistia.

[15] Then the chiefs of Edom were dismayed;
> trembling seized the leaders of Moab;
> all the inhabitants of Canaan melted away.

[16] Terror and dread fell upon them;
> by the might of your arm, they became still as a stone
until your people, O LORD, passed by,
> until the people whom you acquired passed by.

[17] You brought them in and planted them on the mountain of your own possession,
> the place, O LORD, that you made your abode,
> the sanctuary, O LORD, that your hands have established.

[18] The LORD will reign forever and ever."

[19] When the horses of Pharaoh with his chariots and his chariot drivers went into the sea, the Lord brought back the waters of the sea upon them; but the Israelites walked through the sea on dry ground. [20] Then the prophet Miriam, Aaron's sister, took a tambourine in her hand; and all the women went out after her with tambourines and with dancing.

DISCUSSION QUESTIONS

1. How do the hymnic elements (verses 1-18) impact interpretation?
2. How does YHWH's identity as divine warrior play out in the text?
3. What elements of the exodus story are present or absent?
4. How is sea imagery used?

Birth of Sargon

Source: Bill T. Arnold and Bryan E. Beyer, eds., *Readings from the Ancient Near East: Primary Sources for Old Testament Study* (Grand Rapids, Mich.: Baker Academic, 2002).

CLOSE READING TIPS

▶ Note Sargon's real and adoptive parents.
▶ List plot elements.

Sargon, strong king, king of Agade, am I.

My mother was a high priestess, my father I do not know.

My paternal kin inhabit the mountain region.

My city of birth is Azupiranu, which lies on the bank of the Euphrates.

My other, a high priestess, conceived me, in secret she bore me.

She placed me in a reed basket, with bitumen she caulked my hatch.

She abandoned me to the river from which I could not escape.

The river carried me along; to Aqqi, the water drawer, it brought me.

Aqqi, the water drawer, when immersing his bucket lifted me up.

Aqqi, the water drawer, raised me as his adopted son.

Aqqi, the water drawer, set me to his garden work.

During my garden work, Ishtar loved me so that

fifty-five years I ruled as king.

DISCUSSION QUESTION

1. How does Sargon's birth narrative compare with Exodus 2:1-10?

6

The Revelation at Sinai

Key Points

The pivotal moment of the exodus narrative, the crossing of the Reed Sea, is followed immediately by another manifestation of God's power, this time through a theophany on Mount Sinai. It is likely that the Sinai and exodus traditions were originally independent, but in the final form of this book liberation has its fulfillment in the giving of the law. In fact, throughout Exodus 19–40, the primary motivation for keeping the law is the memory of God's deliverance of the Israelites out of slavery in Egypt.

The structure of the Sinai covenant shares many common features with ancient Hittite and Assyrian treaties. At the heart of this treaty structure is a series of stipulations or laws that outline the conditions that lead to blessings or curses. Two types of laws are evident in Exodus: apodictic laws, which are absolute commandments with no qualifications; and casuistic laws, which follow an "if x, then y" pattern.

The Decalogue (Exodus 20) is the most prominent example of apodictic law. Some of these commandments, especially those dealing with the exclusive worship of Yahweh and the prohibition against idols or images, probably do not go back to the time of Moses, but rather reflect later developments in Israelite religion. Though the Decalogue is central to ethical reflection in Judaism and Christianity, there is some variation in how these laws are counted and classified.

The Book of the Covenant (Exodus 21–23) consists of a collection of casuistic laws that qualify the absolute character of apodictic laws. It is difficult to date these laws, though they seem to be presupposed by Deuteronomy. The Book of the Covenant deals with topics such as the rights of slaves, the consequences of violence, the cultic calendar, and dietary restrictions. These laws were likely formulated in a settled, agrarian community and reflect more closely how law was actually practiced in ancient Israel.

Exodus concludes with three additional sections: instructions concerning the tabernacle and its furnishings (chapters 25–31); the Golden Calf affair and the second giving of the law (chapters 32–34); and a description of the construction of the tabernacle (chapters 35–40).

Key Terms

Sinai Sinai is the mountain of YHWH where Moses and the Israelites received the law after escaping Egypt. The revelation of the Sinai law extends from Exodus 19 through Leviticus and Numbers. Most of this material is from the Priestly source, although several legal traditions can be identified.

Covenant A covenant is a formal agreement between two parties, usually with stipulations and sworn under oath. Noah, Abraham, and Moses entered into covenants with God. The Sinai or Mosaic covenant resembles an international treaty. Known primarily from Hittite and Assyrian sources, the treaty was a common covenantal form between a sovereign (suzerain) and an unequal party (vassal).

Ten Commandments The Ten Commandments (Decalogue) appear in Exodus 20:1-17 and Deuteronomy 5:6-21 with some differences in wording. Known as apodictic law, the commands are absolute and without condition. Resembling the exclusive devotion required in a treaty, the first command forbids worship of other gods, setting the Decalogue in a period before monotheism.

Book of the Covenant The Book of the Covenant consists of a self-contained collection of non-priestly law in Exodus 21–23. Written in the form of casuistic or conditional laws, this collection resembles the legal traditions of the ancient Near East and sheds light on the social practices of ancient Israel, addressing topics such as slavery, violence, domesticated animals, and festivals.

Golden calf A festival initiated by Aaron that ends in massacre, the story of the Golden Calf occurs in Exodus 32. There, it displays Israelite vulnerability to idolatry and occasions another legal collection, often called the J Decalogue. A complex story with notable features of polemic, it sheds a negative light on the northern kingdom (1 Kings 12) and the priestly line of Aaron that later officiated in Jerusalem.

Key Personalities

Moses

Chosen by God to lead the Israelites from Egypt to the Promised Land, Moses plays the pivotal role in the revelation at Sinai. He prepares the people for the divine glory to descend on the mountain and then mediates the law when it proves too powerful for them to hear. He spends his time going up and down the mountain, carrying and breaking tablets, leading the Levite massacre in the golden calf episode (Exod. 32), and setting up a tent in which to mediate YHWH to the people (Exod. 33).

Aaron

Aaron plays an important but supporting role in his brother, Moses' career. Earlier in Exodus, he joined Moses in leading the Israelites from Egypt, acting as a spokesperson and playing a key role in the story of the plagues. In Exodus 32, Aaron is portrayed as the villain, collecting gold from the people in order to make a calf, and proclaiming "these are the gods who brought you out of Egypt." The Levite revolt against him in Exodus 32 probably reflects later tensions within the Aaronide line of priests in Jerusalem.

Questions for Study and Discussion

1. Many people claim that our current legal system is a distant cousin of the laws found in the Pentateuch. We live in a "Judeo-Christian Society," we are often told. How are the laws given at Sinai similar to or different from modern laws? What would ancient Israel accept legally that we, as modern Westerners, would reject?

2. The Levites in Exodus 32 are commended for killing some 3,000 of their own neighbors and kin ("brother and friend and neighbor") as retribution for the latter's worship of the golden calf. Given the many problems caused by religious violence in the modern day, how do you respond to the text's claim that, because of their pious violence, the Levites were "blessed" (Exod. 32:29). What kind of status should such texts have in modern society? In religion?

3. The God of Exodus is often depicted in troubling ways. This God is violently jealous for Israel's worship (Exodus 32–34), to the point of nearly destroying his own people (see Exod. 32:9-10). If one generation does sin against God, three to four subsequent generations will suffer (Exod. 20:5-6). How would you respond to the religious person who claims that this very God is the God of the cosmos?

4. How does the God of Sinai, who reveals himself through the law and through powerful displays of nature, compare to the God of the patriarchs?

Primary Texts

Exodus 19

CLOSE READING TIPS

▶ Exodus 19 is a combination of traditions and at times parts of the story seem contradictory or redundant.

▶ Though its actual location is uncertain, Sinai is often associated with a mountain in the southern Sinai Peninsula.

▶ The notion of a "priestly kingdom" can be interpreted in several ways: all Israelites are priestly, Israel played a priestly role among the nations, or Israel's priests had a royal function.

▶ Note the emphasis on the holiness of the mountain itself. This likely corresponds to the holiness of the tabernacle.

▶ Thunder, lightning, a thick cloud, smoke, and violent shaking suggest divine revelation.

[1] On the third new moon after the Israelites had gone out of the land of Egypt, on that very day, they came into the wilderness of Sinai. [2] They had journeyed from Rephidim, entered the wilderness of Sinai, and camped in the wilderness; Israel camped there in front of the mountain. [3] Then Moses went up to God; the LORD called to him from the mountain, saying, "Thus you shall say to the house of Jacob, and tell the Israelites: [4] You have seen what I did to the Egyptians, and how I bore you on eagles' wings and brought you to myself. [5] Now therefore, if you obey my voice and keep my covenant, you shall be my treasured possession out of all the peoples. Indeed, the whole earth is mine, [6] but you shall be for me a priestly kingdom and a holy nation. These are the words that you shall speak to the Israelites."

[7] So Moses came, summoned the elders of the people, and set before them all these words that the LORD had commanded him. [8] The people all answered as one: "Everything that the LORD has spoken we will do." Moses reported the words of the people to the LORD. [9] Then the LORD said to Moses, "I am going to come to you in a dense cloud, in order that the people may hear when I speak with you and so trust you ever after."

When Moses had told the words of the people to the LORD, [10] the LORD said to Moses: "Go to the people and consecrate them today and tomorrow. Have them wash their clothes [11] and prepare for the third day, because on the third day the LORD will come down upon Mount Sinai in the sight of all the people. [12] You shall set limits for the people all around, saying, 'Be careful not to go up the mountain or to touch the edge of it. Any who touch the mountain shall be put to death. [13] No hand shall touch them, but they shall be stoned or shot with arrows; whether animal or human being, they shall not live.' When the trumpet sounds a long blast, they may go up on the mountain." [14] So Moses went down from the mountain to the people. He consecrated the people, and they washed their clothes. [15] And he said to the people, "Prepare for the third day; do not go near a woman."

[16] On the morning of the third day there was thunder and lightning, as well as a thick cloud on the mountain, and a blast of a trumpet so loud that all the people who were in the camp trembled. [17] Moses brought the people out of the camp to meet God. They took their stand at the foot of the mountain. [18] Now Mount Sinai was wrapped in smoke, because the LORD had descended upon it in fire; the smoke went up like the smoke of a kiln, while the whole mountain shook violently. [19] As the blast of the trumpet grew louder and louder, Moses would speak and God would answer him in thunder. [20] When the LORD descended upon Mount Sinai, to the top of the mountain, the LORD summoned Moses to the top of the mountain, and Moses went up. [21] Then the LORD said to Moses, "Go down and warn the people not to break through to the LORD to look; otherwise many of them will perish. [22] Even the priests who approach the LORD must consecrate themselves or the Lord will break out against them." [23] Moses said to the LORD, "The people are not permitted to come up to Mount Sinai; for you yourself warned us, saying, 'Set limits around the mountain and keep it holy.' " [24] The LORD said to him, "Go down, and come up bringing Aaron with you; but do not let either the priests or the people break through to come up to the LORD; otherwise he will break out against them." So Moses went down to the people and told them.

DISCUSSION QUESTIONS

1. How many times does Moses go up and down the mountain in this composite text?
2. In its compact with God, Israel is described as a "treasured possession." How does this compare to the status of covenant partners in Hittite and Assyrian treaties?
3. What role does Moses play in the theophany at Sinai?

Exodus 20:1-17

CLOSE READING TIPS

▶ This set of laws is not titled in Exodus 20; the name is derived from the reference to "ten words" or "ten sayings" in Exodus 34:28.
▶ The commandments are not numbered in the Hebrew Bible and Jewish and Christian traditions count them in slightly different ways.
▶ Note that verse 3 requires the worship of YHWH alone without denying the existence of other gods.
▶ While verse 4 prohibits the making of certain images, certain material objects, such as God's cherubim throne and the ark, are never condemned in the Hebrew Bible.
▶ Note that God's name is often assumed to be a manifestation of (or a metaphor for) divine presence.
▶ Note that the Sabbath commandment is rooted in the P account of creation.
▶ Roman Catholic and Lutheran traditions delineate two different laws in verse 17.

[1] Then God spoke all these words:

[2] I am the LORD your God, who brought you out of the land of Egypt, out of the house of slavery; [3] you shall have no other gods before me.

[4] You shall not make for yourself an idol, whether in the form of anything that is in heaven above, or that is on the earth beneath, or that is in the water under the earth. [5] You shall not bow down to them or worship them; for I the LORD your God am a jealous God, punishing children for the iniquity of parents, to the third and the fourth generation of those who reject me, [6] but showing steadfast love to the thousandth generation of those who love me and keep my commandments.

[7] You shall not make wrongful use of the name of the LORD your God, for the LORD will not acquit anyone who misuses his name.

[8] Remember the sabbath day, and keep it holy. [9] Six days you shall labor and do all your work. [10] But the seventh day is a sabbath to the LORD your God; you shall not do any work—you, your son or your daughter, your male or female slave, your livestock, or the alien resident in your towns. [11] For in six days the LORD made heaven and earth, the sea, and all that is in them, but rested the seventh day; therefore the Lord blessed the sabbath day and consecrated it.

[12] Honor your father and your mother, so that your days may be long in the land that the LORD your God is giving you.

[13] You shall not murder.

[14] You shall not commit adultery.

[15] You shall not steal.

[16] You shall not bear false witness against your neighbor.

[17] You shall not covet your neighbor's house; you shall not covet your neighbor's wife, or male or female slave, or ox, or donkey, or anything that belongs to your neighbor.

DISCUSSION QUESTIONS

1. Why do you think the Ten Commandments begins with a brief historical summary of the exodus from Egypt?
2. How is the commandment about worshipping other gods related to the commandment about making images or idols?
3. While the Ten Commandments are apodictic laws, do any of them seem to allow room for qualifications based on intentionality and context?

Exodus 32

CLOSE READING TIPS

▸ An image such as a calf or young bull could have been seen as an object of worship or, as is the case with the cherubim throne, a pedestal for the (invisible) deity.

▸ Note that Aaron makes one calf but the people say "These are you *gods*." The plural form of gods is likely influenced by 1 Kings 12:25-30, which recounts how Jeroboam set up two calf images, one in Bethel and the other in Dan.

▸ "Stiff-necked" is a common idiom meaning stubborn or obstinate.

▸ Note that verses 7-14 are thought to be a Deuteronomistic addition.

▸ Note how Moses intercedes on behalf of the people (verses 11-13).

▸ It is often assumed that the commandments were divided up between the two tablets. However, it is also possible that the two tablets represent two identical copies, one for each partner in the treaty.

▸ Note Moses' sever reaction to what he sees in the Israelite camp (verses 18-20).

▸ Note how Aaron tries to deny direct responsibility for making the calf in verse 24.

▸ Note that the sons of Levi are rewarded for their violent response.

[1] When the people saw that Moses delayed to come down from the mountain, the people gathered around Aaron, and said to him, "Come, make gods for us, who shall go before us; as for this Moses, the man who brought us up out of the land of Egypt, we do not know what has become of him." [2] Aaron said to them, "Take off the gold rings that are on the ears of your wives, your sons, and your daughters, and bring them to me." [3] So all the people took off the gold rings from their ears, and brought them to Aaron. [4] He took the gold from them, formed it in a mold, and cast an image of a calf; and they said, "These are your gods, O Israel, who brought you up out of the land of Egypt!" [5] When Aaron saw this, he built an altar before it; and Aaron made proclamation and said, "Tomorrow shall be a festival to the LORD." [6] They rose early the next day, and offered burnt offerings and brought sacrifices of well-being; and the people sat down to eat and drink, and rose up to revel.

[7] The LORD said to Moses, "Go down at once! Your people, whom you brought up out of the land of Egypt, have acted perversely; [8] they have been quick to turn aside from the way that I commanded them; they have cast for themselves an image of a calf, and have worshiped it and sacrificed to it, and said, 'These are your gods, O Israel, who brought you up out of the land of Egypt!' " [9] The LORD said to Moses, "I have seen this people, how stiff-necked they are. [10] Now let me alone, so that my wrath may burn hot against them and I may consume them; and of you I will make a great nation."

[11] But Moses implored the LORD his God, and said, "O LORD, why does your wrath burn hot against your people, whom you brought out of the land of Egypt with great power and with a mighty hand? [12] Why should the Egyptians say, 'It was with evil intent that he brought them out to kill them in the mountains, and to consume them from the face of the earth'? Turn from your fierce wrath; change your mind and do not bring disaster on your people. [13] Remember Abraham, Isaac, and Israel, your servants, how you swore to them by your own self, saying to them, 'I will multiply your descendants like the stars of heaven, and all this land that I have promised I will give to your descendants, and they shall inherit it forever.' " [14] And the LORD changed his mind about the disaster that he planned to bring on his people.

[15] Then Moses turned and went down from the mountain, carrying the two tablets of the covenant in his hands, tablets that were written on both sides, written on the front and on the back. [16] The tablets were the work of God, and the writing was the writing of God, engraved upon the tablets. [17] When Joshua heard the noise of the people as they shouted, he said to Moses, "There is a noise of war in the camp."

[18] But he said,

"It is not the sound made by victors,
or the sound made by losers;
it is the sound of revelers that I hear."

[19] As soon as he came near the camp and saw the calf and the dancing, Moses' anger burned hot, and he threw the tablets from his hands and broke them at the foot of the mountain. [20] He took the calf that they had made, burned it with fire, ground it to powder, scattered it on the water, and made the Israelites drink it.

[21] Moses said to Aaron, "What did this people do to you that you have brought so great a sin upon them?" [22] And Aaron said, "Do not let the anger of my lord burn hot; you know the people, that they are bent on evil. [23] They said to me, 'Make us gods, who shall go before us; as for this Moses, the man who

brought us up out of the land of Egypt, we do not know what has become of him.' [24] So I said to them, 'Whoever has gold, take it off'; so they gave it to me, and I threw it into the fire, and out came this calf!"

[25] When Moses saw that the people were running wild (for Aaron had let them run wild, to the derision of their enemies), [26] then Moses stood in the gate of the camp, and said, "Who is on the LORD's side? Come to me!" And all the sons of Levi gathered around him. [27] He said to them, "Thus says the LORD, the God of Israel, 'Put your sword on your side, each of you! Go back and forth from gate to gate throughout the camp, and each of you kill your brother, your friend, and your neighbor.' " [28] The sons of Levi did as Moses commanded, and about three thousand of the people fell on that day. [29] Moses said, "Today you have ordained yourselves for the service of the LORD, each one at the cost of a son or a brother, and so have brought a blessing on yourselves this day."

[30] On the next day Moses said to the people, "You have sinned a great sin. But now I will go up to the LORD; perhaps I can make atonement for your sin." [31] So Moses returned to the LORD and said, "Alas, this people has sinned a great sin; they have made for themselves gods of gold. [32] But now, if you will only forgive their sin—but if not, blot me out of the book that you have written." [33] But the LORD said to Moses, "Whoever has sinned against me I will blot out of my book. [34] But now go, lead the people to the place about which I have spoken to you; see, my angel shall go in front of you. Nevertheless, when the day comes for punishment, I will punish them for their sin."

[35] Then the LORD sent a plague on the people, because they made the calf—the one that Aaron made.

DISCUSSION QUESTIONS

1. How are Aaron and Moses characterized in this story?
2. Do you think the golden calf represented an inappropriate image of Yahweh or an image of another god? How might verse 5 inform your answer?
3. Where in this story do you see evidence for underlying controversies about priests and priesthood?

Treaty between Suppululiuma and Mattiwaza

Source: Bill T. Arnold and Bryan E. Beyer, *Readings from the Ancient Near East*, (Baker Acacemic, 2002), 97-98.

CLOSE READING TIPS

▸ This is a Hittite treaty from the fourteenth century BCE; Suppululiuma is the power king of the Hittites and Mattiwaza is lesser king of Mitanni

▸ It was common to require the depositing of multiple copies of the treaty

▸ Note how various gods are assembled as witnesses to the treaty

▸ Note the curses for not upholding the covenant affect Mattiwaza, his people, and his land

▸ Note the blessings for obedience, like the curses for disobedience, are couched in highly personal terms

A duplicate of this tablet has been deposited before the sun-goddess of Arinna, because the sun-goddess of Arinna regulates kingship and queenship.

In the Mitanni Land *a duplicate* has been deposited before Teshub, the lord of the KURINNU of Kahat. At regular [intervals] shall they read it in the presence of the king of the Mitanni land and in the presence of the sons of the Hurri country. Whoever will remove this tablet from before Teshub, the lord of the KURINNU of the Kahat, and put it in a hidden place, if he breaks it or causes anyone else to change the wording of the tablet—at the conclusion of this treaty we have called the gos to be assembled and the gods of the contracting parties to be present, to listen and to serve as witnesses. . . .

If *on the other hand* you, Mattiwaza, the prince, and *you*, the Hurrians, fulfill this treaty and *this* oath, may these gods protect you, Mattiwaza, together with your wife, the daughter of Hatti land, her children and her children's children, and also *you*, the Hurrians, together with your wives, your children, and your children's children and together with your country. May the Mitanni country return to the place that it occupied before, may it thrive and expand. May you, Mattiwaza, your sons and your sons' sons *descended* from the daughter of the great king of Hatti land, and *you*, the Hurrians, exercise kingship forever. May the throne of your father persist, may the Mitanni country persist.

DISCUSSION QUESTIONS

1. Which parts of the typically Hittite treaty form are *not* included in this excerpt?
2. Where you see parallels to the blessings and curses section of this treaty in the book of Exodus?
3. Does the book of Exodus give any evidence of there being multiple copies of the treaty between Israel and YHWH?

7

The Priestly Theology: Exodus 25–40, Leviticus, and Numbers

Key Points

The Priestly source is evident in editorial additions to Genesis and Exodus 1–24, but it is the dominant thread from Exodus 25 through Leviticus and the first ten chapters of Numbers. For many readers today, this material can be particularly hard to relate to. In fact, many of the specific regulations mentioned here were eventually done away or reinterpreted in Jewish and Christian traditions. Nevertheless, Priestly theology reveals fundamental aspects of Israelite religion. For instance, the sacrificial system provides a symbolic way of expressing gratitude to God and atoning for sins. The tabernacle represents the special dwelling place of God on earth. Impurity laws, especially those dealing with dietary restrictions, attempt to bring order to human experience and give a sense of security in times of crisis. And the priesthood was as a powerful institution through the history of ancient Israel in both cultic and civil matters.

Leviticus 17–26 is known as the Holiness Code (H) and represents a distinct section within the Priestly tradition. It revises P by attempting to integrate ethical concerns with specific cultic and ritual laws. It deals with questions about the slaughter of animals and improper relationships, and it provides a more developed cultic calendar than is evident in either Exodus or Deuteronomy. Its core theology is expressed in Leviticus 19:2, "You shall be holy, for I the LORD your God am holy." The Holiness Code concludes with a list of blessings and curses framed in covenant language.

The book of Numbers primarily deals with issues that arise as Israel travels from Sinai to Canaan. Though the P source describes this journey as an orderly procession, the road to the promised land was somewhat rocky. Enemies to the east pose a threat (Num. 31) and the scarcity of food causes the people to grumble (Num. 11). Korah openly rebels against the authority of the priests (Num. 16) and even Moses and Aaron show a lack of trust in God (Num. 20). Eventually, the people succumb to the worship of the god Baal (Num. 25). Yet the book ends on a positive note in the plains of Moab, where conflicts are resolved and provisions are made for taking possession of the land of Canaan (Num. 34).

Key Terms

Tabernacle   The Tabernacle, a tent shrine, is the visible sign of YHWH's presence in the midst of the tribes. It centralizes worship, houses the ark of the covenant, hosts sacrifices, and mediates YHWH to the people through Moses. The Priestly layer of Exodus includes directions for its construction (chapters 25–31; 35–40), and it is intended to be portable for the wilderness wanderings.

Sacrifice   Sacrifice makes an offering to a god sacred. A number of prescribed rituals for sacrifices are found in Leviticus 1–7. Sacrifices are usually living things such as birds or livestock and they might be offered whole, shared in a sacrificial meal, or partially retained by the priests.

Day of Atonement   Described only in Leviticus 16, the Day of Atonement is designed to expunge impurities from the sanctuary. The blood of two animals is sprinkled and daubed on sacred elements to purge human impurities. A preparation for the coming year, the day includes an annual ritual to dispatch a goat carrying the people's sins to Azazel, a being or demon in the wilderness.

Purity system   Purity systems involve elaborate distinctions between the sacred and profane and the clean and unclean. They are expressed in formal (as in sanctuary rites) and informal (such as dietary laws) social practices. Leviticus 11–15 deals with causes and solutions for impurity, including topics like food, corpses, bodily emissions, clothing, and skin disease.

Holiness Code (H)   Leviticus 17–26 contains another layer of legal material known as the Holiness Code. A later reworking of Priestly tradition, the code resembles the purity laws of Leviticus but integrates the ethical concerns emphasized in Deuteronomy and the Prophets. Leviticus 19 is a primary example.

Key Personalities

Balaam

Balaam is a non-Israelite prophet who features in the J narrative of Numbers 22–24. During the Israelite progression towards the promised land, the Moabite king hires Balaam to curse Israel as it threatens to invade their land. However, Balaam is twice thwarted by YHWH, who intends to bless the Israelites. The famous encounter between Balaam's talking donkey and the angel of the LORD represents a typical Yahwistic legend. Balaam, "a seer of the gods" is attested in an extra-biblical source found in east Jordan dating to the eighth century BCE.

Phinehas

The grandson of Aaron, Phinehas is a priest whose zeal for YHWH in stamping out Israelite apostasy wins him a covenant of eternal priesthood. Specifically, when Israelites begin having sex with the foreign women of Moab, Phinehas follows one couple into their tent and zealously kills them with a spear. This prevents a plague and makes "atonement" for the Israelites. Recounted in Numbers 25, the narrative is Priestly with older J and E elements.

Questions for Study and Discussion

1. According to Mary Douglas, the Priestly laws are meant to provide order to the Israelite's experience of the world. This is one of several interpretations of Priestly law. Do you find her explanation convincing? Are there other explanations you find more compelling?
2. The book of Leviticus is often invoked in contemporary discussions of human sexuality, especially in faith communities for whom this books functions as Scripture. In your view, what role, if any, should Leviticus play in such conversations?
3. Priestly law is clearly ancient law. But in many ways, the problems it tries to solve persist in contemporary culture. What are some of those common problems, and how do modern societies and religious communities address them?
4. It is common for Christians to represent Priestly literature as "legalistic" and as an example of ancient Israel's attempt to earn favor with God. Based on your reading of Leviticus, is this argument convincing?

Primary Texts

The Holiness Code: Leviticus 19

> **CLOSE READING TIPS**
> ▶ Note that the holiness laws in this chapter are addressed not only to priests but all of Israel.
> ▶ The oft-repeated phrase "I am the LORD your God" functions as the motivation for lay holiness in this chapter.
> ▶ Note that several verses, especially verses 3-4 and verses 11-13, have close connections with the Ten Commandments.
> ▶ Verse 10 echoes Deuteronomy 24:19-22 in specifying that the edges of the field should be left un-harvested on behalf of the poor.
> ▶ Verse 19 does not provide an explicit rationale for why certain mixtures are prohibited.
> ▶ Note that the concern for fair treatment of aliens is rooted in the memory that Israel had once been unfairly treated as aliens in Egypt.

[1] The Lord spoke to Moses, saying:

[2] Speak to all the congregation of the people of Israel and say to them: You shall be holy, for I the LORD your God am holy. [3] You shall each revere your mother and father, and you shall keep my Sabbaths :I am the Lord your God. [4] Do not turn to idols or make cast images for yourselves: I am the Lord your God.

[5] When you offer a sacrifice of well-being to the LORD, offer it in such a way that it is acceptable in your behalf. [6] It shall be eaten on the same day you offer it, or on the next day; and anything left over

until the third day shall be consumed in fire. [7] If it is eaten at all on the third day, it is an abomination; it will not be acceptable. [8] All who eat it shall be subject to punishment, because they have profaned what is holy to the LORD; and any such person shall be cut off from the people.

[9] When you reap the harvest of your land, you shall not reap to the very edges of your field, or gather the gleanings of your harvest. [10] You shall not strip your vineyard bare, or gather the fallen grapes of your vineyard; you shall leave them for the poor and the alien: I am the LORD your God.

[11] You shall not steal; you shall not deal falsely; and you shall not lie to one another. [12] And you shall not swear falsely by my name, profaning the name of your God: I am the LORD.

[13] You shall not defraud your neighbor; you shall not steal; and you shall not keep for yourself the wages of a laborer until morning. [14] You shall not revile the deaf or put a stumbling block before the blind; you shall fear your God: I am the LORD.

[15] You shall not render an unjust judgment; you shall not be partial to the poor or defer to the great: with justice you shall judge your neighbor. [16] You shall not go around as a slanderer among your people, and you shall not profit by the blood of your neighbor: I am the LORD.

[17] You shall not hate in your heart anyone of your kin; you shall reprove your neighbor, or you will incur guilt yourself. [18] You shall not take vengeance or bear a grudge against any of your people, but you shall love your neighbor as yourself: I am the LORD.

[19] You shall keep my statutes. You shall not let your animals breed with a different kind; you shall not sow your field with two kinds of seed; nor shall you put on a garment made of two different materials.

[20] If a man has sexual relations with a woman who is a slave, designated for another man but not ransomed or given her freedom, an inquiry shall be held. They shall not be put to death, since she has not been freed; [21] but he shall bring a guilt offering for himself to the LORD, at the entrance of the tent of meeting, a ram as guilt offering. [22] And the priest shall make atonement for him with the ram of guilt offering before the LORD for his sin that he committed; and the sin he committed shall be forgiven him.

[23] When you come into the land and plant all kinds of trees for food, then you shall regard their fruit as forbidden; three years it shall be forbidden to you, it must not be eaten. [24] In the fourth year all their fruit shall be set apart for rejoicing in the LORD. [25] But in the fifth year you may eat of their fruit, that their yield may be increased for you: I am the LORD your God.

[26] You shall not eat anything with its blood. You shall not practice augury or witchcraft. [27] You shall not round off the hair on your temples or mar the edges of your beard. [28] You shall not make any gashes in your flesh for the dead or tattoo any marks upon you: I am the LORD.

[29] Do not profane your daughter by making her a prostitute, that the land not become prostituted and full of depravity. [30] You shall keep my sabbaths and reverence my sanctuary: I am the LORD.

[31] Do not turn to mediums or wizards; do not seek them out, to be defiled by them: I am the LORD your God.

[32] You shall rise before the aged, and defer to the old; and you shall fear your God: I am the LORD.

[33] When an alien resides with you in your land, you shall not oppress the alien. [34] The alien who resides with you shall be to you as the citizen among you; you shall love the alien as yourself, for you were aliens in the land of Egypt: I am the LORD your God.

[35] You shall not cheat in measuring length, weight, or quantity. [36] You shall have honest balances, honest weights, an honest ephah, and an honest hin: I am the LORD your God, who brought you out of the land of Egypt. [37] You shall keep all my statutes and all my ordinances, and observe them: I am the LORD.

DISCUSSION QUESTIONS

1. How does this chapter revise traditional Priestly understandings of holiness?
2. Based on Leviticus 19, how would you characterize the relationship between holiness and justice?
3. What role do you think the concept of lay holiness played in forming Israel's understanding of its identity? Why would this be particularly important in the postexilic period?

The Story of Balaam in Numbers 22 and several other passages (Deut. 23:3-6; Josh. 13:22; 2 Pet. 2:15-16; Rev. 2:14)

CLOSE READING TIPS

▶ In Numbers 22, Balaam is a type of "prophet for hire" whom the king of Moab hires to curse the Israelites.

▶ Divination, which involved decoding messages from the gods by interpreting signs in the natural world, was a common practice in the ancient world.

▶ Deuteronomy 23:3-6 references the story of Balaam in order to justify why no Ammonite or Moabite should be allowed into the assembly of the LORD.

▶ Joshua 13:22 references the story of Balaam as part of its recounting of the Transjordan allotments of land that Moses made in Numbers 34.

▶ 2 Peter 2:15 and Jude 10-11 both follow a postbiblical Jewish tradition that criticizes Balaam for prophesying for financial gain.

▶ The author of Revelation 2:14 addresses an opponent by comparing him to Balaam. This text seems to connect the story of Balaam in Numbers 22–24 to the story of the Israelites having sexual relations with Moabite women in Numbers 25.

NUMBERS 22:1-40

[1] The Israelites set out, and camped in the plains of Moab across the Jordan from Jericho. [2] Now Balak son of Zippor saw all that Israel had done to the Amorites. [3] Moab was in great dread of the people, because they were so numerous; Moab was overcome with fear of the people of Israel. [4] And Moab said to the elders of Midian, "This horde will now lick up all that is around us, as an ox licks up the grass of the field." Now Balak son of Zippor was king of Moab at that time. [5] He sent messengers to Balaam son of Beor at Pethor, which is on the Euphrates, in the land of Amaw, to summon him, saying, "A people has come out of Egypt; they have spread over the face of the earth, and they have settled next to me. [6] Come now, curse this people for me, since they

are stronger than I; perhaps I shall be able to defeat them and drive them from the land; for I know that whomever you bless is blessed, and whomever you curse is cursed."

[7] So the elders of Moab and the elders of Midian departed with the fees for divination in their hand; and they came to Balaam, and gave him Balak's message. [8] He said to them, "Stay here tonight, and I will bring back word to you, just as the Lord speaks to me"; so the officials of Moab stayed with Balaam. [9] God came to Balaam and said, "Who are these men with you?" [10] Balaam said to God, "King Balak son of Zippor of Moab, has sent me this message: [11] 'A people has come out of Egypt and has spread over the face of the earth; now come, curse them for me; perhaps I shall be able to fight against them and drive them out.' " [12] God said to Balaam, "You shall not go with them; you shall not curse the people, for they are blessed." [13] So Balaam rose in the morning, and said to the officials of Balak, "Go to your own land, for the LORD has refused to let me go with you." [14] So the officials of Moab rose and went to Balak, and said, "Balaam refuses to come with us."

[15] Once again Balak sent officials, more numerous and more distinguished than these. 16 They came to Balaam and said to him, "Thus says Balak son of Zippor: 'Do not let anything hinder you from coming to me; [17] for I will surely do you great honor, and whatever you say to me I will do; come, curse this people for me.' " [18] But Balaam replied to the servants of Balak, "Although Balak were to give me his house full of silver and gold, I could not go beyond the command of the LORD my God, to do less or more. [19] You remain here, as the others did, so that I may learn what more the LORD may say to me." [20] That night God came to Balaam and said to him, "If the men have come to summon you, get up and go with them; but do only what I tell you to

do." [21] So Balaam got up in the morning, saddled his donkey, and went with the officials of Moab.

[22] God's anger was kindled because he was going, and the angel of the LORD took his stand in the road as his adversary. Now he was riding on the donkey, and his two servants were with him. [23] The donkey saw the angel of the LORD standing in the road, with a drawn sword in his hand; so the donkey turned off the road, and went into the field; and Balaam struck the donkey, to turn it back onto the road. [24] Then the angel of the LORD stood in a narrow path between the vineyards, with a wall on either side. [25] When the donkey saw the angel of the LORD, it scraped against the wall, and scraped Balaam's foot against the wall; so he struck it again. [26] Then the angel of the LORD went ahead, and stood in a narrow place, where there was no way to turn either to the right or to the left. [27] When the donkey saw the angel of the LORD, it lay down under Balaam; and Balaam's anger was kindled, and he struck the donkey with his staff. [28] Then the LORD opened the mouth of the donkey, and it said to Balaam, "What have I done to you, that you have struck me these three times?" [29] Balaam said to the donkey, "Because you have made a fool of me! I wish I had a sword in my hand! I would kill you right now!" [30] But the donkey said to Balaam, "Am I not your donkey, which you have ridden all your life to this day? Have I been in the habit of treating you this way?" And he said, "No."

[31] Then the LORD opened the eyes of Balaam, and he saw the angel of the LORD standing in the road, with his drawn sword in his hand; and he bowed down, falling on his face. [32] The angel of the LORD said to him, "Why have you struck your donkey these three times? I have come out as an adversary, because your way is perverse before me. [33] The donkey saw me, and turned away from me these three times. If it had not turned away from me, surely

just now I would have killed you and let it live." ³⁴ Then Balaam said to the angel of the LORD, "I have sinned, for I did not know that you were standing in the road to oppose me. Now therefore, if it is displeasing to you, I will return home." ³⁵ The angel of the LORD said to Balaam, "Go with the men; but speak only what I tell you to speak." So Balaam went on with the officials of Balak.

³⁶ When Balak heard that Balaam had come, he went out to meet him at Ir-moab, on the boundary formed by the Arnon, at the farthest point of the boundary. ³⁷ Balak said to Balaam, "Did I not send to summon you? Why did you not come to me? Am I not able to honor you?" ³⁸ Balaam said to Balak, "I have come to you now, but do I have power to say just anything? The word God puts in my mouth, that is what I must say." ³⁹ Then Balaam went with Balak, and they came to Kiriath-huzoth. ⁴⁰ Balak sacrificed oxen and sheep, and sent them to Balaam and to the officials who were with him.

Deuteronomy 23:3-6

³ No Ammonite or Moabite shall be admitted to the assembly of the LORD. Even to the tenth generation, none of their descendants shall be admitted to the assembly of the LORD, ⁴ because they did not meet you with food and water on your journey out of Egypt, and because they hired against you Balaam son of Beor, from Pethor of Mesopotamia, to curse you. ⁵ (Yet the LORD your God refused to heed Balaam; the LORD your God turned the curse into a blessing for you, because the LORD your God loved you.) ⁶ You shall never promote their welfare or their prosperity as long as you live.

Joshua 13:22

²² Along with the rest of those they put to death, the Israelites also put to the sword Balaam son of Beor, who practiced divination.

2 Peter 2:15-16

¹⁵ They have left the straight road and have gone astray, following the road of Balaam son of Bosor, who loved the wages of doing wrong, ¹⁶ but was rebuked for his own transgression; a speechless donkey spoke with a human voice and restrained the prophet's madness.

Jude 10-11

¹⁰ But these people slander whatever they do not understand, and they are destroyed by those things that, like irrational animals, they know by instinct. ¹¹ Woe to them! For they go the way of Cain, and abandon themselves to Balaam's error for the sake of gain, and perish in Korah's rebellion.

Revelation 2:14

¹⁴ But I have a few things against you: you have some there who hold to the teaching of Balaam, who taught Balak to put a stumbling block before the people of Israel, so that they would eat food sacrificed to idols and practice fornication.

Discussion questions

1. Which of these texts portrays Balaam as a positive figure? Which portrays him as a negative figure?
2. How could both ways of understanding Balaam be traced to the story in Numbers 22?
3. Why do you think the story of Balaam continued to be addressed in biblical texts outside of Numbers 22?

8

Deuteronomy

Key Points

The Book of Deuteronomy draws the Pentateuch to a close, yet at the same time it introduces the theological perspectives that will shape how the next chapter of Israelite history is told in Joshua, Judges, Samuel, and Kings. As a second formulation of the law, Deuteronomy repeats but also revises legal traditions found in the book of Exodus. It is framed as the farewell speech of Moses, but its instructions likely reflect reforms initiated by King Josiah of Judah during the late seventh century BCE.

Using direct address and a highly personal tone, the distinctive style of Deuteronomy can be understood as "preached law." The shape of Deuteronomy is influenced by Assyrian treaties, sharing with them common elements, vocabulary, and motivating factors. The key passage is Deuteronomy 6:4-5, which impresses on the Israelites the need for allegiance to YHWH alone.

Cult centralization in Jerusalem is the chief theological concern of Deuteronomy. It not only signals a move toward monotheism but it also transforms how and where Israelites worshiped YHWH. These reforms were also politically expedient insofar as they consolidated power in Jerusalem and established limitations on the king. However, broader humanitarian concerns are also evident in the Deuteronomic laws, especially regarding the release of slaves, remission from debt, care for the poor, and restraint in war. Deuteronomy even exhibits certain parallels with wisdom teaching and it frames its statutes and ordinances as an alternative to the wisdom of other peoples.

Though the primary authors of Deuteronomy were Jerusalem scribes, some of the traditions may have originated in northern Israel, perhaps when refugees traveled south after the fall of Samaria in 722 BCE. This would explain the affinities with the northern prophet Hosea and the location of the covenant ceremony in the northern city of Shechem (chapters 27–28). Scholars have long debated the chronological relationship of Deuteronomy and P, with most now believing that the Priestly legislation is later than the Deuteronomic reforms. In either case, along with the Priestly edition of the Torah the book of Deuteronomy had a lasting influence on Jewish theology in the Second Temple period.

Key Terms

Deuteronomy Literally meaning "second law," Deuteronomy represents another formulation of the Mosaic covenant. The book is presented as Moses' final speech before the Israelites enter the promised land. Best understood as "preached law," Deuteronomy begins with motivational speeches and frames obedience with curses and blessings. The book is associated with a revelation on what the E source calls Mt. Horeb.

Treaty model International treaties functioned politically as loyalty oaths, the stronger kingdom demanding allegiance from obedient vassals. More than the Sinai covenant, Deuteronomy closely resembles these ancient Near Eastern treaty forms. Some analogous elements include love as loyalty, curses, motivational history, invocation of cosmic witnesses, and deposition of the document. The prominence of Assyrian-Israelite treaties in seventh century BCE probably informed Deuteronomy's notion of allegiance to YHWH.

Josiah's reform Josiah, king of Judah in the seventh century, initiated a religious reform that centralized Israelite religion in Jerusalem. Described in 2 Kings 22–23, Josiah finds a book of law, rips his clothes, purges the temple, tears down the "high places," and prescribes a pilgrimage version of the Passover festival. These reforms resemble several of Deuteronomy's unique laws.

Humanitarian laws Beyond its political reforms to Israelite religion (centralization and suppression of local sacrificial worship), Deuteronomy displays a notable concern for the poor and marginal. Deuteronomy contains laws that forgive debt, attend to the release of slaves, protect accused criminals, and address the plight of immigrants, orphans, and widows. These should be read alongside Deuteronomy's more violent prescriptions, such as the total annihilation of enemy civilians in war.

Wisdom and law The book of Deuteronomy shares features with Israelite wisdom. Best exemplified by the book of Proverbs, wisdom is a form of instruction produced not by divine revelation but by tradition and experience. Nevertheless, Deuteronomy contains proverbial topics that are also found in Israelite and international wisdom literature. It even uses the term "wisdom" of its instruction, framing the Torah as an alternative to the wisdom of other peoples.

Key Personalities

Josiah

King of Judah from 649–601 BCE, Josiah centralized Israelite religion while facing two periods of invasion and war. His reign (2 Kings 22–23) followed Manasseh's long and dutiful vassal relationship with Assyria. Because Assyria was on the decline when he took the throne, Josiah asserted Israelite independence from Assyrian treaties, although he would later die in battle during the rise of Babylonia. When his priest discovered a book of the law, Josiah radically and violently reformed Israelite religion. He assassinated regional sacrificial priests, burned down the traditional Israelite high places, and removed all cult objects of non-Yahwistic worship.

The Levites

Traditional Israelite priests known from the narratives of the Pentateuch and Deuteronomistic history, the Levites receive special attention in Deuteronomy.

Traditionally, they oversaw sacrificial practice at regional shrines. However, the centralization of Israelite religion in Jerusalem disenfranchised local worship. In Deuteronomy, Levites were invited to minister at the central temple, an event that contributed to priestly disputes that lasted into and even beyond the Babylonian exile.

Questions for Study and Discussion

1. In a discussion of the relationship between Deuteronomy and the Vassal Treaty of Esarhaddon, the chapter argues that Deuteronomy provides "an alternative to the Assyrian loyalty oaths." This would seem to suggest that Deuteronomy, although couched in the language of divine revelation, is also a deeply political document. Given that the earliest form of Deuteronomy was probably written while Judah was still under Assyrian control, what political, religious, and even social significance might such a document have?

2. Deuteronomy raises serious issues about the relationship between religion and violence. The audience, for instance, is commanded to destroy sacred religious sites of non-Yahwistic cults (see Deut. 12:1-3). Cast in the guise of Deuteronomic theology, Josiah allegedly killed the officials of non-Yahwistic cults (see 2 Kgs. 23:5) in obedience to the Mosaic law. Given Deuteronomy's deeply intolerant orientation toward religious expression that diverges from its own, can the book continue to play a positive role in faith and society today, or is it just another example of religious fanaticism?

3. At the heart of Deuteronomy's claim to authority is its self-presentation as revelation from YHWH, which is in turn handed on by YHWH's authorized servant, Moses. Apart from the biblical text itself, are there modern documents, texts, and other sources that claim similar authority? Do we, in the twenty-first century, continue to appeal to divine authority when attempting to make truth claims? To what other authorities might modern people appeal that ancients might not?

4. At the end of Deuteronomy, Moses dies outside of the promised land, east of the Jordan River. He will never set foot in the land to which he had been leading his people. What are the literary and even theological implications of this fact?

Primary Text

Discovery of Book of the Law and Josiah's Reforms: 2 Kings 22:1-2, 8-13; 23:1-9, 19-25

CLOSE READING TIPS

▶ Josiah is presented as an ideal king, not turning away from the LORD.

▶ Book finding motifs are common in ancient Near Eastern literature and reinforce the authority of the king.

▶ In verse 8, the book of the law is presumably some form of Deuteronomy.

▶ In verse 11, Josiah tore his clothes as a sign of repentance, perhaps in fear of curses like Deuteronomy 28:61 and 29:21.

▶ Note that Josiah himself reads the book of the law to the people (2 Kgs. 23:2).

▶ Note that the statues and symbols of foreign deities are not just removed from the temple but smashed or burned.

▶ In verse 8, sanctuaries are defiled as a way of assuring that worship only occurs at Jerusalem.

▶ The priests of the high places may have been Levites.

▶ Josiah celebrates the Passover according to the instructions in Deuteronomy 16:1-8.

22 ¹ Josiah was eight years old when he began to reign; he reigned thirty-one years in Jerusalem. His mother's name was Jedidah daughter of Adaiah of Bozkath. ² He did what was right in the sight of the LORD, and walked in all the way of his father David; he did not turn aside to the right or to the left.

⁸ The high priest Hilkiah said to Shaphan the secretary, "I have found the book of the law in the house of the LORD." When Hilkiah gave the book to Shaphan, he read it. ⁹ Then Shaphan the secretary came to the king, and reported to the king, "Your servants have emptied out the money that was found in the house, and have delivered it into the hand of the workers who have oversight of the house of the LORD." ¹⁰ Shaphan the secretary informed the king, "The priest Hilkiah has given me a book." Shaphan then read it aloud to the king.

¹¹ When the king heard the words of the book of the law, he tore his clothes. ¹² Then the king commanded the priest Hilkiah, Ahikam son of Shaphan, Achbor son of Micaiah, Shaphan the secretary, and the king's servant Asaiah, saying, ¹³ "Go, inquire of the LORD for me, for the people, and for all Judah, concerning the words of this book that has been found; for great is the wrath of the LORD that is kindled against us, because our ancestors did not obey the words of this book, to do according to all that is written concerning us." ¹⁴ So the priest Hilkiah, Ahikam, Achbor, Shaphan, and Asaiah went to the prophetess Huldah the wife of Shallum son of Tikvah, son of Harhas, keeper of the wardrobe; she resided in Jerusalem in the Second Quarter, where they consulted her. ¹⁵ She declared to them, "Thus says the LORD, the God of Israel: Tell the man who

sent you to me, [16] Thus says the LORD, I will indeed bring disaster on this place and on its inhabitants—all the words of the book that the king of Judah has read. [17] Because they have abandoned me and have made offerings to other gods, so that they have provoked me to anger with all the work of their hands, therefore my wrath will be kindled against this place, and it will not be quenched. [18] But as to the king of Judah, who sent you to inquire of the LORD, thus shall you say to him, Thus says the LORD, the God of Israel: Regarding the words that you have heard, [19] because your heart was penitent, and you humbled yourself before the LORD, when you heard how I spoke against this place, and against its inhabitants, that they should become a desolation and a curse, and because you have torn your clothes and wept before me, I also have heard you, says the LORD. [20] Therefore, I will gather you to your ancestors, and you shall be gathered to your grave in peace; your eyes shall not see all the disaster that I will bring on this place." They took the message back to the king.

23 [1] Then the king directed that all the elders of Judah and Jerusalem should be gathered to him. [2] The king went up to the house of the LORD, and with him went all the people of Judah, all the inhabitants of Jerusalem, the priests, the prophets, and all the people, both small and great; he read in their hearing all the words of the book of the covenant that had been found in the house of the LORD. [3] The king stood by the pillar and made a covenant before the LORD, to follow the LORD, keeping his commandments, his decrees, and his statutes, with all his heart and all his soul, to perform the words of this covenant that were written in this book. All the people joined in the covenant.

[4] The king commanded the high priest Hilkiah, the priests of the second order, and the guardians of the threshold, to bring out of the temple of the LORD all the vessels made for Baal, for Asherah, and for all the host of heaven; he burned them outside Jerusalem in the fields of the Kidron, and carried their ashes to Bethel. [5] He deposed the idolatrous priests whom the kings of Judah had ordained to make offerings in the high places at the cities of Judah and around Jerusalem; those also who made offerings to Baal, to the sun, the moon, the constellations, and all the host of the heavens. [6] He brought out the image of Asherah from the house of the LORD, outside Jerusalem, to the Wadi Kidron, burned it at the Wadi Kidron, beat it to dust and threw the dust of it upon the graves of the common people. [7] He broke down the houses of the male temple prostitutes that were in the house of the LORD, where the women did weaving for Asherah. [8] He brought all the priests out of the towns of Judah, and defiled the high places where the priests had made offerings, from Geba to Beer-sheba; he broke down the high places of the gates that were at the entrance of the gate of Joshua the governor of the city, which were on the left at the gate of the city. [9] The priests of the high places, however, did not come up to the altar of the LORD in Jerusalem, but ate unleavened bread among their kindred.

[19] Moreover, Josiah removed all the shrines of the high places that were in the towns of Samaria, which kings of Israel had made, provoking the LORD to anger; he did to them just as he had done at Bethel. [20] He slaughtered on the altars all the priests of the high places who were there, and burned human bones on them. Then he returned to Jerusalem.

[21] The king commanded all the people, "Keep the passover to the LORD your God as prescribed in this book of the covenant." [22] No such passover had been kept since the days of the judges who judged Israel, or during all the days of the kings of Israel or of the kings of Judah; [23] but in the eighteenth year of

King Josiah this passover was kept to the LORD in Jerusalem.

²⁴ Moreover Josiah put away the mediums, wizards, teraphim, idols, and all the abominations that were seen in the land of Judah and in Jerusalem, so that he established the words of the law that were written in the book that the priest Hilkiah had found in the house of the LORD. ²⁵ Before him there was no king like him, who turned to the LORD with all his heart, with all his soul, and with all his might, according to all the law of Moses; nor did any like him arise after him.

DISCUSSION QUESTIONS

1.   What ideas or policies from the book of Deuteronomy are present in this passage?
2.   Why do you think 2 Kings 22 roots Josiah's reforms in the discovery of a book?
3.   How is Josiah characterized in this passage? What model of kingship can be derived from his example?

The Death of Moses Deuteronomy 34

CLOSE READING TIPS

▶ Chapter 34 more naturally follows after Deuteronomy 32:48-52; it might have originally been linked to Numbers 27, where Moses goes up a mountain to survey the land before his death.
▶ Mount Nebo and Mount Pisgah are in different locations and verse 1 likely joins together two originally separate traditions.
▶ The fact that no one knows were Moses was buried is intended to prevent pilgrimages to the site or the construction of a shrine.
▶ One hundred twenty is the maximum age for humans as stated in Genesis 6:3.
▶ The LORD knew Moses face-to-face instead of through dreams and visions. The former is understood to be a more direct for of communion.

¹ Then Moses went up from the plains of Moab to Mount Nebo, to the top of Pisgah, which is opposite Jericho, and the LORD showed him the whole land: Gilead as far as Dan, ² all Naphtali, the land of Ephraim and Manasseh, all the land of Judah as far as the Western Sea, ³ the Negeb, and the Plain—that is, the valley of Jericho, the city of palm trees—as far as Zoar. ⁴ The LORD said to him, "This is the land of which I swore to Abraham, to Isaac, and to Jacob, saying, 'I will give it to your descendants'; I have let you see it with your eyes, but you shall not cross over there." ⁵ Then Moses, the servant of the LORD, died there in the land of Moab, at the LORD's command. ⁶ He was buried in a valley in the land of Moab, opposite Beth-peor, but no one knows his burial place to this day. ⁷ Moses was one hundred twenty years old when he died; his sight was unimpaired and his vigor had not abated. ⁸ The Israelites wept for Moses in the plains of Moab thirty days; then the period of mourning for Moses was ended.

⁹ Joshua son of Nun was full of the spirit of wisdom, because Moses had laid his hands on him; and the Israelites obeyed him, doing as the LORD had commanded Moses.

[10] Never since has there arisen a prophet in Israel like Moses, whom the LORD knew face to face. [11] He was unequaled for all the signs and wonders that the LORD sent him to perform in the land of Egypt, against Pharaoh and all his servants and his entire land, [12] and for all the mighty deeds and all the terrifying displays of power that Moses performed in the sight of all Israel.

DISCUSSION QUESTIONS

1. Compare Deuteronomy 34:10-11 with 18:18. Are these two perspectives compatible? How do you understand Joshua's leadership in light of these verses?
2. The promise of the land is a major theme throughout the Pentateuch. Why is it significant that the Pentateuch closes with Moses and the Israelites still outside the land?

Comparing laws on slaves: Exodus 21:1-11 and Deuteronomy 15:12-18.

CLOSE READING TIPS

- ▶ Note that in Exodus 21:2, Hebrew slaves are in view.
- ▶ In verses 5-6, if a slave decides to forego freedom, his ear is pierced to mark his continuing status as a slave.
- ▶ The ear-piercing ceremony takes place at a local sanctuary.
- ▶ In verses 7-11, a female slave who becomes a wife in the household she is sold into is afforded certain rights.
- ▶ In Deuteronomy 15:12, "is sold" could also mean "sells himself." Someone in severe debt may decide to work as a slave in order to repay a loan or a thief may decide to serve as a servant as a form of compensation for what he took.
- ▶ The Hebrew noun "slave" (*'eved*) is based on the same root as the verb "to worship" (*'avad*).
- ▶ The ear-piercing ceremony takes place at the house in Deutronomy 15:16-17.

EXODUS 21:1-11

[1] These are the ordinances that you shall set before them:

[2] When you buy a male Hebrew slave, he shall serve six years, but in the seventh he shall go out a free person, without debt. [3] If he comes in single, he shall go out single; if he comes in married, then his wife shall go out with him. [4] If his master gives him a wife and she bears him sons or daughters, the wife and her children shall be her master's and he shall go out alone. [5] But if the slave declares, "I love my master, my wife, and my children; I will not go out a free person," [6] then his master shall bring him before God. He shall be brought to the door or the doorpost; and his master shall pierce his ear with an awl; and he shall serve him for life.

[7] When a man sells his daughter as a slave, she shall not go out as the male slaves do. [8] If she does not please her master, who designated her for

himself, then he shall let her be redeemed; he shall have no right to sell her to a foreign people, since he has dealt unfairly with her. ⁹ If he designates her for his son, he shall deal with her as with a daughter. ¹⁰ If he takes another wife to himself, he shall not diminish the food, clothing, or marital rights of the first wife. ¹¹ And if he does not do these three things for her, she shall go out without debt, without payment of money.

Deuteronomy 15:12-18

¹² If a member of your community, whether a Hebrew man or a Hebrew woman, is sold to you and works for you six years, in the seventh year you shall set that person free. ¹³ And when you send a male slave out from you a free person, you shall not send him out empty-handed. ¹⁴ Provide liberally out of your flock, your threshing floor, and your wine press, thus giving to him some of the bounty with which the LORD your God has blessed you. ¹⁵ Remember that you were a slave in the land of Egypt, and the LORD your God redeemed you; for this reason I lay this command upon you today. ¹⁶ But if he says to you, "I will not go out from you," because he loves you and your household, since he is well off with you, ¹⁷ then you shall take an awl and thrust it through his earlobe into the door, and he shall be your slave forever.

You shall do the same with regard to your female slave.

¹⁸ Do not consider it a hardship when you send them out from you free persons, because for six years they have given you services worth the wages of hired laborers; and the LORD your God will bless you in all that you do.

Discussion questions

1. What are several ways in which Deuteronomy 15:12-18 adjusts the laws in the Book of the Covenant about the release of slaves (Exod. 21:1-11)?
2. How would you characterize these differences?
3. What seems to be the underlying basis for the release of slaves in the account from Deuteronomy?

9

The Book of Joshua

Key Points

The book of Joshua describes the Israelites' swift and decisive conquest of Canaan under Joshua's leadership (chapters 1–12) followed by the allotment of the land among the twelve tribes (chapters 13–21). It is concerned with unity among the tribes (chapter 22), fidelity to the law of Moses (chapter 23), and covenant renewal (chapter 24). While the work as a whole is the product of the Deuteronomistic Historian, the ritualistic actions at Gilgal (chapters. 3–4) and Jericho (chapter 6) and the role of Eleazar in the distribution of the land (chapter 14) suggest the possibility of priestly influence or editing. From a canonical perspective, Joshua links key themes from the Pentateuch, including the promise of land to Abraham's descendents and the exodus from Egypt, with the narrative about the rise and fall of the Israelite kingdom in the rest of the Former Prophets.

The study of the book of Joshua presents two major interpretive problems.

First, it is difficult to reconcile the account of the conquest presented in Joshua 1–12 with other evidence concerning Israel's settlement in Canaan. For one, other biblical texts, such as Joshua 13:1-6 and Judges 1:1—3:6, present a more limited and gradual possession of the land. In addition, a great deal of archaeological evidence weighs against the possibility of a widespread conquest by an ethnically distinct group of outsiders. As a result, scholars have proposed three alternatives to the conquest model that attempt to account for the motivations and mechanisms behind the emergence of Israel in Canaan: (1) the immigration model, (2) the revolt model, and (3) the gradual evolution model. None of these models is fully explanatory. However, the growing consensus in the twenty-first century is that the Israelites were once Canaanites who later developed a distinct identity as they established new settlements in the central highlands region.

Equally problematic is the issue of violence in Joshua. While warfare today is no less violent than it was in the ancient world, it is hard to come to terms with the fact that the *herem* was said to be authorized by God. Multiple perspectives can be potentially helpful in dealing with this issue. First, the *herem* does not provide us with a realistic depiction of war but rather an ideology of conquest framed in ritualistic terms, where defeated people and cities are presented to God as a type of sacrificial offering. Second, it also must be kept in mind that throughout history the Israelites often suffered the kind of violent conquest they had supposedly inflicted. In either case, it is morally and exegetically problematic to invoke the book of Joshua to legitimize conquest.

Key Terms

Tell A tell (or tel) is a flat-topped mound created when a city is repeatedly destroyed and rebuilt over many centuries. Material artifacts discovered in a tell's "destruction layers" reveal important archaeological data about the culture and history of the ancient world. Of the twenty tells that can be identified with cities said to conquered in the book of Joshua, only two show evidence of destruction at the appropriate time.

Merneptah stela The Merneptah stela is a monument commissioned by Pharaoh Merneptah around 1220 BCE. Its inscription boasts of a series of successful Egyptian military victories, including one over Israel. While it is unclear whether Israel is considered a people or a place, the Merneptah stela provides the earliest non-biblical evidence that an entity called Israel existed in the land of Canaan during the Late Bronze Age.

Amarna letters The Amarna letters are fourtheenth century BCE clay tablets written by people in Canaan and addressed to their rulers in Egypt. These letters, which were written in Akkadian, express dissatisfaction with Egyptian rule and often make mention of a group of troublemakers known as Habiru or Hapiru (Abiru or Apiru). Some of the details in the Amarna letters correspond to the biblical description of pre-Israelite Canaan.

Herem The herem, or ban, is a law attributed to God that stipulated all those conquered in battle were to be killed and their property burned. The herem plays a prominent role in the book of Joshua but is also known outside of Israel, such as in the Mesha stela. Rather than providing a factual report of ancient battles, the herem portrays warfare in ritualistic and sacrificial terms.

Amphictyony Amphictyony is a Greek term that refers to a sacred league of people bound together by a common interest in a central shrine. Martin Noth suggested there was an analogy by Greek amphictyonies and the mutual relations that existed among the twelve tribes of Israel during the pre-monarchic period. While the book of Joshua does make mention of a covenant that was periodically renewed at Shechem, the idea of an amphictyony likely does not apply to Israelite tribes.

Key Personalities

Rahab

In Joshua 2, Rahab is the name of a Canaanite prostitute who comes to the aid of Israelite spies. She deceives the king of Jericho and hides the spies on her roof until they can safely escape. As a result, Rahab and her family are spared from the *herem* and allowed to live alongside the Israelites. Her actions are favorably recalled as a model of loyalty and faith in Joshua 6:21-25 as well as in Hebrews 11:31 and James 2:25.

William F. Albright

Albright (1891–1971) was an influential American biblical scholar and archaeologist. He is acknowledged as the founder of the "biblical archaeology" movement and its effort to use archaeological data to corroborate the account of Israelite history provided in the Hebrew Bible. For instance, he advocated the "conquest model" of the settlement of Canaan, which essentially argues that the Israelites took possession of the land through a swift and decisive military campaign sometimes during the mid-thirteenth century. Though Albright's influence should not be downplayed, many of his conclusions were questioned or overturned by the end of the twentieth century.

Questions for Study and Discussion

1. Not unlike Deuteronomy, the book of Joshua raises serious questions about the relationship between religion and violence. Many modern scholars and interpreters of the Bible read the Joshua narrative with a deeply critical lens, arguing that the book effectively sanctions religiously motivated genocide. Do you agree with this analysis? Why or why not?

2. Joshua is a narrative about colonization and displacement. One group, defined by a God named YHWH, is chosen to disinherit Canaan from another group, defined by worship of non-Yahwistic deities. Who within Israel's history would be interested in telling such a story? When? What purpose could such a story possibly serve? Can you think of contemporary "narratives" that serve similar purposes?

3. How would you describe the God of Joshua? What is your reaction to how God is represented in Joshua?

4. The chapter makes the claim that "the account of the conquest in the book of Joshua is not historically accurate, but is a fiction that was composed for ideological reasons at a much later time." Based on your interpretation of the evidence presented in ths chapter, is this a correct assessment?

5. More than many other books, Joshua demonstrates the problems that emerge when one attempts to use the Bible as an historical source. Based on your reading of the chapter, what guidelines, principles, or critical assumptions would you suggest should be in place if one wants to use the Bible to reconstruct ancient Israelite history?

Primary Text

Crossing the Jordan at Gilgal: Joshua 3:1-17; 4:11—5:1

CLOSE READING TIPS

▶ The Jordan river functioned as a symbolic boundary between landlessness and the wilderness wandering.

▶ According to Deuteronomy 31:26, the ark of the covenant was a receptacle for the tablets of the law. However, here the ark was thought to manifest God's presence and power. This is why the Israelites had to sanctify themselves (verse 5).

▶ Note that the only other time the word "heap" (verse 13) is used in the Hebrew Bible is in reference to the dividing of the waters in the story of the Red Sea crossing (Exod. 15:8).

▶ Note that verse 15 specifies that the Jordan is in flood. Otherwise, it is relatively narrow river.

▶ Joshua 4:1-10 is a repetitive unit that seems to preserve different traditions about the crossing of the river and the removal of stones.

▶ Note how Joshua is exalted in verse 14.

▶ The "first month" (verse 19) was in March-April; the first Passover was held on the tenthy day of the first month in Exod. 12:3.

▶ Note the explicit connection between the Jordan crossing and the Red Sea crossing (verses 23-24).

3 ¹ Early in the morning Joshua rose and set out from Shittim with all the Israelites, and they came to the Jordan. They camped there before crossing over. ² At the end of three days the officers went through the camp ³ and commanded the people, "When you see the ark of the covenant of the LORD your God being carried by the levitical priests, then you shall set out from your place. Follow it, ⁴ so that you may know the way you should go, for you have not passed this way before. Yet there shall be a space between you and it, a distance of about two thousand cubits; do not come any nearer to it." ⁵ Then Joshua said to the people, "Sanctify yourselves; for tomorrow the LORD will do wonders among you." ⁶ To the priests Joshua said, "Take up the ark of the covenant, and

pass on in front of the people." So they took up the ark of the covenant and went in front of the people.

⁷ The LORD said to Joshua, "This day I will begin to exalt you in the sight of all Israel, so that they may know that I will be with you as I was with Moses. ⁸ You are the one who shall command the priests who bear the ark of the covenant, 'When you come to the edge of the waters of the Jordan, you shall stand still in the Jordan.' " ⁹ Joshua then said to the Israelites, "Draw near and hear the words of the LORD your God." ¹⁰ Joshua said, "By this you shall know that among you is the living God who without fail will drive out from before you the Canaanites, Hittites, Hivites, Perizzites, Girgashites, Amorites, and Jebusites: ¹¹ the ark of the covenant of the Lord

of all the earth is going to pass before you into the Jordan. [12] So now select twelve men from the tribes of Israel, one from each tribe. [13] When the soles of the feet of the priests who bear the ark of the LORD, the Lord of all the earth, rest in the waters of the Jordan, the waters of the Jordan flowing from above shall be cut off; they shall stand in a single heap."

[14] When the people set out from their tents to cross over the Jordan, the priests bearing the ark of the covenant were in front of the people. [15] Now the Jordan overflows all its banks throughout the time of harvest. So when those who bore the ark had come to the Jordan, and the feet of the priests bearing the ark were dipped in the edge of the water, [16] the waters flowing from above stood still, rising up in a single heap far off at Adam, the city that is beside Zarethan, while those flowing toward the sea of the Arabah, the Dead Sea, were wholly cut off. Then the people crossed over opposite Jericho. [17] While all Israel were crossing over on dry ground, the priests who bore the ark of the covenant of the LORD stood on dry ground in the middle of the Jordan, until the entire nation finished crossing over the Jordan.

4 [11] As soon as all the people had finished crossing over, the ark of the LORD, and the priests, crossed over in front of the people. [12] The Reubenites, the Gadites, and the half-tribe of Manasseh crossed over armed before the Israelites, as Moses had ordered them. [13] About forty thousand armed for war crossed over before the LORD to the plains of Jericho for battle.

[14] On that day the LORD exalted Joshua in the sight of all Israel; and they stood in awe of him, as they had stood in awe of Moses, all the days of his life.

[15] The LORD said to Joshua, [16] "Command the priests who bear the ark of the covenant, to come up out of the Jordan." [17] Joshua therefore commanded the priests, "Come up out of the Jordan." [18] When the priests bearing the ark of the covenant of the LORD came up from the middle of the Jordan, and the soles of the priests' feet touched dry ground, the waters of the Jordan returned to their place and overflowed all its banks, as before.

[19] The people came up out of the Jordan on the tenth day of the first month, and they camped in Gilgal on the east border of Jericho. [20] Those twelve stones, which they had taken out of the Jordan, Joshua set up in Gilgal, [21] saying to the Israelites, "When your children ask their parents in time to come, 'What do these stones mean?' [22] then you shall let your children know, 'Israel crossed over the Jordan here on dry ground.' [23] For the LORD your God dried up the waters of the Jordan for you until you crossed over, as the LORD your God did to the Red Sea, which he dried up for us until we crossed over, [24] so that all the peoples of the earth may know that the hand of the LORD is mighty, and so that you may fear the LORD your God forever."

5 [1] When all the kings of the Amorites beyond the Jordan to the west, and all the kings of the Canaanites by the sea, heard that the LORD had dried up the waters of the Jordan for the Israelites until they had crossed over, their hearts melted, and there was no longer any spirit in them, because of the Israelites.

DISCUSSION QUESTIONS

1. What points of similarity do you see between the crossing of the Jordan in Joshua 3–4 and the crossing of the Red Sea in Exodus 14–15?
2. How would you describe the function of the twelve stones?
3. What affect did the Jordan crossing have on the inhabitants of the land?

Joshua 24:1-28

CLOSE READING TIPS

▸ Shechem is often a site for significant religious events in the Hebrew Bible.

▸ The narrative in verses 2-13 parallels the historical prologue section of Hittite treaties.

▸ The verb "serve" is repeated fourteen times in Joshua 24:14-24. In Hebrew, it can mean "worship" and it is related to the word for "slavery" in verse 17.

▸ Note the role of the stone as a witness to the covenant. This parallels the role of witnesses in ancient Near Eastern treaties.

▸ The Hebrew word for jealous can also mean zeal and implies the desire for an exclusive relationship with Israel.

¹ Then Joshua gathered all the tribes of Israel to Shechem, and summoned the elders, the heads, the judges, and the officers of Israel; and they presented themselves before God. ² And Joshua said to all the people, "Thus says the LORD, the God of Israel: Long ago your ancestors—Terah and his sons Abraham and Nahor—lived beyond the Euphrates and served other gods. ³ Then I took your father Abraham from beyond the River and led him through all the land of Canaan and made his offspring many. I gave him Isaac; ⁴ and to Isaac I gave Jacob and Esau. I gave Esau the hill country of Seir to possess, but Jacob and his children went down to Egypt. ⁵ Then I sent Moses and Aaron, and I plagued Egypt with what I did in its midst; and afterwards I brought you out. ⁶ When I brought your ancestors out of Egypt, you came to the sea; and the Egyptians pursued your ancestors with chariots and horsemen to the Red Sea. ⁷ When they cried out to the LORD, he put darkness between you and the Egyptians, and made the sea come upon them and cover them; and your eyes saw what I did to Egypt. Afterwards you lived in the wilderness a long time. ⁸ Then I brought you to the land of the Amorites, who lived on the other side of the Jordan; they fought with you, and I handed them over to you, and you took possession of their land, and I destroyed them before you. ⁹ Then King Balak son of Zippor of Moab, set out to fight against Israel. He sent and invited Balaam son of Beor to curse you, ¹⁰ but I would not listen to Balaam; therefore he blessed you; so I rescued you out of his hand. ¹¹ When you went over the Jordan and came to Jericho, the citizens of Jericho fought against you, and also the Amorites, the Perizzites, the Canaanites, the Hittites, the Girgashites, the Hivites, and the Jebusites; and I handed them over to you. ¹² I sent the hornet ahead of you, which drove out before you the two kings of the Amorites; it was not by your sword or

by your bow. [13] I gave you a land on which you had not labored, and towns that you had not built, and you live in them; you eat the fruit of vineyards and oliveyards that you did not plant.

[14] "Now therefore revere the LORD, and serve him in sincerity and in faithfulness; put away the gods that your ancestors served beyond the River and in Egypt, and serve the LORD. [15] Now if you are unwilling to serve the LORD, choose this day whom you will serve, whether the gods your ancestors served in the region beyond the River or the gods of the Amorites in whose land you are living; but as for me and my household, we will serve the LORD."

[16] Then the people answered, "Far be it from us that we should forsake the LORD to serve other gods; [17] for it is the LORD our God who brought us and our ancestors up from the land of Egypt, out of the house of slavery, and who did those great signs in our sight. He protected us along all the way that we went, and among all the peoples through whom we passed; [18] and the LORD drove out before us all the peoples, the Amorites who lived in the land. Therefore we also will serve the LORD, for he is our God."

[19] But Joshua said to the people, "You cannot serve the LORD, for he is a holy God. He is a jealous God; he will not forgive your transgressions or your sins. [20] If you forsake the LORD and serve foreign gods, then he will turn and do you harm, and consume you, after having done you good." [21] And the people said to Joshua, "No, we will serve the LORD!" 22 Then Joshua said to the people, "You are witnesses against yourselves that you have chosen the LORD, to serve him." And they said, "We are witnesses." [23] He said, "Then put away the foreign gods that are among you, and incline your hearts to the LORD, the God of Israel." [24] The people said to Joshua, "The LORD our God we will serve, and him we will obey." [25] So Joshua made a covenant with the people that day, and made statutes and ordinances for them at Shechem. [26] Joshua wrote these words in the book of the law of God; and he took a large stone, and set it up there under the oak in the sanctuary of the LORD. [27] Joshua said to all the people, "See, this stone shall be a witness against us; for it has heard all the words of the LORD that he spoke to us; therefore it shall be a witness against you, if you deal falsely with your God." [28] So Joshua sent the people away to their inheritances.

DISCUSSION QUESTIONS

1. According to verses 2-13, what is the beginning point of Israel's relationship with God?
2. What role does God play in Israel's settlement of the land?
3. Why do you think Joshua says that the people "cannot serve the LORD" (verse 19)? What role does this statement play in the covenant renewal ceremony?
4. How do Joshua's words in verses 14-16 reflect Deuteronomic theology?

Excerpts from the Merneptah stela and the Mesha stela

Source: Excerpts from the Merneptah stela and the Mesha Stela from Bill T. Arnold and Bryan E. Beyer, eds., *Readings from the Ancient Near East: Primary Sources for Old Testament Study* (Grand Rapids, Mich.: Baker Academic, 2002), 160–162.

CLOSE READING TIPS

▶ Merneptah reigned near the end of the thirteenth century and led a series of military campaigns around 1208 BCE.

▶ "Shalom" means peace; in this context, the defeated princes are asking for mercy.

▶ In Egyptian art and literature, the nine bows symbolize their traditional enemies.

▶ The word for Israel is accompanied by a grammatical sign that indicates this word should be understood as a people group, not a city-state or nation.

▶ King Mesha of Moab set up this monument around 830 BCE.

▶ Chemosh was one of the primary deities of Moab.

▶ Mesha's victory recalls the conflict between Moab and Israel in 2 Kings 3.

▶ The word used for "devoted" is similar to the word *herem* used in the book of Joshua.

#50: MERNEPTAH STELA

(Lichtheim, *Ancient Egyptian Literature*, 2.77)

One of the last kinds of Egypt's once powerful nineteenth dynasty was Merneptah (1212–1202 BC). Sometime around 1208 BC, he commorated a victory against all his enemies, especially Libyans who had joined with various Sea Peoples and marched into the Delta. Several hymns of victory are preserved on a black granite stela, variously known as the "Merneptah Stela" or the "Israel Stela." Near the end of this long inscription is a section that memorializes what is apparently a separate campaign against Egypt's traditional enemies in Syria-Palestine. Included in the list of conquered groups is the earliest known extrabiblical reference to Israel. Of particular interest to Old Testament studies is a grammatical sign that marks this name not as a city-state or a foreign country but as a people group. Scholars often use this text to demonstrate that in the late thirteenth century BC Israel was present in Syria-Palestine as a people, but not yet viewed by the Egyptians as an established political state.

The princes are prostrate saying:
    Shalom!
Not one of the Nine Bows lifts his head:
Tjehenu is vanquished, Khatti at peace,
Canaan is captive with all woe.
Ashkelon is conquered, Gezer seized,
Yanoam made nonexistent;
Israel is wasted, bare of seed,
Khor is become a widow for Egypt.
All who roamed have been subdued
by the king of Upper and Lower Egypt,
    Banere-meramun,
son of Re, Merneptah, content with
    MAAT,
given life like Re every day.

#51 MESHA STELA

(Gibson, *Textbook of Syrian Semitic Inscriptions,* 1.75-77)

In 1868, a German missionary learned of the existence of a three-and-a-half-foot tall black basalt stela in Dibon, Jordan. The stone contained thirty-four lines of ancient alphabetic script, with no discernible difference from the Paleo-Hebrew script. News of the find spread, and in the ensuing years competition to acquire the stone from the local Bedouin grew fierce between the Germans and the French, exacerbated by the political climate created by the Franco-Prussian War (1870–1). Out of resentment (and perhaps financial motivation), the Bedouin shattered the stone and distributed it among the local tribal leaders. Fortunately, a French scholar had made a facsimile impression, called a "squeeze," of the inscription prior to its destruction. Almost two-thirds of the stone was eventually retrieved, and, with the help of the squeeze, the entire stela was reconstructed and has been on display in the Louvre since 1875. King Mesha of Moab set up this stela around 830 BC to commemorate the construction of a sanctuary and the express gratitude to Chermosh, the god of Moab, for victories over Israel. The inscription has particular importance as a source related to Israel's [161] Omride dynasty and the conflict between Moab and Israel recorded in 2 Kings 3.

I am Mesha, son of Chemosh-yat, king of Moab, the Dibonite. My father was king over Moab for thirty years, and I became king after my father. I built this high place for Chemosh in Qarhoh, a high place of salvation, because he delivered me from all assaults, and because he let me see my desire upon all my adversaries. King Omri of Israel has oppressed Moab many days, for Chemosh was angry with his land. His son succeeded him, and he too said, I will oppress Moab. In my days he said it; but I saw my desire upon him and his house, and Israel has perished utterly forever. Omri had taken possession of the land of Medeba, and dwelled there his days and [162] much of his son's days, forty years; but Chemosh dwelled in it in my days.

I rebuilt Baal-meon, and I made a reservoir in it; and I rebuilt Kiriathaim. Then the men of Gad had settled in the land of Ataroth from of old, and the king of Israel had fortified Ataroth for himself; but I fought against the town and took it; and I slew all the inhabitants of the town, a spectacle for Chemosh and Moab. I brought back from there the lion figure of David, and dragged it before Chemosh at Kerioth; and I settled in it the men of [Sharon] and the men of [Meharit]. Next Chemosh said to me, Go take Nebo from Israel. So I went by night, and fought against it from break of dawn till noon; and I took it and slew all in it, seven thousand men and women, both natives and aliens, and female slaves; for I had devoted it to Ashtar-Chemosh. I took from thence the vessels of YHWH and dragged them before Chemosh. Then the king of Israel had fortified Jahaz, and he occupied it while warring against me; but Chemosh drove him out before me. I took from Moab two hundred men, his whole division, and I led it up against Jahaz and captured it, annexing it to Dibon.

DISCUSSION QUESTIONS

1. How is the fate of Israel described in each of these inscriptions?
2. What light might the Merneptah stela shed on the early history of Israel in the land of Canaan?
3. How does mention of the concept of the *herem* in the Mesha stela further inform your perspective on violence in the book of Joshua?

10

Judges

Key Points

The book of Judges consists of various stories about local heroes that distinguish themselves in battles. With the possible exception of Deborah (Judg. 4:5), these figures were not legal experts associated with court decisions. Rather, the judges are portrayed as military leaders or "deliverers" who God raises up in order to rescue the Israelites from the Canaanites, Midianites, and Philistines. Twelve judges are introduced in all, with some receiving far more attention than others. Some judges are models of faith and justice (such as Othniel in chapter 3). But others are morally problematic and seem to act in rash and excessively violent ways: Abimelech murders his seventy brothers (chapter 9), Jephthah's tragic vow results in the death of his young daughter (chapter 11), and Samson is ultimately undone by the charms of a Philistine woman (chapter 16).

Originally independent folktales about various judges were stitched together into an episodic narrative by the Deuteronomistic Historian. The glue that holds this narrative together is the formulaic pattern or "cycle" of events that is laid out in Judges 2:11-19. This pattern serves as the organizing structure of Judges 3:7—16:31, but in the last four chapters the cycle breaks down. By the end of the book, conditions descend into a state of chaos, civil war, and brutality. Containing some of the most chilling "texts of terror" in the Hebrew Bible, chapters 17–21 are designed to highlight the depravity of the human condition apart from divine mercy and assistance.

Judges connects the deteriorating social conditions with the fact that "in those days there was no king in Israel" (Judg. 17:6; 18:1; 19:1; 21:25). In fact, it is ultimately the failure of Samuel's sons as judges that leads the Israelites to ask for a king to rule over them (1 Sam. 8:6). Nevertheless, the book of Judges as a whole is not uniformly in favor of the kingship. Jotham's fable about the trees (Judg. 9:7-21) likely reflects an independent anti-monarchic tradition and the idolatry of Gideon anticipates the unfaithfulness of future Israelite monarchs.

The summary of Israel's on-going struggle to claim the land (Judg. 1:1—2:5) stands in sharp contrast to the description of the conquest offered in Joshua 1–12. It is widely believed that Judges provides a more realistic picture of Israel's early history in Canaan. However, not unlike the book of Joshua, certain details in Judges are inconsistent with archaeological findings or are impossible to verify. As a result, the primary value of Judges as a historical source lies in its general portrait of conditions in pre-monarchic Israel.

Key Terms

Judge   Rather than being legal experts, judges were local rulers or governors. In the book of Judges, these charismatic figures, who were the successors to Joshua and the precursors to kings, are raised up by YHWH in order to deliver the Israelites from their enemies. While the judges often functioned in a military capacity, they were also responsible for ensuring proper worship of YHWH. Some judges were bringers of justice while others were morally ambiguous characters.

The judges cycle   This schematic structure frames the various stories about judges around a formulaic pattern, or cycle. This pattern, which is most clearly seen in Judges 2:11-19, consists of four parts: 1) the Israelites do evil by going after other gods; 2) YHWH is angered and allows the Israelites to be oppressed by their enemies; 3) in response to the people's groaning or crying out for help, YHWH raises up judges to deliver them; and 4) after the judge dies, the people turn again to idolatry and disobedience. The cycle is not always fully represented, and by the end of the book the people no longer cry out to God and deliverance is barely discernable.

Philistines   The Philistines were a group of sea people who were emerging as a power in the coastal plain region of Canaan during the pre-monarchic period. They worshiped Canaanite deities and are portrayed as one of the chief antagonists in the book of Judges. Their military prowess owes much to their mastery of forging iron (see 1 Sam. 13:19-21). Israelite conflict with the Philistines instigated the people's ultimate acceptance of a king. While the Philistines were eventually destroyed by the Babylonians, this land of Palestine (an early Greek translation of the Hebrew word for Philistia) bears their name.

Nazirite   A nazirite is someone who is devoted or set apart for service to God. They are bound by an oath to allow their hair to grow freely and to abstain from wine. When the angel of the LORD visits Samson's then barren mother, he informs the woman that her future son will be "a nazirite to God from birth" (Judg. 13:5). Later, Samson reveals to Delilah that his uncut hair is the source of his superhuman strength (Judg. 16:17).

Ephod   In the book of Judges, an ephod refers to some sort of illicit cult object. Gideon makes an ephod from precious metal collected from his soldiers and the Israelites subsequently worship it as an idol. In Judges 17–18, an ephod, along with a teraphim and an idol of cast metal, are stolen from Micah's house by the Danites. Though it is uncertain what the ephod consists of in Judges, in other contexts it refers to a priestly garment and may have been associated with divination.

Key Personalities

Jael

Jael is the heroine of Israel's battle with Sisera in Judges 4–5. In the prose version (Judges 4), Jael lures the Canaanite commander into her tent and kills him with a tent-peg while he is asleep. The poetry version (Judges 5) praises Jael as "most blessed among women," though it presents a slightly different picture of her encounter with Sisera. It is notable that Jael, a non-Israelite woman, plays the role of a deliverer in a book that typically focuses on Israelite male judges.

Gideon

Gideon is a judge who leads the Israelites in a regional conflict against the Midianites (chapters 6–8). He is a conflicted figure, showing both positive and negative characteristics. On the positive side, he is visited by the angel of the LORD (Judg. 6:11-18) and follows God's command to tear down the altar of Baal (Judg. 6:25-27). Yet, on the negative side, Gideon devises a series of tests to validate whether God was truly with him (Judg. 6:36-40) and eventually leads the people into idolatry (Judg. 8:24-27). This tension is also evident in Gideon's perspective on his own authority as a leader. While he affirms that YHWH alone rules over the people (Judg. 8:22-23), the name of his son, Abimelech, literally means "my father is king." By the end of chapter 8, it is clear that Gideon is a flawed judge. It is with Gideon that the downward spiral of Israel in chapters 9–21 begins.

Samson

Samson, one of the most prominent and colorful figures in the book of Judges, is raised up as a deliverer when Israel were given over into the hand of the Philistines (chapters 13–16). He was born to a barren woman and set aside as a nazirite. Samson is most well-known for his long hair, which is the source of his superhuman strength. The story of Samson is a popular folktale that seems to share much in common with the Greek legend of Heracles. Though he receives more attention than any other judge, Samson shows little concern for Israel, justice, or the covenant. His story is hailed as a model of faith in Hebrews 11:32, and yet in Judges 13-16 he is portrayed neither as a moral exemplar nor as an ardent defender of Yahwistic worship.

Questions for Study and Discussion

1. The book of Judges is a complex combination of once-independent folkloric stories. Despite the fragmentary nature of the stories, do you detect any unifying themes, questions, or concerns? If so, what kind of society would produce such literature? And to what end?

2. Is Judges helpful as a resource for reconstructing history? What parts are useful? What parts are problematic? From the perspective of historicity, how does Judges compare to Joshua?

3. The narratives in Judges have been reworked by deuteronomistic editors who structured much of the book according to a certain pattern, in which Israel does what is "evil" in the sight of the Lord by worshipping other deities, is handed over to her enemies, cries out to God for relief, and is then delivered by a judge. This pattern assumes a particular theological perspective that places heavy emphasis on obedience to YHWH alone. How would you describe this theology? How does it compare to the theology of other biblical books you have studied?

4. Even though men tend to dominate the narratives in the book of Judges, a handful of women play significant (and sometimes tragic) roles. In your view, what do the stories in Judges tell us about the role of women in Israelite society?

Primary Text

Judges 2:6—3:6

CLOSE READING TIPS

▶ This passage constitutes the second introduction to the book (the other is Judges 1:1—2:5).

▶ Note that verses 6-9 pick up on the narrative sequence from Joshua 24.

▶ The Hebrew verb "to serve" or "to worship" (*'ābad*) is repeated in verses 7, 11, 13, and 19. This verb signals one of the central issues in the book: Who will Israel serve—foreign gods or YHWH?

▶ The use of the plural form Baals (verse 11) and Astartes (verse 13) may suggest a multiplicity of shrines or various manifestations of the gods.

▶ Note God graciously responds to the people's groaning. In other iterations of the cycle, the people cry out to God (see Judges 3:9), which may suggest a more deliberate petition.

▶ The adjective "stubborn" in verse 19 recalls Exodus 32:9; 33:3, 5; and 34:9, where the same word is translated as "stiff-necked." In both cases, this word describes the idolatry of the Israelites.

---

⁶ When Joshua dismissed the people, the Israelites all went to their own inheritances to take possession of the land. ⁷ The people worshiped the LORD all the days of Joshua, and all the days of the elders who outlived Joshua, who had seen all the great work that the LORD had done for Israel. ⁸ Joshua son of Nun, the servant of the LORD, died at the age of one hundred ten years. ⁹ So they buried him within the bounds of his inheritance in Timnath-heres, in the hill country of Ephraim, north of Mount Gaash. ¹⁰ Moreover, that whole generation was gathered to their ancestors, and another generation grew up after them, who did not know the LORD or the work that he had done for Israel.

¹¹ Then the Israelites did what was evil in the sight of the LORD and worshiped the Baals; ¹² and they abandoned the LORD, the God of their ancestors, who had brought them out of the land of Egypt; they followed other gods, from among the gods of the peoples who were all around them, and bowed down to them; and they provoked the LORD to anger. ¹³ They abandoned the LORD, and worshiped Baal and the Astartes. ¹⁴ So the anger of the LORD was kindled against Israel, and he gave them over to plunderers who plundered them, and he sold them into the power of their enemies all around, so that they could no longer withstand their enemies. ¹⁵ Whenever they marched out, the hand of the LORD was against them to bring misfortune, as the LORD had warned them and sworn to them; and they were in great distress.

¹⁶ Then the LORD raised up judges, who delivered them out of the power of those who plundered them. ¹⁷ Yet they did not listen even to their judges; for they lusted after other gods and bowed down to them. They soon turned aside from the way in which their ancestors had walked, who had obeyed the commandments of the LORD; they did not follow their example. ¹⁸ Whenever the LORD raised up judges for them, the LORD was with the judge, and he delivered them from the hand of their enemies all the days of the judge; for the LORD would be moved to pity by their groaning because of those who persecuted and oppressed them. ¹⁹ But whenever the judge died, they would relapse and behave worse than their ancestors, following other gods, worshiping them and bowing down to them. They would not drop any of their practices or their stubborn ways. ²⁰ So the anger of the LORD was kindled against Israel; and he said, "Because this people have transgressed my covenant that I commanded their ancestors, and have not obeyed my voice, ²¹ I will no longer drive out before them any of the nations that Joshua left when he died." ²² In order to test Israel, whether or not they would take care to walk in the way of the LORD as their ancestors did, ²³ the LORD had left those nations, not driving them out at once, and had not handed them over to Joshua.

3 ¹ Now these are the nations that the LORD left to test all those in Israel who had no experience of any war in Canaan ² (it was only that successive generations of Israelites might know war, to teach those who had no experience of it before): ³ the five lords of the Philistines, and all the Canaanites, and the Sidonians, and the Hivites who lived on Mount Lebanon, from Mount Baal-hermon as far as Lebo-hamath. ⁴ They were for the testing of Israel, to know whether Israel would obey the commandments of the LORD, which he commanded their ancestors by Moses. ⁵ So the Israelites lived among the Canaanites, the Hittites, the Amorites, the Perizzites, the Hivites, and the Jebusites; ⁶ and they took their daughters as wives for themselves, and their own daughters they gave to their sons; and they worshiped their gods.

DISCUSSION QUESTIONS

1. What triggers the beginning of the first Judges cycle?
2. Can you identify the verses in Judges 2:11-19 that go with each of the four stages of the Judges cycle?
3. How is God portrayed in this passage—vengeful, merciful, or both?
4. What explanations does Judges 2:20—3:6 give regarding why God allowed non-Israelite nations to remain in the land?

Comparing stories of Jael: Judges 4:1-24; 5:24-31

CLOSE READING TIPS:

▶ Note that none of the human characters in this story is explicitly called a deliverer. The implication is that YHWH is the deliverer (see verses 14-15; 23).
▶ Note Barak's hesitancy to go out to battle (verse 8). This diminishes his heroic status.
▶ Note that the Kenites have dual loyalties—they are tied to the Israelites through the father-in-law of Moses (verse 11) but they also have a peace treaty with the Canaanite king, Jabin.
▶ Under the veil of hospitality, Jael lures Sisera into the tent and then soothes him to sleep with milk.
▶ The poetic account in Judges 5 is often called the Song of Deborah and is widely regarded to be older than Judges 4.
▶ Note that Judges 5 makes no mention of the Kenites' connection to the Israelites or the Canaanites.
▶ Several of the words in Judges 5:27, including "feet" and "lay" can have sexual connotations.
▶ The motif of a woman looking through a window is also found in 2 Samuel 6:16 and 2 Kings 9:30.
▶ Sisera's mother expects her son to return from war having taken women as captives (verse 30). This is perhaps why Sisera entered Jael's tent in the first place.

JUDGES 4:1-24

[1] The Israelites again did what was evil in the sight of the LORD, after Ehud died. [2] So the LORD sold them into the hand of King Jabin of Canaan, who reigned in Hazor; the commander of his army was Sisera, who lived in Harosheth-ha-goiim. [3] Then the Israelites cried out to the LORD for help; for he had nine hundred chariots of iron, and had oppressed the Israelites cruelly twenty years.

[4] At that time Deborah, a prophetess, wife of Lappidoth, was judging Israel. [5] She used to sit under the palm of Deborah between Ramah and Bethel in the hill country of Ephraim; and the Israelites came up to her for judgment. [6] She sent and summoned Barak son of Abinoam from Kedesh in Naphtali, and said to him, "The LORD, the God of Israel, commands you, 'Go, take position at Mount Tabor, bringing ten thousand from the tribe of Naphtali and the tribe of Zebulun. [7] I will draw out Sisera, the general of Jabin's army, to meet you by the Wadi Kishon with his chariots and his troops; and I will give him into your hand.' " [8] Barak said to her, "If you will go with me, I will go; but if you will not go with me, I will not go." 9 And she said, "I will surely go with

you; nevertheless, the road on which you are going will not lead to your glory, for the LORD will sell Sisera into the hand of a woman." Then Deborah got up and went with Barak to Kedesh. [10] Barak summoned Zebulun and Naphtali to Kedesh; and ten thousand warriors went up behind him; and Deborah went up with him.

[11] Now Heber the Kenite had separated from the other Kenites, that is, the descendants of Hobab the father-in-law of Moses, and had encamped as far away as Elon-bezaanannim, which is near Kedesh.

[12] When Sisera was told that Barak son of Abinoam had gone up to Mount Tabor, [13] Sisera called out all his chariots, nine hundred chariots of iron, and all the troops who were with him, from Harosheth-ha-goiim to the Wadi Kishon. [14] Then Deborah said to Barak, "Up! For this is the day on which the LORD has given Sisera into your hand. The Lord is indeed going out before you." So Barak went down from Mount Tabor with ten thousand warriors following him. [15] And the LORD threw Sisera and all his chariots and all his army into a panic before Barak; Sisera got down from his chariot and fled away on foot, [16] while Barak pursued the chariots and the army to Harosheth-ha-goiim. All the army of Sisera fell by the sword; no one was left.

[17] Now Sisera had fled away on foot to the tent of Jael wife of Heber the Kenite; for there was peace between King Jabin of Hazor and the clan of Heber the Kenite. [18] Jael came out to meet Sisera, and said to him, "Turn aside, my lord, turn aside to me; have no fear." So he turned aside to her into the tent, and she covered him with a rug. [19] Then he said to her, "Please give me a little water to drink; for I am thirsty." So she opened a skin of milk and gave him a drink and covered him. [20] He said to her, "Stand at the entrance of the tent, and if anybody comes and asks you, 'Is anyone here?' say, 'No.' " [21] But Jael wife of Heber took a tent peg, and took a hammer in her hand, and went softly to him and drove the peg into his temple, until it went down into the ground—he was lying fast asleep from weariness—and he died. [22] Then, as Barak came in pursuit of Sisera, Jael went out to meet him, and said to him, "Come, and I will show you the man whom you are seeking." So he went into her tent; and there was Sisera lying dead, with the tent peg in his temple.

[23] So on that day God subdued King Jabin of Canaan before the Israelites. [24] Then the hand of the Israelites bore harder and harder on King Jabin of Canaan, until they destroyed King Jabin of Canaan.

JUDGES 5:24-31

[24] "Most blessed of women be Jael,
    the wife of Heber the Kenite,
        of tent-dwelling women most blessed.
[25] He asked water and she gave him milk,
    she brought him curds in a lordly bowl.
[26] She put her hand to the tent peg
    and her right hand to the workmen's
        mallet;
she struck Sisera a blow,
    she crushed his head,
    she shattered and pierced his temple.
[27] He sank, he fell,
    he lay still at her feet;
at her feet he sank, he fell;
    where he sank, there he fell dead.

[28] "Out of the window she peered,
    the mother of Sisera gazed through the
        lattice:
'Why is his chariot so long in coming?
    Why tarry the hoofbeats of his chariots?'
[29] Her wisest ladies make answer,
    indeed, she answers the question herself:

[30] 'Are they not finding and dividing the spoil?

—

A girl or two for every man;
spoil of dyed stuffs for Sisera,
spoil of dyed stuffs embroidered,

two pieces of dyed work embroidered for
my neck as spoil?'

[31] "So perish all your enemies, O LORD!
But may your friends be like the sun as it
rises in its might.

DISCUSSION QUESTIONS

1. Judges 4:9 predicts that "the LORD will sell Sisera into the hand of a woman." Who does this refer to—Deborah or Jael? Why do you think so?

2. Compare Judges 4:17-22 and 5:24-27. What differences do you see in how the prose and poetry accounts describe Jael's encounter with Sisera?

3. What do you think it means that Jael is "most blessed among women" (Judg. 5:24)? Can you think of any reasons why this would be mentioned in Judges 5 but not Judges 4?

4. Some interpreters question the morality of Jael's actions, including her violation of conventions of hospitality. Do you agree? How do the concluding verses of chapter 4 factor into your answer?

Comparing stories of Jephthah's daughter

CLOSE READING TIPS

▶ The spirit of the LORD also comes upon other judges, including Othniel (3:10), Gideon (6:34), and Samson (13:25), though with differing results.

▶ In Hebrew, the vow in verse 31 has two parts joined together with a conjunction: whatever comes out from the doors shall be the LORD's *and* shall be offered up as a burnt offering. Jewish medieval commentator David Kimchi points out that the Hebrew word translated as "and" can also mean "or," thus allowing Jephthah to fulfill his vow by devoting his daughter to the LORD instead of killing her.

▶ Jephthah's words in verse 35 seem to shift the blame on to his daughter.

▶ Note that sacrificing children is prohibited in other parts of the Hebrew Bible (Lev. 18:21; 20:2-5; 2 Kgs. 23:10; Jer. 32:35), though Judges 11:29-40 may have originated prior to these other texts.

▶ Pseudo-Philo's *The Biblical Antiquities* was written near the end of the first century CE. It retells the biblical story from Adam to the death of Saul with numerous modifications.

▶ Note that Pseudo-Philo provides a name for Jephthah's daughter (Seila).

▶ Note how strongly Seila encourages her father to follow through on his vow.

▶ Seila is presented as a faithful martyr, willing to give up her life for the purpose of the vow.

JUDGES 11:29-40

[29] Then the spirit of the LORD came upon Jephthah, and he passed through Gilead and Manasseh. He passed on to Mizpah of Gilead, and from Mizpah of Gilead he passed on to the Ammonites. [30] And Jephthah made a vow to the LORD, and said, "If you will give the Ammonites into my hand, [31] then whoever comes out of the doors of my house to meet me, when I return victorious from the Ammonites, shall be the LORD's, to be offered up by me as a burnt offering." [32] So Jephthah crossed over to the Ammonites to fight against them; and the LORD gave them into his hand. [33] He inflicted a massive defeat on them from Aroer to the neighborhood of Minnith, twenty towns, and as far as Abel-keramim. So the Ammonites were subdued before the people of Israel.

[34] Then Jephthah came to his home at Mizpah; and there was his daughter coming out to meet him with timbrels and with dancing. She was his only child; he had no son or daughter except her. [35] When he saw her, he tore his clothes, and said, "Alas, my daughter! You have brought me very low; you have become the cause of great trouble to me. For I have opened my mouth to the LORD, and I cannot take back my vow." [36] She said to him, "My father, if you have opened your mouth to the LORD, do to me according to what has gone out of your mouth, now that the LORD has given you vengeance against your enemies, the Ammonites." [37] And she said to her father, "Let this thing be done for me: Grant me two months, so that I may go and wander on the mountains, and bewail my virginity, my companions and I." [38] "Go," he said and sent her away for two months.

So she departed, she and her companions, and bewailed her virginity on the mountains. [39] At the end of two months, she returned to her father, who did with her according to the vow he had made. She had never slept with a man. So there arose an Israelite custom that [40] for four days every year the daughters of Israel would go out to lament the daughter of Jephthah the Gileadite.

PSEUDO-PHILO, *BIBLICAL ANTIQUITIES* 40.2-3

And Seila his daughter said unto him: And who is it that can be sorrowful in their death when they see the people delivered? Do you not remember what was in the days of our fathers, when the father set his son for a burnt offering and he did not forbid him, but consented unto him, rejoicing? And he who was offered was ready, and he that offered was glad. 3. Now therefore do not annul anything of what you have vowed, but grant unto me one prayer. I ask of you before I die a small request: I beseech you that before I give up my soul, I may go into the mountains and wander among the hills and walk about among the rocks, I and the virgins that are my companions, and pour out my tears there and tell the affliction of my youth; and the trees of the field shall bewail me and the beasts of the field shall lament for me; for I am not sorrowful that I die, neither does it grieve me that I give up my soul: but whereas my father was overtaken in his vow, [and] if I offer not myself willingly for a sacrifice, I fear lest my death be unacceptable, and that I shall lose my life to no purpose. These things will I say to the mountains, and after that I will return.

DISCUSSION QUESTIONS:

1. Whose perspective are these stories told from? How do they portray Jephthah and his daughter in different ways?

2. What connection, if any, do you see between the spirit of the LORD coming upon Jephthah (verse 29) and the making of the vow (verses 30-31)? Is the vow an appropriate response to verse 29?

3. In light of David Kimchi's suggestion mentioned above, do you think Jephthah's daughter was killed? What clues do you find in the text to support your view?

4. What function does the Israelite custom play at the end of the story?

11

First Samuel

Key Points

First Samuel is a theologically motivated historical narrative that focuses on the period from the end of the judges to the beginning of the monarchy. The main content of the book can be divided into three parts, each of which focuses on a different character: 1) Samuel and the last judges of Israel (chapters 1–7); 2) Saul and the emergence of the monarchy (chapters 8–15); and 3) David's rise to prominence as God's anointed king (chapters 16–31). First Samuel includes many memorable stories, including Hannah's song of praise (1 Sam. 2:1-10), the Ark Narrative (1 Sam. 4:1b-7:1), and David's battle with Goliath (chapter 17). Enduring themes about unconditional obedience, the triumph of underdogs, and loyal friendship are also preserved in the pages of this book.

One of the central interpretive issues in 1 Samuel has to do with its view on the kingship. Two perspectives are evident. One strand looks upon the kingship favorably (such as 1 Sam. 9:1—10:16; 11; 13–14) while a second strand is suspicious of its abuses and pitfalls (such as 1 Sam. 7–8; 10:17-27; 12; 15). These competing viewpoints might derive from different sources or even pre-exilic and exilic editions of the Deuteronomistic History. In either case, the final form of 1 Samuel offers a complex narrative that interweaves a range of attitudes about the monarchy in ancient Israel.

A masterpiece of literature, 1 Samuel does not shy away from presenting multifaceted characters. Samuel not only functions as a prophet, priest, and judge but he also is a king "maker and breaker." Likewise, David is a conflicted figure whose virtues and vices are closely juxtaposed with one another. For instance, chapters 16–18 describe David as a talented musician and valiant warrior who is anointed as God's chosen king. Yet the later chapters of the book reveal that David is engaged in extortion against the farmer Nabal, offers himself as a mercenary for the Philistines, and is complicit in the death of Saul. In light of these tensions in David's character, it is likely that the more positive portrayal of David functioned as an apology or defense of David's legitimate claim to the throne.

While considered part of the Deuteronomistic History, 1 Samuel draws extensively on older sources and is not the product of a single author. As a result, the final form of the book reflects various duplications, including how Saul was elected king and how David came into the service of Saul. In addition, two separate accounts of David's encounter with Goliath are woven together in chapters 17–18. The story of 1 Samuel continues seamlessly into 2 Samuel, and these two books were originally coupled together in the Hebrew. It is only later that the Septuagint divides Samuel into two books and groups them together with 1 and 2 Kings under the titles 1 Reigns through 4 Reigns.

Key Terms

Shiloh   During the pre-monarchic period, Shiloh was the location of the most important Israelite sanctuary. Under Eli's care, the boy Samuel ministers to the LORD at Shiloh. Though referred to as a temple (Heb: *hêkāl*) in 1 Samuel 1:9; 3:3, the sanctuary at Shiloh was likely a portable, tent-like tabernacle. There is a strong tradition that links the ark of God to the shrine at Shiloh (1 Sam. 4:1-7:2; Ps. 78:60-61).

Ark of God   Variously referred to as the ark of God, of YHWH, and of Testimony, this box-like object functions as a receptacle for the stone tablets of the covenant (Deut. 10:1-5). However, in other contexts the ark serves as a powerful symbol of God's presence. It is also closely associated with the cherubim throne as a footstool of the Deity. The capture of the ark by the Philistines in 1 Samuel 4–6 likely mirrors the common ancient Near Eastern practice of carrying off an enemy's gods in the context of war.

Song of Hannah   Found in 1 Samuel 2:1-11, Hannah's song is a general hymn of praise or thanksgiving. It was not likely composed for this context but was later inserted here due to its reference to

the barren having children (verse 5). The theme of the song is that God exalts the lowly (here Hannah) and brings down the mighty. This theme is reiterated throughout 1 and 2 Samuel and 1 and 2 Kings. Hannah's song is echoed in the Magnificat, which is the hymn of praise sung by the virgin Mary in Luke 1:46-55.

Anointing   Anointing involves pouring oil over an object or person in order to confer upon it a special status. Prophets, priests, and kings are often anointed in the Hebrew Bible, and in 1 Samuel 10 Saul is anointed as the first king of Israel. Analogous practices are attested in some other ancient Near Eastern contexts. It is from the Hebrew term translated "anointed"" (*mashiach*) that the word "messiah" is derived.

House of David   This is the name of the ruling family of Judah for around 400 years. Their dynasty was established when Saul was rejected as king and David was anointed in his place by Samuel. While it is difficult to verify historical details about the house of David, this title has been discovered on an inscription from Tel Dan. The story about David and his successors reads like a theological historical novel rather than historiography in the modern sense of the term.

Key Personalities

Eli

Eli is described as the priest at Shiloh (1 Sam. 1:9; 2:11) and a judge in Israel (1 Sam. 4:18). The boy Samuel was brought to the shrine at Shiloh to serve as a nazirite under Eli's care. Samuel's faithful service is contrasted with that of Eli's two sons, Hophni and Phinehas, who "had no regard for the LORD" (1 Sam. 2:12). In 1 Samuel 2:27-36, an unnamed man of God comes to Eli and announces that his family will be cut off from the priesthood as a result of his sons' sins. In their place a "faithful priest" will be raised up to be God's anointed one forever (1 Sam. 2:35). In 1 Kings 2:26-27, this prophecy is to said to be fulfilled when Solomon removes the priest Abiathar (a descendent of Eli through Ahimelech according to 1 Samuel 22:9-20) from his priestly duties leaving Zadok to be the sole high priest.

Samuel

Like Samson, Samuel is born to a barren woman (Hannah) and set apart as a nazirite. He ministers at the shrine in Shiloh under Eli and later becomes judge, though he never functions in a military capacity. He is also called a prophet and a seer (1 Sam. 9:9). When the people reject his sons as judges and demand a king instead, Samuel anoints Saul as the first king of Israel. Although Samuel plays a pivotal role in establishing the monarchy, he has some reservations about this institution. He warns the people about the "ways of the king" (1 Sam. 8:11-18) and writes down the proper rights and duties of the kingship (1 Sam. 10:25). Samuel clashes with Saul on two occasions (1 Sam. 13 and 15), rebuking him for his disobedience and announcing that he will ultimately be replaced by a man after God's own heart (1 Sam. 13:8-14). The conflict between Samuel and Saul likely reflects a struggle between two theologies (unconditional obedience vs. moderate pragmatism) or two sources of authority (religious functionaries vs. secular rulers).

Questions for Study and Discussion

1. At the heart of 1 Samuel is a debate about proper governance: Should Israel have a king like the other nations or should YHWH alone rule, without a human king? Who are the various players in this debate? Who represents the pro-monarchy group and who represents the anti-monarchy group? In your view, was the adoption of a human king ultimately in Israel's best interest?

2. First Samuel focuses largely on powerful men, whose ambitious are actualized through potent prophetic acts, cunning political maneuvering, calculating marriage arrangements, and, of course, violence. One powerful counter-example to this generalization is Hannah, Samuel's mother, who—not unlike the matriarchs in Genesis—not only gives birth to an important figure but also gives voice to a powerful psalm of liberation. Are there any other "exceptions" to the book's general focus on men and their "great" deeds?

3. God is deeply involved in the stories of 1 Samuel, sometimes in overt ways and sometimes in more ambiguous ways. In your own words, how would you describe the God of 1 Samuel? How, moreover, does the God of 1 Samuel compare to how God is depicted in other books of the Hebrew Bible (sich as the Pentateuch, Judges, and so on)?

4. How would you characterize David in 1 Samuel? Is he a hero? A villain? A mercenary? What stories might you draw on to support your claim?

Primary Text

Compare song of Hannah to the Magnificat: 1 Samuel 2:1-10 and Luke 1:39-55

CLOSE READING TIPS

▶ This psalm was inserted into 1 Samuel because its emphasis on thanksgiving and praise mirrors Hannah's attitude.

▶ "Rock" is an often-used metaphor for God in the Psalter (for example, Pss. 18:2; 19:14; 28:1; 31:3, and others).

▶ A bow is a common symbol of strength in ancient art and literature. To break a bow suggests triumphing over the powerful.

▶ Sheol can refer to the grave or the underworld and is typically associated with the abode of the dead. As a metaphor, it implies a state of death-like despair or agony.

▶ Note that the word "anointed" in 1 Samuel 2:10 is a title for the king. In this context, it does not imply the coming of a future messiah.

▶ In the passage leading up to Luke 1:39-55, the angel Gabriel informs Mary, a virgin engaged to Joseph, that she will bear a son who is to be named Jesus.

▶ Elizabeth is a relative of Mary. She was barren but conceives a child through divine intervention (Luke 1:7, 12-13).

▶ Elizabeth's words to Mary—"Blessed are you among women" (Luke 1: 42)—echo words spoken about Jael in Judges 5:24.

▶ Note that in Luke 1:44 the child in Elizabeth's womb is John the Baptist.

▶ Mary's song is called the "Magnificat," which is the Latin translation of the first word in the song (magnifies).

1 SAMUEL 2:1-10

¹ Hannah prayed and said,

> "My heart exults in the LORD;
>> my strength is exalted in my God.
> My mouth derides my enemies,
>> because I rejoice in my victory.
> ² "There is no Holy One like the LORD,
>> no one besides you;
>> there is no Rock like our God.
> ³ Talk no more so very proudly,
>> let not arrogance come from your mouth;
> for the LORD is a God of knowledge,
>> and by him actions are weighed.
> ⁴ The bows of the mighty are broken,
>> but the feeble gird on strength.
> ⁵ Those who were full have hired themselves
>> out for bread,
>> but those who were hungry are fat with
>> spoil.
> The barren has borne seven,
>> but she who has many children is forlorn.
> ⁶ The LORD kills and brings to life;
>> he brings down to Sheol and raises up.
> ⁷ The LORD makes poor and makes rich;
>> he brings low, he also exalts.
> 8 He raises up the poor from the dust;
>> he lifts the needy from the ash heap,
> to make them sit with princes
>> and inherit a seat of honor.
> For the pillars of the earth are the LORD's,
>> and on them he has set the world.
>
> ⁹ "He will guard the feet of his faithful ones,
>> but the wicked shall be cut off in darkness;
>> for not by might does one prevail.
> ¹⁰ The LORD! His adversaries shall be
>> shattered;
>> the Most High will thunder in heaven.

> The LORD will judge the ends of the earth;
>> he will give strength to his king,
>> and exalt the power of his anointed."

LUKE 1:39-55

³⁹ In those days Mary set out and went with haste to a Judean town in the hill country, ⁴⁰ where she entered the house of Zechariah and greeted Elizabeth. ⁴¹ When Elizabeth heard Mary's greeting, the child leaped in her womb. And Elizabeth was filled with the Holy Spirit ⁴² and exclaimed with a loud cry, "Blessed are you among women, and blessed is the fruit of your womb. ⁴³ And why has this happened to me, that the mother of my Lord comes to me? ⁴⁴ For as soon as I heard the sound of your greeting, the child in my womb leaped for joy. ⁴⁵ And blessed is she who believed that there would be a fulfillment of what was spoken to her by the Lord."

⁴⁶ And Mary said,

> "My soul magnifies the Lord,
>> ⁴⁷ and my spirit rejoices in God my Savior,
> ⁴⁸ for he has looked with favor on the lowliness
>> of his servant.
>> Surely, from now on all generations will
>>> call me blessed;
> ⁴⁹ for the Mighty One has done great things for
>> me,
>> and holy is his name.
> ⁵⁰ His mercy is for those who fear him
>> from generation to generation.
> ⁵¹ He has shown strength with his arm;
>> he has scattered the proud in the thoughts
>>> of their hearts.
> ⁵² He has brought down the powerful from
>> their thrones,
>> and lifted up the lowly;
> ⁵³ he has filled the hungry with good things,
>> and sent the rich away empty.

[54] He has helped his servant Israel,
    in remembrance of his mercy,
[55] according to the promise he made to our
    ancestors,

to Abraham and to his descendants
    forever."

DISCUSSION QUESTIONS

1. Why is a psalm of praise appropriate to both Hannah and Mary?
2. What similarities or differences do you see between these two songs?
3. Where do you see the theme of the lowly being exalted and the powerful being brought low in both of these texts? How does this theme fit into the larger context of 1 Samuel?
4. Both songs employ metaphors and other types of figurative language to express praise and thanksgiving. What imagery stands out to you? How does it help to "visualize" the sentiment of Hannah and Mary?

The anointing of David: 1 Samuel 16:1-23.

CLOSE READING TIPS

▸ In verse 4, the elders are trembling perhaps because they fear Saul's wrath if it is found out that they are involved in choosing another king.

▸ It is not certain how Samuel knows which of Jesse's sons will be king. It is possible that he is using a device like the Urim and Thummim, which were used to obtain oracular judgments from God (see 1 Sam. 14:41).

▸ Keeping the sheep (verse 11) can be used as a metaphor for the king, who is a "shepherd" of the people (2 Sam. 5:2).

▸ Though YHWH considers the heart and not outward appearances, note that David is still described as handsome (verse 12).

▸ Note that the anointing of David does not immediately elevate him to the status of a king. This does not happen until 2 Samuel 2:1-11

▸ 1 Samuel 16:14-23 seems to preserve a second tradition concerning the discovery of David. A third tradition can be found in 1 Samuel 17.

▸ The "evil spirit" in verses 14-15 may refer to a mental illness, such as manic depression or bipolar disorder.

▸ Musicians were thought to be able to ward off evil spirits.

¹ The LORD said to Samuel, "How long will you grieve over Saul? I have rejected him from being king over Israel. Fill your horn with oil and set out; I will send you to Jesse the Bethlehemite, for I have provided for myself a king among his sons." ² Samuel said, "How can I go? If Saul hears of it, he will kill me." And the LORD said, "Take a heifer with you, and say, 'I have come to sacrifice to the Lord.' ³ Invite Jesse to the sacrifice, and I will show you what you shall do; and you shall anoint for me the one whom I name to you." ⁴ Samuel did what the LORD commanded, and came to Bethlehem. The elders of the city came to meet him trembling, and said, "Do you come peaceably?" ⁵ He said, "Peaceably; I have come to sacrifice to the LORD; sanctify yourselves and come with me to the sacrifice." And he sanctified Jesse and his sons and invited them to the sacrifice.

⁶ When they came, he looked on Eliab and thought, "Surely the LORD's anointed is now before the LORD." ⁷ But the LORD said to Samuel, "Do not look on his appearance or on the height of his stature, because I have rejected him; for the LORD does not see as mortals see; they look on the outward appearance, but the LORD looks on the heart." ⁸ Then Jesse called Abinadab, and made him pass before Samuel. He said, "Neither has the LORD chosen this one." ⁹ Then Jesse made Shammah pass by. And he said, "Neither has the LORD chosen this one." 10 Jesse made seven of his sons pass before Samuel, and Samuel said to Jesse, "The LORD has not chosen any of these." ¹¹ Samuel said to Jesse, "Are all your sons here?" And he said, "There remains yet the youngest, but he is keeping the sheep." And Samuel said to Jesse, "Send and bring him; for we will not sit down until he comes here." ¹² He sent and brought him in. Now he was ruddy, and had beautiful eyes, and was handsome. The LORD said, "Rise and anoint him; for this is the one." ¹³ Then Samuel took the horn of oil, and anointed him in the presence of his brothers; and the spirit of the LORD came mightily upon David from that day forward. Samuel then set out and went to Ramah.

¹⁴ Now the spirit of the LORD departed from Saul, and an evil spirit from the LORD tormented him. ¹⁵ And Saul's servants said to him, "See now, an evil spirit from God is tormenting you. ¹⁶ Let our lord now command the servants who attend you to look for someone who is skillful in playing the lyre; and when the evil spirit from God is upon you, he will play it, and you will feel better." ¹⁷ So Saul said to his servants, "Provide for me someone who can play well, and bring him to me." ¹⁸ One of the young men answered, "I have seen a son of Jesse the Bethlehemite who is skillful in playing, a man of valor, a warrior, prudent in speech, and a man of good presence; and the Lord is with him." ¹⁹ So Saul sent messengers to Jesse, and said, "Send me your son David who is with the sheep." ²⁰ Jesse took a donkey loaded with bread, a skin of wine, and a kid, and sent them by his son David to Saul. ²¹ And David came to Saul, and entered his service. Saul loved him greatly, and he became his armor-bearer. ²² Saul sent to Jesse, saying, "Let David remain in my service, for he has found favor in my sight." ²³ And whenever the evil spirit from God came upon Saul, David took the lyre and played it with his hand, and Saul would be relieved and feel better, and the evil spirit would depart from him.

DISCUSSION QUESTIONS

1. Compare verses 1-13 and 14-23. What similarities and differences do you see between how David began to rise to prominence in these two accounts?

2. The story of David and Goliath in 1 Samuel 17 reflects a third tradition about David's rise to prominence. Why do you think 1 Samuel preserves multiple accounts of David's early career?

3. How do both of these accounts legitimize David's future claim to the throne?

4. What role does "the spirit of the LORD" play in 1 Samuel 16?

Excerpts from the "Apology of Hattusilis."

Excerpts from *Context of Scripture* (1.77).

CLOSE READING TIPS

▶ Hattusilis was a Hittite king from the mid-thirteenth century BCE. The text is narrated from Hattusilis's first-person perspective.

▶ In section 3, "one-of-the-reins" likely refers to a chariot driver.

▶ In section 4, "became god" is an idiom for died.

▶ The goddess Ištar, also referred to as "My Lady," takes on the role of Hattusilis's special guardian or advocate.

▶ In section 7, note the great odds Hattusilis was up against in battle.

▶ In section 12a-b, note how favorably other kings and even Hattusilis's enemies respond to him.

[. . .]

Ḥóattusûili's early youth; Isûtar's first intervention

§3 (1:9-21) My father Mursûili begot us four children: Ḥóalpasûulupi, Muwatalli, Ḥóattusûili and Masûsûanauzzi, a daughter. Of all these I was the youngest child. As long as I was still a boy, I was a 'one-of-the reins.' [. . .]

Ḥóattusûili under Muwatalli; Armatarh̓unta's first lawsuit

§4 (1:22-60) When my father Mursûili became god, my brother Muwatalli seated himself on the throne of his father, while I became army commander in front of my brother. My brother installed me as Chief of the Royal Bodyguard and gave me the Upper Country to govern. So I was in command of the Upper Country.

[. . .] Since the goddess, My Lady, held me by the hand, she never exposed me to an evil deity (nor) to an evil lawsuit, never did she let an enemy weapon sway over me: Isûtar, My Lady, took me to her in every respect. Whenever illness befell me, sick as I was, I looked on (it) as the goddess' providence. The goddess, My Lady, held me by the hand in every respect. But, since I was a man divinely provided for, since I walked before the gods in divine providence, I never did an evil thing against man. You goddess, My Lady, always take me to you in every respect, wasn't it? The goddess, My Lady, never passed me over in time of fear, she never let me down before the enemy, nor did she ever let me down before my opponent in court (or) before (my) enviers: whether it (concerned) an enemy's word, or <the word> of an opponent or some word from the palace, it was Isûtar, My Lady, who held (her) mantle over me in every respect, took me to her in every respect. Isûtar, My Lady, put my enemies and enviers at my mercy and I finished them off. [...]

Hóattusûili's early military successes

§5 (1:61-74) Now, when my brother Muwatalli looked into the matter, not one evil thing was left against me. So he took me back and put me in charge of all the troops (and) chariots of Hóatti Land, and all the troops (and) chariots of Hóatti Land I commanded. My brother Muwatalli kept sending me out, and now that Isûtar, My Lady, had shown me (her) recognition, wherever I cast my glance towards enemy country, no enemy cast a glance back at me and each of the enemy countries I conquered: the recognition of Isûtar, My Lady, was mine. And whoever was an enemy within the Lands of Hóatti, I expelled him right out of the Lands of Hóatti. Which enemy countries I conquered one after the other, while still young, these I will describe separately on a tablet and I will lay it down before the goddess. [...]

Hóattusûili's further successes against the Kasûkaeans

§7 (2:31-47) It so happened, however, that the Pisûh·urean enemy invaded (the country), and Karah·na (and) Marisûta [were] within the enemy country. On one side the country of Takkasûta was its border, on the other the city of Talmaliya was its border. Eight hundred teams of horses were (there) whereas the troops were innumerable. My brother Muwatalli sent me and he gave me one hundred and twenty teams of horses, but not even a single military man was with me. There too Isûtar, My Lady, marched ahead of me, and there too, I personally

conquered the enemy. When I killed the man who was in command, the enemy fled. The cities of Hóatti Land which had been cut off, they each fought and began to defeat the enemy. A monument(?) in the city of Wisûtawanda I erected. There, too, the recognition of Isûtar, My Lady, was mine. The weapon that I held there, I had it inlaid and I deposited it in front of the goddess, My Lady.

Hóattusûili becomes King of Hóakpisû

§8 (2:48-68) My brother Muwatalli followed me and fortified the cities Anziliya and Tapiqqa, (then) he went right off, did not come near me at all and he let the troops (and) chariots of Hóatti-Land march ahead and led them home. Then he gathered the gods of Hóatti and the Manes on the spot, carried them down to the city of Tarh·untasûsûa and took (up residence in) Tarh·untasûsûa. To Durmitta (and) Kurusûtama, however, he did not go. In these countries he left me (behind), and these desolate countries he gave me to govern. The lands of Isûh·upitta, Marisûta, Hóisûsûasûh·apa, Katapa, Hóanh·ana, Darah·na, Hóattena, Durmitta, Pala, Tumanna, Gasûsûiya, Sûappa, the Hóulana River (and their) chariots and 'golden' chariot fighters I commanded all. The lands of Hóapkisû and Isûtah·ara he gave me in vassalship and in Hóapkisû he made me king. Concerning these desolate countries, which my brother had put me in charge of — because Isûtar, My Lady, held me by the hand, some enemies I defeated, while others concluded peace with me. Isûtar, My Lady, sided with me and these desolate lands I resettled on my own and made them Hittite again. [...]

Hóattusûili's career in retrospect; Kurunta King in Tarh·untasûsûa; transfer of properties to Isûtar; Tuth·aliya priest of Isûtar

§12a (4:41-48) I was a prince and became Chief of the Royal Bodyguard. As Chief of the Royal

Bodyguard I became King of Hóapkisû. As King of Hóapkisû I then became Great King. Finally, Isûtar, My Lady, had put (my) enviers, enemies (and) my opponents in court at my mercy. Some died by the sword, others died on (their appointed) day: all these I finished off. Isûtar, My Lady, had given me kingship over Hóatti Land.

§12b (4:48-80) I had become Great King: She took me as a prince and let me (rise) to kingship. The kings (who were) my elders (and) who had been on good terms with me, they remained on just those good terms with me, and they began to send envoys to me. They began to send gifts to me, and the gifts they ke[ep] sending me, they never sent to any (of my) fathers and grandfathers. The king supposed to respect me, respected me, and the (countries) that had been my enemies, I conquered them. For the Hóatti Lands I [a]nnexed territory upon territory. (Those) who had been enemies in the days of my fathers (and) grandfat[her]s concluded peace with me. Because the goddess, My Lady, had thus shown me (her) recognition, I did not do anything (evil) out of regard for the love for my brother. I took up my [nephew] Kurunta and installed him into kingship there on the spot which my brother Muwatalli had built into the city of Tarhˑuntasûsûa. How often had Isûtar, the Lady, taken me! She had installed me on 'the high place,' into kingship over Hóatti Land! I, then, gave Isûtar, My Lady, the property of Armatarhˑunta: I withdrew it and handed it over. What had been (there) formerly, that I handed over to her, and what I had had, that too I handed over. I withdrew it (all) and handed it over to the goddess.

Discussion questions

1. What similarities do you see between the rise to power of Hattusilis and the rise to power of David?
2. What aspects of this text are designed to defend the legitimacy of Hattusilis's kingship?
3. Where do you see similar themes between this text and the story about David in 1 Samuel 16–31?

12

Second Samuel

Key Points

Second Samuel begins where 1 Samuel left off by narrating the history of David's rise to power. David's path to the throne progresses through various stages: he is chosen as Saul's successor (1 Samuel 16–18), steadily grows in prominence and popularity among the people (1 Samuel 19–31), and, after Saul dies in battle, is anointed as king over the house of Judah at Hebron (2 Samuel 2). Yet in the ensuing chapters the new monarch must still rely on shrewd political maneuvering to consolidate his power. The culmination of David's rise to power comes in 2 Samuel 5, where he is acclaimed as king over all Israel and captures Jerusalem as a new capitol for his kingdom.

One of the most important passages of 2 Samuel—and perhaps all of the Hebrew Bible—is the foundation charter of the Davidic dynasty in 2 Samuel 7. Through an oracle uttered by the prophet Nathan, the LORD promises that David's house, or dynasty, will be established forever. This unconditional promise is best understood in light of the royal ideology expressed in certain psalms that deal with the kingship. In these psalms, the king is described as an adopted "son of God," the rightful ruler of all the earth, and the anointed one of God. While this viewpoint is tempered slightly by Deuteronomistic editors, 2 Samuel 7 remains the basis for the belief that the Davidic dynasty would be restored even after the Babylonian exile. This hope is extremely important to the development of messianism in postexilic Judaism and early Christianity.

The remainder of 2 Samuel (chapters 8–24) consists of a series of traditions about David's reign known as the Court History or Succession Narrative. This literary unit, which culminates in the accession of Solomon in 1 Kings 1–2, includes stories about the wars of David, the Bathsheba affair, the revolt of Absalom, the rape of Tamar, and the census of David. A pattern of sin, repentance, and misplaced punishment emerges. While certainly a flawed figure, David is typically cast in a favorable light by the Court History. Two poetic compositions ascribed to David bring the book to a close. These chapters, along with the notion that David was a skilled musician, helps inform a later tradition in which David is seen as the author of psalms.

Key Terms

Jerusalem   Jerusalem was a moderately sized urban center nestled in the central hill country of ancient Israel. It remained under the control of the Jebusites until David conquered it at the outset of his reign. Jerusalem proved to be an ideal capitol city for the new monarchy because it was easy to defend and was not previously associated with any particular tribe (that is, it was politically neutral). David transfers the ark to Jerusalem, making it a center of Israelite worship.

Temple   A temple was thought to be a sacred place that demarcated the earthly dwelling, or house, of God. In 2 Samuel 7, David proposes to construct a house for YHWH, thus reflecting a common ancient Near Eastern practice whereby the founder of a dynasty builds a temple for this patron god. However, a word of the LORD comes through Nathan that asserts it is not for David to build YHWH a house. Rather, it is YHWH who will establish David's house forever. This oracle plays on the double sense of the word "house" (Heb.: *bayit*) meaning "temple," "palace," or "dynasty."

Royal ideology of Judah   The royal ideology of Judah refers to an understanding of kingship in Jerusalem prior to the Deuteronomic reform. Expressed most clearly in Psalms 2, 45, 72, and 110, royal ideology maintains an exalted view of the king as the rightful ruler of all the earth. The authority of the king comes directly from God and he is often considered the Deity's adopted son. Tasked to uphold truth and righteousness, the king is set in place without condition. Deuteronomistic editors tone down and demythologize

this royal ideology in 2 Samuel 7 in light of the reality of the Babylonian exile.

Messianism   Messianism is the belief in the future restoration of the Davidic dynasty through the coming of "the anointed one [Heb.: *mashiach*] of the LORD" (Ps 89:32). While not fully developed in the Hebrew Bible, messianism is rooted in the unconditional promise in 2 Samuel 7 that David's house will be established forever. Messianism emerges in postexilic Judaism but was not widespread until near the end of the Second Temple period. Early Christianity radically reinterprets Jewish messianism in light of the belief that Jesus was the Christ, the Greek translation of messiah.

Court History of David   Also known as the Succession Narrative, the Court History of David consists of a series of traditions about the reign of David in 2 Samuel 9 through 1 Kings 2. This narrative unit culminates in the accession of Solomon and includes stories about David and Bathsheba, Absalom's revolt, and the rape of Tamar. It generally presents David in a favorable light, though he is far from a flawless character.

Key Personalities

Bathsheba

Seen by David while she was bathing, Bathsheba is invited by the king to the palace and becomes embroiled in an adulterous affair. When David finds out she is pregnant, he attempts to cover up the scandal by arranging for Bathsheba to sleep with her husband, Uriah the Hittite, who had been away at war. However, out of a sense of piety and tradition Uriah refuses to sleep with his wife while his companions are on a military campaign. David arranges for Uriah to be killed in battle and then proceeds to marry Bathsheba. While Nathan rebukes David for his role in "Bathsheba gate," 2 Sam 11–12 gives us little insight into Bathsheba's motivations or emotions. Some believe that she is simply a victim of David's sexual folly and others see her as a one-dimensional agent who merely helps to move forward a plot that is about David's adultery. However, some clues suggest she might have been a co-conspirator with David in a political scheme. Their union is similar to David's other political marriages and in 1 Kings 1–2 she plays an active role in the political intrigue that leads to the rise of Solomon and the death of Adonijah.

Absalom

Absalom is the son of David and Maacah and features prominently in 2 Samuel 13–18, which is part of the Court History of David. When Absalom finds out that his sister, Tamar, has been raped by Amnon (their half-brother) he becomes enraged. Biding his time for two years, Absalom lures Amnon into a trap and kills him. David is grieved, and it is only after several years that he restores Absalom from exile. However, this reconciliation is fleeting. Absalom almost immediately begins a subversive plot against his father and conspires to be made king at Hebron. David eventually flees from Jerusalem. In a later battle, David's forces defeat Absalom. But rather than celebrate the victory, David laments the death of his son in agony. The tragic story of Absalom has often been retold or alluded to in non-biblical sources, including music, art, and literature. Perhaps most notable is the 1936 novel by William Faulkner, *Absalom, Absalom!*

Questions for Study and Discussion

1. Why is 2 Samuel 7 such an important text in the story of David's rise to prominence as the king over all Israel? What significance did this text have for later readers?
2. Like many kingdoms, Judah created its own ideology to bolster and legitimate the Judean kingship. What are some features of that ideology? Do modern day governments—including your own—engage in the creation of power-legitimating ideology? Where might you find examples of such ideology?
3. How is Christian messianism—understood primarily with reference to Jesus of Nazareth—different from or similar to Jewish messianism and the biblical texts on which it is based?
4. Many scholars have characterized Saul as a tragic figure, whose life and reign are fatefully cut short. Do you agree with this evaluation? If so, what texts might you draw on to substantiate your argument?

Primary Text

The LORD's Promise to David: 2 Samuel 7:1-17

> **CLOSE READING TIPS**
>
> ▸ The message in verse 1 seems to be inconsistent with the wars that we hear about in 2 Samuel 8–20.
>
> ▸ The "house" David wants to build for God is a temple; but the "house" that God promises to build for David is a dynasty.
>
> ▸ While YHWH is said to have never lived in a permanent structure in verse 6, the shrine at Shiloh is occasionally described as a temple.
>
> ▸ Note that an agricultural image is used in verse 10 to describe how God will "plant" his people in their place (that is, Jerusalem). In contrast, prophetic literature speaks of the exile as a ruined vineyard and a waterless desert.
>
> ▸ Note that the phrase "to lie down with your ancestors" (verse 12) is a common Hebrew idiom for death.
>
> ▸ The offspring that will build the future temple is David's son Solomon (verses 12-13).
>
> ▸ Note that a king was commonly referred to as an adopted "son of God," as in Psalm 2:7 and Psalm 89:26-27.

¹ Now when the king was settled in his house, and the LORD had given him rest from all his enemies around him, ² the king said to the prophet Nathan, "See now, I am living in a house of cedar, but the ark of God stays in a tent." ³ Nathan said to the king, "Go, do all that you have in mind; for the LORD is with you."

⁴ But that same night the word of the LORD came to Nathan: ⁵ Go and tell my servant David: Thus says the LORD: Are you the one to build me a house to live in? ⁶ I have not lived in a house since the day I brought up the people of Israel from Egypt to this day, but I have been moving about in a tent and a tabernacle. ⁷ Wherever I have moved about among all the people of Israel, did I ever speak a word with any of the tribal leaders of Israel, whom I commanded to shepherd my people Israel, saying, "Why have you not built me a house of cedar?"

⁸ Now therefore thus you shall say to my servant David: Thus says the LORD of hosts: I took you from the pasture, from following the sheep to be prince over my people Israel; ⁹ and I have been with you wherever you went, and have cut off all your enemies from before you; and I will make for you a great name, like the name of the great ones of the earth. ¹⁰ And I will appoint a place for my people Israel and will plant them, so that they may live in their own place, and be disturbed no more; and evildoers shall afflict them no more, as formerly, ¹¹ from the time that I appointed judges over my people Israel; and I will give you rest from all your enemies. Moreover the LORD declares to you that the LORD will make you a house. ¹² When your days are fulfilled and you lie down with your ancestors, I will raise up your offspring after you, who shall come forth from your body, and I will establish his kingdom. ¹³ He shall

build a house for my name, and I will establish the throne of his kingdom forever. [14] I will be a father to him, and he shall be a son to me. When he commits iniquity, I will punish him with a rod such as mortals use, with blows inflicted by human beings. [15] But I will not take my steadfast love from him, as I took it from Saul, whom I put away from before you. [16] Your house and your kingdom shall be made sure forever before me; your throne shall be established forever. [17] In accordance with all these words and with all this vision, Nathan spoke to David.

DISCUSSION QUESTIONS

1. How does the prophet Nathan balance the power and authority of the soon-to-be king David?
2. What problem does the Babylonian exile pose for this Davidic covenant?
3. How can you reconcile the reality of the exile with God's unconditional promise to David?
4. Where do you see evidence in this passage that the king is still subject to some degree of punishment?
5. What language or imagery in this text most clearly reflects Deuteronomistic theology?

Royal Ideology: Psalm 89:19-51

CLOSE READING TIPS

▶ Note that an earlier part of this psalm (verses 3-4) contains a simple statement of the Davidic covenant. Verses 19-37 elaborate on this unconditional promise.

▶ In verse 14, "horn" is a metaphor for strength.

▶ Note that in verse 27, the Davidic king is set above all other earthly kings.

▶ The reference to "my law" in verse 30 likely presupposes Deuteronomic reform.

▶ Note that in verse 38, it is no longer God who speaks. Rather, a representative of the community addresses God directly.

▶ The community speaker claims that God has rejected the Davidic king and renounced his covenant with him (verses 38-45).

▶ The psalm concludes with a passionate plea that God would once again remember his steadfast love for David.

▶ The final verse (verse 52) is not part of the psalm. This doxology of praise was likely inserted by an editor to mark the end of the third division of the Psalter.

[19] Then you spoke in a vision to your faithful
   one, and said:
   "I have set the crown on one who is mighty,
   I have exalted one chosen from the people.
[20] I have found my servant David;
   with my holy oil I have anointed him;

[21] my hand shall always remain with him;
   my arm also shall strengthen him.
[22] The enemy shall not outwit him,
   the wicked shall not humble him.
[23] I will crush his foes before him
   and strike down those who hate him.

[24] My faithfulness and steadfast love shall be
with him;
and in my name his horn shall be exalted.
[25] I will set his hand on the sea
and his right hand on the rivers.
[26] He shall cry to me, 'You are my Father,
my God, and the Rock of my salvation!'
[27] I will make him the firstborn,
the highest of the kings of the earth.
[28] Forever I will keep my steadfast love for him,
and my covenant with him will stand firm.
[29] I will establish his line forever,
and his throne as long as the heavens endure.
[30] If his children forsake my law
and do not walk according to my
ordinances,
[31] if they violate my statutes
and do not keep my commandments,
[32] then I will punish their transgression with
the rod
and their iniquity with scourges;
[33] but I will not remove from him my steadfast
love,
or be false to my faithfulness.
[34] I will not violate my covenant,
or alter the word that went forth from my
lips.
[35] Once and for all I have sworn by my holiness;
I will not lie to David.
[36] His line shall continue forever,
and his throne endure before me like the
sun.
[37] It shall be established forever like the moon,
an enduring witness in the skies."
Selah

[38] But now you have spurned and rejected him;
you are full of wrath against your
anointed.

[39] You have renounced the covenant with your
servant;
you have defiled his crown in the dust.
[40] You have broken through all his walls;
you have laid his strongholds in ruins.
[41] All who pass by plunder him;
he has become the scorn of his neighbors.
[42] You have exalted the right hand of his foes;
you have made all his enemies rejoice.
[43] Moreover, you have turned back the edge of
his sword,
and you have not supported him in battle.
[44] You have removed the scepter from his hand,
and hurled his throne to the ground.
[45] You have cut short the days of his youth;
you have covered him with shame.
Selah

[46] How long, O LORD? Will you hide yourself
forever?
How long will your wrath burn like fire?
[47] Remember how short my time is—
for what vanity you have created all
mortals!
[48] Who can live and never see death?
Who can escape the power of Sheol?
Selah

[49] Lord, where is your steadfast love of old,
which by your faithfulness you swore to
David?
[50] Remember, O Lord, how your servant is
taunted;
how I bear in my bosom the insults of the
peoples,
[51] with which your enemies taunt, O LORD,
with which they taunted the footsteps of
your anointed.

Discussion questions

1. What differences do you see between verses 19-37 and verses 38-51?
2. What historical settings are plausible for these two parts of Psalm 89?
3. What are some similarities between the language of verses 19-37 and 2 Samuel 7:1-17?
4. Verses 46-51 petition God to remember his promise from of old to the Davidic dynasty. On what basis is this appeal made?

David, Bathsheba, and Nathan's Parable: 2 Samuel 11:1—12:14

Close reading tips

- ► In verse 3, David likely inquires whether Bathsheba is married.
- ► The parenthetical note about Bathsheba purifying herself (verse 4) suggests that she was at the most fertile time of her cycle. This assures the reader that the child must be David's.
- ► Note that Uriah refused to go to his house to sleep with Bathsheba out of respect and loyalty to his army.
- ► The story of Abimelech being killed at Thebez is told in Judges 9:50-55.
- ► Note that Nathan is a prophet in David's service, but here he confronts the king for his wrongdoing.
- ► The prediction in 2 Samuel 12:10-11 alludes to the violent events that transpire in 2 Samuel 13–20.
- ► Note that the punishment owed to David (death) is transferred to the child that was born to Bathsheba.

[1] In the spring of the year, the time when kings go out to battle, David sent Joab with his officers and all Israel with him; they ravaged the Ammonites, and besieged Rabbah. But David remained at Jerusalem. [2] It happened, late one afternoon, when David rose from his couch and was walking about on the roof of the king's house, that he saw from the roof a woman bathing; the woman was very beautiful. [3] David sent someone to inquire about the woman. It was reported, "This is Bathsheba daughter of Eliam, the wife of Uriah the Hittite." [4] So David sent messengers to get her, and she came to him, and he lay with her. (Now she was purifying herself after her period.) Then she returned to her house. [5] The woman conceived; and she sent and told David, "I am pregnant."

[6] So David sent word to Joab, "Send me Uriah the Hittite." And Joab sent Uriah to David. [7] When Uriah came to him, David asked how Joab and the people fared, and how the war was going. [8] Then David said to Uriah, "Go down to your house, and wash your feet." Uriah went out of the king's house, and there followed him a present from the king. [9] But Uriah slept at the entrance of the king's house with all the servants of his lord, and did not go down to his house. [10] When they told David, "Uriah did not go down to his house," David said to Uriah, "You have just come from a journey. Why did you not go down to your house?" [11] Uriah said to David, "The

ark and Israel and Judah remain in booths; and my lord Joab and the servants of my lord are camping in the open field; shall I then go to my house, to eat and to drink, and to lie with my wife? As you live, and as your soul lives, I will not do such a thing." [12] Then David said to Uriah, "Remain here today also, and tomorrow I will send you back." So Uriah remained in Jerusalem that day. On the next day, [13] David invited him to eat and drink in his presence and made him drunk; and in the evening he went out to lie on his couch with the servants of his lord, but he did not go down to his house.

[14] In the morning David wrote a letter to Joab, and sent it by the hand of Uriah. [15] In the letter he wrote, "Set Uriah in the forefront of the hardest fighting, and then draw back from him, so that he may be struck down and die." [16] As Joab was besieging the city, he assigned Uriah to the place where he knew there were valiant warriors. [17] The men of the city came out and fought with Joab; and some of the servants of David among the people fell. Uriah the Hittite was killed as well. [18] Then Joab sent and told David all the news about the fighting; [19] and he instructed the messenger, "When you have finished telling the king all the news about the fighting, [20] then, if the king's anger rises, and if he says to you, 'Why did you go so near the city to fight? Did you not know that they would shoot from the wall? [21] Who killed Abimelech son of Jerubbaal? Did not a woman throw an upper millstone on him from the wall, so that he died at Thebez? Why did you go so near the wall?' then you shall say, 'Your servant Uriah the Hittite is dead too.' "

[22] So the messenger went, and came and told David all that Joab had sent him to tell. [23] The messenger said to David, "The men gained an advantage over us, and came out against us in the field; but we drove them back to the entrance of the gate. [24] Then

the archers shot at your servants from the wall; some of the king's servants are dead; and your servant Uriah the Hittite is dead also." [25] David said to the messenger, "Thus you shall say to Joab, 'Do not let this matter trouble you, for the sword devours now one and now another; press your attack on the city, and overthrow it.' And encourage him."

[26] When the wife of Uriah heard that her husband was dead, she made lamentation for him. [27] When the mourning was over, David sent and brought her to his house, and she became his wife, and bore him a son.

But the thing that David had done displeased the LORD,

12 [1] and the LORD sent Nathan to David. He came to him, and said to him, "There were two men in a certain city, the one rich and the other poor. [2] The rich man had very many flocks and herds; [3] but the poor man had nothing but one little ewe lamb, which he had bought. He brought it up, and it grew up with him and with his children; it used to eat of his meager fare, and drink from his cup, and lie in his bosom, and it was like a daughter to him. [4] Now there came a traveler to the rich man, and he was loath to take one of his own flock or herd to prepare for the wayfarer who had come to him, but he took the poor man's lamb, and prepared that for the guest who had come to him." [5] Then David's anger was greatly kindled against the man. He said to Nathan, "As the LORD lives, the man who has done this deserves to die; [6] he shall restore the lamb fourfold, because he did this thing, and because he had no pity."

[7] Nathan said to David, "You are the man! Thus says the LORD, the God of Israel: I anointed you king over Israel, and I rescued you from the hand of Saul; [8] I gave you your master's house, and your master's wives into your bosom, and gave you the

house of Israel and of Judah; and if that had been too little, I would have added as much more. ⁹ Why have you despised the word of the LORD, to do what is evil in his sight? You have struck down Uriah the Hittite with the sword, and have taken his wife to be your wife, and have killed him with the sword of the Ammonites. ¹⁰ Now therefore the sword shall never depart from your house, for you have despised me, and have taken the wife of Uriah the Hittite to be your wife. ¹¹ Thus says the LORD: I will raise up trouble against you from within your own house; and I will take your wives before your eyes, and give them to your neighbor, and he shall lie with your wives in the sight of this very sun. ¹² For you did it secretly; but I will do this thing before all Israel, and before the sun." ¹³ David said to Nathan, "I have sinned against the LORD." Nathan said to David, "Now the LORD has put away your sin; you shall not die. 14 Nevertheless, because by this deed you have utterly scorned the LORD, the child that is born to you shall die."

DISCUSSION QUESTIONS

1. The story begins with a note about David remaining in Jerusalem. Does this paint David in a positive or negative light. Why?

2. How does David abuse his power in chapter 11?

3. What general law or moral issue does the rich man in the parable violate? How does this apply to David's situation?

4. Why do you think it was important for Nathan to articulate his critique of David in the form of a parable?

5. In what ways is the punishment expressed in 2 Samuel 12:10-12 still consistent with God's promise to David in 2 Samuel 7?

13

1 Kings 1–11: Solomon and the Divided Monarchy

Key Points

Mark Twain once remarked, "History doesn't repeat itself, but it often rhymes." Something similar can be said about the history of the monarchic period presented in 1 and 2 Kings. The noticeable "rhyme" of these books, which is provided by Deuteronomistic editors, is especially evident in the recurrence of certain themes and theologies. These include the negative evaluation of all northern kings, the emphasis on centralized worship at the Jerusalem temple, and the continuity of the Davidic covenant. The Deuteronomistic shaping of these books is also apparent in formulaic language about obedience ("with all the heart and soul"), disobedience ("to walk in the sin of Jeroboam"), and the synchronization of the reigns of Israelite and Judean kings.

The content of 1 Kings 1–11 primarily focuses on the reign of Solomon, David's successor. His accession to the throne does not go unchallenged, and as a result, he must rely on court intrigue and the ruthless elimination of his rivals to secure power (chapters 1–2). The early years of his reign are portrayed as a golden age in Israelite history. Solomon demonstrates profound wisdom, establishes extensive international relations, and initiates an ambitious building campaign (chapters 3–5; 9–10). Yet Solomon's crowning achievement is the construction of the temple in Jerusalem (chapters 6–7), which was likely modeled after the typical plan of temples in ancient Syria-Palestine. Through a series of three dedicatory prayers (chapter 8), Solomon articulates the main contours of the Deuteronomist's temple theology. This theology affirms that the temple is a place where God's name dwells and where prayer can be directed.

Despite his many accomplishments, Solomon's reign ends in failure. He sacrifices at high places (1 Kgs. 3:3), conscripts his people into forced labor (1 Kgs. 9:15), and loves many foreign women (1 Kgs. 11:1-8). Led astray into idolatry, God resolves to tear away a large part of the kingdom from Solomon's offspring. However, out of loyalty to the Davidic covenant, God allows two tribes to remain under the control of Solomon's successors. The subsequent division of the "United Monarchy" results in two independent entities—the Northern Kingdom of Israel and the Southern Kingdom of Judah.

The portrait of Solomon's kingdom provided in 1 Kings 1–11 has been challenged by many modern historians. The archaeological record provides little evidence of an expansive kingdom or extensive building projects in and around Jerusalem during the tenth century. Nevertheless, there is good reason to believe that the Deuteronomist did not invent the story of Solomon's reign out of whole cloth. In all likelihood, the golden age of Solomon reflects aspirations of later Judean kings, which are projected onto the more modest historical reality of early Israel.

Key Terms

Solomonic enlightenment   Coined by the German scholar Gerhard von Rad, the Solomonic enlightenment refers to the supposed flourishing of Israelite culture during the mid-tenth century BCE. Von Rad proposed that Solomon's court fostered extensive literary activity, including the composition of the J source of the Pentateuch. Contemporary scholars have come to question the historicity of the Solomonic enlightenment, including the early date of the J source and the extent of literacy in early Israel.

Sins of Jeroboam   This term refers to Jeroboam's construction of worship centers at Dan and Bethel. In the eyes of the Deuteronomist, this action is a violation of the command to centralize worship in Jerusalem. All northern Israelite kings violate this command and thus are said "to walk in the sins of Jeroboam." The story of the golden calf in Exodus 32 likely functions as a polemic against the golden calves Jeroboam sets up at Dan and Bethel. However, Jeroboam likely intended these objects to be pedestals for the invisible deity (like the cherubim throne), not idols.

Corvée   Corvée is a form of forced labor often imposed on people in lieu of taxes. Solomon initiated a corvée during the construction of the temple (1 Kgs. 5:13-14; 9:15). When Solomon's son, Rehoboam, follows the advice of his young advisors to intensify the corvée, the ten northern tribes revolt. There is a parallel between the corvée imposed on the Israelites by Solomon and Rehoboam and the corvée imposed on them by the Egyptians in the exodus story.

Northern Kingdom   After the reign of Solomon, ten tribes break away from Rehoboam's control and form their own nation, known as the Northern Kingdom or "Israel." The Deuteronomist understands this schism as a punishment for Solomon's apostasy, although the socioeconomic reasons for the division are related to the corvée. The capital of the Northern Kingdom was originally located at Shechem but was later transferred to Samaria during the reign of Omri. All northern rulers are evaluated negatively in 1 and 2 Kings.

Cherubim   The term cherubim (plural of cherub) refers to hybrid, winged creatures that include features of various animals. In the inner sanctuary of Solomon's temple, two large cherubim with wings spread open were part of the covering of the ark. The cherubim functioned as resting place or throne for the presence of the invisible God. Two-dimensional cherub imagery is also found in other parts of the temple, including the curtains and veil. Hybrid creatures were popular in ancient Near Eastern art and should not be confused with the chubby, infant-like angelic beings known from Western art.

Key Personalities

Ahijah

Ahijah was a prophet from Shiloh who plays a key role in the Deuteronomistic explanation of the split between the Northern and Southern Kingdoms. When Ahijah meets Jeroboam on the road from Jerusalem, he performs a symbolic act by tearing a garment into twelve pieces. Ten pieces, which symbolize tribes, are taken by Jeroboam as evidence that God is tearing the kingdom from the hand of Solomon due to his apostasy. Ahijah promises Jeroboam that if he walks in God's ways, he will be given "an enduring house" (1 Kgs. 11:38). However, two pieces of the garment, representing Judah and Benjamin, remain with Rehoboam for the sake of the promise made to David in 2 Samuel 7. Rehoboam's refusal to lift the corvée in 1 Kings 12:15 is explained as a fulfillment of Ahijah's prophecy. Later, Ahijah figures prominently in the condemnation of the sin of Jeroboam. Ahijah prophecies not only that Jeroboam's house will be cut off, but that the whole Northern Kingdom will go into exile "beyond the Euphrates" (1 Kgs. 14:12-16). Immediately after uttering these words, Jeroboam's son dies, thus fulfilling part of Ahijah's prophecy. The story of Ahijah anticipates the more prominent role prophets play throughout 1 and 2 Kings.

Hiram of Tyre

Hiram was a tenth century king of Tyre who had contact with both David and Solomon (2 Sam. 5, 1 Kgs. 5). The biblical accounts of Hiram all address commercial relations with Israelite kings, reflecting the fact that Tyre was an important hub of trade located on a small island just off the southern Phoenician coast. In 2 Samuel 5:11, Hiram sends cedar trees, carpenters, and masons to David in order to build him a palace. This gift was likely intended to honor David, who recently captured Jerusalem. In David's view, Hiram's actions confirm that the LORD had established him as king over Israel. Because of Hiram's friendship with David, the king of Tyre also sends servants to greet Solomon after he had been anointed as king. Solomon sends word to Hiram requesting that he once again provide cedars from Lebanon for a royal building project— this time, a "house" (temple) for God. Hiram gladly responds to this request and ships "timber of cedar and cypress" to Israel (1 Kgs. 5:8-10) in return for an annual shipment of oil and wheat (1 Kgs. 5:11-12). Later, Solomon also gives Hiram twenty cities in the Galilee region (1 Kgs. 9:10-14), perhaps because the king was forced into financial difficulty due to his building projects or trade. While Hiram is said to be displeased with these cities, the treaty between the king of Tyre and the king of Israel does not seem to be jeopardized. Later, Hiram provides Solomon with ships and sailors for a fleet of commercial ships that carry precious metals, ivory, and exotic animals (1 Kgs. 9:26-28; 10:11, 22). First Kings 7 specifies that a skilled craftsman, whose name also happens to be Hiram, contributed to the construction of Solomon's temple (1 Kgs. 7:13-47). This Hiram should not be confused with the king of Tyre.

Questions for Study and Discussion

1. Solomon is typically remembered for his wisdom, but a careful reading of the narrative itself reveals that Solomon is not so easily labeled. Is he wise? Foolish? Ironic? What is your view on the matter and what evidence would you point to in support of your view?

2. Writing was a privilege in ancient Israel that was primarily available to privileged men. Temples and palaces in particular are the typical patrons of scribes. Given that King Solomon is ultimately cast in a negative light, who do you think might be responsible for creating these negative images of one of Israel's most famous monarchs?

3. The chapter claims that, "The hand of the Deuteronomistic editors is more obvious in the books of Kings than in those of Samuel." Based on your reading of the chapter, how would you describe Deuteronomistic theology? What are its key features? How does it understand God's

4. The book of Kings is a theological interpretation of Israel's history. For instance, the political rebellion that split the southern and northern kingdoms is understood as God's work, and Solomon's wisdom is attributed to divine action. How do you respond to this kind of historiography? What are its problems? What are its benefits?

Primary Text

The Inauguration of the Temple: 1 Kings 8:1-30, 54-66

CLOSE READING TIPS

▸ Up to this point, the ark had been housed in a tent sanctuary.

▸ Note that the festival mentioned in verse 2 is the festival of booths (also known as tabernacles), which occurs in September-October.

▸ Note that verse 9 emphasizes that the ark was a mere receptacle for the tablets of Moses. The Deuteronomist wanted to counter the notion that the a material object could symbolize God's presence.

▸ Verses 14-21 represent the first of Solomon's three prayers, each of which illuminates the Deuteronomist's temple theology.

▸ In order to avoid saying that God actually dwelled in the temple, Solomon refers to the building as "a house for the name of the LORD, the God of Israel" (verses 17 and 21).

▸ Note that in verses 29-30, prayer should be directed *toward* the temple. This statement may presuppose conditions during the Babylonian exile when it was no longer possible to pray *in* the temple.

> ▶ Note that in the third prayer (verses 54-61), obedience is the proper response to God's past faithfulness to the Israelites.
> ▶ The number of sacrifices said to be offered in verse 63 is highly exaggerated in order to highlight the centrality of the sanctuary to Solomon and his kingship.

¹ Then Solomon assembled the elders of Israel and all the heads of the tribes, the leaders of the ancestral houses of the Israelites, before King Solomon in Jerusalem, to bring up the ark of the covenant of the LORD out of the city of David, which is Zion. ² All the people of Israel assembled to King Solomon at the festival in the month Ethanim, which is the seventh month. ³ And all the elders of Israel came, and the priests carried the ark. ⁴ So they brought up the ark of the LORD, the tent of meeting, and all the holy vessels that were in the tent; the priests and the Levites brought them up. ⁵ King Solomon and all the congregation of Israel, who had assembled before him, were with him before the ark, sacrificing so many sheep and oxen that they could not be counted or numbered. ⁶ Then the priests brought the ark of the covenant of the LORD to its place, in the inner sanctuary of the house, in the most holy place, underneath the wings of the cherubim. ⁷ For the cherubim spread out their wings over the place of the ark, so that the cherubim made a covering above the ark and its poles. ⁸ The poles were so long that the ends of the poles were seen from the holy place in front of the inner sanctuary; but they could not be seen from outside; they are there to this day. ⁹ There was nothing in the ark except the two tablets of stone that Moses had placed there at Horeb, where the LORD made a covenant with the Israelites, when they came out of the land of Egypt. ¹⁰ And when the priests came out of the holy place, a cloud filled the house of the LORD, ¹¹ so that the priests could not stand to minister because of the cloud; for the glory of the LORD filled the house of the LORD.

¹² Then Solomon said,

"The LORD has said that he would dwell in
    thick darkness.
¹³ I have built you an exalted house,
    a place for you to dwell in forever."

¹⁴ Then the king turned around and blessed all the assembly of Israel, while all the assembly of Israel stood. ¹⁵ He said, "Blessed be the LORD, the God of Israel, who with his hand has fulfilled what he promised with his mouth to my father David, saying, ¹⁶ 'Since the day that I brought my people Israel out of Egypt, I have not chosen a city from any of the tribes of Israel in which to build a house, that my name might be there; but I chose David to be over my people Israel.' ¹⁷ My father David had it in mind to build a house for the name of the LORD, the God of Israel. ¹⁸ But the LORD said to my father David, 'You did well to consider building a house for my name; ¹⁹ nevertheless you shall not build the house, but your son who shall be born to you shall build the house for my name.' ²⁰ Now the LORD has upheld the promise that he made; for I have risen in the place of my father David; I sit on the throne of Israel, as the LORD promised, and have built the house for the name of the LORD, the God of Israel. ²¹ There I have provided a place for the ark, in which is the covenant of the LORD that he made with our ancestors when he brought them out of the land of Egypt."

²² Then Solomon stood before the altar of the LORD in the presence of all the assembly of Israel, and spread out his hands to heaven. ²³ He said, "O LORD, God of Israel, there is no God like you in heaven above or on earth beneath, keeping covenant and steadfast love for your servants who walk before you with all their heart, ²⁴ the covenant that you kept for your servant my father David as you declared to him; you promised with your mouth and have this day fulfilled with your hand. ²⁵ Therefore, O LORD, God of Israel, keep for your servant my father David that which you promised him, saying, 'There shall never fail you a successor before me to sit on the throne of Israel, if only your children look to their way, to walk before me as you have walked before me.' ²⁶ Therefore, O God of Israel, let your word be confirmed, which you promised to your servant my father David.

²⁷ "But will God indeed dwell on the earth? Even heaven and the highest heaven cannot contain you, much less this house that I have built! ²⁸ Regard your servant's prayer and his plea, O Lord my God, heeding the cry and the prayer that your servant prays to you today; ²⁹ that your eyes may be open night and day toward this house, the place of which you said, 'My name shall be there,' that you may heed the prayer that your servant prays toward this place. ³⁰ Hear the plea of your servant and of your people Israel when they pray toward this place; O hear in heaven your dwelling place; heed and forgive."

⁵⁴ Now when Solomon finished offering all this prayer and this plea to the LORD, he arose from facing the altar of the LORD, where he had knelt with hands outstretched toward heaven; ⁵⁵ he stood and blessed all the assembly of Israel with a loud voice:

⁵⁶ "Blessed be the LORD, who has given rest to his people Israel according to all that he promised; not one word has failed of all his good promise, which he spoke through his servant Moses. ⁵⁷ The LORD our God be with us, as he was with our ancestors; may he not leave us or abandon us, ⁵⁸ but incline our hearts to him, to walk in all his ways, and to keep his commandments, his statutes, and his ordinances, which he commanded our ancestors. ⁵⁹ Let these words of mine, with which I pleaded before the LORD, be near to the LORD our God day and night, and may he maintain the cause of his servant and the cause of his people Israel, as each day requires; ⁶⁰ so that all the peoples of the earth may know that the LORD is God; there is no other. ⁶¹ Therefore devote yourselves completely to the LORD our God, walking in his statutes and keeping his commandments, as at this day."

⁶² Then the king, and all Israel with him, offered sacrifice before the LORD. ⁶³ Solomon offered as sacrifices of well-being to the LORD twenty-two thousand oxen and one hundred twenty thousand sheep. So the king and all the people of Israel dedicated the house of the LORD. ⁶⁴ The same day the king consecrated the middle of the court that was in front of the house of the LORD; for there he offered the burnt offerings and the grain offerings and the fat pieces of the sacrifices of well-being, because the bronze altar that was before the LORD was too small to receive the burnt offerings and the grain offerings and the fat pieces of the sacrifices of well-being.

⁶⁵ So Solomon held the festival at that time, and all Israel with him—a great assembly, people from Lebo-hamath to the Wadi of Egypt—before the LORD our God, seven days. ⁶⁶ On the eighth day he sent the people away; and they blessed the king, and went to their tents, joyful and in good spirits because of all the goodness that the LORD had shown to his servant David and to his people Israel.

DISCUSSION QUESTIONS

1. What does 1 Kings 8 suggest about the relationship between the king and the temple?

2. Why do you think it is important for the Deuteronomist to emphasize that the temple is a house for God's *name*?

3. How does the first prayer (verses 14-21) attempt to legitimate Solomon's claim to the kingship?

4. How does Solomon's understanding of God's promise to David (verse 23-26) differ from what is found in 2 Samuel 7?

The End of the United Monarchy: 1 Kings 11:1-13, 26-43

CLOSE READING TIPS

▶ In verse 2, the commandment prohibiting intermarriage is from Deuotronomy 7:3-4.

▶ Note that in a polygamous society, a concubine is a woman who lives with a man but has lower status than a wife.

▶ God first appeared to Solomon in a dream at Gibeon (1 Kgs. 3:5). The second appearance is immediately following the inauguration of the temple (1 Kgs. 9:1-9).

▶ Note that the reference to "one tribe" in verse 13 (see also verse 36) likely presupposes that Benjamin had already been absorbed into Judah.

▶ Solomon's son referenced in verse 13 is Rehoboam.

▶ Note that Jeroboam, the future first king of the Northern Kingdom, was originally an overseer of the corvée of Rehoboam.

▶ Ahijah's encounter with Jeroboam has many parallels with Samuel's rejection of Saul in 1 Samuel 15:27-28.

▶ Note that Jeroboam, like David, is promised an "enduring house" (verse 38).

▶ Pharaoh Shishak is mentioned again in 1 Kings 14, when he attacks Jerusalem and takes away treasures from the temple and the palace.

[1] King Solomon loved many foreign women along with the daughter of Pharaoh: Moabite, Ammonite, Edomite, Sidonian, and Hittite women, [2] from the nations concerning which the Lord had said to the Israelites, "You shall not enter into marriage with them, neither shall they with you; for they will surely incline your heart to follow their gods"; Solomon clung to these in love. [3] Among his wives were seven hundred princesses and three hundred concubines; and his wives turned away his heart. [4] For when Solomon was old, his wives turned away his heart after other gods; and his heart was not true to the LORD his God, as was the heart of his father David. [5] For Solomon followed Astarte the goddess of the Sidonians, and Milcom the abomination of the Ammonites. [6] So Solomon did what was evil in the sight of the LORD, and did not completely follow the LORD, as his father David had done. [7] Then

Solomon built a high place for Chemosh the abomination of Moab, and for Molech the abomination of the Ammonites, on the mountain east of Jerusalem. [8] He did the same for all his foreign wives, who offered incense and sacrificed to their gods.

[9] Then the LORD was angry with Solomon, because his heart had turned away from the LORD, the God of Israel, who had appeared to him twice, [10] and had commanded him concerning this matter, that he should not follow other gods; but he did not observe what the LORD commanded. [11] Therefore the LORD said to Solomon, "Since this has been your mind and you have not kept my covenant and my statutes that I have commanded you, I will surely tear the kingdom from you and give it to your servant. [12] Yet for the sake of your father David I will not do it in your lifetime; I will tear it out of the hand of your son. [13] I will not, however, tear away the entire kingdom; I will give one tribe to your son, for the sake of my servant David and for the sake of Jerusalem, which I have chosen."

[26] Jeroboam son of Nebat, an Ephraimite of Zeredah, a servant of Solomon, whose mother's name was Zeruah, a widow, rebelled against the king. [27] The following was the reason he rebelled against the king. Solomon built the Millo, and closed up the gap in the wall of the city of his father David. [28] The man Jeroboam was very able, and when Solomon saw that the young man was industrious he gave him charge over all the forced labor of the house of Joseph. [29] About that time, when Jeroboam was leaving Jerusalem, the prophet Ahijah the Shilonite found him on the road. Ahijah had clothed himself with a new garment. The two of them were alone in the open country [30] when Ahijah laid hold of the new garment he was wearing and tore it into twelve pieces. [31] He then said to Jeroboam: Take for yourself ten pieces; for thus says the LORD, the God of Israel,

"See, I am about to tear the kingdom from the hand of Solomon, and will give you ten tribes. [32] One tribe will remain his, for the sake of my servant David and for the sake of Jerusalem, the city that I have chosen out of all the tribes of Israel. [33] This is because he has forsaken me, worshiped Astarte the goddess of the Sidonians, Chemosh the god of Moab, and Milcom the god of the Ammonites, and has not walked in my ways, doing what is right in my sight and keeping my statutes and my ordinances, as his father David did. [34] Nevertheless I will not take the whole kingdom away from him but will make him ruler all the days of his life, for the sake of my servant David whom I chose and who did keep my commandments and my statutes; [35] but I will take the kingdom away from his son and give it to you—that is, the ten tribes. [36] Yet to his son I will give one tribe, so that my servant David may always have a lamp before me in Jerusalem, the city where I have chosen to put my name. [37] I will take you, and you shall reign over all that your soul desires; you shall be king over Israel. [38] If you will listen to all that I command you, walk in my ways, and do what is right in my sight by keeping my statutes and my commandments, as David my servant did, I will be with you, and will build you an enduring house, as I built for David, and I will give Israel to you. [39] For this reason I will punish the descendants of David, but not forever." [40] Solomon sought therefore to kill Jeroboam; but Jeroboam promptly fled to Egypt, to King Shishak of Egypt, and remained in Egypt until the death of Solomon.

[41] Now the rest of the acts of Solomon, all that he did as well as his wisdom, are they not written in the Book of the Acts of Solomon? [42] The time that Solomon reigned in Jerusalem over all Israel was forty years. [43] Solomon slept with his ancestors and was buried in the city of his father David; and his son Rehoboam succeeded him.

Discussion questions

1. While verse 4 contrasts Solomon and David, what similarities do you see between the transgressions of these two kings?

2. Why does God allow some tribes to remain under the control of Solomon's offspring?

3. Other than Solomon's apostasy, what reason is given in 1 Kings 11 for the division of the United Monarchy?

4. Why is it important to emphasize that the promise to Jeroboam is conditional? How is this consistent with the theology of the Deuteronomist?

5. What similarities do you see between the role of Ahijah and the role of Samuel in terms of their relationship with kings?

14

1 Kings 12—2 Kings 25: Tales of Prophets and the End of the Kingdoms of Israel and Judah

Key Points

The narratives in 1 Kings 12 through 2 Kings 25 bring to a close the Deuteronomistic History, and with it, the part of the Hebrew canon known as the Former Prophets. These chapters primarily contain two types of materials: 1) stories of prophets, especially Micaiah, Elijah, and Elisha (1 Kings 17—2 Kings 13); and 2) a series of annalistic reports on Judean and Israelite kings (1 Kings 12–16 and 2 Kings 10–25). Taken together, they tell the story of the divided monarchy, and with it, riveting accounts of foreign invasions, internal coups, miraculous events, and religious reforms. Second Kings ends with the destruction of Jerusalem and the deportation of part of the Judean population to Babylon.

The principal concern of these chapters is to offer a theological explanation for the tragic events surrounding the fall of Israel (722 BCE) and the fall of Judah (597/586 BCE). In reality, these events were the "collateral damage" of complex geo-political upheavals in the ancient Near Eastern world in the eighth through sixth centuries BCE. Yet the Deuteronomistic explanation is far more simplistic. While the Assyrian exile is the product of Israel following the sins of Jeroboam (2 Kgs. 17:7, 21), the Babylonian exile is brought about by the wickedness of King Manasseh of Judah (2 Kgs. 23:26; 24:3). Thus according to the Deuteronomist, idolatry and disobedience are the root causes of the end of the Northern and Southern Kingdoms.

Nevertheless, this dour portrayal of history is interspersed with glimmers of hope. Josiah (2 Kings 23–24) institutes sweeping religious reforms that reflect or reinforce the centralization of worship in Jerusalem and the emergence of more exclusive forms of monotheism. In addition, the release of Jehoiachin from prison in the final verses of 2 Kings hints at a possible renewal of the Davidic dynasty. Hope for the restoration of the land and the temple will come into fuller bloom in the writings of the Latter Prophets.

The material in 1 Kings 12 through 2 Kings 25 is also important because it provides us with our first sustained encounter with biblical prophets. During the period of the divided monarchy, most prophets were not independent agents but rather were members of a guild and worked in service of the king. However, prophets like Micaiah and Elijah are portrayed as political dissidents, challenging kings on the basis of idolatry and social injustice. These prophets claim to speak the word of the LORD and perform spectacular miracles. Their reputation for being able to access supernatural powers seems to be recognized across ethnic and cultural boundaries. Yet at times, the actions of the prophets are somewhat mysterious, if not morally ambiguous. The phenomenon of prophecy will be discussed in much greater detail in the following chapters.

Key Terms

The vineyard of Naboth   According to 1 Kings 21, Naboth is the victim of a plot by King Ahab's wife, Jezebel. The drama begins when Naboth refuses to sell Ahab his vineyard, which was located near the king's palace in Jezreel. Enraged at Naboth's decision, Jezebel conspires to have him stoned to death by bringing up false charges against him. Elijah condemns Ahab for this abuse of power, predicting that his house will be cut off from the kingship. However, Ahab repents and the punishment is delayed until the next generation.

Elijah's return   Drawing on the story that Elijah was taken up bodily into heaven (2 Kings 2), some interpreters have come to believe that the prophet will one day return to earth. This tradition is first attested in the late-sixth century BCE with the book of Malachi (Mal. 4:5). Later, belief in the return of Elijah gains increasing prominence within Jewish literature of the Hellenistic period. In the New Testament, the return of Elijah is to precede the coming of the Messiah (Mark 9:11; Matt. 17:10).

Jehu's coup   Jehu is an Israelite king who comes to power by overthrowing the Omride dynasty (2 Kings 9–10). He was anointed by a member of Elisha's prophetic group and his actions are said to be a fulfillment of the prophecy Elijah utters against Ahab and Jezebel (2 Kgs. 10:17). While the Deuteronomist seems to look favorably on his attack on the worshipers of Baal, Jehu is nevertheless evaluated negatively for maintaining places of worship outside of Jerusalem (2 Kgs. 10:29).

The fall of Samaria   The fall of Samaria refers to the defeat of Israel's capital city in 722 BCE at the hands of the Assyrians (2 Kgs. 17:5-6, 24). This event signals the end of the Northern Kingdom. Some Israelites were deported to Assyria while others moved to Jerusalem as refugees. Numerous factors contributed to the fall of Samaria, but according to the Deuteronomist this event was the direct result of the apostasy of the Israelites (2 Kgs. 17:7).

Sennacherib's invasion   In order to suppress Hezekiah's rebellion against Assyrian rule, King Sennarcherib invades Judah and lays siege to Jerusalem around 701 BCE. Up against a far superior army, Hezekiah consults the prophet Isaiah, who assures the king that Jerusalem will be delivered. Immediately thereafter, the angle of the LORD is said to have struck down one hundred eighty-five thousand Assyrian soldiers (2 Kgs. 19:35-36). While various explanations are possible for this surprising turn of events, this story contributes to beliefs about the inviolability of Jerusalem.

Key Personalities

Elijah

A series of stories about the prophet Elijah figures prominently in 1 Kings 17–19, 21, and 2 Kings 1–2. His prophetic ministry primarily takes aim at idolatrous worship practices associated with the Northern Kingdom during the reigns of Ahab and Ahaziah. Perhaps most memorable is his confrontation with the prophets of Baal (1 Kings 18), in which he refuses to tolerate the worship of any god but YHWH. In other places, Elijah shows a concern for the unjust abuse of power, as is especially clear in the story of Naboth's vineyard. These two concerns—the exclusive worship of YHWH and a commitment to social justice—reflect the prevailing interests of the prophets in the rest of the Hebrew Bible. As a way of demonstrating that he acts by the power of YHWH, Elijah also performs various miracles, including the multiplication of oil and the raising of a dead child. The Elijah cycle ends in a spectacular fashion: after granting a double share of his spirit to his protégé Elisha, Elijah is taken up to heaven in a whirlwind. Elijah's mysterious disappearance has prompted much speculation in later Jewish and Christian traditions about the prophet one day returning to earth.

Hezekiah

Together with David and Josiah, Hezekiah is one of the most praised kings in the Hebrew Bible. He is well known for initiating religious reforms near the end of the eighth century (2 Kings 18). Doing "what was right in the eyes of the LORD," Hezekiah removed the high places, broke down the pillars, cut down the sacred pole, and broke in pieces the bronze serpent (Nehushtan), which Moses had supposedly made in the wilderness. An even more extensive account of Hezekiah's reforms is found in 2 Chronicles 29–32.

These reforms clearly reflect Deuteronomistic interests, yet they also were motivated by increased need for centralized control in the wake of the Assyrian threat. In either case, the success of Hezekiah's initiatives were short lived. Judah relapses into idolatry under the leadership of Manasseh, Hezekiah's son, and another round of reform is needed when Josiah takes the throne years later. Hezekiah's reign is also notable for his efforts to resist Assyrian control. Despite Hezekiah's praiseworthy track record, the last story about the him ends in controversy. After recovering from a life-threatening illness, Hezekiah entertains a gift-bearing envoy from Babylon (2 Kings 20). In response, Isaiah predicts the future Babylonian exile (2 Kings 24–25).

Omri

Omri is a powerful Israelite king who established the first dynasty in the Northern Kingdom. Supported by part of the army, Omri rises to power in the midst of chaos and revolt in the early ninth century BCE. This king is known for having purchased and fortified the hill of Samaria (1 Kgs. 16:24). This city served as the capital of the Northern Kingdom until it fell to the Assyrians in 722. While Omri is said to have done more evil in the sight of the LORD than all those who preceded him, his son Ahab is even more infamous. Along with his wife Jezebel, Ahab introduces the worship of Baal into the Northern Kingdom. The Omride dynasty remains in place for over thirty years. Omri is the first Israelite king mentioned in extrabiblical sources. His name appears in the inscription of King Mesha of Moab and Assyrian sources refer to Israel as "the land of the house of Omri."

Questions for Study and Discussion

1. The story of Micaiah ben Imlah underscores a number of problems posed by any attempt to authenticate prophecy, or any other form of divination or revelation for that matter. What are those problems and how does the story purport to solve them?

2. In modern American culture, "Jezebel" is often understood to be a power-hungry and manipulative seductress. But is this an accurate picture of the Jezebel of the Hebrew Bible?

3. Jehu's violence against the house of Ahab is couched in religious terms: He wipes out the house of Ahab because Ahab—and especially his wife Jezebel—worship the wrong God. Given that both Christianity and Judaism claim these books as sacred Scripture, does that make them violent religions? How, in your view, should Judaism and Christianity react to such texts?

4. In the book of Kings, two national disasters are attributed to divine judgment: the fall of the Northern Kingdom to Assyrian and the fall of the Southern Kingdom to the Babylonians. In both cases, improper worship provides the fundamental reason behind God's actions. Deeds lead to consequences, which are divinely mediated. How would you respond to a person who utilized a similar "logic" to modern day events—interpreting disasters in light of divine judgment?

Primary Text

Elijah and the Prophets of Baal: 1 Kings 18:1-2, 17-46

CLOSE READING TIPS

- ▸ This narrative is the first sustained discussion of prophecy in the Hebrew Bible.
- ▸ YHWH has brought a drought upon the land (see 1 Kings 18:1) in order to show that he, not Baal, is the true "storm God."
- ▸ The prophets of Asherah (verse 19) play no role in the rest of this story. Their presence here may suggest that Ahab and Jezebel were not just worshipers of Baal but were followers of a broader Canaanite religious system.
- ▸ Mount Carmel is on the northwestern coast of Israel, near modern day Haifa.
- ▸ Note that Elijah claims to be the only remaining prophet of the LORD (verse 24) after Jezebel's killing spree (verses 4, 13). However, these verses suggest that other prophets survived as well.
- ▸ The phrase "he has wandered away" in verse 27 is a euphemism intended to suggest that Baal had gone to the bathroom!
- ▸ The people's exclamation "The LORD indeed is God" (verse 39) closely echoes the meaning of Elijah's name, which is "My God is the LORD."
- ▸ Note that the LORD commands Elijah to follow Ahab to Jezreel for the next confrontation, which occurs in 1 Kings 19:1-18.

[1] After many days the word of the LORD came to Elijah, in the third year of the drought, saying, "Go, present yourself to Ahab; I will send rain on the earth." [2] So Elijah went to present himself to Ahab. The famine was severe in Samaria.

[17] When Ahab saw Elijah, Ahab said to him, "Is it you, you troubler of Israel?" [18] He answered, "I have not troubled Israel; but you have, and your father's house, because you have forsaken the commandments of the LORD and followed the Baals. [19] Now therefore have all Israel assemble for me at Mount Carmel, with the four hundred fifty prophets of Baal and the four hundred prophets of Asherah, who eat at Jezebel's table."

[20] So Ahab sent to all the Israelites, and assembled the prophets at Mount Carmel. [21] Elijah then came near to all the people, and said, "How long will you go limping with two different opinions? If the LORD is God, follow him; but if Baal, then follow him." The people did not answer him a word. [22] Then Elijah said to the people, "I, even I only, am left a prophet of the LORD; but Baal's prophets number four hundred fifty. [23] Let two bulls be given to us; let them choose one bull for themselves, cut it in pieces, and lay it on the wood, but put no fire to it; I will prepare the other bull and lay it on the wood, but put no fire to it. [24] Then you call on the name of your god and I will call on the name of the LORD; the god who answers by fire is indeed God." All the people answered, "Well spoken!" [25] Then Elijah said to the prophets of Baal, "Choose for yourselves one bull and prepare it first, for you are many; then call on the name of your god, but put no fire to it." [26] So they took the bull that was given them, prepared it, and called on the name of Baal from morning until noon, crying, "O Baal, answer us!" But there was no voice, and no answer. They limped about the altar that they had made. [27] At noon Elijah mocked them, saying, "Cry aloud! Surely he is a god; either he is meditating, or he has wandered away, or he is on a journey, or perhaps he is asleep and must be awakened." [28] Then they cried aloud and, as was their custom, they cut themselves with swords and lances until the blood gushed out over them. [29] As midday passed, they raved on until the time of the offering of the oblation, but there was no voice, no answer, and no response.

[30] Then Elijah said to all the people, "Come closer to me"; and all the people came closer to him. First he repaired the altar of the LORD that had been thrown down; [31] Elijah took twelve stones, according to the number of the tribes of the sons of Jacob, to whom the word of the LORD came, saying, "Israel shall be your name"; [32] with the stones he built an altar in the name of the LORD. Then he made a trench around the altar, large enough to contain two measures of seed. [33] Next he put the wood in order, cut the bull in pieces, and laid it on the wood. He said, "Fill four jars with water and pour it on the burnt offering and on the wood." [34] Then he said, "Do it a second time"; and they did it a second time. Again he said, "Do it a third time"; and they did it a third time, [35] so that the water ran all around the altar, and filled the trench also with water.

[36] At the time of the offering of the oblation, the prophet Elijah came near and said, "O LORD, God of Abraham, Isaac, and Israel, let it be known this day that you are God in Israel, that I am your servant, and that I have done all these things at your bidding. [37] Answer me, O LORD, answer me, so that this people may know that you, O LORD, are God, and that you have turned their hearts back." [38] Then the fire of the LORD fell and consumed the burnt offering, the wood, the stones, and the dust, and even licked up the water that was in the trench. [39] When all the people saw it, they fell on their faces and said, "The LORD indeed is God; the LORD indeed is God." [40]

Elijah said to them, "Seize the prophets of Baal; do not let one of them escape." Then they seized them; and Elijah brought them down to the Wadi Kishon, and killed them there.

[41] Elijah said to Ahab, "Go up, eat and drink; for there is a sound of rushing rain." [42] So Ahab went up to eat and to drink. Elijah went up to the top of Carmel; there he bowed himself down upon the earth and put his face between his knees. [43] He said to his servant, "Go up now, look toward the sea." He went up and looked, and said, "There is nothing." Then he said, "Go again seven times." [44] At the seventh time he said, "Look, a little cloud no bigger than a person's hand is rising out of the sea." Then he said, "Go say to Ahab, 'Harness your chariot and go down before the rain stops you.'" [45] In a little while the heavens grew black with clouds and wind; there was a heavy rain. Ahab rode off and went to Jezreel. [46] But the hand of the LORD was on Elijah; he girded up his loins and ran in front of Ahab to the entrance of Jezreel.

DISCUSSION QUESTIONS

1. In what ways does Elijah mock the prophets of Baal?
2. Why does Elijah pour water on the burnt offering and on the wood (verses 33-35)?
3. How does Elijah's prayer in verses 36-37 contrast with the behavior of the prophets of Baal?
4. What do you make of Elijah's massacre of the prophets of Baal in verse 40? Where else do we see this sort of religiously-motivated violence in the Deuteronomistic History?
5. Is the contest set up in this story an adequate way of identifying God? Why or why not?

The End of Judah: 2 Kings 24:1-20; 25:1-21, 27-30

CLOSE READING TIPS

▶ Nebuchadnezzar first came up against Jerusalem in 597 BCE, but the city is spared when Jehoiachin quickly surrenders (2 Kgs. 24:10-12); the final capture of the city occurs in 586.

▶ In ancient Near Eastern warfare, it was common to destroy and or steal objects from the temple and the palace (2 Kgs. 24:13; see also 2 Kgs. 24:13-17).

▶ Note that the last four kings of Judah—Jehoahaz, Jehoiakim, Jehoichin, and Zedekiah—are all said to do what is evil in the sight of the LORD.

▶ It is ironic that the city of Jericho, the place of Israel's first victory in Canaan (Joshua 6), is the site of their final defeat in 2 Kings 25:4-7.

▶ While the ark of God is not mentioned in 2 Kings 25:13-17, some scholars speculate that it was among the treasures taken from the temple.

▶ Note that not all Judeans were exiled from the land. During the postexilic period, tensions would arise between the people who remained in the land and those who returned after the exile was over (538 BCE).

▶ 2 Kings 25:21 was likely the original conclusion to the book of Kings. Verses 27-30 are likely a later addition.

[1] In his days King Nebuchadnezzar of Babylon came up; Jehoiakim became his servant for three years; then he turned and rebelled against him. [2] The LORD sent against him bands of the Chaldeans, bands of the Arameans, bands of the Moabites, and bands of the Ammonites; he sent them against Judah to destroy it, according to the word of the LORD that he spoke by his servants the prophets. [3] Surely this came upon Judah at the command of the LORD, to remove them out of his sight, for the sins of Manasseh, for all that he had committed, [4] and also for the innocent blood that he had shed; for he filled Jerusalem with innocent blood, and the LORD was not willing to pardon. [5] Now the rest of the deeds of Jehoiakim, and all that he did, are they not written in the Book of the Annals of the Kings of Judah? [6] So Jehoiakim slept with his ancestors; then his son Jehoiachin succeeded him. [7] The king of Egypt did not come again out of his land, for the king of Babylon had taken over all that belonged to the king of Egypt from the Wadi of Egypt to the River Euphrates.

[8] Jehoiachin was eighteen years old when he began to reign; he reigned three months in Jerusalem. His mother's name was Nehushta daughter of Elnathan of Jerusalem. [9] He did what was evil in the sight of the LORD, just as his father had done.

[10] At that time the servants of King Nebuchadnezzar of Babylon came up to Jerusalem, and the city was besieged. [11] King Nebuchadnezzar of Babylon came to the city, while his servants were besieging it; [12] King Jehoiachin of Judah gave himself up to the king of Babylon, himself, his mother, his servants, his officers, and his palace officials. The king of Babylon took him prisoner in the eighth year of his reign.

[13] He carried off all the treasures of the house of the LORD, and the treasures of the king's house; he cut in pieces all the vessels of gold in the temple of the LORD, which King Solomon of Israel had made, all this as the LORD had foretold. [14] He carried away all Jerusalem, all the officials, all the warriors, ten thousand captives, all the artisans and the smiths; no one remained, except the poorest people of the land. [15] He carried away Jehoiachin to Babylon; the king's mother, the king's wives, his officials, and the elite of the land, he took into captivity from Jerusalem to Babylon. [16] The king of Babylon brought captive to Babylon all the men of valor, seven thousand, the artisans and the smiths, one thousand, all of them strong and fit for war. [17] The king of Babylon made Mattaniah, Jehoiachin's uncle, king in his place, and changed his name to Zedekiah.

[18] Zedekiah was twenty-one years old when he began to reign; he reigned eleven years in Jerusalem. His mother's name was Hamutal daughter of Jeremiah of Libnah. [19] He did what was evil in the sight of the LORD, just as Jehoiakim had done. [20] Indeed, Jerusalem and Judah so angered the LORD that he expelled them from his presence.

Zedekiah rebelled against the king of Babylon.

25 [1] And in the ninth year of his reign, in the tenth month, on the tenth day of the month, King Nebuchadnezzar of Babylon came with all his army against Jerusalem, and laid siege to it; they built siegeworks against it all around. [2] So the city was besieged until the eleventh year of King Zedekiah. [3] On the ninth day of the fourth month the famine became so severe in the city that there was no food for the people of the land. [4] Then a breach was made in the city wall; the king with all the soldiers fled by night by the way of the gate between the two walls, by the king's garden, though the Chaldeans were all around the city. They went in the direction of the Arabah. [5] But the army of the Chaldeans pursued the king, and overtook him in the plains of Jericho; all

his army was scattered, deserting him. [6] Then they captured the king and brought him up to the king of Babylon at Riblah, who passed sentence on him. [7] They slaughtered the sons of Zedekiah before his eyes, then put out the eyes of Zedekiah; they bound him in fetters and took him to Babylon.

[8] In the fifth month, on the seventh day of the month—which was the nineteenth year of King Nebuchadnezzar, king of Babylon—Nebuzaradan, the captain of the bodyguard, a servant of the king of Babylon, came to Jerusalem. [9] He burned the house of the LORD, the king's house, and all the houses of Jerusalem; every great house he burned down. [10] All the army of the Chaldeans who were with the captain of the guard broke down the walls around Jerusalem. [11] Nebuzaradan the captain of the guard carried into exile the rest of the people who were left in the city and the deserters who had defected to the king of Babylon—all the rest of the population. [12] But the captain of the guard left some of the poorest people of the land to be vinedressers and tillers of the soil.

[13] The bronze pillars that were in the house of the LORD, as well as the stands and the bronze sea that were in the house of the LORD, the Chaldeans broke in pieces, and carried the bronze to Babylon. [14] They took away the pots, the shovels, the snuffers, the dishes for incense, and all the bronze vessels used in the temple service, [15] as well as the firepans and the basins. What was made of gold the captain of the guard took away for the gold, and what was made of silver, for the silver. [16] As for the two pillars, the one sea, and the stands, which Solomon had made for the house of the LORD, the bronze of all these vessels was beyond weighing. [17] The height of the one pillar was eighteen cubits, and on it was a bronze capital; the height of the capital was three cubits; latticework and pomegranates, all of bronze, were on the capital all around. The second pillar had the same, with the latticework.

[18] The captain of the guard took the chief priest Seraiah, the second priest Zephaniah, and the three guardians of the threshold; [19] from the city he took an officer who had been in command of the soldiers, and five men of the king's council who were found in the city; the secretary who was the commander of the army who mustered the people of the land; and sixty men of the people of the land who were found in the city. [20] Nebuzaradan the captain of the guard took them, and brought them to the king of Babylon at Riblah. [21] The king of Babylon struck them down and put them to death at Riblah in the land of Hamath. So Judah went into exile out of its land.

[27] In the thirty-seventh year of the exile of King Jehoiachin of Judah, in the twelfth month, on the twenty-seventh day of the month, King Evil-merodach of Babylon, in the year that he began to reign, released King Jehoiachin of Judah from prison; [28] he spoke kindly to him, and gave him a seat above the other seats of the kings who were with him in Babylon. [29] So Jehoiachin put aside his prison clothes. Every day of his life he dined regularly in the king's presence. [30] For his allowance, a regular allowance was given him by the king, a portion every day, as long as he lived.

DISCUSSION QUESTIONS

1. According to the Deuteronomist, why did Judah go into exile despite the religious reforms of the faithful king, Josiah?
2. What purpose does deportation or exile serve as a military strategy?
3. Why do you think this text gives so much attention to the deportation of the temple furnishings?
4. In what ways does 2 Kings end on a glimmer of hope?

Sennacherib's invasion

Source: Lines 22–34 from the Third Year of the Reign of Sennacherib. In Victor H. Matthews and Don C. Benjamin, *Old Testament Parallels: Laws and Stories from the Ancient Near East*, fully revised and expanded 3d. ed. (New York: Paulist, 2006), 191–92.

CLOSE READING TIPS

▸ This is one of eight accounts of military campaigns that King Sennacherib of Assyria (704–681 BCE) had inscribed on a clay prism.

▸ Less powerful city-states or nations often established alliances with Egypt in order to resist Assyria, and later, Babylonia.

▸ Ashur was the principal Assyrian deity. Assyrian kings often attributed victories to Ashur's divine aid.

▸ Sennacherib's claim that he "personally captured" the enemy forces is likely a form of royal propaganda rather than a straightforward reportage of the facts.

▸ One of the cities in the vicinity of Jerusalem that Sennacherib seized is Lachish. This battle is depicted on a series of massive wall reliefs in the king's royal palace at Nineveh.

The official and ranking citizens of Ekron deposed Padi, their king, and put this loyal covenant partner of Assyria in chains. They placed him in the custody of Hezekiah, the king of Judah. Once they realized what they had done, they called on the pharaohs of Egypt for assistance.

Although the Egyptians marshaled a large army against me, I inflicted a great defeat upon them in the Plains of Eltekeh with the help of Ashur, my divine patron (2 Kgs. 19:9). I personally captured the Egyptian and Ethiopian chariots and their commanders, and then laid siege, conquered, and looted the cities of Eltekeh and Timnah.

Advancing to Ekron, I slew its rebellious officials and ranking citizens and impaled their bodies on the towers of the city (1 Sam. 31:10). All the rest of the people who had raised a hand against me were taken captive. The innocent were spared. King Padi was released from prison in Jerusalem and once again placed on his throne and his tribute payments were reinstated.

Because Hezekiah of Judah did not submit to my yoke, I laid siege to forty-six of his fortified cities and walled forts and to the countless villages in their vicinity. I conquered them using earthen ramps and battering rams. These siege engines were supported by infantry who tunneled under the walls. I took 200,150 prisoners of war, young and old, male and female, from these places. I also plundered more horses, mules, donkeys, camels, large and small cattle than we could count. I imprisoned Hezekiah in Jerusalem like a bird in a cage. I erected siege works to prevent anyone escaping through the city gates. The cities in Judah which I captured I gave to Mitinti, king of Ashdod, and to Padi, king of Ekron, and to Sillibel, king of Gaza. Thus I reduced the land of Hezekiah in this campaign, and I also increased Hezekiah's annual tribute payments.

Hezekiah, who was overwhelmed by my terror-inspiring splendor, was deserted by his elite troops, which he had brought into Jerusalem. He was forced to send me 420 pounds [Akkadian: "thirty talents"] of gold, 11,200 pounds [Akkadian: "eight hundred talents"] of silver, precious stones, couches and chairs inlaid with ivory, elephant hides, ebony wood, boxwood, and all kinds of valuable treasures, his daughters, wives, and males and female musicians. He sent his personal messenger to deliver this tribute and bown down to me (2 Kgs. 18:14-16).

DISCUSSION QUESTIONS

1. Why do you think Sennacherib emphasizes the fact that he spared the innocent in Ekron?
2. How is Hezekiah portrayed in this inscription?
3. What major differences do you see between Sennacherib's account of his invasion of Jerusalem and that which is found in 2 Kings 18:13—19:37?

15

Amos and Hosea

Key Points

The books of Amos and Hosea are centered around prominent eighth century BCE prophets of the Northern Kingdom. Amos and Hosea were not associated with prophetic guilds, and often challenged the religious and political establishment of their time. While they addressed concrete historical situations of their own time, the oracles of these prophets were eventually collected and preserved for future generations by later editors. As a result, it is important to keep in mind the tension between the original contexts of Amos and Hosea and the context of later editors who gave these books their final canonical form. Both of these books were edited in Judah after 722 BCE, and thus include distinctive Judean perspectives and references to later historical developments.

The book of Amos can be divided into three parts. The first two chapters consist of oracles of judgment against the nations Judah and Israel. While these oracles might harken back to a covenant tradition that predates the monarchic period, it is more likely that Amos's preaching helped give shape to later perspectives, especially those found in Deuteronomy. The collection of short oracles in the middle section (chapters 3–6) address topics such as election (Amos 3:2), the link between actions and their consequences (Amos 3:3-8), social injustice (Amos 4:1-3; 6:4-7), and the condemnation of the cult at Bethel (Amos 5:1-27). Five visions are reported in the final section (chapters 7–9), each of which warns of a coming judgment (for example. Amos 8:1-2). A key issue in Amos involves whether the prophet wanted to abolish or merely reform the cult. In theory, Amos does not rule out the possibility that sacrifices and offerings play a role in the worship of God. Yet, his critique of how the cult was actually being practiced is unequivocal: it was offensive to God and had to be rejected.

The book of Hosea is perhaps best known for its first three chapters. Here, marriage is used as a guiding metaphor to talk about the unfaithfulness of Israel in its covenantal relationship with YHWH.

As a form of symbolic action, Hosea's marriage and re-marriage to Gomer points toward God's judgment against idolatry, but also the possibility of restoration. From an ethical perspective, the content of these chapters is arresting. It must be kept in mind that the perspectives it offers on husbands and wives are rooted in cultural norms that are quite foreign to our own.

The remaining material in Hosea (chapters 4–14) focuses on the issue of covenant faithfulness, a theme which is also central to the book of Deuteronomy. Like Amos, Hosea is critical of the cult (chapter 6) and priesthood (chapter 4). He also rails against the political scheming that dominated the Northern Kingdom in its final decades. The fundamental problem was that these kings were looking to political coalitions, not steadfast devotion to God, in order to stave off the ominous Assyrian threat.

Key Terms

The Day of the LORD   This expression typically refers to one of two things: a day of judgment, in which God vindicates Israel by defeating its adversaries in battle; or a cultic celebration, perhaps the Festival of Tabernacles (Sukkoth). Both references were thought to be joyful occasions for Israel. However, Amos 5:18-27 reinterprets this concept, warning that the Day of the LORD will be marked by darkness and gloom because God will judge Israel for its injustice.

Covenant lawsuit   A covenant lawsuit (Heb.: *ribh*) is a legal disputation in which God brings charges against Israel for violating the covenant. Examples can be found in the oracles against Judah and Israel in Amos 2:4-8 or the accusations concerning swearing, lying, murder, stealing, and adultery in Hosea 4:2. The oracle in Hosea 2 is also a covenant lawsuit, though it calls to mind a divorce proceeding rather than a treaty violation.

Marriage metaphor   The first three chapters of Hosea are framed by God's commands to the prophet to marry a promiscuous woman (Gomer) as a metaphor for Israel's unfaithfulness in its relationship with Yahweh. It underscores the conditional nature of the covenant. The marriage metaphor in Hosea reflects common cultural assumptions about the roles of husband and wife. This literary imagery calls for careful interpretation and should not be used to justify violence toward women.

Oracle   An oracle is a general term for prophetic communication. It can also be understood as a specific type of prophetic genre in which a message is delivered to some person, group, situation, or event that is based on God's revelation concerning the realm of human affairs. While some oracles of salvation exist, they often have negative connotations. Oracles of judgment against the nations and against Israel or Judah are both evident in the book of Amos.

Nabi'   *Nabi'* is the most frequent term used for prophets in the Hebrew Bible. Though its etymology is uncertain, it likely refers to an intermediary who is called or authorized to speak on behalf of God. A similar term is found in extrabiblical sources in reference to prophetic figures. The plural of this term, *nabi'im*, is used to indicate the second of three divisions of the Hebrew Bible, consisting of the Former Prophets and the Latter Prophets.

Key Personalities

Amaziah

Amaziah was the priest at the northern sanctuary of Bethel during the reign of Jeroboam II (786–746 BCE). This priest features prominently in the book of Amos, where he openly opposes the prophet's prediction of divine judgment against Israel. Eager to prove his loyalty to the throne, Amaziah warns Jeroboam II that Amos had been prophesying that the king would die by the sword and that Israel would go into exile (Amos 7:11). Amaziah accuses Amos of sedition, telling the "seer" to flee to the land of Judah and to never again prophesy against the king's sanctuary. Amos's response is one of the most well-known passages in the book (Amos 7:14-17). Amos emphasizes that, as a spokesman for YHWH, he is not beholden to the king or priest and is free to openly confront the injustices of Israel. Amos's message is abrasive. Among other things, the prophet claims that Amaziah's wife will become a prostitute and that the priest would die in an unclean land. This prophecy likely functioned as a curse intended to bring about what was predicted. While the text does not reveal what happened to Amaziah or his family, it is unlikely that this prophecy was fulfilled in Amaziah's lifetime. However, the final editors of the book of Amos probably saw the Assyrian exile as the eventual fulfillment of Amos's preaching.

Amos

The prophet Amos hailed from Tekoa, a small village just south of Jerusalem. However, he primarily prophesied in the vicinity of the royal sanctuary of Bethel, which is located near the southern edge of the Northern Kingdom. This geographical setting may suggest that Amos had little regard for the boundary between Israel and Judah or that he was a Davidic loyalist particularly troubled by Jeroboam's rival sanctuaries. The book of Amos emphasizes that he was neither a professional prophet nor a member of a prophetic guild. Since Amos criticized social injustice including the mistreatment of the poor, it has been suggested that the prophet had a very modest background. Indeed, Amos is variously described as a "shepherd" (Amos 1:1), a "herdsman" (Amos 7:14), and "a dresser of sycamore trees" (Amos 7:14). Yet, these terms more likely denote an owner of a large flock or orchard, not a hired worker. In either case, Amos is called by YHWH away from his agricultural profession to prophesy against the people of Israel. His confrontational manner is not designed to gently win over those he condemns. In this sense, Amos's prophetic style is more in the model of Elijah than Nathan. The superscription to the book of Amos places his ministry during the reigns of Jeroboam II of Israel and Uzziah of Judah, "two years before the earthquake." This latter event cannot be precisely dated, though the specificity of this timing may suggest that Amos's prophetic career was quite short.

Hosea

A near contemporary of Amos, Hosea was one of the major eighth century BCE prophets in the Hebrew Bible. He is said to have prophesied during the reigns of Jeroboam II in Israel and Uzziah, Jothan, Ahaz, and Hezekiah in Judah. Since the prophet does not directly reference the fall of Samaria, it is likely that Hosea died sometime before 722 BCE. Like Amos, Hosea's prophetic ministry is situated in the Northern Kingdom. The name Hosea, which was a fairly common in the eighth and seventh centuries and is attested on numerous Israelite seals, is probably a shortened form of a word meaning "YHWH has delivered." Little is know about the prophet's life outside of the introduction to the book of Hosea. In those chapters, it is reported that Hosea, the son of Beeri (Hosea 1:1), is called by God to marry a promiscuous woman named Gomer. Their three children—Jezreel ("God will sow"), Lo-ruhamah ("not pitied"), and Lo-ammi ("not my people")—bear symbolic names that reflect God's judgment on

Israel. At the beginning of chapter three, Hosea is called once again to marry an adulterous woman. This may refer to a second marriage or, more likely, to Hosea's remarriage to Gomer. In either case, it is uncertain whether actual biographical data about the prophet can be gleaned from the extended metaphor in Hosea 1–3. On the whole, Hosea seems to be well-versed in wisdom and covenant traditions as is especially evident in his concern for Israel's lack of knowledge and foolish choices. His critics characterize him as a "fool" and a "mad" person (Hosea 9:7).

Questions for Study and Discussion

1. The oracles against the nations in Amos are often said to reflect a universal view of human "rights." When you consider contemporary views on human rights, do you see points of connection with the book of Amos? Where do modern views on human rights part ways with Amos? Where do they continue on in the tradition of Amos? Do they share common assumptions?
2. Amos clearly has harsh words for the wealthy in Israel. Do his criticisms continue to ring true today? If one were to take up Amos's critique in the modern day, what qualifications would one need to make?
3. The marriage metaphor in Hosea is one of the book's most distinctive features. And yet, for contemporary audiences, it poses a number of problems, not the least of which is the patriarchal (male-dominated) context of the book. In your view, is the "husband" in the metaphor abusive, at least by today's standards? If so, what are the implications for how one thinks about the God of Hosea?

Primary Text

Amos 5:1-27

CLOSE READING TIPS

▶ Verses 1-3 are framed as a lament or funeral speech for Israel, intended to express impending judgment.
▶ The "house of Joseph" in verse 6 refers to the Northern Kingdom.
▶ In verse 7, injustice is compared to wormwood, whose dried leaves are known to be bitter.
▶ In verse 8, the astral bodies attest to God's power; a similar theme is found in Psalm 8:3.

▶ Note that the city gate is the traditional site of legal proceedings, thus it is especially egregious that this is the very place where truth is abhorred, the poor are pushed aside, and bribes are taken (verses 10-11).

▶ The plea for repentance in verses 14-15 echoes that which is found in verses 4-7.

▶ The festivals in verse 21 likely are three pilgrimage feasts (see Exod. 23:14-18; 34:18, 22-23; Deut. 16:16).

▶ The "ever-flowing stream" in verse 24 refers to a riverbed with an abundant water source, in contrast to a wadi which is only occasionally filled with run-off water in the rainy season.

▶ Amos 5:25 was either written before or does not seem to be familiar with the priestly laws of Leviticus, which envision an established sacrificial system in the wilderness.

¹ Hear this word that I take up over you in lamentation, O house of Israel:

² Fallen, no more to rise,
  is maiden Israel;
forsaken on her land,
  with no one to raise her up.

³ For thus says the Lord GOD:
The city that marched out a thousand
  shall have a hundred left,
and that which marched out a hundred
  shall have ten left.

⁴ For thus says the LORD to the house of Israel:
Seek me and live;
  ⁵ but do not seek Bethel,
and do not enter into Gilgal
  or cross over to Beer-sheba;
for Gilgal shall surely go into exile,
  and Bethel shall come to nothing.

⁶ Seek the LORD and live,
  or he will break out against the house of
    Joseph like fire,
  and it will devour Bethel, with no one to
    quench it.
⁷ Ah, you that turn justice to wormwood,

and bring righteousness to the ground!

⁸ The one who made the Pleiades and Orion,
  and turns deep darkness into the morning,
  and darkens the day into night,
who calls for the waters of the sea,
  and pours them out on the surface of the
    earth,
the LORD is his name,
⁹ who makes destruction flash out against the
    strong,
  so that destruction comes upon the
    fortress.

¹⁰ They hate the one who reproves in the gate,
  and they abhor the one who speaks the
    truth.
¹¹ Therefore because you trample on the poor
  and take from them levies of grain,
you have built houses of hewn stone,
  but you shall not live in them;
you have planted pleasant vineyards,
  but you shall not drink their wine.
¹² For I know how many are your
    transgressions,
  and how great are your sins—
you who afflict the righteous, who take a bribe,

and push aside the needy in the gate.
[13] Therefore the prudent will keep silent in such
    a time;
    for it is an evil time.

[14] Seek good and not evil,
    that you may live;
and so the LORD, the God of hosts, will be
    with you,
    just as you have said.
[15] Hate evil and love good,
    and establish justice in the gate;
it may be that the LORD, the God of hosts,
    will be gracious to the remnant of Joseph.

[16] Therefore thus says the LORD, the God of
    hosts, the Lord:
In all the squares there shall be wailing;
    and in all the streets they shall say, "Alas!
    alas!"
They shall call the farmers to mourning,
    and those skilled in lamentation, to
    wailing;
[17] in all the vineyards there shall be wailing,
    for I will pass through the midst of you,
    says the LORD.
[18] Alas for you who desire the day of the
    LORD!
    Why do you want the day of the LORD?
It is darkness, not light;
    [19] as if someone fled from a lion,

and was met by a bear;
or went into the house and rested a hand
    against the wall,
    and was bitten by a snake.
[20] Is not the day of the LORD darkness, not
    light,
    and gloom with no brightness in it?

[21] I hate, I despise your festivals,
    and I take no delight in your solemn
    assemblies.
[22] Even though you offer me your burnt offer-
    ings and grain offerings,
    I will not accept them;
and the offerings of well-being of your fatted
    animals
    I will not look upon.
[23] Take away from me the noise of your songs;
    I will not listen to the melody of your
    harps.
[24] But let justice roll down like waters,
    and righteousness like an ever-flowing
    stream.

[25] Did you bring to me sacrifices and offerings the forty years in the wilderness, O house of Israel? [26] You shall take up Sakkuth your king, and Kaiwan your star-god, your images, which you made for yourselves; [27] therefore I will take you into exile beyond Damascus, says the LORD, whose name is the God of hosts.

DISCUSSION QUESTIONS

1. According to Amos 5, what were the Israelites "seeking" instead of the LORD?

2. In what ways does the prophet seem to reinterpret traditional understandings of the expression "the Day of the LORD?" Why is it a day that the Israelites should *not* desire?

3. Where in this passage do you find language that draws on imagery from the natural world or agriculture? Why do you think this imagery is appealing to Amos?

4. Martin Luther King Jr. quoted Amos 5:24 in his famous "I have a Dream Speech." Understood in the context of Amos 5, how might this verse help inform contemporary ethical and social concerns?

The Judean Edition of Amos: Amos 9:5-6, 11-15

CLOSE READING TIPS

▶ Verses 5-6 represent the third of three short doxologies giving praise to God (see also Amos 4:13; 5:8-9).

▶ In biblical cosmology, there is a celestial barrier, or vault, separating the earth from the waters below (see Gen. 1:6-8).

▶ The phrase "that day" in verse 11 is likely an abbreviated expression that refers to "the Day of the LORD."

▶ Note that the "booth of David" refers to the Davidic dynasty. Booth might indicate a more temporary or fragile structure than a house, thus reflecting the vulnerability of David's line.

▶ Edom (verse 12), which is located in the desert region southeast of Judah, was a traditional enemy of the Southern Kingdom but not necessarily the Northern Kingdom.

⁵ The Lord, GOD of hosts,
he who touches the earth and it melts,
    and all who live in it mourn,
and all of it rises like the Nile,
    and sinks again, like the Nile of Egypt;
⁶ who builds his upper chambers in the
    heavens,
    and founds his vault upon the earth;
who calls for the waters of the sea,
    and pours them out upon the surface of
        the earth—
the LORD is his name.

¹¹ On that day I will raise up

the booth of David that is fallen,
and repair its breaches,
    and raise up its ruins,
    and rebuild it as in the days of old;
¹² in order that they may possess the remnant
    of Edom
    and all the nations who are called by my
        name,
    says the Lord who does this.

¹³ The time is surely coming, says the Lord,
    when the one who plows shall overtake the
        one who reaps,

and the treader of grapes the one who
sows the seed;
the mountains shall drip sweet wine,
and all the hills shall flow with it.
¹⁴ I will restore the fortunes of my people Israel,
and they shall rebuild the ruined cities and
inhabit them;

they shall plant vineyards and drink their wine,
and they shall make gardens and eat their
fruit.
¹⁵ I will plant them upon their land,
and they shall never again be plucked up
out of the land that I have given them,
says the Lord your God.

Discussion questions

1. What indications are there that these verses were added to the book of Amos sometime during or after the Babylonian exile?

2. How does the reference to "that day" in verse 11 contrast with the characterization of "the Day of the LORD" in Amos 5:18?

3. What sort of literary imagery does Amos 9 use to envision future restoration?

Hosea 1–3

Close reading tips

▸ The kings mentioned in Hosea 1:1 reigned mainly during the second half of the eighth century.

▸ Jezreel, meaning "God will sow" (Hosea 1:4), is the place where Jehu initiates his bloody overthrow of the Omride dynasty. King Jeroboam II, mentioned in Hosea 1:1, is the last king of the Jehu dynasty.

▸ Note the distinctly Judean perspective voiced in Hosea 1:6-7.

▸ Note that the language in Hosea 1:9 God seems to reject the covenant, in which he promises the Israelites: "I will take you as my people, and I will be your God" (Exod. 6:7; Deut. 29:13).

▸ Note that Hosea's offspring are now called "children of the living God" (Hosea 1:10) instead of "children of whoredom" (Hosea 1:2).

▸ Hosea 2:2-23 introduces a prophetic speech that indicts Israel for being the unfaithful spouse in the overarching marriage metaphor.

▸ Hosea 2:16 contains a wordplay between two Hebrew words for "husband": Israel is to call YHWH *'ish* instead of *ba'al* since the latter term is also used as the personal name of the Canaanite deity Baal.

▸ Though Gomer is not mentioned by name in chapter 3, the context seems to imply a restoration of Hosea's previous marriage.

▸ The reference to David in Hosea 3:5 likely reflects a later, Judean addition.

¹ The word of the LORD that came to Hosea son of Beeri, in the days of Kings Uzziah, Jotham, Ahaz, and Hezekiah of Judah, and in the days of King Jeroboam son of Joash of Israel.

² When the LORD first spoke through Hosea, the LORD said to Hosea, "Go, take for yourself a wife of whoredom and have children of whoredom, for the land commits great whoredom by forsaking the Lord." ³ So he went and took Gomer daughter of Diblaim, and she conceived and bore him a son.

⁴ And the LORD said to him, "Name him Jezreel; for in a little while I will punish the house of Jehu for the blood of Jezreel, and I will put an end to the kingdom of the house of Israel. ⁵ On that day I will break the bow of Israel in the valley of Jezreel."

⁶ She conceived again and bore a daughter. Then the LORD said to him, "Name her Lo-ruhamah, for I will no longer have pity on the house of Israel or forgive them. ⁷ But I will have pity on the house of Judah, and I will save them by the LORD their God; I will not save them by bow, or by sword, or by war, or by horses, or by horsemen."

⁸ When she had weaned Lo-ruhamah, she conceived and bore a son. ⁹ Then the LORD said, "Name him Lo-ammi, for you are not my people and I am not your God."

¹⁰ Yet the number of the people of Israel shall be like the sand of the sea, which can be neither measured nor numbered; and in the place where it was said to them, "You are not my people," it shall be said to them, "Children of the living God." ¹¹ The people of Judah and the people of Israel shall be gathered together, and they shall appoint for themselves one head; and they shall take possession of the land, for great shall be the day of Jezreel.

2 ¹ Say to your brother, Ammi, and to your sister, Ruhamah.

² Plead with your mother, plead—
    for she is not my wife,
    and I am not her husband—
that she put away her whoring from her face,
    and her adultery from between her breasts,
³ or I will strip her naked
    and expose her as in the day she was born,
and make her like a wilderness,
    and turn her into a parched land,
    and kill her with thirst.
⁴ Upon her children also I will have no pity,
    because they are children of whoredom.
⁵ For their mother has played the whore;
    she who conceived them has acted
      shamefully.
For she said, "I will go after my lovers;
    they give me my bread and my water,
    my wool and my flax, my oil and my
      drink."
⁶ Therefore I will hedge up her way with thorns;
    and I will build a wall against her,
    so that she cannot find her paths.
⁷ She shall pursue her lovers,
    but not overtake them;
and she shall seek them,
    but shall not find them.
Then she shall say, "I will go
    and return to my first husband,
    for it was better with me then than now."
⁸ She did not know
    that it was I who gave her
    the grain, the wine, and the oil,
and who lavished upon her silver
    and gold that they used for Baal.
⁹ Therefore I will take back
    my grain in its time,
    and my wine in its season;
and I will take away my wool and my flax,

which were to cover her nakedness.

[10] Now I will uncover her shame
  in the sight of her lovers,
    and no one shall rescue her out of my
      hand.
[11] I will put an end to all her mirth,
    her festivals, her new moons, her sabbaths,
    and all her appointed festivals.
[12] I will lay waste her vines and her fig trees,
    of which she said,
"These are my pay,
  which my lovers have given me."
I will make them a forest,
    and the wild animals shall devour them.
[13] I will punish her for the festival days of the
      Baals,
    when she offered incense to them
and decked herself with her ring and jewelry,
    and went after her lovers,
    and forgot me, says the LORD.

[14] Therefore, I will now allure her,
    and bring her into the wilderness,
    and speak tenderly to her.
[15] From there I will give her her vineyards,
    and make the Valley of Achor a door of
      hope.
There she shall respond as in the days of her
      youth,
    as at the time when she came out of the
      land of Egypt.

[16] On that day, says the LORD, you will call me, "My husband," and no longer will you call me, "My Baal." [17] For I will remove the names of the Baals from her mouth, and they shall be mentioned by name no more. [18] I will make for you a covenant on that day with the wild animals, the birds of the air, and the creeping things of the ground; and I will abolish the bow, the sword, and war from the land; and I will make you lie down in safety. [19] And I will take you for my wife forever; I will take you for my wife in righteousness and in justice, in steadfast love, and in mercy. [20] I will take you for my wife in faithfulness; and you shall know the LORD.

[21] On that day I will answer, says the LORD,
    I will answer the heavens
      and they shall answer the earth;
[22] and the earth shall answer the grain, the
      wine, and the oil,
      and they shall answer Jezreel;
[23] and I will sow him for myself in the
      land.
And I will have pity on Lo-ruhamah,
    and I will say to Lo-ammi, "You are my
      people";
    and he shall say, "You are my God."

3 [1] The LORD said to me again, "Go, love a woman who has a lover and is an adulteress, just as the LORD loves the people of Israel, though they turn to other gods and love raisin cakes." [2] So I bought her for fifteen shekels of silver and a homer of barley and a measure of wine. [3] And I said to her, "You must remain as mine for many days; you shall not play the whore, you shall not have intercourse with a man, nor I with you." [4] For the Israelites shall remain many days without king or prince, without sacrifice or pillar, without ephod or teraphim. [5] Afterward the Israelites shall return and seek the LORD their God, and David their king; they shall come in awe to the LORD and to his goodness in the latter days.

Discussion questions

1. What role does naming and re-naming play in this text?
2. In what ways is the punishment of stripping (Hosea 2:3) an apt metaphor for the Assyrian exile?
3. In what sense is the worship of Baal a form of "adultery" against YHWH?
4. Where do you see a tension between judgment and restoration in these three chapters?
5. What are some of the potential problems and advantages of using the marriage metaphor as a symbolic vehicle for divine communication?

16

Isaiah, Micah, Nahum, and Zephaniah

Key Points

Events surrounding the ominous advance and eventual demise of the Assyrian empire prompted a flurry of prophetic activity in ancient Judah. Isaiah, Micah, Nahum, and Zephaniah all reflect diverse theological perspectives on the Assyrian crisis, but they also share many common features. These books provide little biographical data about the prophets themselves and reflect—especially in the case of Isaiah—a complex history of composition. In each case, oracles originally spoken by the prophets are supplemented by editors in the exilic and postexilic periods. The reason for the arrangement of oracles in theses books is sometimes difficult to discern, though chronology and common themes can be a factor. While the focus of this chapter is primarily on the original context of these four prophets, attention should also be paid to the final shape and canonical context of these books.

The diverse oracles associated with the prophet Isaiah (chapters 1–39) represent some of the most well-known and oft-debated material in the Hebrew Bible. The prophet interprets the threat of a foreign military invasion as an instrument of divine punishment for the people's idolatry, pride, and disregard for justice. Most notably, Isaiah urges King Ahaz (Isa. 7–8) and King Hezekiah (Isa. 36–38) to trust in YHWH alone, not political alliances, for protection from Assyria. In acts of self-reliance, both rulers fail to heed Isaiah's advice. Thus, it is hardly surprising that many of Isaiah's oracles emphasize that the proud will be brought down (for example, Isa. 14:12-20) and that the "wisdom" of political intrigue will lead to futility (Isa. 29–31). Yet all is not lost. Isaiah holds out hope that God will preserve a remnant of his people and will one day restore an ideal Davidic king to the throne.

Micah, a rural prophet, is less interested than Isaiah in the fate of the Davidic dynasty or the implications of political coalitions. Rather, Micah's preaching offers a biting critique of injustice and inequality. This concern is perhaps best understood as a reaction to Hezekiah's effort to centralize power and wealth in Jerusalem near the close of the eighth century BCE. While effective at asserting Judah's independence from Assyria, Hezekiah's reforms elevated a small minority of people (the "one-percent") at the expense of peasant farmers. In this regard, Micah rarely distinguishes between the sins of Judah and Israel, preferring instead to highlight the pervasiveness of idolatry and the problems of the cult. The core of Micah's message—and perhaps the message of *all* eighth-century prophets—is succinctly expressed in Micah 6:6-8.

Preaching well after their eighth-century counterparts, Nahum and Zephaniah offer a theological response to the fall of Assyria and its capital, Nineveh. While these events were brought on by military incursions by the Babylonians and Medes, Nahum claims that it is none other than YHWH who breaks the yoke of Assyrian oppression (Hah. 1). The "good tidings" of Assyria's demise are cause for celebration, but not complacency. As Zephaniah reminds us, the Day of the LORD will still be one of judgment if the Judeans do not turn away from unbridled apostasy (Zeph. 1 and 3), most vividly embodied in the reign of King Manasseh.

Key Terms

Syro-Ephraimite war   In the mid-730s BCE, Syria (Aram) and Ephraim (Israel) attempted to pressure Judah into joining its coalition against the expanding Assyrian empire. This war forms the historical backdrop of Isaiah's prophecy to King Ahaz of Judah in Isaiah 7–8 (see also 2 Kings 15–16). The prophet lobbies the Judean king not to join this coalition, assuring him that the Syro-Ephraimite campaign would surely fail and Jerusalem would be protected. However, Ahaz does not heed Isaiah's advice and instead appeals to Assyria for help.

'Almah   This Hebrew term, which appears in Isaiah's message to King Ahaz (Isa. 7:14), refers generally to a young woman, not necessarily a virgin. However, the Greek translation of Isaiah uses the word *parthenos*, which specifically indicates a virgin. This Greek translation was used by New Testament authors and later Christian interpreters to support the virgin birth of Jesus (Matt. 1:23).

In the immediate context of Isaiah 7, the prophet was not predicting a miraculous birth in the distant future. Rather, the birth of a child in the time of crisis was supposed to be a sign of assurance to Ahaz that his dynasty would continue.

Remnant   This term generally refers to the portion of a community, typically Israel or Judah, that is left after a catastrophe. It occurs frequently in First Isaiah (fifteen times), Micah (four times), and Zephaniah (four times). It occasionally has a negative connotation, emphasizing that *only* a small remnant will be allowed to survive divine punishment (Zeph. 1:4). Yet more often, the connotation is positive: despite the catastrophe, God graciously preserves a remnant out of which a renewed community will spring (Isa. 1:25-26; 28:5-6). The remnant consists of people who are humble and faithful (for example, Zeph. 2:3; 3:12-13) and is chosen to receive future blessings (as in Mic. 4:6-7; 5:7-8).

Song of the vineyard   Modeled on a song for a wedding day, Isaiah 5:1-7 presents an extended allegory in which a bride is likened to a fertile vineyard. When the vineyard yields sour grapes, its owner decides to remove its protective wall and to allow it to go to ruin. Isaiah uses the song as an indictment against Israel and Judah for failing to do justice. However, in Isaiah 26:2-6 a new vineyard allegory is used to picture restoration. YHWH renews care for his vineyard, causing Judah to take root and Israel to blossom.

The end of Assyria Under stress from revolts in Egypt and Babylonia, Assyria's powerful empire began to weaken in the second half of the seventh century BCE. Nineveh, its capital city, fell to an alliance of Medes and Babylonians in 612 BCE. The decline of Assyria allowed a resurgence of Judean independence, as is likely evident in the reforms of Josiah. Assyria's fall is celebrated in both the oracles of Nahum and Zephaniah.

Key Personalities

Ahaz

Ahaz, the son of Jotham and the father of Hezekiah, was king of Judah during the Syro-Ephraimite war. Various aspects of his reign (c. 742–727 BCE) are discussed in 2 Kings 16, 2 Chronicles 28, and Isaiah 7, as well as several Assyrian annals and inscriptions. These accounts offer different perspectives on Ahaz's life and are extremely difficult to harmonize together. Yet, in general, the Hebrew Bible presents Ahaz in an extremely negative light. He did not do what was right in the sight of the LORD, making illicit offerings on the high places and perhaps even reviving the cult of child sacrifice associated with Molech (2 Kgs. 16:2-4). When Syria and Israel unite to attack Judah, he appeals to King Tiglath-pileser of Assyria for assistance. Ahaz's actions

effectively reduced Judah to the status of an Assyrian vassal-state. Ahaz must pay tribute to Tiglath-pileser, including treasures from the temple. Ahaz also seems to have introduced foreign deities or cult objects into the Jerusalem temple as a result of his contact with Damascus. Ahaz's primary sin was failing to trust in the LORD rather than in political alliances. According to Isaiah 8, Ahaz's refusal to accept God's protection will result in the LORD bringing the destructive—though not yet fatal—floodwaters of Assyrian against Judah.

Isaiah

Isaiah, a name which means "the LORD saves," was an eighth-century BCE prophet from the Southern Kingdom. As is the case with other prophets, it is not always easy to glean biographical data about Isaiah from the diverse oracles found in the book that bears his name. However, some clues are found in chapters 6°8 and 36–39. Though not necessarily his first prophetic experience, the visionary account in chapter 6 describes Isaiah's commission to his role as a prophet. Isaiah sees the LORD seated upon his throne with the hem of his rob filling the temple. Six-winged seraphs or "fiery ones" are in attendance above the LORD of hosts, praising his holiness. Isaiah confesses to being "a man of unclean lips" but is purified when a live coal is placed upon his mouth. Isaiah's visionary experience shares much in common with that of Ezekiel and Micaiah ben Imlah, though it is in contrast to the auditory call of other prophets such as Moses, Amos, and Jeremiah. Outside of this visionary account, Isaiah is perhaps most well known for his encounter with King Ahaz (chapters 7–8) and King Hezekiah (chapters 36–39). In the latter case, it is noteworthy that Isaiah takes on the role of a type of "holy man" by acting as a healer for Hezekiah. While the eighth-century prophet Isaiah is the dominant personality in this book, interpreters as early as the Middle Ages recognized that much of the material in chapters 40–66 presuppose the Babylonian exile and its aftermath. As a result, in modern biblical scholarships it is customary to assume a complex composition history behind the book of Isaiah. In this view, much—but not all—of chapters 1-39 are attributed to the eighth-century prophet Isaiah ben Amoz. The remaining material is thought to be the work of anonymous sixth-century prophets, referred to as "Second Isaiah" (chapters 40–55) and "Third Isaiah" (chapters 56–66).

Questions for Study and Discussion

1. Compare and contrast King Ahaz and King Hezekiah. What do their respective reactions to Isaiah's oracles and urgings say about the editors' assessment of their reigns?

2. Isaiah was an important book for the early Christians. Many texts from Isaiah, for instance, were viewed as prophecies of Christ's coming (see, for example, the reference to the "young woman" who will give birth to a child in Isa. 7:14). How do you respond to these later reappropriations of Isaiah?

3. Many scholars argue that the book of Isaiah does not come from a single person, and not even a single century. The book spans several hundred years, and has been expanded and edited throughout. Is the evidence for this argument compelling? If so, what impact should this knowledge have on one's reading of the book? Should one read the book any differently in light of its complex compositional history?

4. Many prophetic books, including Isaiah and Zephaniah, contain oracles of doom and gloom alongside (often later) oracles of salvation and restoration. What can explain these dramatic shifts in content? And what might they say about Israel's view of its God?

Primary Text

Isaiah 6:1—7:17

CLOSE READING TIPS

▶ Isaiah's vantage point for this vision might reflect that of a royal advisor who stood by the king at the entrance of the temple, able to glimpse into its interior (see 2 Kgs. 11:14; 23:3).

▶ Isaiah's vision of the seraphs ("fiery ones") might call to mind the appearance of a lamp's flame in the midst of the incense smoke that would have filled the temple during worship (Isa. 6:4).

▶ Ancient Mesopotamian priests also went through mouth purification rituals so that they could speak on behalf of the gods.

▶ Isaiah 6:7 does not specify a particular sin or violation. Rather, Isaiah presupposes that all humans are impure in comparison to the holiness of God.

▶ The "us" in Isaiah 6:8 refers to the divine council of heavenly beings (see also Gen. 1:26).

> ▸ Note that the New Testament draws on Isaiah 6:9-10 in reference to why Jesus speaks in parables (Matt. 13:13-15; Mark 4:11-12; Luke 8:9-10).
> ▸ Note that Ephraim is another name for Israel. Aram is a nation located in southern Syria. Together they make up the Syro-Ephraimite alliance.
> ▸ The symbolic name Shear-jashub means "a remnant shall return." It is meant to assure Ahaz that the LORD would defend Jerusalem against any attack.
> ▸ Note that the immediate goal of the attack at Jerusalem was to replace Ahaz with someone named "son of Tabeel" (verse 6), who presumably supported the aims of the Syro-Ephraimite alliance.
> ▸ Isaiah 7:9 features a word play between two forms of a Hebrew verb that can mean either "stand firm (in faith)" or "stand."

¹ In the year that King Uzziah died, I saw the Lord sitting on a throne, high and lofty; and the hem of his robe filled the temple. ² Seraphs were in attendance above him; each had six wings:with two they covered their faces, and with two they covered their feet, and with two they flew. ³ And one called to another and said:

"Holy, holy, holy is the LORD of hosts;
the whole earth is full of his glory."

⁴ The pivots on the thresholds shook at the voices of those who called, and the house filled with smoke. ⁵ And I said: "Woe is me! I am lost, for I am a man of unclean lips, and I live among a people of unclean lips; yet my eyes have seen the King, the LORD of hosts!"

⁶ Then one of the seraphs flew to me, holding a live coal that had been taken from the altar with a pair of tongs. ⁷ The seraph touched my mouth with it and said: "Now that this has touched your lips, your guilt has departed and your sin is blotted out." ⁸ Then I heard the voice of the Lord saying, "Whom shall I send, and who will go for us?" And I said, "Here am I; send me!" 9 And he said, "Go and say to this people:

'Keep listening, but do not comprehend;
keep looking, but do not understand.'
¹⁰ Make the mind of this people dull,
    and stop their ears,
    and shut their eyes,
so that they may not look with their eyes,
    and listen with their ears,
and comprehend with their minds,
    and turn and be healed."
¹¹ Then I said, "How long, O Lord?" And he
    said:
"Until cities lie waste
    without inhabitant,
and houses without people,
    and the land is utterly desolate;
¹² until the LORD sends everyone far away,
    and vast is the emptiness in the midst of
    the land.
¹³ Even if a tenth part remain in it,
    it will be burned again,
like a terebinth or an oak
    whose stump remains standing
    when it is felled."
The holy seed is its stump.

7 ¹ In the days of Ahaz son of Jotham son of Uzziah, king of Judah, King Rezin of Aram and King Pekah son of Remaliah of Israel went up to attack Jerusalem, but could not mount an attack against it. ² When the house of David heard that Aram had allied itself with Ephraim, the heart of Ahaz and the heart of his people shook as the trees of the forest shake before the wind.

³ Then the LORD said to Isaiah, Go out to meet Ahaz, you and your son Shear-jashub, at the end of the conduit of the upper pool on the highway to the Fuller's Field, ⁴ and say to him, Take heed, be quiet, do not fear, and do not let your heart be faint because of these two smoldering stumps of firebrands, because of the fierce anger of Rezin and Aram and the son of Remaliah. ⁵ Because Aram—with Ephraim and the son of Remaliah—has plotted evil against you, saying, ⁶ Let us go up against Judah and cut off Jerusalem and conquer it for ourselves and make the son of Tabeel king in it; ⁷ therefore thus says the Lord GOD:

It shall not stand,
    and it shall not come to pass.
⁸ For the head of Aram is Damascus,
    and the head of Damascus is Rezin.

(Within sixty-five years Ephraim will be shattered, no longer a people.)

⁹ The head of Ephraim is Samaria,
    and the head of Samaria is the son of Remaliah.
If you do not stand firm in faith,
    you shall not stand at all.

¹⁰ Again the LORD spoke to Ahaz, saying, ¹¹ Ask a sign of the LORD your God; let it be deep as Sheol or high as heaven. ¹² But Ahaz said, I will not ask, and I will not put the LORD to the test. ¹³ Then Isaiah said: "Hear then, O house of David! Is it too little for you to weary mortals, that you weary my God also? ¹⁴ Therefore the Lord himself will give you a sign. Look, the young woman is with child and shall bear a son, and shall name him Immanuel. ¹⁵ He shall eat curds and honey by the time he knows how to refuse the evil and choose the good. ¹⁶ For before the child knows how to refuse the evil and choose the good, the land before whose two kings you are in dread will be deserted. ¹⁷ The LORD will bring on you and on your people and on your ancestral house such days as have not come since the day that Ephraim departed from Judah—the king of Assyria."

DISCUSSION QUESTIONS

1. Why you think the visionary account in chapter 6 immediately precedes Isaiah's encounter with King Ahaz in chapter 7?
2. According to Isaiah 6:9-10, what specific task is Isaiah commissioned to do? Why might this be surprising?
3. The image of a stump appears in both Isaiah 6:13 and 7:5. How does it function in each case? Is it a sign of punishment, hope, or both?
4. What message is being communicated through the sign about the "young woman" in Isaiah 7:14-17?

Micah 6

CLOSE READING TIPS

▶ Verses 1-8 function as a legal disputation in which the prophet, as a type of attorney, presents God's case against the community.

▶ As in some ancient Near Eastern treaties, elements of the natural world are invoked as witnesses.

▶ Note that in verse 4, Micah draws on elements of the exodus story.

▶ Note that verse 7 presents a rhetorical question where the implied answer is "no."

▶ Verse 8 is a succinct statement of a key element in the preaching of eighth century prophets.

▶ Verses 9-16 function as the judicial sentence that follows naturally from indictment presented in verses 1-8. Alternatively, it could be a separate oracle.

▶ The city referred to in verse 9 is Jerusalem. Here and elsewhere, Micah makes little distinction between the sin of Judah and Israel.

▶ The curses mentioned in verses 14-15 share much in common with covenant curses in Deuteronomy 28:30-31, 38-40.

---

¹ Hear what the LORD says:
  Rise, plead your case before the
    mountains,
  and let the hills hear your voice.
² Hear, you mountains, the controversy of the
  LORD,
  and you enduring foundations of the
    earth;
for the LORD has a controversy with his
  people,
  and he will contend with Israel.

³ "O my people, what have I done to you?
  In what have I wearied you? Answer me!
⁴ For I brought you up from the land of Egypt,
  and redeemed you from the house of
    slavery;
and I sent before you Moses,
  Aaron, and Miriam.

⁵ O my people, remember now what King
    Balak of Moab devised,
  what Balaam son of Beor answered him,
and what happened from Shittim to Gilgal,
  that you may know the saving acts of the
    LORD."

⁶ "With what shall I come before the LORD,
  and bow myself before God on high?
Shall I come before him with burnt offerings,
  with calves a year old?
⁷ Will the LORD be pleased with thousands of
  rams,
  with ten thousands of rivers of oil?
Shall I give my firstborn for my transgression,
  the fruit of my body for the sin of my
    soul?"
⁸ He has told you, O mortal, what is good;
  and what does the LORD require of you
but to do justice, and to love kindness,
  and to walk humbly with your God?

[9] The voice of the LORD cries to the city
    (it is sound wisdom to fear your name):
Hear, O tribe and assembly of the city!
    [10] Can I forget the treasures of wickedness
        in the house of the wicked,
    and the scant measure that is accursed?
[11] Can I tolerate wicked scales
    and a bag of dishonest weights?
[12] Your wealthy are full of violence;
    your inhabitants speak lies,
    with tongues of deceit in their mouths.
[13] Therefore I have begun to strike you down,
    making you desolate because of your sins.
[14] You shall eat, but not be satisfied,

and there shall be a gnawing hunger
    within you;
you shall put away, but not save,
    and what you save, I will hand over to the
    sword.
[15] You shall sow, but not reap;
    you shall tread olives, but not anoint your-
    selves with oil;
    you shall tread grapes, but not drink wine.
[16] For you have kept the statutes of Omri
    and all the works of the house of Ahab,
    and you have followed their counsels.
Therefore I will make you a desolation, and
    your inhabitants an object of hissing;
    so you shall bear the scorn of my people.

DISCUSSION QUESTIONS

1. The first eight verses contain numerous shifts in speakers. Where do you see these shifts and who is speaking in each case?
2. How does reference to the exodus story (verse 4) function to strengthen God's case against Israel?
3. How would you summarize the central message of verses 6-8? In what other prophetic books have you encountered a similar perspective?
4. What is the nature of the curses in verse 14-15?

Nahum 1

CLOSE READING TIPS:

▶ "Jealous" (1:2) is a familiar characteristic of God in the Hebrew Bible (for example, Exod. 34:6; Jon. 4:2). It can be used in a positive sense (to zealously work for someone's benefit) or a negative sense (to bear a grudge or resent).

▶ Throughout the Hebrew Bible, "vengeance" does not imply illegitimate or unrestrained revenge but rather God's willingness to uphold lawfulness and justice.

▶ Verses 3b-5 draw on a common stock of imagery about the divine warrior. It emphasizes God's cosmic power.

▶ In verses 9-15, the identity of the addresses is sometimes ambiguous. The "you" (feminine singular in Hebrew) in verses 9-13 and 15 likely refers to Judah while the "you" (masculine singular in Hebrew) in verse 14 likely refers to the king of Assyria.

▶ Note that in the verse 12 "they" is Assyria. "His yoke" in verse 13 is the political and military oppression of Assyria.

▶ References to one who brings "good tidings" and "peace" can also be found in 2 Samuel 18:27, 31 and Isaiah 40:9; 41:27.

[1] An oracle concerning Nineveh. The book of the vision of Nahum of Elkosh.

[2] A jealous and avenging God is the LORD,
   the LORD is avenging and wrathful;
the LORD takes vengeance on his adversaries
   and rages against his enemies.
[3] The LORD is slow to anger but great in power,
   and the LORD will by no means clear the
      guilty.

His way is in whirlwind and storm,
   and the clouds are the dust of his feet.
[4] He rebukes the sea and makes it dry,
   and he dries up all the rivers;
Bashan and Carmel wither,
   and the bloom of Lebanon fades.
[5] The mountains quake before him,
and the hills melt;
the earth heaves before him,
   the world and all who live in it.

[6] Who can stand before his indignation?
   Who can endure the heat of his anger?
His wrath is poured out like fire,
   and by him the rocks are broken in pieces.
[7] The LORD is good,
   a stronghold in a day of trouble;
he protects those who take refuge in him,
   [8] even in a rushing flood.
He will make a full end of his adversaries,
   and will pursue his enemies into darkness.
[9] Why do you plot against the LORD?
   He will make an end;

no adversary will rise up twice.
[10] Like thorns they are entangled,
   like drunkards they are drunk;
   they are consumed like dry straw.
[11] From you one has gone out
   who plots evil against the Lord,
   one who counsels wickedness.

[12] Thus says the LORD,
"Though they are at full strength and many,
   they will be cut off and pass away.
Though I have afflicted you,
   I will afflict you no more.
[13] And now I will break off his yoke from you
   and snap the bonds that bind you."

[14] The LORD has commanded concerning you:
   "Your name shall be perpetuated no
      longer;
from the house of your gods I will cut off
   the carved image and the cast image.
I will make your grave, for you are worthless."

[15] Look! On the mountains the feet of one
   who brings good tidings,
   who proclaims peace!
Celebrate your festivals, O Judah,
   fulfill your vows,
for never again shall the wicked invade you;
   they are utterly cut off.

DISCUSSION QUESTIONS

1. How does the emphasis on God's jealousy and vengeance relate to the specific issue of the fall of Nineveh?
2. Why might it be comforting for Judean readers to see YHWH described as a powerful warrior capable of controlling natural forces?
3. What is the nature of the each of the threats against the king of Assyria in verse 14?
4. What good tidings are being delivered in verse 15? Why would this news enable the people of Judah to celebrate festivals and fulfill vows?

Zephaniah 1:2—2:3

CLOSE READING TIPS

▶ Note that "from the face of the earth" begins an ends verses 2-3. This is called an "inclusio."
▶ Judgment is announced against all of creation in verses 2-3. Focus narrows on Judah and Jerusalem in the subsequent verses.
▶ Many of the religious offenses referenced in verses 4-6 call to mind the account of Manasseh's idolatry in 2 Kings 21. This might provide a plausible historical backdrop for Zephaniah's prophecy.
▶ The "Fish Gate," "Second Quarter," and "Mortar wall" likely refer to wealthy areas within Jerusalem where traders work.
▶ Note that the final verse of chapter 1 returns to the cosmic scope of verses 2-3.
▶ Zephaniah 2:1-3 hold out the promise that destruction will be averted if the people repent.

² I will utterly sweep away everything
    from the face of the earth, says the LORD.
³ I will sweep away humans and animals;
    I will sweep away the birds of the air
    and the fish of the sea.
I will make the wicked stumble.
    I will cut off humanity
    from the face of the earth, says the LORD.
⁴ I will stretch out my hand against Judah,
    and against all the inhabitants of
        Jerusalem;
and I will cut off from this place every remnant
    of Baal
    and the name of the idolatrous priests;
⁵ those who bow down on the roofs

to the host of the heavens;
    those who bow down and swear to the LORD,
    but also swear by Milcom;
⁶ those who have turned back from following
    the LORD,
who have not sought the LORD or inquired of
    him.

⁷ Be silent before the Lord GOD!
    For the day of the LORD is at hand;
the LORD has prepared a sacrifice,
    he has consecrated his guests.
⁸ And on the day of the LORD's sacrifice
I will punish the officials and the king's sons
    and all who dress themselves in foreign
        attire.

⁹ On that day I will punish
    all who leap over the threshold,
who fill their master's house
    with violence and fraud.

¹⁰ On that day, says the LORD,
    a cry will be heard from the Fish Gate,
a wail from the Second Quarter,
    a loud crash from the hills.
¹¹ The inhabitants of the Mortar wail,
    for all the traders have perished;
    all who weigh out silver are cut off.
¹² At that time I will search Jerusalem with
    lamps,
    and I will punish the people
who rest complacently on their dregs,
    those who say in their hearts,
"The LORD will not do good,
    nor will he do harm."
¹³ Their wealth shall be plundered,
    and their houses laid waste.
Though they build houses,
    they shall not inhabit them;
though they plant vineyards,
    they shall not drink wine from them.

¹⁴ The great day of the LORD is near,
    near and hastening fast;
the sound of the day of the LORD is bitter,
    the warrior cries aloud there.
¹⁵ That day will be a day of wrath,
    a day of distress and anguish,
a day of ruin and devastation,
    a day of darkness and gloom,
a day of clouds and thick darkness,
    ¹⁶ a day of trumpet blast and battle cry
against the fortified cities
    and against the lofty battlements.

¹⁷ I will bring such distress upon people
    that they shall walk like the blind;
    because they have sinned against the
        LORD,
their blood shall be poured out like dust,
    and their flesh like dung.
¹⁸ Neither their silver nor their gold
    will be able to save them
    on the day of the LORD's wrath;
in the fire of his passion
    the whole earth shall be consumed;
for a full, a terrible end
    he will make of all the inhabitants of the
        earth.

2 ¹ Gather together, gather,
    O shameless nation,
² before you are driven away
    like the drifting chaff,
before there comes upon you
    the fierce anger of the LORD,
before there comes upon you
    the day of the LORD's wrath.
³ Seek the LORD, all you humble of the land,
    who do his commands;
seek righteousness, seek humility;
    perhaps you may be hidden
    on the day of the LORD's wrath.

DISCUSSION QUESTIONS

1. What similarities and differences do you see between Zephaniah 1:2—2:3 and Amos 5 in terms of how both prophets present the Day of the LORD?

2. What sorts of sins does Zephaniah target in this oracle? Are they more related to idolatry or social injustice?

3. How might a seventh-century BCE audience have understood references to "ruin," "devastation," and a "battle cry against the fortified city?"

4. If Zephaniah spoke during the early reign of Josiah, how might the words of Zephaniah 2:3 motivate the king's religious reforms?

17

The Babylonian Era: Habakkuk, Jeremiah, and Lamentations

Key Points

Writing is often a means by which communities recount, process, and cope with trauma. The books of Habakkuk, Jeremiah, and Lamentations are no exception. Set against the backdrop of the fall of Jerusalem in 587 BCE, these books attempt to come to terms with the cause of the Babylonian exile. From a geo-political perspective, this tragic event was a product of Babylonian expansion and conquest under King Nabopolassar (626–605 BCE) and King Nebuchadnezzar II (605–562 BCE). However, in the theological perspective of these three books, the Babylonian exile was a form of divine punishment. Though Habakkuk, Jeremiah, and Lamentations generally agree that this punishment is deserved, each of these texts offer some hope for future consolation.

One of the twelve Minor Prophets, the book of Habakkuk is notable for its first-person style and sustained reflection on the problem of theodicy. The major section of the book (Hab. 1:2-17; 2:1-20) features a series of first-person speeches in which Habakkuk voices the community's complaint against God concerning the actions of the Babylonians. God's responses do not directly address the prophet's concerns, but instead indict the proud and the wealthy. The final chapter includes a reassuring vision of the theophany of the divine warrior. As in later apocalyptic literature, Habakkuk's prophecy looks to the future in order to resolve the problem of injustice in the present.

Jeremiah is an exceedingly complex book, consisting of poetic oracles, narratives about the prophet, prose sermons in a Deuteronomic style, and oracles against the nations. Scholars disagree on whether the bulk of this material preserves Jeremiah's original words or reflects the work of anonymous scribes in the postexilic period. In either case, the content of the book is arranged in a roughly chronological fashion, stretching from the time of Josiah's reforms through the final deportation. Distinguishing features of Jeremiah's preaching includes his announcement of impending doom for Jerusalem, his biting criticism of certain Judean kings, scribes, and prophets, and his acquiescence to Babylonian rule. Not surprisingly, Jeremiah's message was met with considerable resistance. Perhaps more than any other prophet, Jeremiah experiences bitterness and isolation, as is evident in the so-called "laments" of Jeremiah (Jer. 11–20). Nevertheless, the book of Jeremiah also contains several hopeful oracles about the restoration of Jerusalem and the return of "the voice of gladness" to the towns of Judah (Jer. 30–33).

The five highly stylized poems in the book of Lamentations share much in common with the city lament, a literary genre well attested in the ancient Near East since the end of the third millennium. Using lurid detail, Lamentations brings the reader face-to-face with the horrific devastation of Jerusalem. Though Lamentations believes this punishment is deserved, it nevertheless professes confidence in "the steadfast love of the LORD" (Lam. 3:22). This book is most well-known for its heart-wrenching expression of grief over God abandoning his people and disavowing his sanctuary. These words of lament have resonated with readers throughout the ages and have been incorporated into Jewish and Christian liturgies (the Ninth of Ab and Good Friday, respectively) that commemorate past tragedies.

Key Terms

Chaldeans   Of Aramean origins, the Chaldeans were a heterogeneous population that settled between the Tigris and Euphrates rivers early in the first millennium BCE. This southern Mesopotamian region would later be called the "Land of the Chaldeans." Under King Nabopolassar (626–605 BCE), the Chaldeans became one of the dominant elements of the Neo-Babylonian Empire. In much of the Hebrew Bible, the term Chaldeans is used as a synonym for Babylonians.

Lament   A lament is a literary genre that expresses grief or sorrow. Various types of laments are known from the Hebrew Bible and ancient Near Eastern literature. For instance, the book of Lamentations is modeled on Mesopotamian city laments while the material in Jeremiah 11–20 reflects individual laments. The Psalter features communal laments while the funeral dirge is evident in several prophetic texts. During the time of exile, the lament was an appropriate response

to loss and the experience of divine punishment and abandonment.

The Ninth of Ab   In later Jewish tradition, the Ninth of Ab is an annual fast that commemorates not only the destruction of the first temple (587 BCE) but also the fall of the second temple to the Romans (70 CE) and the defeat of Bar Kochba (132 CE). By virtue of being used in the liturgy for the Ninth of Ab, the book of Lamentations becomes a lament for all major tragedies in Jewish history. This tradition may originate in a much earlier time when mourning rituals were used in connection with the Babylonian exile (see Jer. 41:5; Zech. 7:3; 8:19).

Greek Jeremiah   The Greek translation of Jeremiah differs in significant ways from the Hebrew version preserved in the Masoretic Text. Not only is the Greek text one-eighth shorter, but the oracles against foreign nations are located after Jeremiah 25:13 instead of at the end of the Hebrew text (Jer. 46–51). It was initially believed that the Greek translator abridged and rearranged the Hebrew.

However, evidence from the Dead Sea Scrolls suggests that the Greek preservers an older form of the book.

Acrostic An acrostic is a literary composition in which the first word of each stanza or line begins with a consecutive letter of the alphabet. Lamentations 1, 2, and 4 are simple acrostics with twenty-two stanzas each (to match the twenty-two letters in the Hebrew alphabet). A more complex acrostic is found in Lamentations 3, where the three lines of each of the twenty-two stanzas all begin with the appropriate letter. Lamentations 5 has twenty-two lines but breaks from the acrostic pattern, perhaps suggesting the inability to bring closure to the lament.

Key Personalities

Jeremiah

The prophet Jeremiah was a descendant of Abiathar, a Levite who served (along with Zadok) as one of David's two chief priests. Abiathar was eventually exiled to Anathoth when he supported Adonijah, the king's rival to the throne. Subsequently, control of the Jerusalem priesthood fell into the hands of Zadok and his descendants. Jeremiah's critique of the Davidic dynasty and Jerusalem temple, as well as his emphasis on the exodus tradition, likely owes much to his association with Abiathar and the town of Anathoth. Jeremiah's prophetic call, which is placed during the thirteenth year of King Josiah (627 BCE), shares much in common with the call of Moses. Both prophets have an auditory experience, initially resist God on the basis of their unsuitability for the mission, and ultimately are assured that they have been appointed by YHWH. The details of his prophetic career are somewhat difficult to reconstruct, although it is clear that Jeremiah's ministry was closely intertwined with the critical events surrounding Josiah's reforms, two unsuccessful revolts against Babylonia, and the comprehensive deportation in 586 BCE. While Jeremiah initially chose to stay in Jerusalem after it fell, he was later forced to accompany a group of exiles seeking refuge in Egypt. The book of Lamentations is often attributed to Jeremiah, though the Hebrew Bible never makes this claim. Nevertheless, the prophet's doleful tone is the most prominent aspect of the book that bears his name, thus giving rise to the term "jeremiad," which refers to a speech or writing that expresses mournful complaint.

Baruch

Baruch was a scribe and close associate of the prophet Jeremiah. Almost every time he is mentioned in the book of Jeremiah, he is referred to as the "son of Neriah" (Jer. 32:12, 16; 36:4, 8, 14, 32; 43:3, 6; 45:1). It is believed that Baruch was a royal scribe in Jerusalem in part because of a discovery of a seal impression in a royal archive with the inscription "Berechiah, son of Neriah, the scribe" (Berechiah is the long form of the name Baruch). During the siege of Jerusalem, Baruch functions as a witness to Jeremiah's purchase of a piece of land in Anathoth, an act meant to symbolize that land would one day be restored to Israel. In Jeremiah 36, the prophet receives a command from the LORD to write on a scroll all the words that were spoken to him. Instead of doing this himself, Jeremiah has Baruch write on the scrolls as he dictates what the LORD had told him. Since Jeremiah was barred from entering the temple, he calls on Baruch to read the scroll in the house of the LORD on a fast day. Baruch also reads from the scroll in the presence of the King Jehoiakim's officials at the royal palace.

When the scroll was read again in the presence of the king (though not by Baruch), Jehoiakim burns the scroll. After escaping, Jeremiah once again dictates words to Baruch for another scroll. Some scholars consider Baruch as Jeremiah's biographer and others suggest that Baruch was responsible for writing large portions of the book's prose. Jeremiah's relationship with Baruch is an obvious exception to the prophet's critical view of scribes. Baruch is a popular figure in later Jewish tradition. An apocryphal letter from the second center BCE is attributed to Baruch, as are several other texts.

Questions for Study and Discussion

1. Societies tend to silence voices that cry out for unpopular change. Jeremiah's situation was no different. He preached a deeply unpopular message to a largely resistant audience. Can you think of any modern day "Jeremiahs"? How do their messages, lives, and reception within the society parallel the literary portrayal of Jeremiah?
2. The book of Jeremiah is dominated by oracles that announce impending judgment. But there are also oracles about Israel's future—both in and after exile. What kind of future does Jeremiah envision? How do these visions of the future compare to other utopian visions of the future of which you are aware?
3. Both Habakkuk and Jeremiah identify Babylon as a divinely commissioned agent of violence and judgment. According to these two books, God uses Babylon to accomplish God's will in the world. Throughout history, both ancient and modern, religious leaders have tended to associated might, power, and influence with God's will. What is your reaction to this tendency?
4. Habakkuk and Jeremiah, in their own ways, highlight the problem of evil in the world. Habakkuk wonders why God delays in his response to prayer. For his part, Jeremiah cries out, "Why does the way of the wicked prosper?" In your view, how do these two books respond to these questions, if at all? What is your own response to these questions?

Primary Text

Lamentation Over the Destruction of Ur

Source: Victor H. Matthews and Don C. Benjamin, *Old Testament Parallels: Laws and Stories from the Ancient Near East*, fully revised and expanded 3d. ed. (New York: Paulist, 2006), 249–55

CLOSE READING TIPS

▶ Ur was a Sumerian city located in southern Mesopotamia that was destroyed around 2000 BCE.
▶ Note that defeat in war is interpreted as a sign that the deities have abandoned their cities or temples.
▶ The goddess Ningal, the wife of Nanna, mourns for the city as a mother mourns for her child.

▶ The expression "the Day of the Dust Storm" is used in a somewhat similar way as the biblical expression "the Day of the LORD" or "that day."

▶ Note that no explanation is provided for the divine assembly's decision.

▶ On a mythopoetic level, the city is laid waste by a violent dust storm sent by the god Enlil. In historical terms, the city fell to the Elamites and Amorites (lines 171–206).

▶ The text describes the bloody aftermath of the destruction. Note the graphic nature of this description.

▶ Note that the text beseeches Anu and Enlil to end the destruction and to permit the rebuilding of Ur. This lamentation likely would have been sung during various stages of the rebuilding process.

FIRST LAMENT

Enlil, the shepherd of Sumer, has fled Nippur
  His sheep are without a shepherd.
Enlil, divine patron of the Earth, has abandoned Nippur,
  His sheep are without a shepherd.
Enlil has left Nippur,
  His sheep are without a shepherd.
Ninlil, wife of Enlil, has fled Nippur,
  Her sheep are without a shepherd.
Ninlil has abandoned her temple,
  Her sheep are without a shepherd. . .

SECOND LAMENT

Cities of Sumer, weep bitter tears!
  Cities of Sumer, mourn!
Weep bitter tears for Ur, the faithful city!
  Mourn with Nanna, the divine patron of
    the city!
Cities of Sumer, mourn!
  Weep bitter tears over the ruins of Ur.
Mourn with Nanna,
  Weep bitter tears as long as Nanna
    mourns!
Weep bitter tears over the walls of Ur!
  Mourn for Ekishnugal, the temple of
    Nanna. . .

THIRD LAMENT

That Night, I could not go to bed,
  That Night, I could not fall asleep.
Night after night, I could not go to bed,
  Night after night, I could not fall asleep.
The land of Ur is filled with sorrow,
  Sorrow fated for my land.
Although I screamed for the life of my calf,
  cried out for its release,
  I could not save my land from its misery.
My land was in distress,
  Distress that condemned my city to death.
Even if I could flap my wings like a bird,
  Even if I could fly to save my city,
Still my city would be destroyed,
  Still my city would be razed to its
    foundations,
  Still my Ur would be destroyed where it
    lays.

FOURTH LAMENT

The Day of the Dust Storm struck Ur over and
  over,
  I watched the destruction of my city. . . ,
The Day of the Dust Storm, the divine assembly condemned my city,

Enlil commanded the total destruction of
     my city and its people,
The Day of the Dust Storm, I did not abandon
     my city,
     I did not forget my land.
I shed tears of sorrow before Anu,
     I uttered prayers of supplication before
          Enlil.
     I repeated cried, "Spare the city and its
          people!"

But Anu and Enlil did not relent;
     They gave no comfort to my heart.
Their command remained to destroy my city.
     Their decree was to kill my people. . . .

"Spare my city from destruction," I asked.
     "Spare Ur from destruction," I begged.
     "Spare its people from death," I pleaded
          with Anu and Enlil.

Anu would not listen to me,
     Enlil would not sooth my distress,
     He would not decree: "Grant her petition!"
Instead, Enlil and Anu ordered the city
     destroyed,
     They ordered Ur destroyed.
The fate of Ur was sealed,
     The people of Ur were sentenced to death.

FIFTH LAMENT

Enlil prepares the dust storm,
     And the people of Ur mourn.
He withholds the rain from the land;
     And the people of Ur mourn.
He delays the winds that water the corps of
     Sumer,
     And the people of Ur mourn.
He gives the winds that dry the land their
     orders,

And the people of Ur mourn.
Enlil orders Kingaluda, the dust storm, to put
     the city to death,
     And the people of Ur mourn.
He prepares the winds that dry the land,
     And the people of Ur mourn.
Enlil orders Gibil, the lightning, to prepare the
     dust storms.
     And the people of Ur mourn.
The winds that dry the land howl.
     And the people of Ur mourn.
The storm sweeps across the land,
     And the people of Ur mourn.
The winds that dry the land rush unrestrained
     to the sea,
     And the people of Ur mourn.
Great waves swallow the city's ships,
     And the people of Ur mourn.
Earthquakes rock the pillars of the earth,
     And the people of Ur mourn.
Lightning flashes and explodes in the dust
     storms.
     And the people of Ur mourn.
The dust storm leaves the city and the Temple
     of Nanna in ruins,
     And the people of Ur mourn.
The dust storm scatters bodies everywhere like
     broken pots,
     And the people of Ur mourn. . . .
The walls are breached and corpses block the
     gates,
     And the people of Ur mourn. . . .

The main streets are choked with the dead.
     Bodies fill the streets.
Where crowds once celebrated festivals, bodies
     lie in every street,
     Corpses are piled on every road.
In the squares where people danced,

Heaps of corpses lie.
The blood of the dead fills every crevice,
    Like molten metal in a worker's mold.
The bodies of the dead melt,
    Their flesh is like the fat of sheep left in the
        sun.
Warriors wounded by an ax bleed to death.
    Warriors wounded by a lance go untended.
Soldiers lie in the dust,
    Fighters gasp like gazelles pierced by
        hunters' spears. . . .

The elders of Ur are slaughtered,
    And the people of Ur mourn.
The wise of Ur are scattered,
    And the people of Ur mourn.
Mothers turn their backs on their daughters,
    And the people of Ur mourn.
Fathers walk away from their sons,
    And the people of Ur mourn.
Women, children, and houses are abandoned
    and looted. . . .

Seventh Lament

All the buildings outside the walls are
    destroyed.
    And the people of Ur say: "Our poor city!"
All the buildings inside the walls are destroyed.

And the people of Ur say: "Our poor city!"
Ur, my fertile ewe, has been slaughtered.
    Its good shepherd is gone.
My strong ox no longer stands in its stable.
    Its oxherd is gone.
The daughters and sons of Ur have been car-
    ried away in ships.
    And the people of Ur say: "Our poor
        children!"

My poor city and temple are destroyed,
    The Temple of Nanna is destroyed, and the
        people of Ur are dead.
Poor me, I have no place to sit or stand.
    Poor me, ruins I do not recognize stand in
        place of my city.

Eighth Lament

May Anu, divine patron of the sky, decree:
    "Enough!"
    May Enlil, divine patron of the winds,
        grant Ningal a better fate.
May Anu rebuild Ur,
    May he restore the Temple of Ningal.
May Anu return your city to its former
    grandeur,
    May he make you, once again, its queen.

Discussion question

1. What is the underlying reason why Ur is allowed to be destroyed? How does this compare or contrast
    with the explanation given in Jeremiah or the book of Lamentations?
2. In this lament, the goddess Ningal mourns for the desolation of her city. What character plays a similar
    role in the book of Lamentations?
3. The profession of the steadfast love of YHWH (Lam. 3:22-24) interjects hope into the biblical lament. Do
    you see any future oriented hope in the Lamentation Over the Destruction of Ur? Where?
4. Why do you think the author of this lament, much like the author of Jeremiah and Lamentations,
    included such graphic depictions of violence and desolation? What affect does this have on the reader?

Jeremiah 29

CLOSE READING TIPS

▶ The time frame for this letter is several years (C. 594–593) after the first wave of exiles were deported from Jerusalem.

▶ The purpose of the commands in verses 4-7 is to emphasize that the exiles should not expect an immediate restoration as some false prophets had been predicting (verses 9-10).

▶ The prediction of a seventy year exile (verse 10) is difficult to account for. It may refer to the period between the destruction of the temple (587 BCE) and its rebuilding (516–515 BCE). More likely, it is a typological figure representing the period of a normal life span.

▶ The purpose of verses 16-20 is to critique those who remained behind in Jerusalem, including King Zedekiah and his officials. The imagery of rotten figs is also used in a similar message in chapter 24.

▶ Note that Shemaiah had attempted to have Jeremiah imprisoned.

[1] These are the words of the letter that the prophet Jeremiah sent from Jerusalem to the remaining elders among the exiles, and to the priests, the prophets, and all the people, whom Nebuchadnezzar had taken into exile from Jerusalem to Babylon. [2] This was after King Jeconiah, and the queen mother, the court officials, the leaders of Judah and Jerusalem, the artisans, and the smiths had departed from Jerusalem. [3] The letter was sent by the hand of Elasah son of Shaphan and Gemariah son of Hilkiah, whom King Zedekiah of Judah sent to Babylon to King Nebuchadnezzar of Babylon. It said: [4] Thus says the LORD of hosts, the God of Israel, to all the exiles whom I have sent into exile from Jerusalem to Babylon: [5] Build houses and live in them; plant gardens and eat what they produce. [6] Take wives and have sons and daughters; take wives for your sons, and give your daughters in marriage, that they may bear sons and daughters; multiply there, and do not decrease. [7] But seek the welfare of the city where I have sent you into exile, and pray to the LORD on its behalf, for in its welfare you will find your welfare. [8] For thus says the LORD of hosts, the God of Israel: Do not let the prophets and the diviners who are among you deceive you, and do not listen to the dreams that they dream, [9] for it is a lie that they are prophesying to you in my name; I did not send them, says the LORD.

[10] For thus says the LORD: Only when Babylon's seventy years are completed will I visit you, and I will fulfill to you my promise and bring you back to this place. [11] For surely I know the plans I have for you, says the LORD, plans for your welfare and not for harm, to give you a future with hope. [12] Then when you call upon me and come and pray to me, I will hear you. [13] When you search for me, you will find me; if you seek me with all your heart, [14] I will let you find me, says the LORD, and I will restore your fortunes and gather you from all the nations and all the places where I have driven you, says the LORD, and I will bring you back to the place from which I sent you into exile.

[15] Because you have said, "The LORD has raised up prophets for us in Babylon,"— [16] Thus says the

LORD concerning the king who sits on the throne of David, and concerning all the people who live in this city, your kinsfolk who did not go out with you into exile: ¹⁷ Thus says the LORD of hosts, I am going to let loose on them sword, famine, and pestilence, and I will make them like rotten figs that are so bad they cannot be eaten. ¹⁸ I will pursue them with the sword, with famine, and with pestilence, and will make them a horror to all the kingdoms of the earth, to be an object of cursing, and horror, and hissing, and a derision among all the nations where I have driven them, ¹⁹ because they did not heed my words, says the LORD, when I persistently sent to you my servants the prophets, but they would not listen, says the LORD. ²⁰ But now, all you exiles whom I sent away from Jerusalem to Babylon, hear the word of the LORD: 21 Thus says the LORD of hosts, the God of Israel, concerning Ahab son of Kolaiah and Zedekiah son of Maaseiah, who are prophesying a lie to you in my name: I am going to deliver them into the hand of King Nebuchadnezzar of Babylon, and he shall kill them before your eyes. ²² And on account of them this curse shall be used by all the exiles from Judah in Babylon: "The LORD make you like Zedekiah and Ahab, whom the king of Babylon roasted in the fire," ²³ because they have perpetrated outrage in Israel and have committed adultery with their neighbors' wives, and have spoken in my name

lying words that I did not command them; I am the one who knows and bears witness, says the LORD.

24 To Shemaiah of Nehelam you shall say:25 Thus says the LORD of hosts, the God of Israel: In your own name you sent a letter to all the people who are in Jerusalem, and to the priest Zephaniah son of Maaseiah, and to all the priests, saying, ²⁶ The LORD himself has made you priest instead of the priest Jehoiada, so that there may be officers in the house of the LORD to control any madman who plays the prophet, to put him in the stocks and the collar. ²⁷ So now why have you not rebuked Jeremiah of Anathoth who plays the prophet for you? ²⁸ For he has actually sent to us in Babylon, saying, "It will be a long time; build houses and live in them, and plant gardens and eat what they produce."

²⁹ The priest Zephaniah read this letter in the hearing of the prophet Jeremiah. ³⁰ Then the word of the LORD came to Jeremiah: ³¹ Send to all the exiles, saying, Thus says the LORD concerning Shemaiah of Nehelam: Because Shemaiah has prophesied to you, though I did not send him, and has led you to trust in a lie, ³² therefore thus says the LORD: I am going to punish Shemaiah of Nehelam and his descendants; he shall not have anyone living among this people to see the good that I am going to do to my people, says the LORD, for he has spoken rebellion against the LORD.

DISCUSSION QUESTIONS

1. Where in this passage do you see Jeremiah challenging other religious authorities? What does this suggest about his prophetic leadership?
2. What specific issue causes conflict between Jeremiah and other prophets?
3. How is Jeremiah's command in verses 4-8 consistent with his theological assessment of the exile?
4. Why might Jeremiah's perspective on submitting to Babylon not sit well most of his audience?

Habakkuk 1

CLOSE READING TIPS

▶ The term "prophet" (verse 1) is only used in the superscriptions to two other books, Haggai and Zechariah.

▶ Habakkuk's language in verses 2-4 is typical of the complaint section of the lament genre (see Ps. 13).

▶ Note that the term "violence" occurs six times in this short book (Hab. 1:2, 3, 4, 9; 2:18, 17).

▶ In verses 5-11, the speaker seems to be God but is never identified as such.

▶ Chaldeans (verse 6) is another name for the Babylonians.

▶ Habakkuk is the speaker once again in verses 12-17. Here he offers a second complaint (verse 17).

▶ Note that verses 14-16 employs an extended analogy between fish and people, where the enemy (Babylon) is a fisherman.

---

¹ The oracle that the prophet Habakkuk saw.

² O LORD, how long shall I cry for help,
    and you will not listen?
Or cry to you "Violence!"
    and you will not save?
³ Why do you make me see wrongdoing
    and look at trouble?
Destruction and violence are before me;
    strife and contention arise.
⁴ So the law becomes slack
    and justice never prevails.
The wicked surround the righteous—
    therefore judgment comes forth perverted.

⁵ Look at the nations, and see!
    Be astonished! Be astounded!
For a work is being done in your days
    that you would not believe if you were told.
⁶ For I am rousing the Chaldeans,
    that fierce and impetuous nation,
who march through the breadth of the earth
    to seize dwellings not their own.

⁷ Dread and fearsome are they;
    their justice and dignity proceed from
        themselves.
⁸ Their horses are swifter than leopards,
    more menacing than wolves at dusk;
    their horses charge.
Their horsemen come from far away;
    they fly like an eagle swift to devour.
⁹ They all come for violence,
    with faces pressing forward;
    they gather captives like sand.
¹⁰ At kings they scoff,
    and of rulers they make sport.
They laugh at every fortress,
    and heap up earth to take it.
¹¹ Then they sweep by like the wind;
    they transgress and become guilty;
    their own might is their god!

¹² Are you not from of old,
    O LORD my God, my Holy One?
    You shall not die.
O LORD, you have marked them for judgment;

and you, O Rock, have established them
   for punishment.
[13] Your eyes are too pure to behold evil,
   and you cannot look on wrongdoing;
why do you look on the treacherous,
   and are silent when the wicked swallow
   those more righteous than they?
[14] You have made people like the fish of the sea,
   like crawling things that have no ruler.

[15] The enemy brings all of them up with a hook;
   he drags them out with his net,
he gathers them in his seine;
   so he rejoices and exults.
[16] Therefore he sacrifices to his net
   and makes offerings to his seine;
for by them his portion is lavish,
   and his food is rich.
[17] Is he then to keep on emptying his net,
   and destroying nations without mercy?

DISCUSSION QUESTIONS

1. What sort of problem—sin within Judah or an external threat—do you think Habakkuk is referring to in the opening verses?
2. What instrument does God use to respond to the violence and wrongdoing that Habakkuk observers?
3. Is the prophet persuaded that God's solution to his first complaint will work? Why or why not?

18

The Exilic Period: Ezekiel and Obadiah

Key Points

For many readers, the prophecies found in the book of Ezekiel are as provocative and perplexing as any other part of the Hebrew Bible. Bizarre symbolic actions and vivid metaphors are coupled with fantastic imagery about God's "mobile" throne (chapter 1), a life-giving river flowing from the temple (chapter 47), and valley full of dry bones (chapter 37). Though diverse in subject matter, the contents of Ezekiel are highly structured. The first twenty-four chapters are set before the fall of Jerusalem and feature oracles of judgment against Judah (chapters 12–24) as well as symbolic predictions of the coming exile (chapters 3–11). The second half of the book offers a more hopeful message for Israel. After a series of oracles against the nations (chapters 25–32, see Obadiah for similar oracles), the prophet focuses his attention on the restoration of Judah (chapters 33–39), and with it, the blueprint for the restored temple and land (chapters 40–48).

The book of Ezekiel is marked by priestly concerns, many of which display strong conceptual correspondences with the Holiness Code (Leviticus 17–26). From the perspective of Ezekiel and his later editors, the fall of Jerusalem to the Babylonians was a direct result of the defilement of the temple through a number of idolatrous practices and cultic offenses (chapters 8–9). This impurity is an affront to the holiness of YHWH, and as a result the people must be cut off from the land and the glory of the LORD must depart from the temple. The responsibility for such offenses lay primarily at the feet of the people who remained in the city with Zedekiah, the puppet ruler installed by the Babylonians after the first deportation.

At the same time, Ezekiel's oracles of restoration also have a priestly ring to them. The landscape of the sanctified city is dominated by the temple and the primary authority lay not with the Davidic "prince" but rather with the Zadokite priests, who exclusively control cultic operations. While Ezekiel's vision never comes to fruition, it becomes a model for utopian prescriptions for a New Jerusalem in the Second Temple period.

Ezekiel's prophecies are also distinguished by several notable literary features. Several terms and phrases are often repeated, including "mortal," "for the sake of my holy name," and "so that you [or they] will know that I am the LORD." The prophet also frequently employs political allegories (chapters 17 and 19), marital metaphors (chapter 16), mythic allusions (chapters 26–28), theophanies (chapters 1 and 10), and symbolic action reports (chapters 3–6) in order to probe transcendent realities and divine perspectives. One of the most important theological contributions of the book is its extended discourse on personal responsibility in chapter 18. In contrast to other biblical traditions that emphasize that the blessings and curses of the covenant are applied to the people as a whole, Ezekiel calls for discrimination on the basis of the behavior of individuals. While this theology is not without its problems, it does enable Ezekiel to emphasize that the exiles in Babylon were more righteous than the other Judeans who perished in Jerusalem.

Key Terms

Chariot-throne   The prophet Ezekiel envisions God's throne as a chariot-like vehicle, borne aloft by four winged creatures (chapter 1). The chariot-throne also has four wheels that can move in any direction the spirit leads. The fact that God's throne is mobile is crucial for Ezekiel's theology insofar as it symbolizes that God is not tied down to the Jerusalem temple. This vision becomes a cornerstone of later Jewish mysticism, which derives its name, *Merkavah*, from the Hebrew word for chariot.

The glory of the LORD   This expression indicates the presence of God in the book of Ezekiel and throughout the Priestly tradition. It emphasizes the transcendent, surpassing, and immaterial nature of God. Priestly theology emphasizes that the glory (Heb.: *kabod*) of the LORD dwells in the temple, in contrast to ancient Near Eastern religions where a divine cult statue had a similar function. In Ezekiel, the glory of the LORD departs from the temple at the time of the exile and travels with the Judeans to Babylon.

Symbolic actions   Symbolic actions are embodied signs intended to attract public attention. Often performed by prophets, they are a characteristic way in which divine messages are communicated. Symbolic actions are prominent in the book of Ezekiel and include such things as the prophet shaving his head and beard (chapter 5) and sleeping on his left and right side for a prescribed period of time (chapter 4). The prophet often explains the lessons conveyed through these actions.

Zadokite priests   This branch of priests traces its lineage through Zadok, one of David's two chief priests. After Zadok became the sole chief priest under Solomon, his descendants controlled the priesthood in Jerusalem up until the time of the exile. In his vision of the New Jerusalem, Ezekiel, likely a Zadokite himself, reserves the priesthood for the Zadokites. In contrast, the levitical priests are punished for contributing to Israel's past idolatry and are only allowed to perform menial tasks in the temple.

Prince   In the P source of the Pentateuch, the term prince (Heb.: *naśi'*) is used to refer to the lay leader of the tribes. Ezekiel applies the same term to David in a messianic oracle concerning the future restoration (Ezek. 34:23-24). While the prince has a place of honor in Ezekiel's elaborate vision of the New Jerusalem (chapters 40–48), he retains little power. The description of the curtailed power of the prince in Ezekiel anticipates the reality of Second Temple Judaism, where the high priest became the primary Jewish ruler.

Key Personalities

Ezekiel

The prophet Ezekiel lived during the Babylonian exile and was among the first group of citizens who were deported to Babylon when Nebuchadnezzar conquered Jerusalem in 597 BCE. He lived among the deportees in a settlement at Tel-abib along the Chebar river (Ezek. 3:15). It is likely that Ezekiel was already in Babylon when he received his inaugural vision (Ezek. 1:1), which is said to have occurred in the fifth year of the exile of Jehoiachin. Ezekiel was married (Ezek. 24:18) and seems to have been a figure of considerable importance among the exiles (Ezek. 8:1; 14:1; 20:1). Like Jeremiah, Ezekiel can trace his lineage through a priestly clan. However, Ezekiel, or at least those who compiled and edited his prophecies, was associated with the dominant Zadokite priestly line in Jerusalem. The specific priestly theology of the Zadokites, which is preserved in the Holiness Code (Lev. 17–26), permeates Ezekiel's writing. This is especially evident in the prophet's focus on purity and his frequent coupling of moral and ritual concerns. In addition to his priestly interests, Ezekiel is also well known for his symbolic actions. Some scholars have attempted to associate this bizarre behavior with an unusual psychological condition, but this is not a necessary conclusion. Though the Hebrew Bible does not report on his death, Jewish tradition preserves the notion that Ezekiel was buried in a tomb at al-Kifl, which is near ancient Babylon.

Gog

In Ezekiel 38, Gog is described as "the chief prince of Meshech and Tubal" from the land of Magog. He is said to be a leader of an army of nations who advance against Israel from the north. The name Gog is likely derived from Gyges, King of Lydia, who is also known as *gugu* in Assyrian texts. However, this Gyges lived a century before Ezekiel and had no contact with Israel. As a result, rather than being a historical person, the Gog of Ezekiel 38–39 is probably a legendary figure who plays a part in a mythic conflict between YHWH and the nations. In Ezekiel's prophecy, YHWH rouses Gog to go against Israel, but this is merely a pretext for God to vindicate his holiness before the nations (Ezek. 38:16) and to make his power known (Ezek. 38:23). Gog ultimately falls on the mountains of Israel (Ezek. 39:4), his entire army is wiped out, and his land is burned (Ezek. 39:5-6). A macabre sacrificial feast is described in which Gog is devoured by birds and wild animals (Ezek. 39:18). This disturbing final scene emphasizes that there are no limits to the destruction that is wished upon the nations who rise up against YHWH and his people. Ultimately, the punishment of Gog is linked to the restoration of Israel and the promise that God will never again abandon his people (Ezek. 39:25-19). Ezekiel's description of Gog had some influence on the New Testament. In Revelation 20:8-9, Gog and Magog are described as nations of the earth that Satan gathers in battle against the saints and God's "beloved city."

Questions for Study and Discussion

1. The depiction of Jerusalem as a promiscuous whore, deserving of capital punishment, is certainly disturbing, especially when one considers that the book of Ezekiel is understood to be sacred by Jewish and Christian faith communities. Can or do texts like Ezekiel 16 contribute to violence against women? If so, how should society respond to such texts?

2. Ezekiel 18 argues against the notion of collective judgment, which states that later generations can suffer the consequences of their "fathers'" sins. Instead, he states that people only suffer the consequences of their own wrongdoings, not those of others. With which side do you agree? Are there other options you prefer?

3. When national disasters hit, in antiquity or in modernity, people are often on the lookout for causes. Who is to blame? Who can be brought to justice? How does Ezekiel's priestly background inform his own response to these questions?

4. As a priest, Ezekiel came from an elite level of society. How do you see his social setting expressed in his criticisms of Jerusalem and in his hopes for the future? Thinking in particular of Ezekiel 40–48, which are utopian in nature, how do the values of his elite social class come through in his hopes for the future?

Primary Text

Ezekiel's Commissioning: Ezekiel 1:28b—3:15

CLOSE READING TIPS

▶ Note that the term "mortal" or "son of man" (Heb: *ben 'adam*) is used ninety-three times in this book in reference to Ezekiel.

▶ The term "rebellious house" (Ezek. 2:5, 6, 7) is unique to Ezekiel. It emphasizes Judah's contempt for God's holiness.

▶ Note that the role of the prophet is to deliver God's word, regardless of how his audience responds (Ezek. 2:7; 3:11).

▶ The scroll in Ezekiel 2:8—3:3 is inscribed with bad news. Words of lamentation, mourning, and woe may reflect funeral rites.

▶ "Obscure speech and difficult language" (Ezek. 3:5) is a reference to Akkadian, a complex cuneiform language of ancient Mesopotamia.

▶ Note that in Hebrew, the term for "spirit" (Ezek. 3:12, 14) can also be translated as "wind." This wind or spirit also moves the prophet in Ezekiel 8:3; 11:1, 23; 43:5.

---

²⁸ᵇ When I saw it, I fell on my face, and I heard the voice of someone speaking.

2 ¹ He said to me: O mortal, stand up on your feet, and I will speak with you. ² And when he spoke to me, a spirit entered into me and set me on my feet; and I heard him speaking to me. ³ He said to me, Mortal, I am sending you to the people of Israel, to a nation of rebels who have rebelled against me; they and their ancestors have transgressed against me to this very day. ⁴ The descendants are impudent and stubborn. I am sending you to them, and you shall say to them, "Thus says the Lord GOD." ⁵ Whether they hear or refuse to hear (for they are a rebellious house), they shall know that there has been a prophet among them. ⁶ And you, O mortal, do not be afraid of them, and do not be afraid of their words, though briers and thorns surround you and you live among scorpions; do not be afraid of their words, and do not be dismayed at their looks, for they are a rebellious house. ⁷ You shall speak my words to them, whether they hear or refuse to hear; for they are a rebellious house.

⁸ But you, mortal, hear what I say to you; do not be rebellious like that rebellious house; open your mouth and eat what I give you. ⁹ I looked, and a hand was stretched out to me, and a written scroll was in it. ¹⁰ He spread it before me; it had writing on the front and on the back, and written on it were words of lamentation and mourning and woe.

3 ¹ He said to me, O mortal, eat what is offered to you; eat this scroll, and go, speak to the house of Israel. ² So I opened my mouth, and he gave me the scroll to eat. ³ He said to me, Mortal, eat this scroll that I give you and fill your stomach with it. Then I ate it; and in my mouth it was as sweet as honey.

⁴ He said to me: Mortal, go to the house of Israel and speak my very words to them. ⁵ For you are not sent to a people of obscure speech and difficult language, but to the house of Israel— ⁶ not to many peoples of obscure speech and difficult language, whose words you cannot understand. Surely, if I sent you to them, they would listen to you. ⁷ But the house of Israel will not listen to you, for they are not willing to listen to me; because all the house of Israel have a hard forehead and a stubborn heart. ⁸ See, I have made your face hard against their faces, and your forehead hard against their foreheads. ⁹ Like the hardest stone, harder than flint, I have made your forehead; do not fear them or be dismayed at their looks, for they are a rebellious house. ¹⁰ He said to me: Mortal, all my words that I shall speak to you receive in your heart and hear with your ears; ¹¹ then go to the exiles, to your people, and speak to them. Say to them, "Thus says the Lord GOD"; whether they hear or refuse to hear.

¹² Then the spirit lifted me up, and as the glory of the LORD rose from its place, I heard behind me the sound of loud rumbling; ¹³ it was the sound of the wings of the living creatures brushing against one another, and the sound of the wheels beside them, that sounded like a loud rumbling. ¹⁴ The spirit lifted me up and bore me away; I went in bitterness in the heat of my spirit, the hand of the LORD being strong upon me. ¹⁵ I came to the exiles at Tel-abib, who lived by the river Chebar. And I sat there among them, stunned, for seven days.

DISCUSSION QUESTIONS

1.   How do you understand the description of Ezekiel as a "mortal" or "son of man" in light of the book's emphasis on God's holiness and purity?
2.   What indications does this passage give about how the people will respond to Ezekiel's prophecy?
3.   Ezekiel's eating of the scroll is the first of many symbolic actions performed by the prophet. What message is being conveyed through this action?

God's judgment and promise: Ezekiel 11

CLOSE READING TIPS

▶ Note that the term "officials of the people" only occurs in postexilic literature. It often distinguishes lay leaders from priestly leaders.
▶ The "wicked counsel" in verse 2 might refer to the misguided plan of Zedekiah to join with Egypt against the Babylonian king Nebuchadnezzar.
▶ In verse 3, the "pot" is a sturdy metal cauldron where food was safely stored. This imagery symbolizes false confidence in the security and invulnerability of Jerusalem.
▶ Ezekiel's plea in verse 13 is responded to in a reassuring way in verses 14-21.
▶ Note that those who remained in the land claimed that it was the exiles who were bearing the brunt of God's punishment (verse 15). However, the prophet argues that the exiles are the true Israel.
▶ The fact that God has been a "sanctuary" to the exiles (verse 16) suggests that the glory of the LORD dwelled with the people into the Babylonian exile.
▶ Note that upon the return from exile, the land would need to be purified from detestable things and abominations (verse 18).
▶ The chariot-throne of the LORD departs from Jerusalem and settles upon the mountain east of the city, which is the Mount of Olives.

1 The spirit lifted me up and brought me to the east gate of the house of the LORD, which faces east. There, at the entrance of the gateway, were twenty-five men; among them I saw Jaazaniah son of Azzur, and Pelatiah son of Benaiah, officials of the people. ² He said to me, "Mortal, these are the men who devise iniquity and who give wicked counsel in this city; ³ they say, 'The time is not near to build houses; this city is the pot, and we are the meat.' ⁴ Therefore prophesy against them; prophesy, O mortal."

⁵ Then the spirit of the LORD fell upon me, and he said to me, "Say, Thus says the LORD: This is what you think, O house of Israel; I know the things that come into your mind. ⁶ You have killed many in this city, and have filled its streets with the slain. ⁷ Therefore thus says the Lord GOD: The slain whom you have placed within it are the meat, and this city is the pot; but you shall be taken out of it. ⁸ You have feared the sword; and I will bring the sword upon you, says the Lord GOD. ⁹ I will take you out of it and give you

over to the hands of foreigners, and execute judgments upon you. [10] You shall fall by the sword; I will judge you at the border of Israel. And you shall know that I am the LORD. [11] This city shall not be your pot, and you shall not be the meat inside it; I will judge you at the border of Israel. [12] Then you shall know that I am the LORD, whose statutes you have not followed, and whose ordinances you have not kept, but you have acted according to the ordinances of the nations that are around you."

[13] Now, while I was prophesying, Pelatiah son of Benaiah died. Then I fell down on my face, cried with a loud voice, and said, "Ah Lord GOD! will you make a full end of the remnant of Israel?"

[14] Then the word of the LORD came to me: [15] Mortal, your kinsfolk, your own kin, your fellow exiles, the whole house of Israel, all of them, are those of whom the inhabitants of Jerusalem have said, "They have gone far from the LORD; to us this land is given for a possession." [16] Therefore say: Thus says the Lord GOD: Though I removed them far away among the nations, and though I scattered them among the countries, yet I have been a sanctuary to them for a little while in the countries where they have gone. [17] Therefore say: Thus says the Lord GOD: I will gather you from the peoples, and assemble you out of the countries where you have been scattered, and I will give you the land of Israel. [18] When they come there, they will remove from it all its detestable things and all its abominations. [19] I will give them one heart, and put a new spirit within them; I will remove the heart of stone from their flesh and give them a heart of flesh, [20] so that they may follow my statutes and keep my ordinances and obey them. Then they shall be my people, and I will be their God. [21] But as for those whose heart goes after their detestable things and their abominations, I will bring their deeds upon their own heads, says the Lord GOD.

[22] Then the cherubim lifted up their wings, with the wheels beside them; and the glory of the God of Israel was above them. [23] And the glory of the LORD ascended from the middle of the city, and stopped on the mountain east of the city. [24] The spirit lifted me up and brought me in a vision by the spirit of God into Chaldea, to the exiles. Then the vision that I had seen left me. [25] And I told the exiles all the things that the LORD had shown me.

DISCUSSION QUESTIONS

1. What are the leaders, or "officials of the people" accused of in this passage?
2. Why do you think the people who remained in the land thought that the exiles were the ones bearing God's punishment?
3. In contrast, what is Ezekiel's perspective on the exiles? How does he support this view?
4. During the future restoration, what will enable the people to faithfully carry out God's statutes and ordinances?

Vision of a restored Jerusalem: Ezekiel 43:1-12; 47:1-12

CLOSE READING TIPS

▶ God's chariot-throne returns to the temple by the east gate (Ezek. 43:4). Earlier, the chariot-throne departs the temple through the east gate (Ezek. 10:18-19; 11:22-23).

▶ The "man" mentioned in Ezekiel 43:6 is the supernatural figure who had guided Ezekiel on his tour of the new temple (see Ezek. 40:3-4).

▶ The water flowing from the temple (Ezek. 47:1) does not refer to an actual river running through Jerusalem. Rather, this imagery reflects the motif of the temple as the deity's garden or paradise.

▶ Note that the warnings against defiling the temple especially focus on issues related to the kings and their encroachment on the temple.

▶ Note that the "sea of stagnant waters" (Ezek. 47:8) refers to the Dead Sea, a body of water whose high salt and mineral content makes it virtually uninhabitable.

▶ A "place for the spreading of nets" (Ezek. 47:10) indicates an area for excellent fishing.

43 ¹ Then he brought me to the gate, the gate facing east. ² And there, the glory of the God of Israel was coming from the east; the sound was like the sound of mighty waters; and the earth shone with his glory. ³ The vision I saw was like the vision that I had seen when he came to destroy the city, and like the vision that I had seen by the river Chebar; and I fell upon my face. ⁴ As the glory of the LORD entered the temple by the gate facing east, ⁵ the spirit lifted me up, and brought me into the inner court; and the glory of the LORD filled the temple.

⁶ While the man was standing beside me, I heard someone speaking to me out of the temple. ⁷ He said to me: Mortal, this is the place of my throne and the place for the soles of my feet, where I will reside among the people of Israel forever. The house of Israel shall no more defile my holy name, neither they nor their kings, by their whoring, and by the corpses of their kings at their death. ⁸ When they placed their threshold by my threshold and their doorposts beside my doorposts, with only a wall

between me and them, they were defiling my holy name by their abominations that they committed; therefore I have consumed them in my anger. ⁹ Now let them put away their idolatry and the corpses of their kings far from me, and I will reside among them forever.

¹⁰ As for you, mortal, describe the temple to the house of Israel, and let them measure the pattern; and let them be ashamed of their iniquities. ¹¹ When they are ashamed of all that they have done, make known to them the plan of the temple, its arrangement, its exits and its entrances, and its whole form—all its ordinances and its entire plan and all its laws; and write it down in their sight, so that they may observe and follow the entire plan and all its ordinances. ¹² This is the law of the temple: the whole territory on the top of the mountain all around shall be most holy. This is the law of the temple.

47 ¹ Then he brought me back to the entrance of the temple; there, water was flowing from below the threshold of the temple toward the east (for the

temple faced east); and the water was flowing down from below the south end of the threshold of the temple, south of the altar. ² Then he brought me out by way of the north gate, and led me around on the outside to the outer gate that faces toward the east; and the water was coming out on the south side.

³ Going on eastward with a cord in his hand, the man measured one thousand cubits, and then led me through the water; and it was ankle-deep. ⁴ Again he measured one thousand, and led me through the water; and it was knee-deep. Again he measured one thousand, and led me through the water; and it was up to the waist. ⁵ Again he measured one thousand, and it was a river that I could not cross, for the water had risen; it was deep enough to swim in, a river that could not be crossed. ⁶ He said to me, "Mortal, have you seen this?"

Then he led me back along the bank of the river. ⁷ As I came back, I saw on the bank of the river a great many trees on the one side and on the other. ⁸ He said to me, "This water flows toward the eastern region and goes down into the Arabah; and when it enters the sea, the sea of stagnant waters, the water will become fresh. ⁹ Wherever the river goes, every living creature that swarms will live, and there will be very many fish, once these waters reach there. It will become fresh; and everything will live where the river goes. ¹⁰ People will stand fishing beside the sea from En-gedi to En-eglaim; it will be a place for the spreading of nets; its fish will be of a great many kinds, like the fish of the Great Sea. ¹¹ But its swamps and marshes will not become fresh; they are to be left for salt. ¹² On the banks, on both sides of the river, there will grow all kinds of trees for food. Their leaves will not wither nor their fruit fail, but they will bear fresh fruit every month, because the water for them flows from the sanctuary. Their fruit will be for food, and their leaves for healing."

DISCUSSION QUESTIONS:

1. According to Ezekiel, why was defiling the temple (Ezek. 43:7) such a grave offense? What were its results?
2. What is the plan of the temple intended to do?
3. What effect does the river from the temple have on the land?
4. How does this imagery reinforce Ezekiel's view of the temple and its place in the New Jerusalem?
5. What parallels do you see between Ezekiel 47 and the description of the Garden of Eden in Genesis 2 or the description of the river of life in Revelation 22?

19

The Additions to the Book of Isaiah

Key Points

As a type of anthology, the book of Isaiah is a collection of loosely-related materials from different authors spanning several hundred years. The oracles that can be associated with the eighth-century prophet are located in chapters 1–39 and are commonly referred to as First Isaiah. The remaining chapters, which are typically referred to as Second Isaiah (40–55) and Third Isaiah (56–66), come from anonymous prophets sometime during or after the Babylonian exile. Yet even these divisions do not capture the full complexity of the book. For instance, the line between Second and Third Isaiah is not always clear (for examples, chapters 60–62) and discrete literary units, such as the "Isaiah Apocalypse" (chapters 24–27), are later inserted back into First Isaiah. Nevertheless, there are still notable continuities that run throughout the book, including an interest in Zion, the designation of God as "the Holy One" and "King" of Israel, and the frequent use of light imagery. The presence of these common themes reflects the fact that later editors, perhaps even Second Isaiah, had a hand in shaping the original oracles of Isaiah.

Delivered within a year or two after the fall of Babylon, Second Isaiah marks a turning point in the history of Hebrew prophecy. In these chapters, oracles of judgment against Israel and Judah generally give way to words of comfort and salvation. The return from exile is heralded as a "new exodus" through which God's past deliverance is reenacted in the present. By affirming God's universal power and mocking the cult statues of other deities, Second Isaiah offers one of the earliest articulations of monotheism in the biblical tradition. The most well-known feature of Second Isaiah are four the so-called "Servant Songs" (Isa. 42:1-4; 49:1-6; 50:4-9; and 52:13—53:12). Whether understood as a certain individual or as Israel itself, the figure in question is endowed with the spirit of YHWH, is given a mission to be a light to the nations, and is called to bear the iniquities of others. As with other prophets, the words of Second Isaiah were apparently met with some resistance. In order to reassure the people, chapters 49–55 promise that God will establish an everlasting covenant of peace as a fulfillment of the Davidic covenant.

One of the distinctive features of Third Isaiah is its glorious vision of the restoration of Jerusalem in chapters 60–62. Yet, many other oracles in Third Isaiah suggest that this restoration did not materialize as quickly or fully as expected. In addition, a tension is evident between the prophet and the Jerusalem priesthood. Not only does Third Isaiah critique aspects of the cult, but he is also at odds with the theological vision of the Zadokites insofar as he emphasizes open access, not exclusion, from the temple. Finally, it should be noted that certain elements of Third Isaiah, such as its expectation in a radical reversal of fortune (Isa. 65:13-14) and hope in a new creation (Isa. 65:17; 66:22), anticipate key elements of later Apocalyptic literature.

Key Terms

The new exodus A recurring theme in Second Isaiah, the new exodus describes the return from Babylon in terms similar to God's deliverance of Israel from Egypt. The prophet speaks of preparing the way of the LORD in the wilderness (Isa. 40:5), making a path in the sea (Isa. 43:16), and giving the people water in the desert (Isa. 43:18-20). In each case, the restoration of Jerusalem after the fall of Babylon is presented as a reenactment of the pattern of divine intervention found in the exodus story.

Monotheism Monotheism is the doctrine or belief that there is only one God. It should be distinguished from monolatry or henotheism, which asserts the supremacy of one god without denying the existence of others. While early forms of Israelite religion were henotheistic, Second Isaiah represents one of the first articulations of a truly monotheistic tradition (for examples, Isa. 40:10-11; 44:6; 46:9). This view is especially evident in the idol parodies as well as the emphasis that YHWH is a universal God, not just a national one.

Idol parodies Idol parodies refer to a series of mocking critiques of pagan cult statues in Second Isaiah (for example, Isa. 40:18-20; 41:6-7;

44:9-20). In these passages, the prophet ridicules idol worshipers and insists that cult statues are lifeless, senseless, and impotent objects, the mere work of human hands. These parodies are best understood in light of the use of cult statues as a symbol of the deity's presence in ancient Mesopotamian religions.

Vicarious suffering This concept, which is associated with the Servant Song in Isaiah 52:13—53:12, refers to the idea that the sufferings of one person can atone for the sin of another. In the context of Second Isaiah, the exaltation of the suffering servant leads onlookers to turn to YHWH out of their astonishment. This passage highlights a positive understanding of suffering, an idea that is expanded in the book of Daniel, the Dead Sea Scrolls, and Christian perspectives on the death of Jesus.

The Isaiah apocalypse Dubbed the "Isaiah apocalypse," chapters 24–27 are often singled out from the rest of the book of Isaiah due to their unique content. These chapters share much in common with later apocalyptic literature, especially in their interest in eschatology, cosmic destruction, the resurrection of the dead, and future judgment. Lacking explicit references to historical events or people, the Isaiah apocalypse draws on ancient myths to describe the future.

Key Personalities

King Cyrus II of Persia

Cyrus II was the king of Persia from 558–530 BCE and was the founder of the Achaemenid Empire. After consolidating his power in the heartland of Persia, Cyrus embarked on an aggressive campaign to expand his empire. He first moved against the Lydian kingdom before attacking King Nabonidus and the Babylonian Empire. By 539 BCE, Cyrus conquered Babylon, effectively gaining control over most of the Near Eastern world. While motivated more by shrewd political strategies than humanitarian concerns, Cyrus is known to have implemented a policy that was generally favorable to subject people. For instance, an inscription on a clay barrel known as the Cyrus Cylinder recounts how the Persian king allowed for the restoration of Babylonian gods to their shrines. According to Ezra 1:2-4 and 2 Chronicles 36:22, Cyrus initiated a similar policy toward the Judeans. Even though the authenticity of the document referred to by Ezra and Chronicles has been questioned, it is nevertheless the case that Cyrus authorized the Judeans to return to Jerusalem and to rebuild their temple. From the vantage point of Second Isaiah, Cyrus was God's "shepherd" (Isa. 44:28) and God's "anointed" (Isa. 45:1). Some have suggested that the figure referenced in the first Servant Song (Isa. 42:1-4) is Cyrus. In extra-biblical sources, Cyrus became somewhat of a legendary figure. The Greek writer Xenophon and the Jewish historian Josephus both praise this Persian king for establishing one of the most formidable empires known in the ancient world.

The servant of the LORD

The Hebrew Bible describes many figures as "servants" of God, including Abraham, Moses, Joshua, David, and Hezekiah. However, in Second Isaiah, four poems—known as the Servant Songs—center around the theme of "the servant of the LORD." The servant is variously described as: one who is humble, does no violence, and brings justice (Isa. 42:1-4); one called before birth to be God's instrument to restore Israel and to be a light to the nation (Isa. 49:1-6); a teacher who listens carefully to God's word and is faithful despite insult and injury (Isa. 50:4-9); and, perhaps most famously, one who suffers on behalf of the sins and transgressions of others (Isa. 52:13—53:12). The identity of the servant is widely debated in each of these cases, with suggestions including Cyrus, a new Moses, Jeremiah, the prophet behind Second Isaiah, or, in early Christian tradition, Jesus. In certain instances, it is possible to understand the servant as an individual, especially in cases where this figure is given a mission to Israel or the nations. However, many cases allow, if not demand, a collective sense of the term in which exiled Israel is the servant. For instance, God's servant is directly identified as Israel or Jacob (Isa. 41:8; 44:1-2; 44:21; 45:4). It is also possible that Israel is restored by virtue of being a servant to God. Alternatively, the servant may be an idealized, faithful remnant of Israel, called by God to help liberate (or suffer on behalf of) the rest of the people. Even in the last poem it is possible that the servant is Israel, albeit through a metaphor that pictures the nation as a suffering individual. Nevertheless, it is important to note that there is some degree of ambiguity in identifying the servant in each of these four poems.

Questions for Study and Discussion

1. The Servant Songs of Second Isaiah (Isa. 42:1-4; 49:1-6; 50:4-9; and 52:13—53:12) have received a great deal of attention. One of the most perplexing questions these texts raise, however, concerns the identity of the servant or servants. Who is the servant? What are some of the options? How might one go about arguing for a given position? (Responding to this question is easier if one has read the Servant Songs themselves, alongside the textbook's comments.)

2. Third Isaiah imagines a glorious future in which the heavens and earth are completely remade, with Jerusalem and YHWH's chosen people at the center of the cosmos. What is your response to this vision of the future? What problems does it try to solve? What problems does it create?

3. Isaiah 24–27 utilizes older mythological material, both from Israel's own texts and from the mythological collections of other Ancient Near Eastern cultures. What are some of these borrowed motifs and how does this section of Isaiah rework them?

Primary Text

Ezra 1:2-4 and the Cyrus Cylinder

Source: Irving Finkel, *Translation of the text on the Cyrus Cylinder*, (The British Museum, 2014), https://www.britishmuseum.org/explore/highlights/articles/c/cyrus_cylinder_-_translation.aspx

---

CLOSE READING TIPS:

▶ Cyrus reviews the history of his rise to power by describing how the gods of Babylon (in particular, Marduk) acted to save their city in response to the evil deeds carried out by the Babylonian king Nabonidus.

▶ Note how Marduk selects and empowers Cyrus, here described as the deity's "friend."

▶ Cyrus claims that Marduk enabled him to enter Babylon without resistance. This is likely because Persian forces had already secured the city by the time the king arrived.

▶ Note how the Babylonians respond to Cyrus. While this is surely hyperbole, Nabonidus was unpopular and had many detractors, especially among the Babylonian priests.

▶ Cyrus is depicted as worshiping Marduk, though the chief Persian god was Ahura Mazda.

▶ Note that Cyrus provides for the return of the gods (in the form of cult statues) to their shrines.

▶ In Ezra 1, Cyrus allows the exile to return to Jerusalem in order to rebuild the temple, which had been destroyed by the Babylonians almost fifty years earlier.

THE CYRUS CYLINDER

[When ... Mar]duk, king of the whole of heaven and earth, the .... who, in his ..., lays waste his.......

[...]
broad? in intelligence, ... who inspects (?) the wor]ld quarters (regions)

[...….]   his [first]born (=Belshazzar), a low person, was put in charge of his country,

but [..
........] he set [a (...) counter]feit over them.

He ma[de] a counterfeit of Esagil, [and ......….......]... for Ur and the rest of the cult-cities.

Rites inappropriate to them, [impure] fo[od-offerings …..] disrespectful [...] were daily gabbled, and, as an insult,

he brought the daily offerings to a halt; he inter[fered with the rites and] instituted […......] within the sanctuaries. In his mind, reverential fear of Marduk, king of the gods, came to an end.

He did yet more evil to his city every day; . . . his [people …................], he brought ruin on them all by a yoke without relief.

Enlil-of-the-gods became extremely angry at their complaints, and [...] their territory. The gods who lived within them left their shrines,

angry that he had made (them) enter into Shuanna (Babylon). Ex[alted Marduk, Enlil-of-the-Go]ds, relented. He changed his mind about all the settlements whose sanctuaries were in ruins,

and the population of the land of Sumer and Akkad who had become like corpses, and took pity on them. He inspected and checked all the countries,

seeking for the upright king of his choice. He took the hand of Cyrus, king of the city of Anshan, and called him by his name, proclaiming him aloud for the kingship over all of everything.

He made the land of Guti and all the Median troops prostrate themselves at his feet, while he shepherded in justice and righteousness the black-headed people

whom he had put under his care. Marduk, the great lord, who nurtures his people, saw with pleasure his fine deeds and true heart,

and ordered that he should go to Babylon. He had him take the road to Tintir (Babylon), and, like a friend and companion, he walked at his side.

His vast troops whose number, like the water in a river, could not be counted, were marching fully-armed at his side.

He had him enter without fighting or battle right into Shuanna; he saved his city Babylon from hardship. He handed over to him Nabonidus, the king who did not fear him.

All the people of Tintir, of all Sumer and Akkad, nobles and governors, bowed down before him and kissed his feet, rejoicing over his kingship and their faces shone.

The lord through whose help all were rescued from death and who saved them all from distress and hardship, they blessed him sweetly and praised his name.

I am Cyrus, king of the universe, the great king, the powerful king, king of Babylon, king of Sumer and Akkad, king of the four quarters of the world,

son of Cambyses, the great king, king of the city of Anshan, grandson of Cyrus, the great king, ki[ng of the ci]ty of Anshan, descendant of Teispes, the great king, king of the city of Anshan,

the perpetual seed of kingship, whose reign Bel (Marduk)and Nabu love, and with whose kingship, to their joy, they concern themselves. When I went as harbinger of peace i[nt]o Babylon

I founded my sovereign residence within the palace amid celebration and rejoicing. Marduk, the great lord, bestowed on me as my destiny the great magnanimity of one who loves Babylon, and I every day sought him out in awe.

My vast troops were marching peaceably in Babylon, and the whole of [Sumer] and Akkad had nothing to fear.

I sought the safety of the city of Babylon and all its sanctuaries. As for the population of Babylon [..., w]ho as if without div[ine intention] had endured a yoke not decreed for them,

I soothed their weariness; I freed them from their bonds(?). Marduk, the great lord, rejoiced at [my good] deeds,

and he pronounced a sweet blessing over me, Cyrus, the king who fears him, and over Cambyses, the son [my] issue, [and over] my all my troops,

that we might live happily in his presence, in well-being. At his exalted command, all kings who sit on thrones,

from every quarter, from the Upper Sea to the Lower Sea, those who inhabit [remote distric]ts (and) the kings of the land of Amurru who live in tents, all of them,

brought their weighty tribute into Shuanna, and kissed my feet. From [Shuanna] I sent back to their places to the city of Ashur and Susa,

Akkad, the land of Eshnunna, the city of Zamban, the city of Meturnu, Der, as far as the border of the land of Guti—the sanctuaries across the river Tigris—whose shrines had earlier become dilapidated,

the gods who lived therein, and made permanent sanctuaries for them. I collected together all of their people and returned them to their settlements,

and the gods of the land of Sumer and Akkad which Nabonidus—to the fury of the lord of the

gods—had brought into Shuanna, at the command of Marduk, the great lord,

I returned them unharmed to their cells, in the sanctuaries that make them happy. May all the gods that I returned to their sanctuaries,

every day before Bel and Nabu, ask for a long life for me, and mention my good deeds, and say to Marduk, my lord, this: "Cyrus, the king who fears you, and Cambyses his son,

may they be the provisioners of our shrines until distant (?) days, and the population of Babylon call blessings on my kingship. I have enabled all the lands to live in peace."

Every day I increased by [… ge]ese, two ducks and ten pigeons the [former offerings] of geese, ducks and pigeons.

I strove to strengthen the defences of the wall Imgur-Enlil, the great wall of Babylon,

and [I completed] the quay of baked brick on the bank of the moat which an earlier king had bu[ilt but not com]pleted its work.

[I …… which did not surround the city] outside, which no earlier king had built, his workforce, the levee [from his land, in/int]o Shuanna.

[… ………………………………………………………… with bitum]en and baked brick I built anew, and [completed] its [work].

[…………………………………………………] great [doors of cedar wood] with bronze cladding,

[and I installed] all their doors, threshold slabs and door fittings with copper parts. [………………]. I saw within it an inscription of Ashurbanipal, a king who preceded me;

[……………………………………] in its place. May Marduk, the great lord, present to me as a gift a long life and the fullness of age, [a secure throne and an enduring rei]gn, [and may I ...... in] your heart forever.

 a. [Written and check]ed [from a...]; (this) tablet (is) of

 b. Qishti-Marduk, son of [...].

Ezra 1:1-4

[1] In the first year of King Cyrus of Persia, in order that the word of the LORD by the mouth of Jeremiah might be accomplished, the LORD stirred up the spirit of King Cyrus of Persia so that he sent a herald throughout all his kingdom, and also in a written edict declared:

[2] "Thus says King Cyrus of Persia: The LORD, the God of heaven, has given me all the kingdoms of the earth, and he has charged me to build him a house at Jerusalem in Judah. [3] Any of those among you who are of his people—may their God be with them! —are now permitted to go up to Jerusalem in Judah, and rebuild the house of the LORD, the God of Israel—he is the God who is in Jerusalem; [4] and let all survivors, in whatever place they reside, be assisted by the people of their place with silver and gold, with goods and with animals, besides freewill offerings for the house of God in Jerusalem."

DISCUSSION QUESTIONS:

1. Where do you see evidence of Cyrus's benevolent attitude to conquered people in both of these texts?
2. Why do you think Cyrus boasts of being commissioned by foreign deities to overthrow Babylon and to rebuild the Jerusalem temple?
3. In the Cyrus Cylinder, what does the king request from the gods in return for restoring them to their sanctuaries?
4. Do you think these edicts reflect humanitarian concerns or political savvy (or both)? Where do you see evidence of each?

Isaiah 40:1-31 and Luke 3:1-6

CLOSE READING TIPS:

▶ Isaiah 40:1-11 functions as a renewal of the prophet's commission to speak on behalf of the LORD.

▶ Note that verse 2 suggests that the exile was a punishment for Israel's sin, but that this punishment was excessive.

▶ The way in the wilderness referenced in verse 3 evokes a tradition in which the people traveled along the King's Highway in the Transjordan on their way back to Israel (see Num. 20:17; 21:22; Deut. 2:8).

▶ The eternality of God's word is contrasted with the ephemeral nature of humanity (verses 6-8).

▶ The imagery of YHWH as a shepherd draws on traditional royal imagery in which kings care for their "flock," or people (verse 11).

▶ Note that the series of rhetorical questions in verses 12-14 are meant to highlight God's power and wisdom. See also verses 21-24 for a similar technique.

> ▶ Mesopotamian texts specify that divine cult statues were made from special wood selected by the gods (verse 19).
> ▶ The Hebrew word translated as "created" (*bara'*) in verse 26 is primarily restricted to Genesis 1 and other texts in Second Isaiah.
> ▶ Waiting for God is a common theme that runs through much of the book of Isaiah (Isa. 8:17; 30:18; 49:23; 64:4).
> ▶ Earlier in Luke, the birth of John the Baptist is described (Luke 1:5-20). It is said that John will be endowed with the spirit and power of Elijah and that he will turn the hearts of the people to God.

Isaiah 40:1-31

¹ Comfort, O comfort my people,
    says your God.
² Speak tenderly to Jerusalem,
    and cry to her
that she has served her term,
    that her penalty is paid,
that she has received from the LORD's hand
    double for all her sins.

³ A voice cries out:
"In the wilderness prepare the way of the
    LORD,
make straight in the desert a highway for our
    God.
⁴ Every valley shall be lifted up,
    and every mountain and hill be made low;
the uneven ground shall become level,
    and the rough places a plain.
⁵ Then the glory of the Lord shall be revealed,
    and all people shall see it together,
    for the mouth of the LORD has spoken."

⁶ A voice says, "Cry out!"
    And I said, "What shall I cry?"
All people are grass,
    their constancy is like the flower of the
        field.

⁷ The grass withers, the flower fades,
    when the breath of the LORD blows upon it;
    surely the people are grass.
⁸ The grass withers, the flower fades;
    but the word of our God will stand forever.
⁹ Get you up to a high mountain,
    O Zion, herald of good tidings;
lift up your voice with strength,
    O Jerusalem, herald of good tidings,
    lift it up, do not fear;
say to the cities of Judah,
    "Here is your God!"
¹⁰ See, the Lord GOD comes with might,
    and his arm rules for him;
his reward is with him,
    and his recompense before him.
¹¹ He will feed his flock like a shepherd;
    he will gather the lambs in his arms,
and carry them in his bosom,
    and gently lead the mother sheep.

¹² Who has measured the waters in the hollow
    of his hand
    and marked off the heavens with a span,
enclosed the dust of the earth in a measure,
    and weighed the mountains in scales
    and the hills in a balance?
¹³ Who has directed the spirit of the LORD,

or as his counselor has instructed him?

¹⁴ Whom did he consult for his enlightenment,
and who taught him the path of justice?
Who taught him knowledge,
and showed him the way of understanding?

¹⁵ Even the nations are like a drop from a
bucket,
and are accounted as dust on the scales;
see, he takes up the isles like fine dust.

¹⁶ Lebanon would not provide fuel enough,
nor are its animals enough for a burnt
offering.

¹⁷ All the nations are as nothing before him;
they are accounted by him as less than
nothing and emptiness.

¹⁸ To whom then will you liken God,
or what likeness compare with him?

¹⁹ An idol? —A workman casts it,
and a goldsmith overlays it with gold,
and casts for it silver chains.

²⁰ As a gift one chooses mulberry wood
—wood that will not rot—
then seeks out a skilled artisan
to set up an image that will not topple.

²¹ Have you not known? Have you not heard?
Has it not been told you from the
beginning?
Have you not understood from the
foundations of the earth?

²² It is he who sits above the circle of the earth,
and its inhabitants are like grasshoppers;
who stretches out the heavens like a curtain,
and spreads them like a tent to live in;

²³ who brings princes to naught,
and makes the rulers of the earth as
nothing.

²⁴ Scarcely are they planted, scarcely sown,

scarcely has their stem taken root in the
earth,
when he blows upon them, and they wither,
and the tempest carries them off like
stubble.

²⁵ To whom then will you compare me,
or who is my equal? says the Holy One.

²⁶ Lift up your eyes on high and see:
Who created these?
He who brings out their host and numbers
them,
calling them all by name;
because he is great in strength,
mighty in power,
not one is missing.

²⁷ Why do you say, O Jacob,
and speak, O Israel,
"My way is hidden from the LORD,
and my right is disregarded by my God"?

²⁸ Have you not known? Have you not heard?
The LORD is the everlasting God,
the Creator of the ends of the earth.
He does not faint or grow weary;
his understanding is unsearchable.

²⁹ He gives power to the faint,
and strengthens the powerless.

³⁰ Even youths will faint and be weary,
and the young will fall exhausted;

³¹ but those who wait for the Lord shall renew
their strength,
they shall mount up with wings like eagles,
they shall run and not be weary,
they shall walk and not faint.

LUKE 3:1-6

¹ In the fifteenth year of the reign of Emperor
Tiberius, when Pontius Pilate was governor of Judea,

and Herod was ruler of Galilee, and his brother Philip ruler of the region of Ituraea and Trachonitis, and Lysanias ruler of Abilene, ² during the high priesthood of Annas and Caiaphas, the word of God came to John son of Zechariah in the wilderness. ³ He went into all the region around the Jordan, proclaiming a baptism of repentance for the forgiveness of sins,

⁴ as it is written in the book of the words of the prophet Isaiah,

"The voice of one crying out in the wilderness:
  'Prepare the way of the Lord,
make his paths straight.
⁵ Every valley shall be filled,
    and every mountain and hill shall be made low,
and the crooked shall be made straight,
    and the rough ways made smooth;
⁶ and all flesh shall see the salvation of God.' "

DISCUSSION QUESTIONS

1. In drawing on the words of Second Isaiah, who or what does the prophecy in Luke's gospel refer to?
2. Carefully compare the wording of Luke 3:4 and Isaiah 40:3. What differences do you notice and how do these differences affect the interpretation of the prophecy?
3. Where in Isaiah 40 do you see evidence of Second Isaiah's monotheistic perspective?
4. What is the basis of Second Isaiah's critique of idols in verses 18-20?
5. Throughout Isaiah 40, YHWH is presented as a cosmic deity rather than a national deity. Why is this portrayal significant in light of the historical context of Second Isaiah?

Isaiah 66

CLOSE READING TIPS

▸ Note that Isaiah downplays the centrality of the Jerusalem temple, emphasizing that heaven is God's true dwelling place (verse 1).

▸ One interpretation of the syntax in verse 3 is that cultic practices were equivalent to murder or profanity. In another interpretation, the one who sacrifices is also the one who commits the moral offenses.

▸ In verses 6-9, God's restoration of the righteous and punishment of the wicked are as immanent and natural as a woman in labor giving birth to a child.

▸ Note that fire is associated with theophany and divine judgments (verses 15-16) in other parts of Isaiah as well (Isa. 26:11; 29:5-6; 30:27, 33; 31:9; 33:12, 14; 34:10).

▸ Eating the flesh of pigs in verse 17 would have been a horrific violation of Israelite dietary restrictions. As in Isaiah 65:4, the reference here may function as an intentional exaggeration that highlights the seriousness of the abominations targeted by the prophet.

▸ Note the universal scope of the prophet's vision of restoration (verses 18-20).

▸ The new creation pictured in verses 22-23 is picked up on in the last chapters of the book of Revelation.

---

¹ Thus says the LORD:
Heaven is my throne
    and the earth is my footstool;
what is the house that you would build for me,
    and what is my resting place?
² All these things my hand has made,
    and so all these things are mine,
        says the LORD.
But this is the one to whom I will look,
    to the humble and contrite in spirit,
    who trembles at my word.

³ Whoever slaughters an ox is like one who kills
    a human being;
    whoever sacrifices a lamb, like one who
        breaks a dog's neck;
whoever presents a grain offering, like one who
    offers swine's blood;
    whoever makes a memorial offering of
        frankincense, like one who blesses an
        idol.
These have chosen their own ways,
    and in their abominations they take
        delight;
⁴ I also will choose to mock them,
    and bring upon them what they fear;
because, when I called, no one answered,
    when I spoke, they did not listen;
but they did what was evil in my sight,
    and chose what did not please me.

⁵ Hear the word of the LORD,
    you who tremble at his word:
Your own people who hate you
    and reject you for my name's sake
have said, "Let the LORD be glorified,
    so that we may see your joy";
    but it is they who shall be put to shame.

⁶ Listen, an uproar from the city!

A voice from the temple!
The voice of the LORD,
    dealing retribution to his enemies!

⁷ Before she was in labor
    she gave birth;
before her pain came upon her
    she delivered a son.
⁸ Who has heard of such a thing?
    Who has seen such things?
Shall a land be born in one day?
    Shall a nation be delivered in one
        moment?
Yet as soon as Zion was in labor
    she delivered her children.
⁹ Shall I open the womb and not deliver?
    says the LORD;
shall I, the one who delivers, shut the womb?
    says your God.

¹⁰ Rejoice with Jerusalem, and be glad for her,
    all you who love her;
rejoice with her in joy,
    all you who mourn over her—
¹¹ that you may nurse and be satisfied
    from her consoling breast;
that you may drink deeply with delight
    from her glorious bosom.

¹² For thus says the LORD:
I will extend prosperity to her like a river,
    and the wealth of the nations like an over-
        flowing stream;
and you shall nurse and be carried on her arm,
    and dandled on her knees.
¹³ As a mother comforts her child,
    so I will comfort you;
    you shall be comforted in Jerusalem.

¹⁴ You shall see, and your heart shall rejoice;

your bodies shall flourish like the grass;
and it shall be known that the hand of the
LORD is with his servants,
and his indignation is against his enemies.
[15] For the LORD will come in fire,
and his chariots like the whirlwind,
to pay back his anger in fury,
and his rebuke in flames of fire.
[16] For by fire will the LORD execute judgment,
and by his sword, on all flesh;
and those slain by the LORD shall be
many.

[17] Those who sanctify and purify themselves to go into the gardens, following the one in the center, eating the flesh of pigs, vermin, and rodents, shall come to an end together, says the LORD.

[18] For I know their works and their thoughts, and I am coming to gather all nations and tongues; and they shall come and shall see my glory, [19] and I will set a sign among them. From them I will send survivors to the nations, to Tarshish, Put, and Lud—which draw the bow—to Tubal and Javan, to the coastlands far away that have not heard of my fame or seen my glory; and they shall declare my glory among the nations. [20] They shall bring all your kindred from all the nations as an offering to the LORD, on horses, and in chariots, and in litters, and on mules, and on dromedaries, to my holy mountain Jerusalem, says the LORD, just as the Israelites bring a grain offering in a clean vessel to the house of the LORD. [21] And I will also take some of them as priests and as Levites, says the LORD.

[22] For as the new heavens and the new earth,
which I will make,
shall remain before me, says the Lord;
so shall your descendants and your name
remain.
[23] From new moon to new moon,
and from sabbath to sabbath,
all flesh shall come to worship before me,
says the LORD.

[24] And they shall go out and look at the dead bodies of the people who have rebelled against me; for their worm shall not die, their fire shall not be quenched, and they shall be an abhorrence to all flesh.

DISCUSSION QUESTIONS

1. How would you characterize the prophet's attitude toward the priesthood or cultic system in this passage?
2. What other biblical prophets offer a similar perspective on priests and sacrifices?
3. Why do think imagery about rejoicing (verse 14) is juxtaposed so closely with imagery about judgment (verses 15-16)? Who is each message intended for?
4. Where in this passage do you see evidence of Third Isaiah's emphasis on the universal scope of restoration?

20

Postexilic Prophecy: Haggai, Zechariah, Malachi, Joel

Key Points

Concluding the survey of the Minor Prophets, this chapter explores Haggai, Zechariah, Malachi, Joel, and Jonah. These books were written during the postexilic period and cover a wide range of issues, including the rebuilding of the temple, the dual leadership (or dyarchy) of the high priest and governor, messianic hope, critique of improper worship, and the repentance of foreigners. The Minor Prophets have long been grouped together as one book. Though arranged in a roughly chronological fashion, the order of the books in the Hebrew and Greek versions differ slightly. The most important common feature of the book of the Twelve Prophets are themes and imagery related to eschatology, or the end times.

Haggai and Zechariah 1–8 (or "First Zechariah") are both set during the early years of Darius's reign (c. 520-515 BCE). A considerable amount of time had passed since the initial return under Cyrus but the restoration was far from complete. The prophet Haggai indicts the people for living in lavish houses while the temple still lay in ruins (Hag. 1:1-11). Haggai promises that the splendor of new temple will surpass that of the old temple (Hag. 1:15b—2:9). Haggai ends with the rededication of the temple and the prediction that Zerubbabel would achieve royal status as God's "signet ring" (Hag. 2:23).

The revelation of First Zechariah comes in the form of visions seen at night, each of which is interpreted by an angel. These chapters envision divine horsemen patrolling the earth (Zech. 1), a city walled by fire (Zech. 2), the high priest and "the Satan" (Zech. 3), a gold lampstand (Zech. 4), a flying scroll (Zech. 5), and the Branch (Zech. 6). Like Second Isaiah, First Zechariah views Persia in a positive light and even imagines the cosmic rule of YHWH in terms similar to the earthly reign of Darius.

The book of Malachi and the last six chapters of Zechariah (or "Second Zechariah") likely represent anonymous oracles that were only later added to the book of the Twelve Prophets. In fact, the division between this material is unclear since the heading "an oracle" is repeated in Zechariah 9:1; 12:1 and Malachi 1:1. The content of Second Zechariah is difficult to locate historically, and in general its "proto-apocalyptic" oracles look beyond history to a time when the kingship of God would be fully revealed. Malachi consists of six speeches or disputations followed by two appendices. Three interpretive issues are of note: 1) the concern for the integrity of worship in Malachi 2:4-9; 2) the meaning of the difficult passage on divorce in Malachi 2:10-16; and 3) the identity of the messenger of the covenant in Malachi 2:17-3:5.

In the Hebrew canon, Joel is placed second among the Twelve Prophets due to its thematic correspondence with Amos. However, it is probably the last of the Minor Prophets to be written. The most striking features of Joel are the description of the plague of locusts (Joel 1:1—2:17) and the eschatological prediction that the Spirit of the LORD will be poured out on all people (Joel 2:28-29). The book of Jonah is unique among the Minor Prophets not only because it consists of a narrative rather than a series of oracles, but also because of its compassionate portrayal of a foreign people. The surprising responsiveness of the Ninevites to God's message highlights the stubbornness of Israel and the reluctance of the prophet.

Key Terms

Nineveh   Nineveh was the capital of the Assyrian Empire and was destroyed by a combined force of Medes and Babylonians in 612 BCE. Jonah is sent to Nineveh, but instead flees in the opposite direction to Tarshish (Spain). When Jonah eventually delivers God's message, the Ninevites immediately believe the prophet and repent Jonah is resentful of the compassion God extends to the Ninevites.

Signet ring   Much like a notary public's stamp today, signet rings were used in the ancient world to authenticate documents by pressing the design of the ring into wet clay or wax. By extension, the king's signet ring came to symbolize his authority. In Haggai's last oracle, the prophet declares that god will make Zerubbabel "like a signet ring" (Hag. 2:23). While this statement clearly indicates that God will exercise his authority through Zerubbabel, it is uncertain whether Haggai pictures Zerubbabel as the restorer of the Davidic kingship.

Branch   The word Branch (Heb.: *tsemach*) refers to a future Davidic ruler who is associated with the restoration of postexilic Israel. In Jeremiah 23:5 and 33:5, the figure described as a "righteous Branch" is left unspecified. However, in the context of Zechariah 3:8 and 6:12, Branch clearly refers to the governor Zerubbabel. This term came to have messianic overtones, though its use in a third century Phoenician inscription suggests its basic meaning is that of a legitimate heir to the throne.

Dyarchy   A dyarchy is a government by two independent authorities. This model of leadership is evident in postexilic Israel, where the high priest and governor shared power. This concept is implicit in the imagery of "two sons of oil" in Zechariah 4:14 as well as the description of a priest by the throne of the royal figure, or Branch, in Zechariah 6:13. This new order is presupposed in the Dead Sea Scrolls, which speak of two Messiahs—one from the priestly line of Aaron and the other from Israel.

Eschatology   Eschatology, which comes from a Greek word (*eschatos*) meaning "last," concerns teachings about the end times. Directed beyond the bounds of history, eschatological hope envisions a future time when God will redeem Israel, bring judgment against the wicked, restore the land and temple, and gather the nations to Jerusalem. Eschatological language plays a major role in the book of the Twelve Prophets and later becomes a dominant focus of Jewish apocalyptic texts and early Christian literature.

Key Personalities

Darius I of Persia

Darius I was the king of Persia from 522–486 BCE. Belonging to a branch of the Achaemenid family, he came to power only after Cambyses, Cyrus II's son, died suddenly without a clear heir to the throne. With the support of several key leaders, Darius conspired to overthrow a rival named Gaumata. These events trigged great tumult throughout the empire, and as such, Darius spent the greater part of his first year as king suppressing rebellions. Darius then proceeded with an aggressive plan of expansion aimed especially at the western peripheries of his empire. Throughout his reign, Darius relied on savvy as much as brute force. He is known for organizing the Persian empire into twenty administrative units, or satrapies, for the purposes of regulating tax collection and maintaining local control. The postexilic community of Yehud was in a satrapy called Eber-Nari ("Beyond the River"). According to the biblical record, Darius was supportive of the temple rebuilding project even in the face of local opposition (Ezra 5–6). The prophets Zechariah and Haggai were both active during the early years of Darius's reign. While Zerubbabel and Joshua certainly had some autonomy as leaders of Yehud, their power was derived from the local satrap, and ultimately, Darius himself. Darius is most well known for massive building campaigns at Susa and Persepolis and the introduction of imperial coinage, which featured a royal figure as an armed archer. The imagery on these coins reflects a larger artistic program instituted to communicate messages about imperial power and control.

Joshua the high priest

Joshua son of Jehozadak was the high priest in the postexilic period who supervised the rebuilding of the temple. He was born in Babylon, but later returned to Judah with other exiles around 522 BCE. Under the new reality of Persian control, the high priest was no longer subordinate to the royal figure. By virtue of sharing leadership with the governor Zerubbabel, Joshua came to possess prominence and authority unprecedented for preexilic priests. The book of Haggai presumes this dyarchic model of leadership, though the final oracle (Hag. 2:23) might suggest that Zerubbabel was seen as a slightly more important figure. Zechariah's vision in Zechariah 3 pictures Joshua in a divine assembly where his filthy clothes are replaced with festal garments. This purification ceremony prepares Joshua to take up the office of high priest after the defilement of the exile. Zechariah's vision of the "two sons of oil" in Zechariah 4 confirms the dyarchic model of leadership. In Zechariah 6:9, the prophet is told to crown the high priest. However, since the following oracle seems to apply more closely to Zerubbabel, it has been suggested that the original text of Zechariah 6 made reference to two crowns—one for Joshua and the other for Zerubbabel. The most detailed narrative about this high priest is found in Ezra-Nehemiah, where his name is spelled Jeshua. In this book, the high priest and governor are represented on equal footing, with both working to reestablish the cult. Though he is not mentioned in Chronicles, his father's genealogy is traced through Eleazar to Aaron (1 Chron. 6:1-15).

Questions for Study and Discussion

1. Prophecy seems to taper off in the postexilic period, especially in the time after Haggai and Zechariah. To whom does revelatory authority shift? What sorts of changes—social, economic, religious or otherwise—might account for this important shift in Israelite religion?
2. Respond to the following claim: The book of Zechariah contains a clear reference to the Devil—Satan—the same evil figure who is known from the New Testament.
3. Malachi 1:11 makes the following claim: "from the rising of the sun to its setting my name is great among the nations, and in every place incense is offered to my name, and a pure offering." Within the larger context of the Hebrew Bible, why is this such an astonishing claim? What, in your view, could have given rise to such a statement?
4. What is Malachi's view of divorce, and how does it relate to other biblical texts on divorce?
5. The book of Jonah is full of comic material. Give some examples from your reaching of both the chapter and the book itself. Are there other biblical stories or books you are familiar with that also contain humorous material?

Primary Text

Haggai 1:1-15a

> **CLOSE READING TIPS**
>
> ▶ The first day of the month (verse 1) was typically a time for special rituals; though here this reference is ironic because the place for such rituals—the temple—still lay in ruins.
> ▶ The reason for the delay in rebuilding the temple is unclear (verse 2). Based on Jeremiah's prophecy about a seventy year period in which Jerusalem would be desolate (Jer. 25:11; 29:10), some may have believed that the time for rebuilding had not yet come.
> ▶ "Paneled houses" (verse 4) refers to lavish accommodations. Solomon's palace was paneled with cedar (1 Kgs. 7:7).
> ▶ Note that Haggai draws on a mythological idea that establishing a deity's temple would bring abundant fertility to the land (verses 9-11). This is highlighted by a wordplay between the Hebrew term for ruins (ⱨareb) and drought (ⱨoreb).
> ▶ Note that the expression "I am with you" (verse 13) is often used in oracles of salvation.

[1] In the second year of King Darius, in the sixth month, on the first day of the month, the word of the LORD came by the prophet Haggai to Zerubbabel son of Shealtiel, governor of Judah, and to Joshua son of Jehozadak, the high priest: [2] Thus says the LORD of hosts: These people say the time has not yet come to rebuild the LORD's house. [3] Then the word of the LORD came by the prophet Haggai, saying: [4] Is it a time for you yourselves to live in your paneled houses, while this house lies in ruins? [5] Now therefore thus says the LORD of hosts: Consider how you have fared. [6] You have sown much, and harvested little; you eat, but you never have enough; you drink, but you never have your fill; you clothe yourselves, but no one is warm; and you that earn wages earn wages to put them into a bag with holes.

[7] Thus says the LORD of hosts: Consider how you have fared. [8] Go up to the hills and bring wood and build the house, so that I may take pleasure in it and be honored, says the LORD. [9] You have looked for much, and, lo, it came to little; and when you brought it home, I blew it away. Why? says the LORD of hosts. Because my house lies in ruins, while all of you hurry off to your own houses. [10] Therefore the heavens above you have withheld the dew, and the earth has withheld its produce. [11] And I have called for a drought on the land and the hills, on the grain, the new wine, the oil, on what the soil produces, on human beings and animals, and on all their labors.

[12] Then Zerubbabel son of Shealtiel, and Joshua son of Jehozadak, the high priest, with all the remnant of the people, obeyed the voice of the LORD their God, and the words of the prophet Haggai, as the LORD their God had sent him; and the people feared the LORD. [13] Then Haggai, the messenger of the LORD, spoke to the people with the LORD's message, saying, I am with you, says the LORD. [14] And the LORD stirred up the spirit of Zerubbabel son of Shealtiel, governor of Judah, and the spirit of Joshua son of Jehozadak, the high priest, and the spirit of all the remnant of the people; and they came and worked on the house of the LORD of hosts, their God, [15] on the twenty-fourth day of the month, in the sixth month.

DISCUSSION QUESTIONS

1. From Haggai's perspective, why should rebuilding the temple be the top priority for the community?
2. How do the people respond to Haggai's message? Is this like or not like how people respond to many earlier prophets?
3. In what other prophetic books do you find a close connection between the temple cult and agricultural abundance or the restoration of the land?
4. How does this passage characterize the relationship between the governor Zerubbabel and the high priest Joshua?

Zechariah 3:1-10

CLOSE READING TIPS

▶ The Hebrew term translated "the Satan" in verse 1 means the adversary. This is only one of three times that this figure appears in the Hebrew Bible.

▶ Note that the nature of the accusation brought against Joshua is not specified. It seems to have something to do with not being worthy of the position of high priest.

▶ The reference to "filthy clothes" (verse 3-4) implies that the high priest was ritually unclean.

▶ The turban is the traditional headgear associated with the high priest, though here the Hebrew word is different from the one used in Leviticus 8:9.

▶ Note that "those who are standing here" refers to the divine council. In other places, access to this council is a privilege extended to the prophets (see Jer. 23:18).

▶ "Branch" refers to a ruler from the line of David. Here it is Zerubbabel, the governor.

▶ Note that the "stone with seven facets" probably indicates the engraved gold plaque on the turban of the high priest. In Exodus 28:36-38 this plaque is associated with removing guilt from the people.

---

¹ Then he showed me the high priest Joshua standing before the angel of the LORD, and Satan standing at his right hand to accuse him. ² And the LORD said to Satan, "The LORD rebuke you, O Satan! The LORD who has chosen Jerusalem rebuke you! Is not this man a brand plucked from the fire?" ³ Now Joshua was dressed with filthy clothes as he stood before the angel. ⁴ The angel said to those who were standing before him, "Take off his filthy clothes." And to him he said, "See, I have taken your guilt away from you, and I will clothe you with festal apparel." ⁵ And I said, "Let them put a clean turban on his head." So they put a clean turban on his head and clothed him with the apparel; and the angel of the LORD was standing by.

⁶ Then the angel of the LORD assured Joshua, saying ⁷ "Thus says the LORD of hosts: If you will walk in my ways and keep my requirements, then you shall rule my house and have charge of my courts, and I will give you the right of access among those who are standing here. ⁸ Now listen, Joshua, high priest, you and your colleagues who sit before you! For they are an omen of things to come: I am going to bring my servant the Branch. ⁹ For on the stone that I have set before Joshua, on a single stone with seven facets, I will engrave its inscription, says the LORD of hosts, and I will remove the guilt of this land in a single day. ¹⁰ On that day, says the LORD of hosts, you shall invite each other to come under your vine and fig tree."

DISCUSSION QUESTIONS

1. What role does "the Satan" play at the beginning of this passage?

2. What does putting on the "festal apparel" symbolize in verse 4?

3. After being commissioned as high priest, what two promises are given to Joshua?

Malachi 2:17—3:12

CLOSE READING TIPS

▶ The fifth of six disputations in the book of Malachi begins at Malachi 2:17. The last disputation starts at Malachi 3:6.

▶ "Where is the God of justice?" is a succinct articulation of the problem of theodicy. This language echoes the psalms of lament.

▶ In the Hebrew, the word translated "my messenger" is *mal'aki*; in Malachi 1:1. This same Hebrew word is translated as "Malachi," the name of the prophet.

▶ Note that the second appendix of Malachi (Mal. 4:5-6) identifies the messenger as the prophet Elijah. In the New Testament, the messenger is identified as John the Baptist (Matt. 11:10; Mark 1:2; Luke 1:17, 76).

▶ Note that fullers' soap (Mal. 3:2) is used as a whitening and cleansing agent in the manufacture of textiles.

▶ All the infractions listed in Malachi 3:5 also appear in the book of Deuteronomy.

▶ Note that issues surrounding the tithe are also addressed in other postexilic texts (see Neh. 10:35, 37-40).

▶ Note that the theme of locusts destroying the land also appears in Joel 1–2.

---

[17] You have wearied the LORD with your words. Yet you say, "How have we wearied him?" By saying, "All who do evil are good in the sight of the LORD, and he delights in them." Or by asking, "Where is the God of justice?"

3 [1] See, I am sending my messenger to prepare the way before me, and the Lord whom you seek will suddenly come to his temple. The messenger of the covenant in whom you delight—indeed, he is coming, says the LORD of hosts. [2] But who can endure the day of his coming, and who can stand when he appears?

For he is like a refiner's fire and like fullers' soap; [3] he will sit as a refiner and purifier of silver, and he will purify the descendants of Levi and refine them like gold and silver, until they present offerings to the LORD in righteousness. [4] Then the offering of Judah and Jerusalem will be pleasing to the LORD as in the days of old and as in former years.

[5] Then I will draw near to you for judgment; I will be swift to bear witness against the sorcerers, against the adulterers, against those who swear falsely, against those who oppress the hired workers in their wages, the widow and the orphan, against those who thrust aside the alien, and do not fear me, says the LORD of hosts.

[6] For I the LORD do not change; therefore you, O children of Jacob, have not perished. [7] Ever since the days of your ancestors you have turned aside from my statutes and have not kept them. Return to me, and I will return to you, says the LORD of hosts. But you say, "How shall we return?"

[8] Will anyone rob God? Yet you are robbing me! But you say, "How are we robbing you?" In your

tithes and offerings! [9] You are cursed with a curse, for you are robbing me—the whole nation of you! [10] Bring the full tithe into the storehouse, so that there may be food in my house, and thus put me to the test, says the LORD of hosts; see if I will not open the windows of heaven for you and pour down for you an overflowing blessing. [11] I will rebuke the locust for you, so that it will not destroy the produce of your soil; and your vine in the field shall not be barren, says the LORD of hosts. [12] Then all nations will count you happy, for you will be a land of delight, says the LORD of hosts.

DISCUSSION QUESTIONS:

1. How does God respond to the people's complaint at the end of Malachi 2:17?
2. What does it entail for the messenger to "prepare the way" before the LORD?
3. What similarities or differences do you see between the theophany pictured in this passage and the theme of "the Day of the LORD" in other prophetic books?
4. How would you characterize Malachi's perspective on sacrifices and offerings in Malachi 3:6-12? How does this compare with the perspective on display in other prophets, such as Amos, Third Isaiah, or Ezekiel?

Jonah 3–4

CLOSE READING TIPS

▶ Note that this is the second time that the word of the LORD had come to Jonah (see Jon. 1:1-2).
▶ Nineveh was a very large city, but the description of its size in Jonah 3:3 is an exaggeration.
▶ Note that even the animals undergo customs of mourning and repentance (Jon. 3:8).
▶ Jonah's characterization of God in Jonah 4:2 draws on language from Exodus 34:6-7.
▶ Note that booths (Jon. 4:5) were constructed to protect the crop during harvest season.
▶ The "east wind" refers to a scorching wind that blew off the desert. Elsewhere in the Hebrew Bible it is associated with divine judgment (for example, Exod. 10:13; Isa. 27:8; Jer. 18:17; Ezek. 17:10; Hos. 13:15).

---

3 [1] The word of the LORD came to Jonah a second time, saying, [2] "Get up, go to Nineveh, that great city, and proclaim to it the message that I tell you." [3] So Jonah set out and went to Nineveh, according to the word of the LORD. Now Nineveh was an exceedingly large city, a three days' walk across. [4] Jonah began to go into the city, going a day's walk. And he cried out, "Forty days more, and Nineveh shall be overthrown!" [5] And the people of Nineveh believed God; they proclaimed a fast, and everyone, great and small, put on sackcloth.

[6] When the news reached the king of Nineveh, he rose from his throne, removed his robe, covered himself with sackcloth, and sat in ashes. [7] Then he had a proclamation made in Nineveh: "By the decree of the king and his nobles: No human being or

animal, no herd or flock, shall taste anything. They shall not feed, nor shall they drink water. [8] Human beings and animals shall be covered with sackcloth, and they shall cry mightily to God. All shall turn from their evil ways and from the violence that is in their hands. [9] Who knows? God may relent and change his mind; he may turn from his fierce anger, so that we do not perish."

[10] When God saw what they did, how they turned from their evil ways, God changed his mind about the calamity that he had said he would bring upon them; and he did not do it.

4 [1] But this was very displeasing to Jonah, and he became angry. [2] He prayed to the LORD and said, "O LORD! Is not this what I said while I was still in my own country? That is why I fled to Tarshish at the beginning; for I knew that you are a gracious God and merciful, slow to anger, and abounding in steadfast love, and ready to relent from punishing. [3] And now, O LORD, please take my life from me, for it is better for me to die than to live." [4] And the LORD said, "Is it right for you to be angry?" [5] Then Jonah went out of the city and sat down east of the city, and made a booth for himself there. He sat under it in the shade, waiting to see what would become of the city.

[6] The LORD God appointed a bush, and made it come up over Jonah, to give shade over his head, to save him from his discomfort; so Jonah was very happy about the bush. [7] But when dawn came up the next day, God appointed a worm that attacked the bush, so that it withered. [8] When the sun rose, God prepared a sultry east wind, and the sun beat down on the head of Jonah so that he was faint and asked that he might die. He said, "It is better for me to die than to live."

[9] But God said to Jonah, "Is it right for you to be angry about the bush?" And he said, "Yes, angry enough to die." [10] Then the LORD said, "You are concerned about the bush, for which you did not labor and which you did not grow; it came into being in a night and perished in a night. [11] And should I not be concerned about Nineveh, that great city, in which there are more than a hundred and twenty thousand persons who do not know their right hand from their left, and also many animals?"

DISCUSSION QUESTIONS

1. Closely compare Jonah 3:1-3 and Jonah 1:1-3. What differences do you see? Do you think the nature of Jonah's mission had changed?
2. How does the response of the Ninevites in Jonah 3:5-9 contrast with the behavior and attitude of the prophet in chapter 4?
3. Why does Jonah object to God's decision to extend mercy to the Ninevites?
4. How does Jonah's perspective on Nineveh compare with that of Nahum?

21

Ezra and Nehemiah

Key Points

The books of Ezra and Nehemiah are the work of a single author or editor, and as a result it is customary to refer to them collectively as Ezra-Nehemiah. This material was originally grouped together as one book in the Hebrew Bible and only later was separated in the Greek Bible. While these books appear in the section of the Hebrew canon known as the Writings (*K^etubim*), in the Christian Old Testament they are included among the historical books, immediately following 1 and 2 Chronicles. Many modern scholars contend that Ezra-Nehemiah is part of the Chronicler's History. However, despite numerous points of affinity with 1 and 2 Chronicles, it is best to regard Ezra-Nehemiah as an independent composition that gives its own perspective on the reconstruction of Jewish life under Persian control.

The primary content of these books is laid out in three main sections: 1) the initial return and the restoration of the temple (Ezra 1–6); 2) the account of Ezra's career (Ezra 7–10; Neh. 8–9); and 3) the account of Nehemiah's career (Neh. 1–7; 11–13). Though following a roughly chronological framework, some of the material is clearly out of order. For instance, the letter in Ezra 4:11-22 is addressed to Artaxerxes I (465–424 BCE) and concerns the rebuilding of the city walls while the letter in Ezra 5:6-17 is addressed to Darius (522–486 BCE) and is focused on the rebuilding of the temple.

Ezra and Nehemiah were both Persian loyalists who carried out their respective missions under the authorization of the king (likely Artaxerxes I). Ezra's career centered on a variety of religious reforms, most notably those associated with the problem of intermarriage (Ezra 9–10). He also is said to have read and interpreted "the book of the law of Moses" in the presence of the community (Neh. 8:1-8), re-initiated the festival of booths (Neh. 8:9-18), and led people in confession and re-commitment to the law (Neh. 9–10). Nehemiah's career focuses specifically on the rebuilding of the Jerusalem wall. Despite considerable opposition (Neh. 1–7), Nehemiah finishes the project and dedicates the wall (Neh. 11–12).

The book concludes with a retrospective sometime after 433 BCE, when Nehemiah returns to Jerusalem and responds to violations pertaining to the purity of the temple, observance of the Sabbath, and intermarriage (Neh. 13).

In Ezra-Nehemiah, the returned exiles are portrayed as a godly remnant charged with the task of maintaining their distinct ethnic and religious identity within the vast, multicultural Persian empire. This involved not only rebuilding the temple and restoring the cult but also establishing boundaries between the Jewish community and their neighbors both physically (as with the wall) and relationally (as with prohibitions against intermarriage). A renewed commitment to the covenant teachings would help the people avoid the mistakes that led to the exile and successfully negotiate the new demands of life in the Diaspora.

Key Terms

Nehemiah memoir   The Nehemiah memoir refers to the first-person, autobiographical narrative of the career of Nehemiah. It consists of Nehemiah 1–7 as well as parts of chapters 11–13. Nehemiah's account is distinguished by its apologetic character and its frequent call on God "to remember." The genre of the memoir shares much in common with ancient Near Eastern royal inscriptions and Egyptian autobiographical texts addressed to the deity and deposited in a temple. Comparisons have also been made with psalms of individual complaint.

The book of the law of Moses   In Ezra 8, the reconstruction of the temple culminates when Ezra is summoned to read "the book of the law of Moses" before the community. Most scholars conclude that this law was the Torah in form similar to what we have it today, including Deuteronomy and the Priestly code. Nevertheless, there are certain discrepancies between Ezra's law and the final form of the Pentateuch, especially regarding the cultic calendar and the temple tax. Ezra's public reading of Scripture initiates a similar practice in later Jewish and Christian traditions.

Intermarriage   During the postexilic period, the problem of intermarriage involved returning exiles marrying "the peoples of the lands" (Ezra 9:1). While some intermarriages may have occurred with non-Israelites, the primary issue involved non-exiled Judeans and Samaritans. For a variety of reasons, Ezra and Nehemiah are only concerned about Jewish men entering into such marriages. Ezra's prohibition is based on Deuteronomy 7 and 23:3-8, though it also speaks to a more extreme fear of contact with outsiders.

1 Esdras   1 Esdras is an apocryphal book that consists of a Greek translation of 2 Chronicles 35–36, Ezra 1–10, and Nehemiah 8:1-13, as well as an additional story about three young men (including Zerubbabel) in the court of Darius. It bears witness to an alternative arrangement to the material in Ezra-Nehemiah. This book, which is called 3 Ezra in the Latin Vulgate, was likely composed during the late-second century BCE and displays stylistic similarities with Esther and Daniel.

Prince of Judah In Ezra 1:8 this title is applied to Sheshbazzar, the first governor of Judah and the predecessor to Zerubbabel. Since the term prince (Heb.: *nasi'*) is used in Ezekiel to refer to the Davidic ruler, it might imply that Sheshbazzar was descended from the line of David. However, his genealogy is not specified either here or in Chronicles. The fact that the editors of Ezra-Nehemiah were loyal Persian subjects suggests that the title "Prince of Judah" did not have strong messianic connotations in this context.

Key Personalities

Ezra

Ezra was a religious reformer during the reconstruction of Jerusalem. According to Ezra 7:7-8, Ezra came to Jerusalem during the seventh year of King Artaxerxes in 458 BCE, thirteen years prior to the arrival of Nehemiah. This chronology assumes that the Persian king mentioned with respect to both Ezra and Nehemiah was Artaxerxes I (465–424 BCE). However, there is much scholarly debate on the timing of Ezra's activities, with some placing his work after Nehemiah and during the reign of Artaxerxes II (c. 398 BCE). In either case, the account of Ezra's activities are found in the so-called Ezra Memoir (Ezra 7–10; Neh. 8–9). He is described as both "a scribe skilled in the law of Moses" and as a priest descended from Zadok and Aaron (Ezra 7:1-6). He was sent to Jerusalem at the behest of the king and his mission is best understood in light of the Persian policy of co-opting loyal subjects and allowing them to regulate the cult of local communities. At the rededication of the temple, Ezra publically read the law and reinstituted the festival of booths (Neh. 8). Yet, the major issue Ezra addressed is the problem of intermarriage between exiles and those Judeans who remained in the land. His command that all such marriages should be dissolved is not required by Deuteronomy but instead reflects an emerging self-understanding of the exilic community as a pure, "holy seed" that tolerated little to no contact with outsiders. It is uncertain how long Ezra remained in Jerusalem, though it seems likely that references to Nehemiah and Ezra being contemporaries (Neh. 8:9; 12:26, 36) are anachronistic redactions. His reforms were somewhat short-lived and he disappears quickly from the scene in Ezra-Nehemiah. His name is associated with several apocryphal books.

Sanballat and Tobiah

According to a fifth-century BCE document from the Jewish community in Elephantine, Egypt, Sanballat was the governor of Samaria. Though his name honors the Babylonian moon god, Sin (*Sin-ubal-lit* in Akkadian means "may Sin give him life"), it is still likely that he was a Yahwistic Jew. Sanballat's son-in-law was the grandson of the high priest Eliashib. Tobiah is described as an Ammonite official, thus suggesting he exercised some control over Ammon, a nation which was to be excluded from the Israelite community (Deut. 23:3-8). Tobiah maintained close connections with nobles in Judah (Neh. 6:17) and was the head of the powerful Tobiad family, which remained prominent in Jerusalem into the Hellenistic period. Eliashib allowed him to live within the temple precincts (Neh. 13:4-5), but when Nehemiah returned to the city Tobiah was evicted. Sanballat and Tobiah were the two leaders of the opposition to Nehemiah's rebuilding of the walls in Jerusalem (Neh. 2). While they are never said to make a formal complaint to the Persian court, they ridicule the wall-building effort (Neh. 4:1-3) and are prepared to use force to stop Nehemiah (Neh. 4:8). Along with

Geshem, they unsuccessfully try to lure Nehemiah into a trap (Neh. 6:1-9). Further, they accuse Nehemiah of rebelling against the Persian king (Neh. 2:19) and contend that he was attempting to reestablish a Judean monarchy (Neh. 6:6-7). While Nehemiah was not likely trying to gain independence from Persia, he probably did hope to free Jerusalem from the influence of its immediate neighbors, most notably Samaria and Ammon.

Questions for Study and Discussion

1. Ezra-Nehemiah raise some troubling questions about the relationship between religious law that is allegedly revealed by the deity and human ethics. Are there situations in which divinely revealed law should override or suspend broader ethical norms? Should ethics ever be subordinated to revelation?

2. The establishment and maintenance of a post-exilic communal identity is a key concern of Ezra-Nehemiah. To this end, reforms are made, economic problems are addresses, walls are built. Can you think of other, modern day communities, that employ social, economic, and religious strategies analogous to those found in Ezra-Nehemiah?

Primary Text

Ezra 9:1—10:6

CLOSE READING TIPS

▶ Note that there were probably no surviving Canaanites, Hittites, Perizzites, Jebusites, or Amorites still in Palestine during the time of Ezra. The primary target of this prohibition were Judeans who had never gone into exile.

▶ Note that the term "holy seed" draws on imagery from Isaiah 6:13 as well as God's blessings to Abraham (Gen. 12:7; 13:14-16; 17:1-8).

▶ Spreading out the palms upward (Ezra 9:5) is a gesture of supplication in prayer in ancient Near Eastern art.

▶ The notion that the land had been made unclean by the previous inhabitants is laid out in Levitucs 18:24-30.

▶ Note that in Ezra 9:12 and elsewhere, the concern is specifically with Jewish men entering into mixed marriages.

▶ The phrase "to send away" (Ezra 10:3) means to divorce. Though this is done "according to the law," the Pentateuch does not include a law that demands mixed marriages be dissolved.

▶ The threat of confiscation of goods and excommunication from the community was aimed at people who did not participate in the communal decision-making process, not those who disagreed with Shecaniah's resolution.

---

9 ¹ After these things had been done, the officials approached me and said, "The people of Israel, the priests, and the Levites have not separated themselves from the peoples of the lands with their abominations, from the Canaanites, the Hittites, the Perizzites, the Jebusites, the Ammonites, the Moabites, the Egyptians, and the Amorites. ² For they have taken some of their daughters as wives for themselves and for their sons. Thus the holy seed has mixed itself with the peoples of the lands, and in this faithlessness the officials and leaders have led the way." ³ When I heard this, I tore my garment and my mantle, and pulled hair from my head and beard, and sat appalled. ⁴ Then all who trembled at the words of the God of Israel, because of the faithlessness of the returned exiles, gathered around me while I sat appalled until the evening sacrifice.

⁵ At the evening sacrifice I got up from my fasting, with my garments and my mantle torn, and fell on my knees, spread out my hands to the LORD my God, ⁶ and said,

"O my God, I am too ashamed and embarrassed to lift my face to you, my God, for our iniquities have risen higher than our heads, and our guilt has mounted up to the heavens. ⁷ From the days of our ancestors to this day we have been deep in guilt, and for our iniquities we, our kings, and our priests have been handed over to the kings of the lands, to the sword, to captivity, to plundering, and to utter shame, as is now the case. ⁸ But now for a brief moment favor has been shown by the LORD our God, who has left us a remnant, and given us a stake in his holy place, in order that he may brighten our eyes and grant us a little sustenance in our slavery. ⁹ For we are slaves; yet our God has not forsaken us in our slavery, but has extended to us his steadfast love before the kings of Persia, to give us new life to set up the house of our God, to repair its ruins, and to give us a wall in Judea and Jerusalem.

¹⁰ "And now, our God, what shall we say after this? For we have forsaken your commandments, ¹¹ which you commanded by your servants the prophets, saying, 'The land that you are entering to possess is a land unclean with the pollutions of the peoples of the lands, with their abominations. They have filled it from end to end with their uncleanness. ¹² Therefore do not give your daughters to their sons, neither take their daughters for your sons, and never seek their peace or prosperity, so that you may be strong and eat the good of the land and leave it for an inheritance to your children forever.' ¹³ After all that has come upon us for our evil deeds and for our great guilt, seeing that you, our God, have punished us less than our iniquities deserved and have given us such a remnant as this, ¹⁴ shall we break your commandments again and intermarry with the peoples who practice these abominations? Would you not be angry with us until you destroy us without remnant or survivor? ¹⁵ O LORD, God of Israel, you are just, but we have escaped as a remnant, as is now the case. Here we are before you in our guilt, though no one can face you because of this."

10 ¹ While Ezra prayed and made confession, weeping and throwing himself down before the house of God, a very great assembly of men, women, and children gathered to him out of Israel; the people also wept bitterly. ² Shecaniah son of Jehiel, of the descendants of Elam, addressed Ezra, saying, "We have broken faith with our God and have married foreign women from the peoples of the land, but even now there is hope for Israel in spite of this. ³ So now let us make a covenant with our God to send away all these wives and their children, according to the counsel of my lord and of those who tremble at the commandment of our God; and let it be done

according to the law. [4] Take action, for it is your duty, and we are with you; be strong, and do it." [5] Then Ezra stood up and made the leading priests, the Levites, and all Israel swear that they would do as had been said. So they swore.

[6] Then Ezra withdrew from before the house of God, and went to the chamber of Jehohanan son of Eliashib, where he spent the night. He did not eat bread or drink water, for he was mourning over the faithlessness of the exiles. [7] They made a proclamation throughout Judah and Jerusalem to all the returned exiles that they should assemble at Jerusalem, [8] and that if any did not come within three days, by order of the officials and the elders all their property should be forfeited, and they themselves banned from the congregation of the exiles.

DISCUSSION QUESTIONS

1. In the book of Deuteronomy, intermarriage is prohibited primarily because contact with outsiders could lead to idolatry. What new rationale does Ezra provide for this prohibition?
2. What does Ezra fear will happen to the "remnant" (Ezra 9:8, 13) if intermarriages continue?
3. Why do you think Ezra is only concerned about intermarriage when it comes to Jewish men?
4. How does Shecaniah's recommendation (Ezra 10:1-6) compare with Malachi's discussion of divorce in Malachi 2:10-16?

Nehemiah 2:1-20

CLOSE READING TIPS

▶ Note that the reference in verse 1 is likely to Artaxerxes I, placing the mission of Nehemiah in 445 BCE, thirteen years after Ezra came on the scene.
▶ Nehemiah starts off as a cupbearer in the court of the Persian king. The cupbearer would have been a highly trusted official since he had the duty of sampling wine for safety purposes.
▶ Nehemiah was "very much afraid" to respond to the king lest his request be interpreted as a sign of disloyalty.
▶ The queen's presence (verse 6) may suggest an intimate setting for this conversation.
▶ Sanballat and Tobiah were governors of the provinces of Samaria and Ammon, respectively. These were the most immediate neighbors of Judah.
▶ Nehemiah seems to move in a counterclockwise fashion around the city; some of the features he inspects can no longer be identified.
▶ Sanballat, Tobiah, and Geshem imply that Nehemiah is attempting an insurrection by rebuilding the walls of the city (verse 19).

¹ In the month of Nisan, in the twentieth year of King Artaxerxes, when wine was served him, I carried the wine and gave it to the king. Now, I had never been sad in his presence before. ² So the king said to me, "Why is your face sad, since you are not sick? This can only be sadness of the heart." Then I was very much afraid. ³ I said to the king, "May the king live forever! Why should my face not be sad, when the city, the place of my ancestors' graves, lies waste, and its gates have been destroyed by fire?" ⁴ Then the king said to me, "What do you request?" So I prayed to the God of heaven. ⁵ Then I said to the king, "If it pleases the king, and if your servant has found favor with you, I ask that you send me to Judah, to the city of my ancestors' graves, so that I may rebuild it." ⁶ The king said to me (the queen also was sitting beside him), "How long will you be gone, and when will you return?" So it pleased the king to send me, and I set him a date. ⁷ Then I said to the king, "If it pleases the king, let letters be given me to the governors of the province Beyond the River, that they may grant me passage until I arrive in Judah; ⁸ and a letter to Asaph, the keeper of the king's forest, directing him to give me timber to make beams for the gates of the temple fortress, and for the wall of the city, and for the house that I shall occupy." And the king granted me what I asked, for the gracious hand of my God was upon me.

⁹ Then I came to the governors of the province Beyond the River, and gave them the king's letters. Now the king had sent officers of the army and cavalry with me. ¹⁰ When Sanballat the Horonite and Tobiah the Ammonite official heard this, it displeased them greatly that someone had come to seek the welfare of the people of Israel.

¹¹ So I came to Jerusalem and was there for three days. ¹² Then I got up during the night, I and a few men with me; I told no one what my God had put into my heart to do for Jerusalem. The only animal I took was the animal I rode. ¹³ I went out by night by the Valley Gate past the Dragon's Spring and to the Dung Gate, and I inspected the walls of Jerusalem that had been broken down and its gates that had been destroyed by fire. ¹⁴ Then I went on to the Fountain Gate and to the King's Pool; but there was no place for the animal I was riding to continue. ¹⁵ So I went up by way of the valley by night and inspected the wall. Then I turned back and entered by the Valley Gate, and so returned. 16 The officials did not know where I had gone or what I was doing; I had not yet told the Jews, the priests, the nobles, the officials, and the rest that were to do the work.

¹⁷ Then I said to them, "You see the trouble we are in, how Jerusalem lies in ruins with its gates burned. Come, let us rebuild the wall of Jerusalem, so that we may no longer suffer disgrace." ¹⁸ I told them that the hand of my God had been gracious upon me, and also the words that the king had spoken to me. Then they said, "Let us start building!" So they committed themselves to the common good. ¹⁹ But when Sanballat the Horonite and Tobiah the Ammonite official, and Geshem the Arab heard of it, they mocked and ridiculed us, saying, "What is this that you are doing? Are you rebelling against the king?" ²⁰ Then I replied to them, "The God of heaven is the one who will give us success, and we his servants are going to start building; but you have no share or claim or historic right in Jerusalem."

1. What details in this story reflect the fact that Nehemiah's mission was supported by Persia?

2. Why do think Sanballat and Tobiah were displeased when they heard of Nehemiah's mission? What did they fear he might do?

3. What does Nehemiah discover when he goes out to examine the walls of Jerusalem? Why might he have done this at night?

4. In verses 17-18, what rhetorical means does Nehemiah employ in order to convince the people to join him in the rebuilding process?

5. What does a rebuilt wall symbolize for the people of Jerusalem both spiritually and politically?

Nehemiah 8:1-18

CLOSE READING TIPS

▶ Note that "the book of the law of Moses" (verse 1) likely refers to the Torah in a form that closely resembles what we have today.

▶ The first day of the seventh month (verse 2) is the date set for Rosh Hashanah, the New Year Festival, in Leviticus 23:24. However, this festival is not specifically mentioned in Nehemiah 8.

▶ Note that the reference to opening the book in verse 5 means that Ezra unrolled a scroll. Book technology did not become more prominent until the first century CE.

▶ Ezra's assistants "helped the people understand the law" (verse 7) either by translating the Hebrew into the more familiar Aramaic language or by clarifying the content through interpretation.

▶ Note that verse 9 implies that Ezra and Nehemiah were contemporaries. However, the usual chronology suggests that Ezra was active thirteen years prior to Nehemiah and there otherwise is no evidence that they had contact with one another.

▶ Yom Kippur, or the Day of Atonement, is set on the tenth day of the seventh month (Lev. 23:27), but there is no mention of Yom Kippur here.

▶ Living in booths or tabernacles was a way of commemorating the Israelites' journey through the wilderness (Lev. 23:42).

▶ Note that Deuteronomy 31:10-13 requires the public reading of the Torah during the feast of booths every seventh year.

[1] All the people gathered together into the square before the Water Gate. They told the scribe Ezra to bring the book of the law of Moses, which the LORD had given to Israel. [2] Accordingly, the priest Ezra brought the law before the assembly, both men and women and all who could hear with understanding. This was on the first day of the seventh month. [3] He read from it facing the square before the Water Gate from early morning until midday, in the presence of the men and the women and those who could

understand; and the ears of all the people were attentive to the book of the law. ⁴ The scribe Ezra stood on a wooden platform that had been made for the purpose; and beside him stood Mattithiah, Shema, Anaiah, Uriah, Hilkiah, and Maaseiah on his right hand; and Pedaiah, Mishael, Malchijah, Hashum, Hash-baddanah, Zechariah, and Meshullam on his left hand. ⁵ And Ezra opened the book in the sight of all the people, for he was standing above all the people; and when he opened it, all the people stood up. ⁶ Then Ezra blessed the LORD, the great God, and all the people answered, "Amen, Amen," lifting up their hands. Then they bowed their heads and worshiped the LORD with their faces to the ground. ⁷ Also Jeshua, Bani, Sherebiah, Jamin, Akkub, Shabbethai, Hodiah, Maaseiah, Kelita, Azariah, Jozabad, Hanan, Pelaiah, the Levites, helped the people to understand the law, while the people remained in their places. ⁸ So they read from the book, from the law of God, with interpretation. They gave the sense, so that the people understood the reading.

⁹ And Nehemiah, who was the governor, and Ezra the priest and scribe, and the Levites who taught the people said to all the people, "This day is holy to the LORD your God; do not mourn or weep." For all the people wept when they heard the words of the law. ¹⁰ Then he said to them, "Go your way, eat the fat and drink sweet wine and send portions of them to those for whom nothing is prepared, for this day is holy to our LORD; and do not be grieved, for the joy of the LORD is your strength." ¹¹ So the Levites stilled all the people, saying, "Be quiet, for this day is holy; do not be grieved." ¹² And all the people went their way to eat and drink and to send portions and to make great rejoicing, because they had understood the words that were declared to them.

¹³ On the second day the heads of ancestral houses of all the people, with the priests and the Levites, came together to the scribe Ezra in order to study the words of the law. ¹⁴ And they found it written in the law, which the LORD had commanded by Moses, that the people of Israel should live in booths during the festival of the seventh month, ¹⁵ and that they should publish and proclaim in all their towns and in Jerusalem as follows, "Go out to the hills and bring branches of olive, wild olive, myrtle, palm, and other leafy trees to make booths, as it is written." ¹⁶ So the people went out and brought them, and made booths for themselves, each on the roofs of their houses, and in their courts and in the courts of the house of God, and in the square at the Water Gate and in the square at the Gate of Ephraim. ¹⁷ And all the assembly of those who had returned from the captivity made booths and lived in them; for from the days of Jeshua son of Nun to that day the people of Israel had not done so. And there was very great rejoicing. ¹⁸ And day by day, from the first day to the last day, he read from the book of the law of God. They kept the festival seven days; and on the eighth day there was a solemn assembly, according to the ordinance.

DISCUSSION QUESTIONS

1. Where do you see evidence of Ezra playing the role of both scribe and priest in this passage?
2. If Ezra and Nehemiah were *not* contemporaries, what point does the author try to make by placing them together in verse 9? What do both figures symbolize for the community?
3. Why might the people have mourned or wept after hearing the law read and interpreted for them?
4. What do you make of the fact that there are certain discrepancies between the cultic calendar in Nehemiah 8 and that of the Priestly code in Leviticus?

22

The Book of Chronicles

Key Points

Like the books of Samuel and Kings, 1 and 2 Chronicles were originally grouped together as one book. This material can be understood as a highly selective retelling of the Deuteronomistic History. While Chronicles draws on some independent traditions, the places where it diverges from Samuel and Kings owe mostly to differing theological perspectives. Dating Chronicles is notoriously difficult. Nevertheless, since its language is regarded as Late Biblical Hebrew, it likely emerged sometime after the Priestly source and the book of Ezekiel (c. 400 BCE).

The Chronicle's historical survey begins with a list of extensive genealogies (1 Chron. 1–9). Special prominence is given to Judah (1 Chron. 2:3—4:23), Levi (1 Chron. 6), and Benjamin (1 Chron. 8), no doubt because these tribes remained faithful to the Davidic line. The other nine tribes are treated far more briefly. The introduction also includes a list of those who returned from the exile, focusing especially on the priests, Levites, and temple functionaries (1 Chron. 9).

The remainder of the book consists of a continuous narrative stretching from the beginning of the Davidic dynasty to the end of the Babylonian exile. David and Solomon each receive considerable attention (1 Chron. 10 through 2 Chron. 9). The hallmark of their reigns centers on the building of the temple and the organizing of the cult. After the division of the monarchy, Chronicles only follows the history of Judahite kings (2 Chron. 10–36). On the whole, Chronicles offers a negative assessment of the Northern Kingdom primarily on the basis of its rejection of centralized worship in Jerusalem. However, in some instances, such as Hezekiah's celebration of the Passover and Josiah's reforms, the possibility is left open for Northerners to participate in proper cultic worship. The book ends on a hopeful note by mentioning the edict of Cyrus (2 Chron. 36:22-23), which allowed for the return of the exiles to Jerusalem.

Several distinctive characteristics of the Chronicler's version of history should be noted. First, Chronicles tends to present David and Solomon as ideal kings. In this regard, David's affair with Bethsheba is omitted and no mention is made of Solomon's apostasy. Both kings are portrayed as models of piety so as to underscore their worthiness as founders of the Jerusalem temple. Second, the Chronicler's view of history is primarily focused on the temple and cultic leadership. The greatest achievement of a king is the proper functioning of the cult, not political independence, and the responsibilities of the priests and Levites are continually emphasized. This portrait of a temple-centered kingdom likely functions to legitimize the postexilic theocracy in Judah. Third, in comparison to the Deuteronomistic History, Chronicles offers a different evaluation of certain kings. Most notably, Hezekiah, not Josiah, is the Chronicler's ideal king and Manasseh, the most reviled of Judahite rulers in 2 Kings, is moved to repentance and carries out cult reform in 2 Chronicles 33. These differences reflect a theological interpretation of history that is rooted in a strict principle of retribution—that is, Manasseh's peaceful death must indicate conversion while Josiah's violent death in his battle with Pharaoh Neco must be the result of sin.

Key Terms

Paralipomena Meaning "things omitted" or "passed over," this Greek term is used as a title of Chronicles in the Septuagint. It recognizes the secondary character of 1 and 2 Chronicles as an alternative account of the historical narrative in 2 Samuel and 1 and 2 Kings. However, the term *Paralipomena* is somewhat of a misnomer. Rather than consisting of things left out of earlier biblical history, Chronicles is best understood as a highly selective, theologically-motivated retelling of older material.

Geneology　A genealogy is a record of an individual's or clan's descent from an ancestor. In the Hebrew Bible, genealogies (Heb.: *tôlēdôt*) are not always complete and often contain inconsistences. They functioned not only as a family tree but also as a way of conferring status or legitimacy by virtue of kinship ties to certain individuals. Genealogies are prominent in the Pentateuch,

Ruth, Ezra-Nehemiah, and 1 and 2 Chronicles. The latter includes extensive genealogies from the time of Adam down through the postexilic period (1 Chronicles 1–9).

Hezekiah's Passover　In 2 Chronicles 30, Hezekiah calls Judah and Israel to Jerusalem in order to reinstitute the Passover celebration. Hezekiah appears to incorporate the originally distinct, seven-day Festival of Unleavened Bread into Passover. In contrast, 2 Kings contends that Josiah was the first to celebrate Passover since the days of the judges (2 Kgs. 23:22). This discrepancy is characteristic of Chronicles, which consistently portrays Hezekiel in a better light than Josiah.

The Prayer of Manasseh　This pseudepigraphical composition is a prayer of confession offered by Manasseh while imprisoned in Babylon. It is preserved in later editions of the Septuagint and the Protestant version of the Apocrypha. Drawing on the language of a penitential psalm, Manasseh acknowledges his sin of idolatry and desperately calls on God for forgiveness. The Chronicler includes this prayer (2 Chron. 33:19) in order to help explain why Manasseh was never punished for his many misdeeds.

Levites As described in Chronicles, the Levites are cult personnel of a lower order than the Aaronide priests. Within the well-established temple hierarchy, they have both religious and civil duties. They serve as gatekeepers, oversee the temple treasuries, are in charge of the temple furniture and utensils, instruct people in the law, and contribute singing and music to temple services. The delineation of these roles emerges over time and is only partially evident in Ezekiel 40–48 and Ezra-Nehemiah.

Key Personalities

Manasseh

Manasseh was the king of Judah from 697–642 BCE. In the Deuteronomistic History, he is condemned as the most wicked king of Judah because he erected altars for Baal, made a sacred pole, and committed a host of other cultic offenses (2 Kgs. 21:1-17). Manasseh's actions effectively reverse the reforms of his father Hezekiah and are said to be the ultimate cause of the fall of Judah. Even the reforms of his grandson, Josiah, cannot reverse the negative effects of Manasseh's abominations (2 Kgs. 24:3-4). In Chronicles, Manasseh's reign is also marked by evil and apostasy—so much so that God brings the king of Assyria against him in order to imprison the Judahite king in Babylon. From here, however, the Chronicler's treatment of Manasseh diverges sharply from that which is found in 2 Kings. While in prison, Manasseh is said to have prayed to

God in order confess his sins. God hears his plea and restores him to his land. Thus in Chronicles Manasseh becomes a model of the repentant sinner. A much later pseudepigraphical composition, called the Prayer of Manasseh, purports to record the content of the king's confession. As a result of his forgiveness, Manasseh carries out significant political, military, and religious reforms (2 Chron. 33:14-17). Most scholars contend that the Chronicler freely adds this account of Manasseh's conversion in order to explain the unprecedented length of this reign. However, it is also possible that the Deuteronomistic Historian exaggerates Manasseh's wickedness in order to account for the fall of Jerusalem despite the religious reform of the ideal king, Josiah.

The Chronicler's David

The portrayal of David in 1 Chronicles differs from that which is found in 1 Samuel 16 through 1 Kings 2 on several key points. First, David's rise to power is significantly contracted. The Chronicler omits stories about the civil war between Saul and David as well as the various accounts of how God chose David from among his brothers. Instead, he is unanimously appointed king at Hebron immediately following Saul's death. A second distinguishing mark of the Chronicler's treatment of David is the king's extensive involvement with the temple. For instance, the narrative concerning the transfer of the ark to Jerusalem is greatly expanded in 1 Chronicles 15–16 (compare with 2 Samuel 6). In addition, he designates the site for the temple, provides Solomon with a blueprint for its construction, and sets aside a great quantity of resources from his own treasury in order to fund the project. Third, the Chronicle's David plays a major role in organizing cultic personnel. This activity includes assigning specialized tasks to the Levites and dividing the priests into twenty-four divisions for the purposes of overseeing temple worship. Finally, it should be noted that the Chronicler consistently shows David in a favorable light. He excludes stories that would be potentially scandalous, including the king's affair with Bathsheba, the murder of Uriah, the complaint of Michal about the king's dancing, Amnon's rape of Tamar, and Absalom's subsequent rebellion. In a similar vein, Nathan's oracle about the Davidic covenant makes no mention of punishment in the event of sin. Even when David does err by taking the census, the Chronicle adds that the king was incited by the Satan.

Questions for Study and Discussion

1. Chronicles is clearly missing much of the material found in Samuel and Kings. In many cases, the material that paints David negatively is missing (for example, his affair with Bathsheba, the rape of Tamar by Amnon, and the rebellion of Absalom). In your view, why might such material missing from Chronicles?
2. In many ways, the book of Chronicles is redundant. It retells a story that is already available in Kings, albeit from a different angle. In your view, what might motivate someone to write another history of Israel's monarchy? Can you think of other, perhaps even modern, alternative historiographies? How might these shed light on the Chronicler's distinct emphasis, for instance, on the temple?

Primary Text

The Prayer of Manasseh

Source: J. H. Charlesworth, "Prayer of Manasseh," *The Old Testament Pseudepigrapha* 2:634–5

> **CLOSE READING TIPS**
> ▶ This prayer likely was from a Jewish author from the second or first century BCE. It is uncertain if the original language was Greek or Hebrew.
> ▶ The prayer is in the form of a penitential psalm and shares much in common with Psalm 51.
> ▶ Note that the opening of the prayer functions as an invocation that sets the stage for Manasseh's confession. A similar element is found in penitential psalms and individual psalms of lament.
> ▶ The text seems to describe Manasseh's physical imprisonment in Babylon.
> ▶ Note that Manasseh's inability to lift up his eyes implies his guilt and shame in the presence of God.
> ▶ Note that Manasseh acknowledges that his punishment is deserved. This is a typical element of a penitential psalm.
> ▶ "Bending the knees of my heart" is a metaphor for bowing in worship. Here Manasseh directs his worship to God, an appropriate reversal of his previous setting up of idols.

O Lord, God of our father,
>   God of Abraham, Isaac, Jacob, and their
>   righteous offspring;
He who made the heaven and the earth
>   with all their beauty;
He who bound the sea
>   and established it by the command of his
>   word,
he who closed the bottomless pit
>   and sealed it by his powerful and glorious
>   name;
You (before) whom all things fear and tremble;
>   (especially) before your power.
Because your awesome magnificence
>   cannot be endured;
none can endure or stand before
>   your anger and your fury against sinners;
But unending and immeasurable
>   are your promised mercies;
Because you are Lord,
>   long-suffering, merciful, and greatly
>   compassionate;
and you feel sorry over the evils of men.
You, O Lord, according to your gentle grace,
>   promised forgiveness to those who repent
>   of their sins,
>   and in your manifold mercies
>   appointed repentance for sinners as the
>   (way to) salvation.
You, therefore, O Lord, God of the righteous,
>   did not appoint grace for the righteous,
>   such as Abraham, Isaac, and Jacob,
>   those who did not sin against you;
>   but you appointed grace for me, (I) who
>   am a sinner.
Because my sins exceeded the number of the
>   sand(s) of the sea,

and on account of the multitude of my
>   inituities,
>   I have no strength to lift up my eyes.
And now, O Lord, I am justly afflicted,
>   and I am deservedly harassed;
>   already I am ensnared.
And I am bent by many iron chains,
>   so that I cannot lift up my head;
for I do not deserve to lift up my eyes
>   and look to see the height of heaven,
because of the gross iniquity of my wicked
>   deeds,
>   because I did evil things before you,
>   and provoked your fury,
>   and set up idols and multiplied impurity.
And now behold I am bending the knees of my
>   heart before you;
and I am beseeching your kindness.
I have sinned, O Lord, I have sinned;
and I certainly know my sins.
I beseech you;
>   forgive me, O Lord, forgive me!
Do not destroy me with my transgressions;
do not be angry against me forever;
do not remember my evils;
and do not condemn me and banish me to the
>   depths of the earth!
For you are the God of those who repent.
In me you will manifest all your grace;
and although I am not worthy,
>   you will save me according to your mani
>   fold mercies.
Because of this (salvation) I shall praise you
>   continually
>   all the days of my life;
because all the hosts of heaven praise you,
>   and sing to you forever and ever.

DISCUSSION QUESTIONS

1.   Compare verses 9-12 of Manasseh's prayer with 2 Chronicles 33:6-12. What evidence do you see of the prayer incorporating details from the story of Manasseh in the Chronicler's account?

2.   In Manasseh's invocation (verses 1-7), what aspects of God's character does he appeal to as a basis for his confession of sin?

3.   Where do you see signs of Manasseh's desperation in this prayer? How does this enhance the sincerity of his plea?

4.   What parallels do you see between Manasseh's physical imprisonment and spiritual condition?

5.   What does Manasseh promise to do if God forgives him? How does Manasseh respond to forgiveness in 2 Chronicles 33:14-17?

1 Chronicles 28:1-11, 19-21; 29:1-13; 20-25

CLOSE READING TIPS

▶ Note that David's last act is to charge the people to back Solomon as his successor.

▶ Note the two reasons given for why David himself did not build the temple (1 Chron. 28:3).

▶ As in Deuteronomy, Israel's possession of the land is conditioned on their obedience (1 Chron. 28:8).

▶ Just as David gives Solomon a plan for the temple (1 Chron. 28:11), so too did God give Moses instructions for the tabernacle in Exodus 25:9. Detailed plans for the new temple are also given in Ezekiel 40–48.

▶ Note that David's plans for the temple come from divine inspiration (1 Chron. 28:19).

▶ There is an analogy between how David invites the people to contribute to the temple and how Moses asks the people to contribute to the tabernacle (Exod. 35:4-9; 35:20-29).

▶ Note that "darics" (1 Chron. 29:7) are a type of gold coin instituted by Darius I near the end of the sixth century. The reference to a daric in the time of David and Solomon is highly anachronistic.

▶ 1 Chronicles 29:11 is the source of the concluding doxology to the Lord's Prayer that appears in late manuscripts of Matthew 6:13.

▶ Note that David had already designated Solomon as king over Israel (2 Chron. 23:1). Here in 1 Chronicles 29:22, the people publically affirm David's choice of Solomon.

---

28 ¹ David assembled at Jerusalem all the officials of Israel, the officials of the tribes, the officers of the divisions that served the king, the commanders of the thousands, the commanders of the hundreds, the stewards of all the property and cattle of the king and his sons, together with the palace officials, the mighty warriors, and all the warriors. ² Then King David rose to his feet and said: "Hear me, my brothers and my people. I had planned to build a house of rest for the ark of the covenant of the LORD, for

the footstool of our God; and I made preparations for building. ³ But God said to me, 'You shall not build a house for my name, for you are a warrior and have shed blood.' ⁴ Yet the LORD God of Israel chose me from all my ancestral house to be king over Israel forever; for he chose Judah as leader, and in the house of Judah my father's house, and among my father's sons he took delight in making me king over all Israel. ⁵ And of all my sons, for the LORD has given me many, he has chosen my son Solomon to sit upon the throne of the kingdom of the LORD over Israel. ⁶ He said to me, 'It is your son Solomon who shall build my house and my courts, for I have chosen him to be a son to me, and I will be a father to him. ⁷ I will establish his kingdom forever if he continues resolute in keeping my commandments and my ordinances, as he is today.' ⁸ Now therefore in the sight of all Israel, the assembly of the LORD, and in the hearing of our God, observe and search out all the commandments of the LORD your God; that you may possess this good land, and leave it for an inheritance to your children after you forever.

⁹ "And you, my son Solomon, know the God of your father, and serve him with single mind and willing heart; for the LORD searches every mind, and understands every plan and thought. If you seek him, he will be found by you; but if you forsake him, he will abandon you forever. ¹⁰ Take heed now, for the LORD has chosen you to build a house as the sanctuary; be strong, and act."

¹¹ Then David gave his son Solomon the plan of the vestibule of the temple, and of its houses, its treasuries, its upper rooms, and its inner chambers, and of the room for the mercy seat.

¹⁹ "All this, in writing at the LORD's direction, he made clear to me—the plan of all the works."

²⁰ David said further to his son Solomon, "Be strong and of good courage, and act. Do not be afraid or dismayed; for the LORD God, my God, is with you. He will not fail you or forsake you, until all the work for the service of the house of the LORD is finished. ²¹ Here are the divisions of the priests and the Levites for all the service of the house of God; and with you in all the work will be every volunteer who has skill for any kind of service; also the officers and all the people will be wholly at your command."

29 ¹ King David said to the whole assembly, "My son Solomon, whom alone God has chosen, is young and inexperienced, and the work is great; for the temple will not be for mortals but for the LORD God. ² So I have provided for the house of my God, so far as I was able, the gold for the things of gold, the silver for the things of silver, and the bronze for the things of bronze, the iron for the things of iron, and wood for the things of wood, besides great quantities of onyx and stones for setting, antimony, colored stones, all sorts of precious stones, and marble in abundance. ³ Moreover, in addition to all that I have provided for the holy house, I have a treasure of my own of gold and silver, and because of my devotion to the house of my God I give it to the house of my God: ⁴ three thousand talents of gold, of the gold of Ophir, and seven thousand talents of refined silver, for overlaying the walls of the house, ⁵ and for all the work to be done by artisans, gold for the things of gold and silver for the things of silver. Who then will offer willingly, consecrating themselves today to the LORD?"

⁶ Then the leaders of ancestral houses made their freewill offerings, as did also the leaders of the tribes, the commanders of the thousands and of the hundreds, and the officers over the king's work. ⁷ They gave for the service of the house of God five thousand talents and ten thousand darics of gold, ten thousand talents of silver, eighteen thousand talents of bronze, and one hundred thousand talents of

iron. [8] Whoever had precious stones gave them to the treasury of the house of the LORD, into the care of Jehiel the Gershonite. [9] Then the people rejoiced because these had given willingly, for with single mind they had offered freely to the LORD; King David also rejoiced greatly.

[10] Then David blessed the LORD in the presence of all the assembly; David said: "Blessed are you, O LORD, the God of our ancestor Israel, forever and ever. [11] Yours, O LORD, are the greatness, the power, the glory, the victory, and the majesty; for all that is in the heavens and on the earth is yours; yours is the kingdom, O LORD, and you are exalted as head above all. [12] Riches and honor come from you, and you rule over all. In your hand are power and might; and it is in your hand to make great and to give strength to all. [13] And now, our God, we give thanks to you and praise your glorious name.

[20] Then David said to the whole assembly, "Bless the LORD your God." And all the assembly blessed the LORD, the God of their ancestors, and bowed their heads and prostrated themselves before the LORD and the king. [21] On the next day they offered sacrifices and burnt offerings to the LORD, a thousand bulls, a thousand rams, and a thousand lambs, with their libations, and sacrifices in abundance for all Israel; [22] and they ate and drank before the LORD on that day with great joy.

They made David's son Solomon king a second time; they anointed him as the LORD's prince, and Zadok as priest. [23] Then Solomon sat on the throne of the LORD, succeeding his father David as king; he prospered, and all Israel obeyed him. [24] All the leaders and the mighty warriors, and also all the sons of King David, pledged their allegiance to King Solomon. [25] The LORD highly exalted Solomon in the sight of all Israel, and bestowed upon him such royal majesty as had not been on any king before him in Israel.

DISCUSSION QUESTIONS

1. On what basis should the people back Solomon as the next king?
2. While David himself does not build the temple, in what ways is he involved in the preparations for this future project?
3. How does the account in 1 Chronicles 29:20-25 contrast with Solomon's ascension to the throne in 1 Kings 1–2?
4. In what ways does this passage reflect characteristic concerns of the Chronicler's vision of history?

The death of Josiah: 2 Chronicles 34:22-28; 35:20-27

CLOSE READING TIPS

▸ Huldah is a prophetess from Jerusalem. Her prophecy is also recorded in 2 KIngs 22:14-20.
▸ The "curses that are written in the book" (2 Chron. 34:24) refer to curses associated with the covenant in the book of Deuteronomy. These curses will come upon Judah despite Josiah's sweeping reforms.

▸ Because of his faithfulness, Josiah will be allowed to die in peace and he will be spared from having to see the fall of Jerusalem (2 Chron. 34:28).

▸ Neco was king of Egypt from 610–595 BCE. His encounter with Josiah is recorded in 2 Kings 23:29-30.

▸ In an effort to stave off the advancing power of the Babylonians, Neco may have traveled to Carcamesh to support the Assyrians (2 Chron. 35:20).

▸ Since he is sent by God, Neco assumes that anyone who opposes him also opposes God (2 Chron. 35:21).

▸ The battle occurs at Megiddo, a town along an important pass leading from the coastal plain into the Jezreel Valley. It was the site of numerous battles in the Hebrew Bible.

▸ It is not entirely clear why Josiah would go against King Neco (2 Chron. 35:22-23). Perhaps it was because he was anti-Assyria or because he simply wanted to maintain his independence.

▸ Note that in 2 Kings 23, Josiah dies at Megiddo and is then brought to Jerusalem to be buried. This might suggest that Josiah was executed on the battle field.

▸ The "Laments" mentioned in 2 Chronicles 35:25 do not refer to the book of Lamentations, although like Lamentations, they are said to be associated with the prophet Jeremiah.

34 [22] So Hilkiah and those whom the king had sent went to the prophet Huldah, the wife of Shallum son of Tokhath son of Hasrah, keeper of the wardrobe (who lived in Jerusalem in the Second Quarter) and spoke to her to that effect. [23] She declared to them, "Thus says the LORD, the God of Israel: Tell the man who sent you to me, [24] Thus says the LORD: I will indeed bring disaster upon this place and upon its inhabitants, all the curses that are written in the book that was read before the king of Judah. [25] Because they have forsaken me and have made offerings to other gods, so that they have provoked me to anger with all the works of their hands, my wrath will be poured out on this place and will not be quenched. [26] But as to the king of Judah, who sent you to inquire of the LORD, thus shall you say to him: Thus says the LORD, the God of Israel: Regarding the words that you have heard, [27] because your heart was penitent and you humbled yourself before God when you heard his words against this place

and its inhabitants, and you have humbled yourself before me, and have torn your clothes and wept before me, I also have heard you, says the LORD. [28] I will gather you to your ancestors and you shall be gathered to your grave in peace; your eyes shall not see all the disaster that I will bring on this place and its inhabitants." They took the message back to the king.

35 [20] After all this, when Josiah had set the temple in order, King Neco of Egypt went up to fight at Carchemish on the Euphrates, and Josiah went out against him. [21] But Neco sent envoys to him, saying, "What have I to do with you, king of Judah? I am not coming against you today, but against the house with which I am at war; and God has commanded me to hurry. Cease opposing God, who is with me, so that he will not destroy you." [22] But Josiah would not turn away from him, but disguised himself in order to fight with him. He did not listen to the words of Neco from the mouth of God, but joined

battle in the plain of Megiddo. [23] The archers shot King Josiah; and the king said to his servants, "Take me away, for I am badly wounded." [24] So his servants took him out of the chariot and carried him in his second chariot and brought him to Jerusalem. There he died, and was buried in the tombs of his ancestors. All Judah and Jerusalem mourned for Josiah. [25] Jeremiah also uttered a lament for Josiah, and all the singing men and singing women have spoken of Josiah in their laments to this day. They made these a custom in Israel; they are recorded in the Laments. [26] Now the rest of the acts of Josiah and his faithful deeds in accordance with what is written in the law of the LORD, [27] and his acts, first and last, are written in the Book of the Kings of Israel and Judah.

Discussion questions

1. According to the prophetess Huldah, is Josiah's death a sign of divine punishment or an act of divine mercy?
2. How does your view of the reason for Josiah's death change in light of 2 Chronicles 35?
3. 2 Chronicles 35:21-22 is entirely absent in the account of Josiah's death in 2 Kings 23. Why do you think the Chronicler added these details? How is it consistent with his theological perspective of retribution?
4. How does the portrayal of Josiah in this story differ from the characterization of Josiah in the Deuteronomistic History?

23

The Psalms and Song of Songs

Key Points

The book of Psalms (the Psalter) includes some of the most often quoted and deeply cherished materials in the Hebrew Bible. Though traditionally associated with David, the 150 psalms in this book were composed over the course of many centuries. The psalms are organized into five sections, or books, each of which ends in a short hymn of praise. Smaller groupings of psalms are also evident, such as the Psalms of Asaph (Pss. 50, 73–83) and the Songs of Ascent (Pss. 130–134). Some notable differences are evident between the order and content of the Masoretic Psalter and that which is attested in both the Greek Bible and Psalms Scroll at Qumran.

Rather than being spontaneous prayers of individuals, the psalms reflect relatively fixed literary forms that were originally designed for use in the context of communal worship. Hymns, or songs of praise, celebrate God's power, majesty, and kingship and were likely associated with festivals or enthronement liturgies. Complaints, which are the most common genre in the Psalter, are formulaic expressions emerging from either individual experiences of sin or trauma or the community's response to war, exile, or other calamities. Psalms of individual and communal thanksgiving consist of grateful responses to God for acts of deliverance and are often associated with processions or other ritual contexts. In addition, there are a number of psalms that do not strictly fit into one of these three main categories. Some poems, such as the royal psalms and wisdom psalms, can be grouped together based on a consistent set of themes.

Although the book of Psalms is best understood as a loosely edited anthology, several common features are evident. First, the psalms provide a window into ancient Israelite spirituality, probing the depths of despair, the reality of death, and longings for YHWH's life-giving presence and deliverance. In this sense, the psalms lend themselves to liturgical use and theological reflection. Second, the psalms are poems written with careful attention to their rhetorical and aesthetic qualities. As such, they employ a variety of literary devices, including parallelism, acrostics, inclusios, chiastic arrangements, and figurative language. Finally, while certain psalms may have played a role in moral instruction, the Psalter as a whole functions to mirror or elicit human emotions, often unfiltered and cathartic.

Like the Psalms, the Song of Songs is a collection of poems that utilizes evocative imagery and gives expression to raw human emotion—in this case, love. It consists of a series of dialogues between two young lovers, both of whom freely express romantic and erotic love for one another. In this sense, the Song of Songs shares much in common with ancient Near Eastern love poetry. One notable feature of the Song of Songs is that it is one of only two books in the Hebrew Bible that does not mention God. As a result, questions were originally raised among the rabbis about whether this book should be included in the Hebrew Bible. Nevertheless, the canonical status of the Song of Songs has been vigorously defended. In Jewish and Christian traditions, this book has traditionally been interpreted as an allegory for YHWH's love for Israel or Christ's love for the church, respectively.

Key Terms

Psalms of Enthronement   This term refers to a distinct group of hymns in the Psalter (Pss. 93, 97, 99) that affirm the greatness of YHWH as king. Each begins with an acclamation that can be rendered either "YHWH is king" or "YHWH has become king." Sigmund Mowinckel argued that these psalms reflect a festival celebrating the enthronement of YHWH. While no such event is explicitly mentioned in the Hebrew Bible, parallels are found in the recitation of the *Enuma Elish*, which celebrates Marduk's enthronement during the Babylonian New Year festival.

The Psalms Scroll   This scroll from the Qumran community (known as 11Q5) contains the last third of the book of Psalms, though in a slightly different arrangement than the Masoretic Psalter. It also includes several apocryphal psalms as well as some previously unknown materials. Among the Dead Sea Scrolls are other portions of the Psalter, most of which correspond closely to the

first three books of the Masoretic Psalter. This suggests that the content and order of the latter part of the Psalms were still in flux in the second century BCE.

Wisdom psalms   This category of psalms is distinguished by its meditative tone and close affinity with themes found in wisdom literature. These psalms show much interest in the fate of the righteous and the wicked. The Torah figures prominently in these psalms, thus suggesting that the Psalter should be read in light of the Torah as a source of wisdom (for example, Pss. 1, 19, and 119). Some have suggested that the didactic quality of the wisdom psalms means that they were used for moral instruction or were developed outside of liturgical contexts.

Parallelism   Parallelism refers to the correspondence of content or grammatical structure in two consecutive lines of poetry. The nature of this correspondence varies widely, with the most common forms being synonymous (using near equivalent terms or sentiments), antithetic (using opposite terms or sentiments), and synthetic (using a similar form of construction). Parallelism is the most prominent rhetorical feature of Hebrew poetry and is also widely attested in ancient Near Eastern literature.

Five scrolls (*Megillot*)   The term *Megillot*, which means "scrolls" in Hebrew, is used to indicate a collection of five books, each of which is associated with a specific Jewish festival: Song of Songs (Passover), Ruth (Feast of Weeks), Lamentations (ninth of Ab), Qoheleth (Sukkoth or Tabernacles), and Esther (Purim). In the Hebrew Bible, these books appear together within the Writings. In the Christian Old Testament, these books are distributed among the historical books, prophets, and wisdom literature mostly based on thematic considerations.

Hallelujah   Hallelujah is a transliteration of a Hebrew imperative meaning "Praise Yah(weh)!" This word occurs twenty-four times in psalms that are categorized as hymns. In these contexts, the congregation is called on to praise YHWH either for his mighty work as creator (for example, Pss. 8 and 104) or his historical acts of deliverance (as in Ps. 114). In both Jewish and Christian liturgies today, the word Hallelujah is used extensively.

Key Personalities

The young lovers

Two young, unnamed lovers are the main characters in the Song of Songs. They address each other through a series of dialogues, though occasionally the woman also speaks to "the daughters of Jerusalem." These dialogues or "songs" allow the reader to listen in on the young lovers' intimate conversations. Through evocative similes and vivid imagery drawn from nature, the man and woman praise each other's physical beauty. Though not married, their celebration of sexual love is joyful and uninhibited. The romantic and erotic feelings freely expressed by the lovers contrasts with the more guarded and restrictive sexual ethic found elsewhere in the Hebrew Bible. Perhaps because of their uneasiness with this language, rabbinic interpreters claimed that the Song of Songs was an allegory for the love between YHWH and Israel. Many Christians have employed a similar line of reasoning, suggesting that the lovers represent Christ and the church. Without dismissing the value of these later interpretations, it should be noted that the young lovers would not likely have been understood as allegorical figures by the original readers of the Song of Songs. In fact, the sensual descriptions of physical beauty exchanged between the young lovers is typical of Mesopotamian and Egyptian love poetry.

The divine king

The central image used to describe God throughout the Psalter is that of kingship. The Psalms of Enthronement proclaim that YHWH is or has become king. Other psalms celebrate the justice and righteousness associated with his universal reign. As in Canaanite myths, the psalms attest that God was established as king by virtue of defeating chaos (Ps. 93:3-4) or by triumphing over Yamm, the sea (Ps. 89:9-10). In these cosmic battles, the divine king, not unlike Baal, manifests his power through thunder, lightning, wind, and rain (as in Psalm 29). However, in most cases the psalms dealing with the divine king demythologize the combat tradition. Instead, YHWH is shown as the supreme creator, bringing order and fertility to the land (Ps. 104). As such, even the natural world itself bears witness to the glory and majesty of YHWH's kingship (for example, Pss. 19:1; 97:6; 93:3). The universal scope of Yahweh's reign has a clear eschatological dimension. It is significant to note that the kingship of YHWH is closely tied to the Davidic kingship. Though subordinate to the divine king, the earthly king is called YHWH's son (Ps. 2:7) and is invited to sit at his right hand (Ps. 110:1). Like his heavenly counterpart, the human king is associated with justice and righteousness (Ps. 72). Finally, the human kingship also has an eschatological aspect to it, as is especially evident in many of the royal psalms.

Questions for Study and Discussion

1. How do the psalms give interpreters a glimpse into the human condition? What does one learn about humanity, the world, and God, in other words, from Israel's ancient prayers and hymns?

2. The Psalms seems to have two conflicting views on death and the afterlife. One of these views is dominant and the other provides a minority report. What are these two conflicting views and to what texts would you refer when making your argument?

3. As prayers, the psalms clearly have an interest in communicating with God. But what kind of God do they interact with? Describe as many characteristics of the Psalter's theology that you can, even if certain features seem to be in conflict with one another.

4. The psalms of vengeance raise an interesting set of ethical questions: Since the Psalms likely have an instructional function, how should one react to the various calls for God to enact vengeance upon enemies?

Primary Text

Psalm 151

CLOSE READING TIPS

▶ Though not appearing in the Masoretic Text, this is the final psalm in the Greek Bible. Slightly longer versions of this psalm are found in the Psalms Scroll at Qumran and in the Syriac translation of the Hebrew Bible.

▶ Psalm 151 was likely written in the third century BCE.

▶ Note that musical ability (verse 2) was thought to be closely related to the art of poetry.

▶ Verses 4-5 reference the story about how David was chosen from among his many brothers as the future king (see 1 Sam. 16:1-13).

▶ In verses 6-7, the focus of the psalms shifts to David's slaying of the Philistine, Goliath; the reference to Goliath cursing David by his idols, or gods, is found in 1 Samuel 17:43.

¹ I was small among my brothers,
    and the youngest in my father's house;
I tended my father's sheep.
² My hands made a harp;
    my fingers fashioned a lyre.
³ And who will tell my Lord?
    The Lord himself; it is he who hears.
⁴ It was he who sent his messenger
    and took me from my father's sheep,
    and anointed me with his anointing oil.
⁵ My brothers were handsome and tall,
    but the Lord was not pleased with them.
⁶ I went out to meet the Philistine,
    and he cursed me by his idols.
⁷ But I drew his own sword;
    I beheaded him, and took away disgrace
    from the people of Israel.

DISCUSSION QUESTIONS

1. What type of psalm is this—a hymn, a prayer of thanksgiving, a complaint, or something else?
2. Compare this psalm with the end of the Masoretic Psalter (especially Pss. 146–150). To what extent do you think Psalm 151 fits with these other psalms? Why?
3. How does this text contribute to the tradition that David was the author of the psalms?

Psalm 51

CLOSE READING TIPS

▶ Note that the superscription is not an original part of Psalm 51. It was added by later editors.
▶ In the Christian tradition, this psalm is considered one of the seven penitential psalms (Pss. 6; 32; 38; 51; 102; 130; 143) due to its emphasis on contrition or penitence.
▶ Note that the verbs "blot out" and "wash" are repeated in verses 1-9.
▶ "Born guilty" in verse 5 underscores the depth of human sin and is not exactly an affirmation of the Christian doctrine of original sin.
▶ The branches of hyssop were used for sprinkling liquids in purification rituals (see Lev. 14:2-9, 48-53; Num. 19:6, 18).
▶ It is thought that verses 18-19 are a later addition to Psalm 51.
▶ "Right sacrifices" in verse 19 may refer to sacrifices offered with the proper attitude or sacrifices made according to the appropriate prescriptions of the law.

To the leader. A Psalm of David, when the prophet Nathan came to him, after he had gone in to Bathsheba.

¹ Have mercy on me, O God,
    according to your steadfast love;
according to your abundant mercy
    blot out my transgressions.
² Wash me thoroughly from my iniquity,
    and cleanse me from my sin.
³ For I know my transgressions,
    and my sin is ever before me.
⁴ Against you, you alone, have I sinned,

and done what is evil in your sight,
so that you are justified in your sentence
    and blameless when you pass judgment.
⁵ Indeed, I was born guilty,
    a sinner when my mother conceived me.

⁶ You desire truth in the inward being;
    therefore teach me wisdom in my secret
        heart.
⁷ Purge me with hyssop, and I shall be clean;
    wash me, and I shall be whiter than snow.
⁸ Let me hear joy and gladness;
    let the bones that you have crushed rejoice.
⁹ Hide your face from my sins,
    and blot out all my iniquities.

¹⁰ Create in me a clean heart, O God,
    and put a new and right spirit within me.
¹¹ Do not cast me away from your presence,
    and do not take your holy spirit from me.
¹² Restore to me the joy of your salvation,
    and sustain in me a willing spirit.

¹³ Then I will teach transgressors your ways,
    and sinners will return to you.
¹⁴ Deliver me from bloodshed, O God,
    O God of my salvation,
    and my tongue will sing aloud of your
        deliverance.

¹⁵ O Lord, open my lips,
    and my mouth will declare your praise.
¹⁶ For you have no delight in sacrifice;
    if I were to give a burnt offering, you
        would not be pleased.
¹⁷ The sacrifice acceptable to God is a broken
    spirit;
    a broken and contrite heart, O God, you
        will not despise.

¹⁸ Do good to Zion in your good pleasure;
    rebuild the walls of Jerusalem,
¹⁹ then you will delight in right sacrifices,
    in burnt offerings and whole burnt
        offerings;
then bulls will be offered on your altar.

DISCUSSION QUESTIONS

1. Where do you see the typical elements of the complaint psalm in this text?
2. What metaphors for sin are used throughout this psalm?
3. What does the psalmist promise to do in response to receiving a "clean heart?"
4. What attitude is expressed in this psalm to cultic sacrifices?

Psalm 118

CLOSE READING TIPS

▶ This psalm was likely used in a liturgical procession that leads into the temple. THE first-person speaker is possibly the king (see verse 10-14), though he could be any representative of the community.
▶ Note that "steadfast love" is a covenant term (Heb.: ⊠*esed*) that has to do with the LORD's fidelity to past promises.
▶ In Deuteronomy 1:44, bees are also used as a metaphor for Israel's enemies (verse 12).

> ▸ Verses 15-16 reflects an ancient victory song.
> ▸ Verse 19 seems to imagine the individual entering the temple precincts and asking to be admitted through the temple gates. The requirements for admission are stated in verse 20.
> ▸ In verse 21, the individual gives thanks again, having been admitted into the sanctuary.
> ▸ The transition from low to high in verse 22 is a result of divine intervention. This verse is quoted multiple times in the New Testament in reference to Jesus (see Matt. 21:42; Mark 12:10; Luke 20:17; Acts 4:11; 1 Pet. 2:7).
> ▸ "Save us" in verse 25 translates the Hebrew word "Hosanna."
> ▸ The horns of the altar (verse 27) refer to four projections at the corners of the altar. Their function is not entirely clear.

[1] O give thanks to the LORD, for he is good;
  his steadfast love endures forever!

[2] Let Israel say,
  "His steadfast love endures forever."
3 Let the house of Aaron say,
  "His steadfast love endures forever."
[4] Let those who fear the LORD say,
  "His steadfast love endures forever."

[5] Out of my distress I called on the LORD;
  the LORD answered me and set me in a
    broad place.
[6] With the LORD on my side I do not fear.
  What can mortals do to me?
[7] The LORD is on my side to help me;
  I shall look in triumph on those who hate
    me.
[8] It is better to take refuge in the LORD
  than to put confidence in mortals.
[9] It is better to take refuge in the LORD
  than to put confidence in princes.

[10] All nations surrounded me;
  in the name of the LORD I cut them off!
[11] They surrounded me, surrounded me on
  every side;

  in the name of the LORD I cut them off!
[12] They surrounded me like bees;
  they blazed like a fire of thorns;
  in the name of the LORD I cut them off!
[13] I was pushed hard, so that I was falling,
  but the LORD helped me.
[14] The LORD is my strength and my might;
  he has become my salvation.

[15] There are glad songs of victory in the tents of
  the righteous:
    "The right hand of the LORD does
      valiantly;
[16] the right hand of the LORD is exalted;
  the right hand of the LORD does
    valiantly."
[17] I shall not die, but I shall live,
  and recount the deeds of the LORD.
[18] The LORD has punished me severely,
  but he did not give me over to death.

[19] Open to me the gates of righteousness,
  that I may enter through them
  and give thanks to the LORD.

[20] This is the gate of the LORD;
  the righteous shall enter through it.

²¹ I thank you that you have answered me
  and have become my salvation.
²² The stone that the builders rejected
  has become the chief cornerstone.
²³ This is the LORD's doing;
  it is marvelous in our eyes.
²⁴ This is the day that the LORD has made;
  let us rejoice and be glad in it.
²⁵ Save us, we beseech you, O LORD!
  O LORD, we beseech you, give us success!

²⁶ Blessed is the one who comes in the name of
  the LORD.

We bless you from the house of the LORD.
²⁷ The LORD is God,
  and he has given us light.
Bind the festal procession with branches,
  up to the horns of the altar.

²⁸ You are my God, and I will give thanks to
  you;
you are my God, I will extol you.

²⁹ O give thanks to the LORD, for he is good,
  for his steadfast love endures forever.

Discussion questions

1. Where do you see the typical elements of a psalm of thanksgiving in this text?
2. How does the psalmist describe the circumstances that lead to this expression of thanksgiving?
3. Although this is an individual thanksgiving, in what sense does it have a collective aspect?
4. Where do you see evidence of an inclusio in Psalm 118?
5. Where are several places you see parallelism in this poem? What type of parallelism is evident in each case?

Song of Songs 1:7—2:7

Close reading tips

▸ In Song of Songs 1:7, "veiled" may refer to the guise of a harlot.
▸ Note that Song of Songs 1:8 may be spoken by the man or by the women of Jerusalem who appear earlier in this chapter.
▸ The comparison of the woman to a fine horse is a common form of praise in ancient literature.
▸ Note that in Song of Songs 1:12-14, the woman refers to her beloved as "the king." Rather than actually imply the youth was royalty, this expression may suggest that he was reclining like a king on a lavish couch.
▸ Nard, myrrh, and henna blossoms all are costly aromatics used as a type of perfume.
▸ Sharon is the coastal plane between Jaffa and Mount Carmel. The woman's statement that she is a rose is not a boast but rather a modest way of saying that she is but one flower out of thousands.
▸ The "banquet house" literally is the house of wine (Song of Songs 2:5). It suggests the "intoxicating" quality of the young couple's love.
▸ Note that in Song of Songs 2:7 love is personified.

1 ⁷ Tell me, you whom my soul loves,
> where you pasture your flock,
> where you make it lie down at noon;
> for why should I be like one who is veiled
> beside the flocks of your companions?

⁸ If you do not know,
> O fairest among women,
> follow the tracks of the flock,
> and pasture your kids
> beside the shepherds' tents.

⁹ I compare you, my love,
> to a mare among Pharaoh's chariots.
¹⁰ Your cheeks are comely with ornaments,
> your neck with strings of jewels.
¹¹ We will make you ornaments of gold,
> studded with silver.

¹² While the king was on his couch,
> my nard gave forth its fragrance.
¹³ My beloved is to me a bag of myrrh
> that lies between my breasts.
¹⁴ My beloved is to me a cluster of henna
> blossoms
> in the vineyards of En-gedi.

¹⁵ Ah, you are beautiful, my love;
> ah, you are beautiful;

> your eyes are doves.
¹⁶ Ah, you are beautiful, my beloved,
> truly lovely.
Our couch is green;
> ¹⁷ the beams of our house are cedar,
> our rafters are pine.

2 ¹ I am a rose of Sharon,
> a lily of the valleys.

² As a lily among brambles,
> so is my love among maidens.

³ As an apple tree among the trees of the wood,
> so is my beloved among young men.
With great delight I sat in his shadow,
> and his fruit was sweet to my taste.
⁴ He brought me to the banqueting house,
> and his intention toward me was love.
⁵ Sustain me with raisins,
> refresh me with apples;
> for I am faint with love.
⁶ O that his left hand were under my head,
> and that his right hand embraced me!
⁷ I adjure you, O daughters of Jerusalem,
> by the gazelles or the wild does:
do not stir up or awaken love
> until it is ready!

DISCUSSION QUESTIONS

1. There are several changes of speaker in this short passage. Can you identify when the woman is speaking and when the man is speaking?
2. What similes or figures of speech are used here in order to describe physical beauty? Do they share any common theme?
3. In the context of this passage, is love "ready" (Song of Songs 2:7) between these two people? Why or why not?
4. If you read this text as an allegory for YHWH's love for Israel, how would you interpret Song of Songs 2:4-7?

24

Proverbs

Up to this point in our study of the Hebrew Bible, we have not encountered a book quite like Proverbs. In stark contrast to the Pentateuch or Prophets, Proverbs makes hardly any mention of the Torah, the exodus, the Davidic covenant, or the sacrificial cult. Rather, what Proverbs offers are a number of pithy instructions often framed as advice from a father to a son. These instructions attempt to define wisdom and folly and to confer practical advice about cultivating a fruitful life.

Proverbs is traditionally associated with King Solomon. However, Solomon is best understood as the patron saint of wisdom, not the author of this book. Wisdom literature tends to originate in two different settings: oral traditions that preserved wise sayings among families and tribes or the well-attested genre of instructions that developed in the context of a royal court. Both settings likely apply in the case of Proverbs. In either case, the book of Proverbs can be situated within an extensive tradition of wisdom literature in the ancient Near East and Egypt. In addition, wisdom literature can also be found in Qoheleth and Job as well as the deuterocanonical books Ben Sira and the Wisdom of Solomon.

Though the arrangement of individual sayings is often random, the book as a whole is divided into seven collections of proverbs, each of which is set off by a superscription. The core of the book (chapters 10–29) consists of a series of short sayings, some of which are clustered thematically (for example, Prov. 25:1-7) and others of which reflect similar forms, such as the numerical sayings in Proverbs 30:15-33. Chapters 1–9 offer more general instructions and are notable for their personification of wisdom as a woman. Proverbs concludes with a laudatory poem about "the capable wife," perhaps as a way of counterbalancing the image of "the strange woman" in the opening of the book.

Three particular features of the book of Proverbs should be carefully noted. First, God plays a far more indirect role in human affairs than in most other biblical books. Yet, wisdom is impossible without God. By guaranteeing the cosmic order, God makes it possible to base instruction on an observable chain of cause and effect. As such, Proverbs repeatedly affirms that "the Fear of the LORD is the beginning of knowledge." Second, Proverb's ethical system is driven by pragmatism—its basic premise is that righteousness is the most profitable course of action. Yet complexities abound. Because the path of wisdom can vary depending on a given situation, the instructions given throughout the book occasionally contradict one another (for example, Prov. 26:4-5). In general, this pragmatism is balanced with a strain of idealism that affirms, among other things, the importance of caring for the poor. Finally, proverbial wisdom is rooted in everyday experience, not divine revelation or the Torah. This means that the claims Proverbs makes are verifiable by observation and can be extended through the use of analogies. However, as we will see in the books of Job and Qoheleth, the reliability of the connection between act and consequence, observation and conclusion are not always as certain as Proverbs would have us believe.

Key Terms

Instruction of Amenemope   The Instruction of Amenemope is an Egyptian wisdom text from around the twelfth century BCE. Framed as the teachings of Amenemope to his youngest son, this didactic text emphasizes honesty in personal and professional affairs, care for the poor, self control, and reverence for "the Lord of all." The Instruction of Amenemope shares thematic and structural similarities with the book of Proverbs (especially Prov. 22:18—23:11), suggesting that the Egyptian text served as a model for the biblical composition.

The fear of the LORD   Summarizing the theology of Proverbs, Proverbs 1:7 declares that "the fear of the LORD is the beginning of knowledge." This expression, which occurs sixteen times throughout the book, introduces a divine dimension to the pursuit of wisdom. It acknowledges the limitations of human experience and affirms all of creation's dependence on God. While characteristic of the Proverbs, the sentiment behind the fear of the LORD is also present in other ancient Near Eastern wisdom texts.

Folly   Taken together, folly and the related terms "fool" and "foolish" occur seventy-seven times in Proverbs and generally describe that which is opposite of wisdom. Specifically, the fool despises instruction, speaks without restraint, does not heed parental advice, and is quick to anger. Folly leads to ruin and shame. The book of Proverbs displays little sympathy for the fool and sharply contrasts the foolish woman with personified Wisdom (Prov. 9:1-18).

The capable wife   The capable wife refers to the woman described in the acrostic poem at the end of the book of Proverbs (Prov. 31:10-31). As a counterbalance to the "strange woman" in chapters 1–9, the capable wife is praised for her industriousness and wisdom, and as such is said to be "far more precious than jewels" (Prov. 31:10). Though complementary in its tone, Proverbs 31:10-31 is patriarchal in its perspective. In this poem, the woman herself is silent and her virtues are defined according to the husband's (or male's) point of view.

"Created" or "acquired" (*qanah*)   Proverbs 8:22 affirms that God "created" (Heb.: *qanah*) wisdom at the beginning of this work. The verb *qanah* can also mean "acquired," which would imply that wisdom existed independently and aligned with YHWH at creation. In either case, the book of Proverbs affirms that wisdom is embedded in the very fabric of the universe. This is the basis of a type of natural theology in which one can arrive at knowledge of God by studying the order of the universe.

Key Personalities

Lady Wisdom

In Proverbs 1–9, wisdom is personified as a woman. She is the embodiment of wisdom, offering its fruit to humanity. Not unlike a prophet, Lady Wisdom cries out to the people in a public setting (Prov. 1:20-21) and occasionally has a reproving tone (Prov. 1:26-32). She extols the many benefits of seeking instruction and urges the people to follow the path of the righteous rather than the path of the wicked (chapter 4). Lady Wisdom's advice is grounded in practical admonitions and includes warnings about the temptations of the strange woman (chapters 5 and 7) and the foolish woman (chapter 9). She claims to give long life and prosperity to those who lay hold of her (Prov. 3:16-18). The most developed depiction of Lady Wisdom is found in chapter 8. Here we are told that Lady Wisdom was created or acquired (Heb.: *qanah*) at the beginning of God's work (Prov. 8:22). While the best translation of the verb *qanah* is debated, the rest of Proverbs 8 makes it clear that Lady Wisdom accompanied God as a "master worker" (Prov. 8:30) in creation. Due to the nature of her speech and her association with truth and righteousness, some scholars have speculated that Lady Wisdom was originally conceived of as a goddess. However, even if the portrayal of Lady

Wisdom was influenced by depictions of Egyptian goddesses such as Isis and Maat, there is no explicit evidence that she was regarded as a deity in ancient Israel. Instead, the personification of Lady Wisdom is best understood as a literary device common in the Hebrew Bible and other ancient literature.

The strange woman

Introduced in Proverbs 2:16-19, the strange woman (NRSV: "loose woman") is the primary metaphor of temptation in the book of Proverbs. As the antithesis of Lady Wisdom, she is associated with the adulteress and her path leads to death. Her words drip honey, but in the end she only offers bitterness to those who pursue her (Prov. 5:3-4). Rather than keeping to the path of life, her ways wander (Prov. 5:6). In Proverbs 7, she is pictured as actively trying to seduce the "young man without sense," accosting him in the streets and luring him to her house with seductive words. The author admonishes the reader not to turn their hearts to the strange woman, lest he "goes like an ox to the slaughter" (Prov. 7:22). The strange woman can be interpreted in a variety of ways. She may be a mythological figure modeled on certain dangerous goddesses (namely, Ishtar) in ancient Near Eastern literature. Alternatively, her seductive behavior has led some to think of her as a type of cult prostitute who lures men into the worship of a goddess. Recognizing that the Hebrew word translated as "strange" (*zarah*) can also mean "foreign," a third option is that she is a non-Israelite women. While the book of Proverbs lends little support to this idea, it does correspond with warnings about inter-marriage in Ezra-Nehemiah. The most plausible option is that the strange woman is the wife of another man. As such, the primary danger is that of adultery, which not only threatens the social order but also takes on symbolic significance as a deviation from the way of wisdom.

Questions for Study and Discussion

1. Much of biblical literature is depicted as divine revelation from YHWH (such as the law at Sinai, and prophetic speeches). How does revelation occur in Proverbs? How is this different or similar to other forms of revelation found elsewhere in the Hebrew Bible. Moreover, each of these modes of revelation pose unique challenges to later interpreters of biblical literature, and especially those who consider the Hebrew Bible to be Scripture. What are those problems? And what are some possible responses to them?

2. The chapter describes a tension between pragmatism and idealism. Describe this tension and how it plays out in specific ways in the book of Proverbs. Then, thinking about modern sources of wisdom, reflect on whether you see similar points of tension? Sources of wisdom could include: parental wisdom, self-help books, the American meritocratic myth, and so forth.

3. Respond to the following statement: "Proverbs 31 is clearly an example of a virtuous and industrious wife—a true example for young women who want to live wisely in the twenty-first century."

4. The many ancient Near Eastern—and especially Egyptian—parallels in Proverbs suggest that the book of Proverbs drew on many non-Israelite sources. Implicitly at least, Israel does not claim to have a corner on wisdom. What might this imply about Israel's understanding of God and the world God has created?

Primary Text

Proverbs 8

CLOSE READING TIPS

▶ As in Proverb 1, Lady wisdom appears in verses 1-3 as a prophet or street teacher, addressing the people from public spaces. In the Hellenistic world, teachers and philosophers often sought pupils in public spaces such as those mentioned in these verses.

▶ "Simple ones" in verse 5 refers to those who can still learn and benefit from wisdom's instructions.

▶ Note that proper and truthful speech is a central concern of the wisdom tradition. Listening and speaking well are barometers of success and necessary for an orderly society.

▶ Wicked and righteous, much like wise and foolish, are commonly employed word pairs in Proverbs.

▶ Note that wisdom is accessible to those who seek it (verse 17).

▶ The word translated as "prosperity" (verse 18) and "righteousness" (verse 20) goes back to the same Hebrew word (*tsedaqah*).

▶ The Hebrew word translated as "set up" in verse 23 is elsewhere used to refer to God's installation of the king in Jerusalem.

▶ An alternative reading for "Master worker" is little child. This reading fits well with verse 24, where "brought forth" implies the birthing of a child. Comparisons can be made with the Egyptian goddess Maat, who is sometimes depicted as a little child playing on the lap of her father, the creator god Amum Re.

¹ Does not wisdom call,
    and does not understanding raise her
        voice?
² On the heights, beside the way,
    at the crossroads she takes her stand;
³ beside the gates in front of the town,
    at the entrance of the portals she cries out:
⁴ "To you, O people, I call,
    and my cry is to all that live.
⁵ O simple ones, learn prudence;
    acquire intelligence, you who lack it.
⁶ Hear, for I will speak noble things,
    and from my lips will come what is right;
⁷ for my mouth will utter truth;
    wickedness is an abomination to my lips.
⁸ All the words of my mouth are righteous;
    there is nothing twisted or crooked in
        them.
⁹ They are all straight to one who understands
    and right to those who find knowledge.
¹⁰ Take my instruction instead of silver,
    and knowledge rather than choice gold;
¹¹ for wisdom is better than jewels,
    and all that you may desire cannot
        compare with her.
¹² I, wisdom, live with prudence,
    and I attain knowledge and discretion.
¹³ The fear of the LORD is hatred of evil.
Pride and arrogance and the way of evil
    and perverted speech I hate.
¹⁴ I have good advice and sound wisdom;
    I have insight, I have strength.

¹⁵ By me kings reign,
    and rulers decree what is just;
¹⁶ by me rulers rule,
    and nobles, all who govern rightly.
¹⁷ I love those who love me,
    and those who seek me diligently find me.
¹⁸ Riches and honor are with me,
    enduring wealth and prosperity.
¹⁹ My fruit is better than gold, even fine gold,
    and my yield than choice silver.
²⁰ I walk in the way of righteousness,
    along the paths of justice,
²¹ endowing with wealth those who love me,
    and filling their treasuries.
²² The LORD created me at the beginning of his
        work,
    the first of his acts of long ago.
²³ Ages ago I was set up,
    at the first, before the beginning of the
        earth.
²⁴ When there were no depths I was brought
        forth,
    when there were no springs abounding
        with water.
²⁵ Before the mountains had been shaped,
    before the hills, I was brought forth—
²⁶ when he had not yet made earth and fields,
    or the world's first bits of soil.
²⁷ When he established the heavens, I was
        there,
    when he drew a circle on the face of the
        deep,

28 when he made firm the skies above,
when he established the fountains of the deep,
29 when he assigned to the sea its limit,
so that the waters might not transgress his command,
when he marked out the foundations of the earth,
30 then I was beside him, like a master worker;
and I was daily his delight,
rejoicing before him always,
31 rejoicing in his inhabited world
and delighting in the human race.

32 And now, my children, listen to me:
happy are those who keep my ways.
33 Hear instruction and be wise,
and do not neglect it.
34 Happy is the one who listens to me,
watching daily at my gates,
waiting beside my doors.
35 For whoever finds me finds life
and obtains favor from the LORD;
36 but those who miss me injure themselves;
all who hate me love death."

DISCUSSION QUESTIONS

1. Why is it important that Lady Wisdom is pictured as teaching in a public setting instead of, say, the temple or royal court? How is this consistent with the nature of wisdom literature?
2. How are the words of Lady Wisdom in verses 6-9 in contrast to what you know about the words of the strange woman (see especially Prov. 5:3-4; 7:11-12, 21-22)?
3. What role does Lady Wisdom's self praise (verses 15-21) play in the overall message of Proverbs 8?
4. As in other places in Proverbs, verses 18-21 links moral well-being to material well-being. In what ways does this reflect the underlying logic of wisdom literature? Why is a straightforward connection between the moral and the material problematic?
5. According to verses 32-35, what are the results of listening to Lady Wisdom?

Proverbs 14

CLOSE READING TIPS

▶ Note that Proverbs 10:1—22:16 contains a continuous series of two-line sayings. In chapter 14, these sayings are characterized by the use of antithetic parallelism, where the second line restates the first line in a contrasting way.
▶ Verse 1 calls to mind the contrast between Lady Wisdom and the foolish woman in chapter 9.
▶ Note that the ox was highly valued for its use in physical labor (verse 4).
▶ In biblical Hebrew, the heart (verse 10) is the seat of human emotions.
▶ Note that wisdom involves more than just knowledge. It entails wise judgment (verses 15-18).

▶ According to verse 28, a large population is a sign of blessing on a ruler. This echoes the connection between blessing and fertility found throughout the Hebrew Bible.

▶ "Passion" in verse 30 generally refers to unrestrained emotion, not specifically to sexual attraction.

▶ Though appearing in verses 28 and 35, references to royalty are relatively rare in the book of Proverbs.

¹ The wise woman builds her house,
   but the foolish tears it down with her own hands.
² Those who walk uprightly fear the LORD,
   but one who is devious in conduct despises him.
³ The talk of fools is a rod for their backs,
   but the lips of the wise preserve them.
⁴ Where there are no oxen, there is no grain;
   abundant crops come by the strength of the ox.
⁵ A faithful witness does not lie,
   but a false witness breathes out lies.
⁶ A scoffer seeks wisdom in vain,
   but knowledge is easy for one who understands.
⁷ Leave the presence of a fool,
   for there you do not find words of knowledge.
⁸ It is the wisdom of the clever to understand where they go,
   but the folly of fools misleads.
⁹ Fools mock at the guilt offering,
   but the upright enjoy God's favor.
¹⁰ The heart knows its own bitterness,
   and no stranger shares its joy.
¹¹ The house of the wicked is destroyed,
   but the tent of the upright flourishes.
¹² There is a way that seems right to a person,
   but its end is the way to death.
¹³ Even in laughter the heart is sad,
   and the end of joy is grief.
¹⁴ The perverse get what their ways deserve,
   and the good, what their deeds deserve.
¹⁵ The simple believe everything,
   but the clever consider their steps.
¹⁶ The wise are cautious and turn away from evil,
   but the fool throws off restraint and is careless.
¹⁷ One who is quick-tempered acts foolishly,
   and the schemer is hated.
¹⁸ The simple are adorned with folly,
   but the clever are crowned with knowledge.
¹⁹ The evil bow down before the good,
   the wicked at the gates of the righteous.
²⁰ The poor are disliked even by their neighbors,
   but the rich have many friends.
²¹ Those who despise their neighbors are sinners,
   but happy are those who are kind to the poor.
²² Do they not err that plan evil?
   Those who plan good find loyalty and faithfulness.
²³ In all toil there is profit,
   but mere talk leads only to poverty.
²⁴ The crown of the wise is their wisdom,
   but folly is the garland of fools.
²⁵ A truthful witness saves lives,

but one who utters lies is a betrayer.

[26] In the fear of the LORD one has strong confidence,
and one's children will have a refuge.

[27] The fear of the LORD is a fountain of life,
so that one may avoid the snares of death.

[28] The glory of a king is a multitude of people;
without people a prince is ruined.

[29] Whoever is slow to anger has great understanding,
but one who has a hasty temper exalts folly.

[30] A tranquil mind gives life to the flesh,
but passion makes the bones rot.

[31] Those who oppress the poor insult their Maker,
but those who are kind to the needy honor him.

[32] The wicked are overthrown by their evil-doing,
but the righteous find a refuge in their integrity.

[33] Wisdom is at home in the mind of one who has understanding,
but it is not known in the heart of fools.

[34] Righteousness exalts a nation,
but sin is a reproach to any people.

[35] A servant who deals wisely has the king's favor,
but his wrath falls on one who acts shamefully.

DISCUSSION QUESTIONS

1.   What do you learn from this passage about the view of the poor and poverty in wisdom literature?
2.   How would you characterize the emotional life of the wise person? Of the fool?
3.   Where do you see a tension in this chapter between pragmatism and idealism? Is one side of this tension emphasized more than the other?
4.   Consider verses 27-33. In each verse, what opposition is emphasized by the antithetical parallelism? Why might this technique be a helpful way of communicating wisdom sayings?

Instruction of Amenemope

Source: Miriam Lichtheim, trans. *Context of Scripture* 1.47.

CLOSE READING TIPS

▶ The Instruction of Amenemope consists of thirty chapters with a prologue and colophon. It is highly unified and consists of a number of similes and metaphors.

▶ The prologue deals with proper behavior and success in life, both in terms of relationships and work.

▶ Note that the instructions are given to Amenemope's youngest son (II.10-15). In Proverbs, wisdom sayings are also framed as advice from a father to a son.

▶ As in proverbs, wisdom here is described as a source of life and prosperity (IV.1).

> ▶ Note that the "heated man" (V.15) is the antithesis to the silent man. This theme appears frequently throughout the instruction.
> ▶ Reverence for "the lord of all" (VIII.14) is a common feature of this instruction. It is broadly analogous with "the fear of the LORD" in Proverbs.
> ▶ Similar language about the tongue as a rudder (XX.5) is also present in James 3:4-5.
> ▶ Concern for widows XXVI.9 is often an extension of a broader concern for the poor.
> ▶ Note how the instruction concludes by reinforcing the goals of wisdom.

Prologue

I.1   Beginning of the teaching for life,
      The instructions for well-being,
      Every rule for relations with elders,
      For conduct toward magistrates;

5   Knowing how to answer one who speaks, To
      reply to one who sends a message.
      So as to direct him on the paths of life,
      To make him prosper upon earth;
      To let his heart enter its shrine,

10   Steering clear of evil;
      To save him from the mouth of strangers,
      To let (him) be praised in the mouth of
      people.
      Made by the overseer of fields, experienced
      in his office,
      The offspring of a scribe of Egypt,

15   The overseer of grains who controls the
      measure,
      Who sets the harvest-dues for his lord,
      Who registers the islands of new land,
      In the great name of his majesty,
      Who records the markers on the borders of
      fields,

II.1 Who acts for the king in his listing of taxes,
      Who makes the land-register of Egypt;
      The scribe who determines the offerings for
      all the gods.
      Who gives land-leases to the people,

5   The overseer of grains, [provider of] foods,
      Who supplies the granary with grains;
      The truly silent in This of Ta-wer,
      The justified in Ipu,
      Who owns a tomb on the west of Senu,

10   Who has a chapel at Abydos,
      Amenemope, the son of Kanakht,
      The justified in Ta-wer.
      <For> his son, the youngest of his children,
      The smallest of his family,

15   The devotee of Min-Kamutef,
      The water-pourer of Wennofer,
      Who places Horus on his father's throne,
      Who guards him in his noble shrine,
      Who ———

III.1 The guardian of the mother of god,
      Inspector of the black cattle of the terrace of
      Min,
      Who protects Min in his shrine:
      Hor-em-maakher is his true name,

5   The child of a nobleman of Ipu,
      The son of the sistrum-player of Shu and
      Tefnut,
      And chief songstress of Horus, Tawosre.

Chapter 1

III. He says:
      Give your ears, hear the sayings,

10   Give your heart to understand them;

It profits to put them in your heart,
Woe to him who neglects them!
Let them rest in the casket of your belly,
May they be bolted in your heart;

15   When there rises a whirlwind of words,
They'll be a mooring post for your tongue.
If you make your life with these in your heart,
You will find it a success;

IV.1   You will find my words a storehouse for life,
Your being will prosper upon earth.

Chapter 3

V. 10   Don't start a quarrel with a hot-mouthed man,
Nor needle him with words.
Pause before a foe, bend before an attacker,
Sleep (on it) before speaking.
A storm that bursts like fire in straw,

15   Such is the heated man in his hour.
Withdraw from him, leave him alone,
The god knows how to answer him.
If you make your life with these (words) in your heart,
Your children will observe them.

Chapter 6

VIII. 9. Beware of destroying the borders of fields,

10   Lest a terror carry you away;
One pleases god with the might of the lord
When one discerns the borders of fields.
Desire your being to be sound,
Beware of the Lord of All;

15   Do not erase another's furrow,
It profits you to keep it sound.
Plow your fields and you'll find what you need,

You'll receive bread from your threshing-floor.
Better is a bushel given you by the god,

20   Than five thousand through wrongdoing.

IX.1   They stay not a day in bin and barn,
They make no food for the beer jar,
A moment is their stay in the granary,
Comes morning they have vanished.

5   Better is poverty in the hand of the god,
Than wealth in the storehouse;

Better is bread with a happy heart
Than wealth with vexation.

Chapter 11

XIV. 5   Do not covet a poor man's goods,
Nor hunger for his bread;
A poor man's goods are a block in the throat,
It makes the gullet vomit.
He who makes gain by lying oaths,

10   His heart is misled by his belly;
Where there is fraud success is feeble,
The bad spoils the good.

Chapter 18

10   Do not lie down in fear of tomorrow:
"Comes day, how will tomorrow be?"
Man ignores how tomorrow will be;
God is ever in his perfection,

15   Man is ever in his failure.
The words men say are one thing,
The deeds of the god are another.
Do not say: "I have done no wrong,"
And then strain to seek a quarrel;

20   The wrong belongs to the god,
He seals (the verdict) with his finger.
There is no perfection before the god,
But there is failure before him;

XX.1   If one strains to seek perfection,
        In a moment he has marred it.
        Keep firm your heart, steady your heart,
        Do not steer with your tongue;
5   If a man's tongue is the boat's rudder,
        The Lord of All is yet its pilot.

Chapter 28
XXVI. 9 Do not pounce on a widow when you find
        her in the fields
10   And then fail to be patient with her reply.
        Do not refuse your oil jar to a stranger,
        Double it before your brothers.
        God prefers him who honors the poor

To him who worships the wealthy.

Chapter 30
XXVII.7 Look to these thirty chapters,
        They inform, they educate;
        They are the foremost of all books,
10   They make the ignorant wise.
        If they are read to the ignorant,
        He is cleansed through them.
        Be filled with them, put them in your heart,
        And become a man who expounds them,
15   One who expounds as a teacher.
        The scribe who is skilled in his office,
        He is found worthy to be a courtier.

DISCUSSION QUESTIONS

1.   Exhortations to honesty and warnings about dishonesty is a basic theme in the Instruction of Amenemope. Where do you see this in the following excerpt?

2.   What attitude does this text express about the poor? How does this compare to what is found in the book of Proverbs?

3.   What role does restraint, especially in speech, play in the cultivation of wisdom? What is this in contrast to?

4.   What sorts of relationships are mentioned in this text? What does this suggest about the scope of wisdom?

25

Job and Qoheleth

Key Points

Job and Qoheleth (or Ecclesiastes) represent a crisis within the biblical wisdom tradition. These two books question the assumptions upon which the standard view of wisdom—embodied in the book of Proverbs—is based. These texts view wisdom as far more elusive and far less explanatory than what is promised in the world of Proverbs, and they are skeptical of the connection between acts and consequences. In contrast, they provide an alternative reflection on wisdom that speaks to basic human questions about why the righteous suffer (Job) and how one finds enjoyment despite the "vanity" of life and the finality of death (Qoheleth).

The book of Job consists of a narrative prologue and epilogue (Job 1–2; 42:7-17) that frame a series of poetic speeches, including the dialogue between and Job and his three friends (Job 3–31), a lengthy speech of Elihu (Job 32–37), and divine speeches, with Job's responses (Job 38:1—42:6). A number of sections show evidence of secondary additions (for example, the wisdom poem in Job 28) or accidents of transmission (for example, the omission of Zophar's speech in the third cycle of dialogues). In either case, redundancies in the final form of the book function to reinforce certain basic themes such as the inadequacy of the "normal" wisdom tradition to account for Job's suffering.

Although Job has had an enduring impact in later theology and literature, it is not an easy book to read. Two difficult interpretive issues should be kept in view. First, one of the main problems in the book has to do with the tensions between the narrative frame and the poetic speeches. Job is a model of piety and resignation in the prologue, but in the dialogues he complains bitterly, objects to the fairness of his trial before God, and offers an elaborate self-justification for this past actions. While it is possible that the narrative frame represents an originally independent folktale, these tensions aptly reflect broader points of conflict within Israelite religion and biblical theology. Second, God's response from the "whirlwind" constitutes something of a non-response. Rather than answering any of the questions Job raises, God asserts that the universe does not revolve around Job's fate, nor humanity as a whole. As such, God's justice—and the link between suffering and sin, fruitfulness and faithfulness—cannot be understood in any simplistic manner.

Like Job, Qoheleth presents several interpretive challenges. A wide range of dates are proposed for its composition (fifth through second century BCE) and early on its place in the canon was vigorously questioned. Its structure is difficult to discern, though one may identify two halves: Ecclesiastes 1:1—6:9, which is distinguished by the well-known refrain "all is vanity and chasing after the wind"; and Ecclesiastes 6:10—12:8, which underscores the limits of knowledge and the elusiveness of wisdom. While there is no clear progression of thought, Qoheleth's basic message focuses on the transitoriness of life, the impermanence of wealth and fame, and the futility of transcending death. In the world of Qoheleth, the wicked and the righteous come to the same fate and knowing when it is the right time to kill or heal, mourn or dance, and so forth (Eccles. 3:1-9) is beyond human grasp. Yet, from these observations Qoheleth reaches a surprising conclusion. Rather than descending into nihilism, he affirms that people should eat, drink, and take pleasure in all their toil, enjoying the everyday gifts of life.

Key Terms

Elihu's speech   In his lengthy speech in Job 32–37, Elihu son of Barachel expresses opposition to both Job and the three friends. Though generally representing traditional positions, he questions certain assumptions about wisdom including the notion that the aged are more wise than youth. Most scholars agree that Elihu's speech is a secondary addition since Elihu is not mentioned in either the prologue or the epilogue. In addition, God's response (Job 38–39) would seem to follow more naturally after the end of Job's final speech (Job 29–31).

The wisdom poem   Found in Job 28, this poem emphasizes the elusiveness of wisdom. In contrast to Proverbs 8, Wisdom does not cry out in the streets for all to hear. Rather, only God knows where wisdom is hidden and it is generally inaccessible to people. This theme meshes well with Job's emphasis on human limitation. While the

poem seems to be part of Job's speech, it is likely an independent tradition whose position here interrupts the dialogues.

Epilogues to Qoheleth   Qoheleth concludes with three epilogues in Ecclesiastes 12:9-10, 11-12, and 13-14. These epilogues likely come from a different author than the rest of the book and are somewhat at odds with the teachings of Qoheleth. Among other things, the epilogues describe the author as a teacher of traditional wisdom, warn against the making of many books, and reduce the complexity of Qoheleth's perspective to a matter of keeping the commandments.

Vanity   The term vanity (Heb.: *hebel*) literally means "vapor" but in Qoheleth it primarily conveys the idea of transitoriness. This concept is introduced in the opening verses of the book ("vanity of vanities," Eccles. 1:2) and is frequently repeated through the refrain "all is vanity and a chasing after the wind" (Eccles. 1:14, 17; 2:11,

17, 26; 4:4, 6; 16; 6:9). The notion of vanity summarizes one of the basic themes of Qoheleth. Job uses the same Hebrew word when he dismisses the speeches of his three friends as "vain" (Job 27:12).

Profit The term "profit" (Heb.: *yitron*) comes from the world of business and generally means "that which is left over." One of the central concerns of the book of Qoheleth is whether any profit can be gained from life (Eccles. 1:2). In Qoheleth's perspective, there is no enduring profit in wealth, labor, or even wisdom. Yet life still can be enjoyed by appreciating everyday activities (such as eating and drinking) and the toil God has given human beings.

Key Personalities

The three friends

A large portion of the book of Job (chapters 3–31) is taken up by a series of dialogues between Job and his three friends, Eliphaz the Temanite, Bildad the Shuhite, and Zophar the Naamathite. Little biographical data can be gleaned about these figures, though the content of their speeches suggest that they represent traditional wisdom perspectives. Eliphaz, a well-attested Edomite name, is the first to speak after Job's bitter curse. He counters Job's profession of innocence by affirming the common idea that no human can be fully righteous before God (Job 4:7). In his later speeches, Eliphaz's accusations become more severe as he deduces from Job's suffering that he must be guilty of numerous transgressions (for example, Job 22:5-9). Bildad is the second speaker in each of the three cycles. He affirms the justice of God (Job 8:3), and by extension, the fate of the wicked (Job 18). But he holds out hope that if

Job makes supplication to God, he will be restored to his rightful place. Zophar speaks last in the first two cycles and is absent from the third cycle. He is arguably the most aggressive and contemptuous of the three friends. He emphasizes God's inscrutability, stresses the unavoidable fate of the wicked, and even implies that Job has not been punished as much as he deserves. Job answers each of his friends in turn, accusing them of speaking falsely and charging them with failing to offer consolation in his suffering. Against their accusations, Job does not waiver in asserting his innocence.

Qoheleth

Qoheleth (occasionally spelled Qohelet or Koheleth) is the name of the primary speaker in the book of Ecclesiastes. The meaning of this name is open to several interpretations. The Greek translation, Ecclesiastes, means "member of an assembly" and assumes that the Hebrew Qoheleth is derived from *qahal*, "assembly." A closely related idea is that Qoheleth is derived from a Hebrew verbal noun meaning "one who assembles or gathers (people) together." This idea is reflected in the translation of the KJV ("the Preacher"). However, Qoheleth is more of a philosopher than a preacher and so the NRSV's "the Teacher" is a more suitable English translation. It is also possible that Qoheleth means "a gatherer (of wisdom)." In either case, the superscription of the book portrays Qoheleth as "the son of David, king in Jerusalem" (Eccles. 1:1) and later he is represented as the king over Israel (Eccles. 1:12). While a Jewish tradition maintains that Solomon wrote this book in his old age, evidence of Solomonic authorship is completely lacking. In fact, in the rest of the book Qoheleth appears as a teacher and a wise man, suggesting the role of a sage rather than a king. Qoheleth is most well known for questioning traditional wisdom perspectives.

Questions for Study and Discussion

1. Both Job and Qoheleth represent critical attitudes toward the kind of wisdom found in the book of Proverbs. Describe the critical debate happening among these three books. What are the underlying assumptions in the argument, theological and otherwise? What are the various authoritative sources appealed to? Finally, offer your own assessment of the debate.

2. In your opinion, what kind of response does God give to Job? Is it angry? Compassionate? What is the purpose of God's speech to Job near the end of the book?

3. The problem of evil's presence in the world has exercised great minds for millennia. Why do disasters occur? What link is there between sin and disaster? What is God's (or the gods') role in bringing about or preventing evil? Many of these problems are only heightened when one asks them within the context of a monotheistic religion. In your view, how do Proverbs, Job, and Qoheleth address these questions?

4. Qoheleth is described in this chapter as a work that is skeptical of the wisdom tradition. Of what is it skeptical and why? Moreover, how do you respond to Qoheleth's understanding of the world? Is it convincing?

5. You have now been exposed to a wide range of wisdom texts, with their plurality of views on the world. If you had to locate your own take on wisdom within the world of biblical wisdom literature, where would you stand?

Primary Text

The Babylonian Theodicy

CLOSE READING TIPS

- ▶ Composed in 1000 BCE, this acrostic poem has twenty-seven stanzas of a eleven lines each; the acrostic spells out the expression, "I, Saggil-kinam-ubbib, the incantation priest, a worshipper of god and king."
- ▶ The word "sage" in the opening address implies that the friend is a wise and learned scholar.
- ▶ Note the respect with which the sufferer and friend treat one another; this is often different than what is find in the dialogues of Job 3–31.
- ▶ In the sufferer's second speech (III), nothing in life is enjoyable or satisfying anymore. Physical pain and mental anguish overwhelm him.
- ▶ Note that in VII, the sufferer compliments the advice of the friend, but objects to the notion that faithfulness to the deities will lead to blessing while those who ignore the gods can still be successful.
- ▶ In XXIII, the sufferer is lamenting the inequality between two sons.
- ▶ In XXIV, the friend construes the sufferer's lament as a form of blasphemy against the gods.
- ▶ In XXV, the sufferer describes an upside-down social order where the expected linkage between act and consequence is severed.

I. *Sufferer*

O sage, [. . .], come, [let] me speak to you,

[. . .], let me recount to you,

[. . .],

[I . . .], who have suffered greatly, let me always
    praise you,

Where is one whose reflective capacity is as
    great as yours?

Who is he whose knowledge could rival yours?

Wh[ere] is the counsellor to whom I can tell of
    woe?

I am without recourse, heartache has come
    upon me.

I was the youngest child when fate claimed
    (my) father,

My mother who bore me departed to the land
    of no return,

My father and mother left me, and with no one
    my guardian!

II. *Friend*

Considerate friend, what you tell is a sorrowful
    tale,

My dear friend, you have let your mind harbor
    ill.

You make your estimable discretion
    feeble-minded,

You alter your bright expression to a scowl.

Of course our fathers pay passage to go death's
    way,

I too will cross the river of the dead,
    as is commanded from of old.

When you survey teeming mankind all
    together,

The poor man's son advanced, someone helped
    him get rich,

Who did favors for the sleek and wealthy?

He who looks to his god has a protector,

The humble man who reveres his goddess will
    garner wealth.

III. *Sufferer*

My friend, your mind is a wellspring of depth
    unplumbed,

The upsurging swell of the ocean that brooks
    no inadequacy.

To you, then, let me pose a question, learn
    [what I would say].

Hearken to me but for a moment, hear my
    declaration.

My body is shrouded, craving wears me
    do[wn],

My assets have vanished, my res[ouces?]
    dwindled.

My energies have turned feeble, my prosperity
    is at a standstill,

Moaning and woe have clouded [my] features.

The grain of my mead is nowhere near satisfy-
    ing [me],

Beer, the sustenance of mankind, is far from
    being enough.

Can a happy life be a certainty? I wish I knew
    how that might come about!

IV. *Friend*

My well-thought-out speech is the ulti[mate]
    in good advice,

But you [make?] your well-ordered insight
    [sound] like babble.

You force [your . . .] to be [sca]tter-brained,
    irrational,

You render your choicest offerings without
    conviction.

As to your [ever]lasting, unremitting desire
    [. . .],

The [fore]most protection [. . .] in prayer:

The reconciled goddess returns to [. . .]

The re[conciled gods] will take pity on the
      fool(?), the wrong-doer.

Seek constantly after the [rites?] of justice.

Your mighty [. . .] will surely show kindness,

[. . .] . . . will surely grant mercy.

VII. *Sufferer*

Your reasoning is a cool breeze, a breath of
      fresh air for mankind,

Most particular friend, your advice is
      e[xcellent].

Let me [put] but one matter before you:

Those who seek not after a god can go the road
      of favor,

Those who pray to a goddess have grown poor
      and destitute.

Indeed, in my youth I tried to find out the will
      of (my) god,

With prayer and supplication I besought my
      goddess.

I bore a yoke of profitless servitude:

(My) god decreed (for me) poverty instead of
      wealth.

A cripple rises above me, a fool is ahead of me,

Rogues are in the ascendant, I am demoted.

VIII. *Friend*

O just, knowledgeable one, your logic is
      perverse,

You have cast off justice, you have scorned
      divine design.

In your emotional state you have an urge to
      disregard divine ordinances,

[. . .] the sound rules of your goddess.

The strategy of a god is [as remote as] inner-
      most heaven,

The command of a goddess cannot be dr[awn
      out].

Teeming humanity well understands trouble,

XXIII. *Sufferer*

I have looked around in society, indications are
      the contrary:

God does not block the progress of a demon.

A father hauls a boat up a channel,

While his first-born sprawls in bed.

The eldest son makes his way like a lion,

The second son is content to drive a donkey.

The heir struts the street like a peddler,

The younger son makes provision for the
      destitute.

What has it profited me that I knelt before my
      god?

It is I who must (now) bow before my inferior!

The riffraff despise me as much as the rich and
      proud.

XXIV. *Friend*

Adept scholar, master of erudition,

You blaspheme in the anguish of your
      thoughts.

Divine purpose is as remote as innermost
      heaven,

It is too difficult to understand, people cannot
      understand it.

Among all creatures the birth goddess formed,

Why should offspring be completely
      unmatched(?)?

The cow's first calf is inferior,

Her subsequent offspring is twice as big.

The first child is born a weakling,

The second is called a capable warrior.

Even if one (tries to) apprehend divine inten-
      tion, people cannot understand it.

XXV. *Sufferer*

Pay attention, my friend, learn my (next) parry,

Consider the well-chosen diction of my speech.

They extol the words of an important man who
    is accomplished in murder,

They denigrate the powerless who has commit-
    ted no crime.

They esteem truthful the wicked to whom
    tr[uth] is abhorrent,

They reject the truthful man who he[eds] the
    will of god.

They fill the oppressor's st[rongroom] with
    refined gold,

They empty the beggar's larder of [his]
    provisions.

They shore up the tyrant whose all is crime,

They ruin the weak, they oppress the
    powerless.

And as for me, without means, a parvenu
    harasses me.

XXVI. *Friend*

Enlil, king of the gods, who created teeming
    mankind,

Majestic Ea, who pinched off their clay,

The queen who fashioned them, mistress
    Mami,

Gave twisted words to the human race,

They endowed them in perpetuity with lies and
    falsehood.

Solemnly they speak well of a rich man,

"He's the king," they say, "he has much wealth."

They malign a poor man as a thief,

They lavish mischief upon him, they conspire
    to kill him.

They make him suffer every evil because he has
    no wherewithal(?).

They bring him to a horrible end, they snuff
    him out like an ember.

DISCUSSION QUESTIONS

1. What does the acrostic reveal about the author? Why would this information be important in light of the content of the sufferer's lament?

2. What circumstances have led to the distress of the sufferer? How is this similar to what Job experiences in the prologue?

3. Imagine a conversation between the friend in this passage and Eliphaz, Bildad, and Zophar. What would they agree about? On what points would their worldviews differ?

4. In several instances, the friend emphasizes that the divine purpose is "as remote as the innermost heaven." How is this statement meant to reassure the sufferer? What does it have in common with YHWH's two speeches in Job 38:1—42:6?

5. Compare the tone and language of the sufferer and that of Job in the dialogue (Job 3–31). What similarities or differences do you observe?

Job 6:14—7:21

CLOSE READING TIPS

▶ This passage represents Job's response to Eliphaz's first speech. Job 6:1-13, which is not included here, offers a soliloquy seemingly addressed to no one.

▶ The "torrent-bed" and "freshets" (Job 6:15) both refer to wadis, which are only full during the rainy season but are dry in the summer when water is most needed.

▶ In Job 6:24, Job asks to be taught about where he has sinned. His objection suggestions that Eliphaz has inferred that Job is guilty based on his suffering, not actual evidence that he has sinned.

▶ The language in Job 6:29 might imply that the friends had literally turned their back on Job and were walking aw, or it might simply be a metaphor for Job's experience of abandonment.

▶ Beginning in Job 7:1, Job addresses God. An allusion is perhaps made here to the *Enuma Elish*, in which the gods created humans for menial labor.

▶ A Hellenistic Jewish writing called *The Testament of Job* expands on the imagery of Job 7:5 by claiming that Job picked up a worm that had fallen off his skin and put it back in place.

▶ Note that the sea and the Dragon (Job 7:12) are classic enemies in ancient Mesopotamian myths. Job claims that God is treating him like these creatures.

▶ Note that Job 7:17-18 are a parody of Psalm 8:4.

---

6 ¹⁴ "Those who withhold kindness from a friend
forsake the fear of the Almighty.
¹⁵ My companions are treacherous like a torrent-bed,
like freshets that pass away,
¹⁶ that run dark with ice,
turbid with melting snow.
¹⁷ In time of heat they disappear;
when it is hot, they vanish from their place.
¹⁸ The caravans turn aside from their course;
they go up into the waste, and perish.
¹⁹ The caravans of Tema look,
the travelers of Sheba hope.
²⁰ They are disappointed because they were confident;

they come there and are confounded.
²¹ Such you have now become to me;
you see my calamity, and are afraid.
²² Have I said, 'Make me a gift'?
Or, 'From your wealth offer a bribe for me'?
²³ Or, 'Save me from an opponent's hand'?
Or, 'Ransom me from the hand of oppressors'?

²⁴ "Teach me, and I will be silent;
make me understand how I have gone wrong.
²⁵ How forceful are honest words!
But your reproof, what does it reprove?
²⁶ Do you think that you can reprove words,
as if the speech of the desperate were wind?

²⁷ You would even cast lots over the orphan,
and bargain over your friend.

²⁸ "But now, be pleased to look at me;
for I will not lie to your face.
²⁹ Turn, I pray, let no wrong be done.
Turn now, my vindication is at stake.
³⁰ Is there any wrong on my tongue?
Cannot my taste discern calamity?

7 ¹ "Do not human beings have a hard service
on earth,
and are not their days like the days of a
laborer?
² Like a slave who longs for the shadow,
and like laborers who look for their wages,
³ so I am allotted months of emptiness,
and nights of misery are apportioned to me.
⁴ When I lie down I say, 'When shall I rise?'
But the night is long,
and I am full of tossing until dawn.
⁵ My flesh is clothed with worms and dirt;
my skin hardens, then breaks out again.
⁶ My days are swifter than a weaver's shuttle,
and come to their end without hope.

⁷ "Remember that my life is a breath;
my eye will never again see good.
⁸ The eye that beholds me will see me no more;
while your eyes are upon me, I shall be
gone.
⁹ As the cloud fades and vanishes,
so those who go down to Sheol do not
come up;

¹⁰ they return no more to their houses,
nor do their places know them any more.

¹¹ "Therefore I will not restrain my mouth;
I will speak in the anguish of my spirit;
I will complain in the bitterness of my soul.
¹² Am I the Sea, or the Dragon,
that you set a guard over me?
¹³ When I say, 'My bed will comfort me,
my couch will ease my complaint,'
¹⁴ then you scare me with dreams
and terrify me with visions,
¹⁵ so that I would choose strangling
and death rather than this body.
¹⁶ I loathe my life; I would not live forever.
Let me alone, for my days are a breath.
¹⁷ What are human beings, that you make so
much of them,
that you set your mind on them,
¹⁸ visit them every morning,
test them every moment?
¹⁹ Will you not look away from me for a while,
let me alone until I swallow my spittle?
²⁰ If I sin, what do I do to you, you watcher of
humanity?
Why have you made me your target?
Why have I become a burden to you?
²¹ Why do you not pardon my transgression
and take away my iniquity?
For now I shall lie in the earth;
you will seek me, but I shall not be."

DISCUSSION QUESTIONS

1.   According to Job, what are his friends guilty of (Job 6:14-29)?
2.   What complaint does Job level against God in Job 7:12-21?
3.   For Job, is the attention of God a good thing (see especially Job 7:18-21)? Why or why not?
4.   In what ways does this speech encapsulate Job's skepticism about the traditional perspective on wisdom as represented by his three friends and the book of Proverbs?

Qoheleth 2:12—3:13

CLOSE READING TIPS

▶ Much like Proverbs, Qoheleth clearly affirms the superiority of wisdom over folly (Eccles. 2:12-14); yet, he affirms that the same fate comes upon both types of people.

▶ "Chasing after the wind" in Ecclesiastes 2:17 refers to a futile pursuit. This same phrase is used four other times in Ecclesiastes 1–6 (Eccles. 1:14; 2:11; 2:26; 6:9).

▶ In the Hebrew Bible, the phrase "under the sun" (Eccles. 2:18-20, 22) only occurs in Qoheleth. It refers to the realm of the living rather than the realm of the dead; the similar phrase "under the heavens" typically has more of a spatial connotation.

▶ Note that "toil" in Ecclesiastes 2:18-23 seems to refer both to the process of work as well as its result (that is, wealth).

▶ The last part of Ecclesiastes 2:26 ("This also is vanity. . .") may refer either to the "gathering and heaping" or to his own conclusions about toil and profit.

▶ The seven sets of paired opposites (Eccles. 3:1-9) symbolically represent the totality and variety of circumstances one might encounter.

▶ In Ecclesiastes 3:11, Qoheleth, like Proverbs, affirms that wisdom is situational. The primary difference, however, is that Qoheleth is skeptical about whether humans can ever known what a given situation requires.

---

2 ¹² So I turned to consider wisdom and madness and folly; for what can the one do who comes after the king? Only what has already been done. ¹³ Then I saw that wisdom excels folly as light excels darkness.

14 The wise have eyes in their head,
    but fools walk in darkness.

Yet I perceived that the same fate befalls all of them. ¹⁵ Then I said to myself, "What happens to the fool will happen to me also; why then have I been so very wise?" And I said to myself that this also is vanity. ¹⁶ For there is no enduring remembrance of the wise or of fools, seeing that in the days to come all will have been long forgotten. How can the wise die just like fools? ¹⁷ So I hated life, because what is done under the sun was grievous to me; for all is vanity and a chasing after wind.

[18] I hated all my toil in which I had toiled under the sun, seeing that I must leave it to those who come after me [19] and who knows whether they will be wise or foolish? Yet they will be master of all for which I toiled and used my wisdom under the sun. This also is vanity. [20] So I turned and gave my heart up to despair concerning all the toil of my labors under the sun, [21] because sometimes one who has toiled with wisdom and knowledge and skill must leave all to be enjoyed by another who did not toil for it. This also is vanity and a great evil. [22] What do mortals get from all the toil and strain with which they toil under the sun? [23] For all their days are full of pain, and their work is a vexation; even at night their minds do not rest. This also is vanity.

[24] There is nothing better for mortals than to eat and drink, and find enjoyment in their toil. This also, I saw, is from the hand of God; [25] for apart from him who can eat or who can have enjoyment? [26] For to the one who pleases him God gives wisdom and knowledge and joy; but to the sinner he gives the work of gathering and heaping, only to give to one who pleases God. This also is vanity and a chasing after wind.

3 [1] For everything there is a season, and a time for every matter under heaven:

[2] a time to be born, and a time to die;
a time to plant, and a time to pluck up what is
   planted;
[3] a time to kill, and a time to heal;
a time to break down, and a time to build up;
[4] a time to weep, and a time to laugh;
a time to mourn, and a time to dance;
[5] a time to throw away stones, and a time to
   gather stones together;
a time to embrace, and a time to refrain from
   embracing;
[6] a time to seek, and a time to lose;
a time to keep, and a time to throw away;
[7] a time to tear, and a time to sew;
a time to keep silence, and a time to speak;
[8] a time to love, and a time to hate;
a time for war, and a time for peace.

[9] What gain have the workers from their toil? [10] I have seen the business that God has given to everyone to be busy with. [11] He has made everything suitable for its time; moreover he has put a sense of past and future into their minds, yet they cannot find out what God has done from the beginning to the end. [12] I know that there is nothing better for them than to be happy and enjoy themselves as long as they live; [13] moreover, it is God's gift that all should eat and drink and take pleasure in all their toil.

DISCUSSION QUESTIONS

1. In Ecclesiastes 2:12-17, what leads Qoheleth to conclude that he hates life?

2. What might the author of Proverbs say in response to the perspective articulated in Ecclesiastes 2:12-26?

3. In light of what you read in Ecclesiastes 2:12-23, does Qoheleth's conclusion in Ecclesiastes 2:24 surprise you?

4. In your opinion, is the notion that there is an appropriate time for all the things listed in Ecclesiastes 3:1-9 consistent with the ethical perspective offered in the rest of the Hebrew Bible? Why or why not?

5. What underlying assumptions about the world prompt Qoheleth to assert that "all should eat and drink and take pleasure in all their toil" (Eccles. 3:13)? To what extent does this view summarize his life philosophy?

26

The Hebrew Short Story: Ruth, Esther, Tobit, Judith

Key Points

The short story, or novella, is an important literary genre in the Hebrew Bible and early Jewish writing. Novellas such as the story about Joseph (Gen. 37–50) are often embedded within larger literary settings. However, several books in the Hebrew Bible (Ruth and Esther) and the Apocrypha (Tobit and Judith) are novellas in their own right. Rather than summarizing their content, it will be most helpful to highlight three key issues that emerge in this literature.

First, each of these novellas give superficial trappings of a historical narrative. However, many of the details are problematic. For instance, certain people and places in Judith are completely fictitious and Nebuchadnezzar is referred to as the ruler of the Assyrians, not the Babylonians. Likewise, in Esther the number of Ahasuerus's provinces is inaccurate and there is no record of a Persian decree that would annihilate the Jews. As a result, instead of being seen as history writing, these novellas should be read as artfully composed legends. Careful attention should be paid to how certain literary features, such as irony, hyperbole, characterization, and plot, contribute to the message of the story.

Second, these short stories display markedly different attitudes toward non-Israelites. The books of Esther and Judith share a militant attitude toward Gentiles. The arch-enemies of these stories, Haman and Holofernes, are portrayed as trying to oppress the Jews through a military assault or annihilate them through a decree. Their plans are ultimately thwarted and their deaths are celebrated. In contrast, the heroine of the book of Ruth is a Moabite woman who shows extraordinary faithfulness to the Israelite, Naomi, and is said to be the great-grandmother of David. The situation in Tobit is a bit more neutral, though this man from the tribe of Naphtali does find favor with the Assyrian king. In either case, these stories should be read against the backdrop of life in the Diaspora, where issues surrounding Jewish-Gentile relationships were paramount to social, economic, and religious dimensions of Jewish life.

Finally, the religious character of each of these books varies widely. Esther is one of two books in the Hebrew Bible not to mention God. Though Esther should not be considered a "secular" story, divine intervention plays a minimal role and the characters make little reference to YHWH or his laws. However, the additions present in the Greek version of Esther make religious aspects of the text far more explicit and leave no doubt about the piety of Esther and Mordecai. In a similar fashion, the characters in Tobit frequently praise God and make repeated references to the law of Moses. The angel Raphael plays an essential role in the development of the plot. Judith likewise is exemplary in her observance of Jewish law and utters an impassioned prayer prior to embarking on her mission to slay Holofernes. These stories may provide a glimpse into popular religious piety in Second Temple Judaism.

Key Terms

Purim   Purim is a spring festival in the Jewish liturgical calendar that celebrates the defeat of Haman and the survival of the Jews in the book of Esther. The word Purim is Hebrew for "lots" and refers to Haman's casting of lots in order to decide the date for the mass killing of the Persian Jews. While it is not clear whether the book or the festival originated first, Esther is traditionally read in its entirety during the synagogue service on Purim.

The novella   The novella, or short story, is a relatively simple prose narrative that describes an initial complication or crisis followed by its resolution. The Hebrew Bible significantly contributes to the development of this literary genre. Biblical novellas are distinguished by their artful composition and often deal with quasi-historical situations (such as Joseph in Egypt). Novellas are embedded in Genesis and the Deuteronomistic History but also can constitute books themselves, such as Ruth, Esther, Jonah, Judith, and Tobit.

Levirate marriage   Levirate marriage stipulated that if a man died without a son, his brother would marry the widow and raise up an heir.

This practice is known throughout the ancient Near East, but in the Hebrew Bible is most clearly expressed in Deuteronomy 25. The issue of levirate marriage also plays a role in the first chapter of Ruth. Its primary purpose was to provide the deceased man with a son and heir, as well as to prevent the widow from marrying outside the family. The law also functioned to provide care for a widow.

Additions to Esther   The additions to Esther refer to content found in the Greek translation (the Septuagint, or LXX) of this book that has no counterpart in the Hebrew (Mesoretic Text or MT). These additions consist of six passages, often labeled A–F, with a total of 107 verses. They do not necessarily come from the same source and were added sometime after the Hebrew edition was composed. This material has the effect of enhancing the piety of characters in the story and making God's role more explicit.

Raphael   Raphael is an angel first mentioned in Jewish literature during the postexilic period. In the book of Tobit, Raphael is described as "one of the seven angels who stand ready and enter before the glory of the Lord" (Tob. 12:15). In addition to binding the demon Asmodeus, Raphael enters the earthly sphere in order to help Tobit and Sarah. He is initially mistaken for a human and only is recognized as an angel at the end of the story. He exhorts Tobias and Tobit to piety and commissions them to write an account of what happened.

Diaspora This term generally refers to the geographical dispersion of any people from their homeland. More specially, the Diaspora is used to describe the situation of those Jews living outside of Israel beginning with the Assyrian and Babylonian exiles. Subsequently, large Jewish populations appeared across the ancient world, including key cities in Egypt, Greece, and Rome. Increased contact between Jews and Gentiles in the Diaspora gave rise to new practices, laws, and literature that helped Jewish communities maintain a distinct identity in a heterogeneous cultural and religious context.

Key Personalities

Mordecai

Mordecai is one of the main characters in the book of Esther. A Jew living in the citadel of Susa, he is identified as Esther's cousin and becomes her foster father when her parents die. He counsels Esther not to reveal to the king that she is a Jew. He gains favor with King Ahasuerus when he informs him, via Esther, of an assassination attempt. However, the plot of the book centers on Mordecai's conflict with Haman, the highest official of Ahasuerus. Infuriated when Mordecai refuses to bow down or do obeisance to the king, Haman plots to destroy all the Jews. Haman convinces the king to issue a decree that called for the mass killing of the Jews on a day established by casting lots. When Mordecai hears of the decree, he

laments and beseeches Esther to use her position in the king's inner court to intercede on behalf of the Jews. The plan eventually succeeds, thus triggering a stunning reversal of fortunes. The king remembers Mordecai's past faithfulness and lavishes upon him honors that Haman expected for himself. Haman is eventually hung on the very gallows he had prepared for Mordecai. In the end, the Jews are spared and Queen Esther puts Mordecai in charge of Haman's property. Under the authority of the king, Mordecai issues a decree that grants Jews the permission to kill any people who might attack them. This occasion, which is celebrated during the festival of Purim, is referred to as "Mordecai's day" in 2 Maccabees 15:36.

Judith

Judith is the heroine of the book that bears her name. She is said to be from a fictional town called Bethulia, where Nebuchadnezzar's general Holofernes tries to subdue the Israelites. Her name means "Jewish woman," though it also might call to mind the name Judah the Maccabee, the greatest defender of Jewish freedom during the Maccabean era. She is described as a widow of great beauty and piety who develops a plot deceive the Assyrians. After gaining entrance to the Assyrian camp, she gives Holofernes false information about their attack on Bethulia. One evening, she kills Holofernes in his sleep, cutting off his head and taking it with her in a bag. After escaping from the city, she returns to Bethulia, where she is widely praised. Her piety is especially on display in her refusal to eat the food of the Gentiles and the song of praise that she utters at the conclusion of the book. Judith shares much in common with Esther, who also risks her life to save her people. A close parallel is also evident with Jael, who uses deceptions in order to kill the enemy Sisera in his sleep, all of which helps lead to the deliverance of the Israelites.

Questions for Study and Discussion

1. The short stories related in this chapter depict many examples of boundary crossing. What are some of those boundaries and how are they either transgressed or renegotiated in these stories?
2. The Persian and Hellenistic periods presented Jews with a number of challenges related to their national, ethnic, and religious identity: How does one express Jewish identity while living under the shadow of empire? Where does cultural compromise become an offense against God? How do you see these questions being worked out in the Hebrew short stories addressed in this chapter?
3. How does Judith—the slayer of Holofernes—both affirm and subvert traditional women's roles?
4. To be sure, many of the Hebrew short stories were meant for entertainment. But what other function might they have had in the early years of Judaism? Keep in mind that many of these stories—if not all of them—were written when Jews were living under the oppressive rule of foreign empires.

Primary Text

Ruth 1

CLOSE READING TIPS

▶ In the Christian Old Testament, Ruth is placed just after the book of Judges, in part due to the opening line "in the days when the judges ruled" (verse 1).

▶ The word Bethlehem literally means "the house of bread." The name of the city underscores the irony of the famine.

▶ In Hebrew, the names Mahlon and Chilion are related to the words for "sickness" and "destruction," respectively.

▶ Note that the words "return" (verses 6, 10, 15, and 22), "turn back" (verses 11, 12, and 16) and "go back" (verse 7, 8, and 15) all come from the same Hebrew root.

▶ Note how both Orpah and Ruth both initially express an interest in staying with Naomi.

▶ Orpah means "back of the neck" and implies her turning away from Naomi.

▶ Note that Ruth does not expect any reward for her faithfulness to Naomi.

▶ In Hebrew, the name Naomi means "pleasant" while Mara means "bitter."

---

¹ In the days when the judges ruled, there was a famine in the land, and a certain man of Bethlehem in Judah went to live in the country of Moab, he and his wife and two sons. ² The name of the man was Elimelech and the name of his wife Naomi, and the names of his two sons were Mahlon and Chilion; they were Ephrathites from Bethlehem in Judah. They went into the country of Moab and remained there. ³ But Elimelech, the husband of Naomi, died, and she was left with her two sons. ⁴ These took

Moabite wives; the name of the one was Orpah and the name of the other Ruth. When they had lived there about ten years, ⁵ both Mahlon and Chilion also died, so that the woman was left without her two sons and her husband.

⁶ Then she started to return with her daughters-in-law from the country of Moab, for she had heard in the country of Moab that the LORD had considered his people and given them food. ⁷ So she set out from the place where she had been living, she and her two daughters-in-law, and they went on their way to go back to the land of Judah. ⁸ But Naomi said to her two daughters-in-law, "Go back each of you to your mother's house. May the LORD deal kindly with you, as you have dealt with the dead and with me. ⁹ The LORD grant that you may find security, each of you in the house of your husband." Then she kissed them, and they wept aloud. ¹⁰ They said to her, "No, we will return with you to your people." ¹¹ But Naomi said, "Turn back, my daughters, why will you go with me? Do I still have sons in my womb that they may become your husbands? ¹² Turn back, my daughters, go your way, for I am too old to have a husband. Even if I thought there was hope for me, even if I should have a husband tonight and bear sons, ¹³ would you then wait until they were grown? Would you then refrain from marrying? No, my daughters, it has been far more bitter for me than for you, because the hand of the LORD has turned against me." ¹⁴ Then they wept aloud again. Orpah kissed her mother-in-law, but Ruth clung to her.

¹⁵ So she said, "See, your sister-in-law has gone back to her people and to her gods; return after your sister-in-law." ¹⁶ But Ruth said,

"Do not press me to leave you
    or to turn back from following you!
Where you go, I will go;
    Where you lodge, I will lodge;
your people shall be my people,
    and your God my God.
¹⁷ Where you die, I will die—
    there will I be buried.
May the LORD do thus and so to me,
    and more as well,
if even death parts me from you!"

¹⁸ When Naomi saw that she was determined to go with her, she said no more to her.

¹⁹ So the two of them went on until they came to Bethlehem. When they came to Bethlehem, the whole town was stirred because of them; and the women said, "Is this Naomi?" ²⁰ She said to them,

"Call me no longer Naomi,
    call me Mara,
        for the Almighty has dealt bitterly with me.
²¹ I went away full,
    but the LORD has brought me back
        empty;
why call me Naomi
    when the LORD has dealt harshly with me,
    and the Almighty has brought calamity
        upon me?"

²² So Naomi returned together with Ruth the Moabite, her daughter-in-law, who came back with her from the country of Moab. They came to Bethlehem at the beginning of the barley harvest.

DISCUSSION QUESTIONS

1. How do the names of the characters symbolize their roles in this story?
2. Why does Naomi urge Orpah and Ruth to return to their mothers' houses?
3. How does the idea of the levirate law help explain Naomi's words in verses 12-14?
4. What is the nature of the commitment that Ruth makes to Naomi in verses 15-17?

Esther 4

CLOSE READING TIPS

▶ "All that had been done" refers to Haman's plot to annihilate the Jews, described in chapter 3.

▶ Note that sackcloth, ashes, and torn clothing are all traditional signs of mourning and repentance.

▶ Remember that when Esther first hears of Mordecai's mourning, she is not yet aware of the king's degree allowing Haman to destroy the Jews.

▶ A eunuch (verse 5) is a castrated official who is deemed appropriate to serve the queen in the royal courts.

▶ Susa (verse 8) was the location of Ahasuerus's winter capital. This city is located in northwestern Iran, east of ancient Babylon.

▶ Note that we do not directly get to see Esther's reaction to finding out about the degree.

▶ The expression "Who knows?" often precedes an expression of hope in divine mercy (see 2 Sam. 12:22; Joel 2:14; Jon. 3:9).

▶ After verse 16, the Greek version of Esther includes prayers by both Mordecai and Esther.

[1] When Mordecai learned all that had been done, Mordecai tore his clothes and put on sackcloth and ashes, and went through the city, wailing with a loud and bitter cry; [2] he went up to the entrance of the king's gate, for no one might enter the king's gate clothed with sackcloth. [3] In every province, wherever the king's command and his decree came, there was great mourning among the Jews, with fasting and weeping and lamenting, and most of them lay in sackcloth and ashes.

[4] When Esther's maids and her eunuchs came and told her, the queen was deeply distressed; she sent garments to clothe Mordecai, so that he might take off his sackcloth; but he would not accept them.

[5] Then Esther called for Hathach, one of the king's eunuchs, who had been appointed to attend her, and ordered him to go to Mordecai to learn what was happening and why. [6] Hathach went out to Mordecai in the open square of the city in front of the king's gate, [7] and Mordecai told him all that had happened to him, and the exact sum of money that Haman had promised to pay into the king's treasuries for the destruction of the Jews. [8] Mordecai also gave him a copy of the written decree issued in Susa for their destruction, that he might show it to Esther, explain it to her, and charge her to go to the king to make supplication to him and entreat him for her people.

9 Hathach went and told Esther what Mordecai had said. 10 Then Esther spoke to Hathach and gave him a message for Mordecai, saying, 11 "All the king's servants and the people of the king's provinces know that if any man or woman goes to the king inside the inner court without being called, there is but one law—all alike are to be put to death. Only if the king holds out the golden scepter to someone, may that person live. I myself have not been called to come in to the king for thirty days." 12 When they told Mordecai what Esther had said, 13 Mordecai told them to reply to Esther, "Do not think that in the king's palace you will escape any more than all the other Jews. 14 For if you keep silence at such a time as this, relief and deliverance will rise for the Jews from another quarter, but you and your father's family will perish. Who knows? Perhaps you have come to royal dignity for just such a time as this." 15 Then Esther said in reply to Mordecai, 16 "Go, gather all the Jews to be found in Susa, and hold a fast on my behalf, and neither eat nor drink for three days, night or day. I and my maids will also fast as you do. After that I will go to the king, though it is against the law; and if I perish, I perish." 17 Mordecai then went away and did everything as Esther had ordered him.

Discussion questions

1. Why does the crisis facing Mordecai and the Jews present a special dilemma for Esther?
2. What reasons does Esther initially give for why she cannot carry out Mordecai's request (verse 11)?
3. On what basis does Mordecai try to convince Esther to take action (verses 13-14)?
4. How does Esther's actions in verses 1-13 compare with those in verses 15-17? How do they compare with her actions in the rest of the story?

Judith 11:1-23; 12:10-20; 13:1-10a

Close reading tips

▸ In anticipation of entering into the camp of Holofernes, Judith utters an elaborate prayer (Jth. 9) and beautifies herself (Jth. 10:1-5).

▸ Earlier Achior told Holofernes that he would only be able to triumph over the Jews if they had offended their God. Judith assures Holofernes that the Jews had indeed committed a sin that provoked their God to anger (Jth. 11:11-15).

▸ Note the use of irony in Judith 11:16—the world will be astonished not by what Holofernes does but by what Judith does to Holofernes.

▸ Note that even Judith's pious statement in Judith 11:17 is intended to deceive Holofernes.

▸ In Judith 11:22-23, Holofernes unknowingly hints at the conclusion to this story.

▸ Note that both Holofernes and Bagoas are taken captive to Judith's beauty. As a result, she is fully in charge of the situation.

> ▶ Note that Judith collects the canopy of the bed and Holofernes's decapitated head as trophies of war (Jth. 12:6-10).
> ▶ Judith is able to escape unnoticed because she had previously gained permission to go out every night into the valley in order to pray for information regarding the timing of Holofernes's attack (Jth. 11:16-19).

11 [1] Then Holofernes said to her, "Take courage, woman, and do not be afraid in your heart, for I have never hurt anyone who chose to serve Nebuchadnezzar, king of all the earth. [2] Even now, if your people who live in the hill country had not slighted me, I would never have lifted my spear against them. They have brought this on themselves. [3] But now tell me why you have fled from them and have come over to us. In any event, you have come to safety. Take courage! You will live tonight and ever after. [4] No one will hurt you. Rather, all will treat you well, as they do the servants of my lord King Nebuchadnezzar."

[5] Judith answered him, "Accept the words of your slave, and let your servant speak in your presence. I will say nothing false to my lord this night. [6] If you follow out the words of your servant, God will accomplish something through you, and my lord will not fail to achieve his purposes. [7] By the life of Nebuchadnezzar, king of the whole earth, and by the power of him who has sent you to direct every living being! Not only do human beings serve him because of you, but also the animals of the field and the cattle and the birds of the air will live, because of your power, under Nebuchadnezzar and all his house. [8] For we have heard of your wisdom and skill, and it is reported throughout the whole world that you alone are the best in the whole kingdom, the most informed and the most astounding in military strategy.

[9] "Now as for Achior's speech in your council, we have heard his words, for the people of Bethulia spared him and he told them all he had said to you. [10] Therefore, lord and master, do not disregard what he said, but keep it in your mind, for it is true. Indeed our nation cannot be punished, nor can the sword prevail against them, unless they sin against their God.

[11] "But now, in order that my lord may not be defeated and his purpose frustrated, death will fall upon them, for a sin has overtaken them by which they are about to provoke their God to anger when they do what is wrong. [12] Since their food supply is exhausted and their water has almost given out, they have planned to kill their livestock and have determined to use all that God by his laws has forbidden them to eat. [13] They have decided to consume the first fruits of the grain and the tithes of the wine and oil, which they had consecrated and set aside for the priests who minister in the presence of our God in Jerusalem—things it is not lawful for any of the people even to touch with their hands. [14] Since even the people in Jerusalem have been doing this, they have sent messengers there in order to bring back permission from the council of the elders. [15] When the response reaches them and they act upon it, on that very day they will be handed over to you to be destroyed.

[16] "So when I, your slave, learned all this, I fled from them. God has sent me to accomplish with

you things that will astonish the whole world wherever people shall hear about them. [17] Your servant is indeed God-fearing and serves the God of heaven night and day. So, my lord, I will remain with you; but every night your servant will go out into the valley and pray to God. He will tell me when they have committed their sins. [18] Then I will come and tell you, so that you may go out with your whole army, and not one of them will be able to withstand you. [19] Then I will lead you through Judea, until you come to Jerusalem; there I will set your throne. You will drive them like sheep that have no shepherd, and no dog will so much as growl at you. For this was told me to give me foreknowledge; it was announced to me, and I was sent to tell you."

[20] Her words pleased Holofernes and all his servants. They marveled at her wisdom and said, [21] "No other woman from one end of the earth to the other looks so beautiful or speaks so wisely!" [22] Then Holofernes said to her, "God has done well to send you ahead of the people, to strengthen our hands and bring destruction on those who have despised my lord. [23] You are not only beautiful in appearance, but wise in speech. If you do as you have said, your God shall be my God, and you shall live in the palace of King Nebuchadnezzar and be renowned throughout the whole world."

12 [10] On the fourth day Holofernes held a banquet for his personal attendants only, and did not invite any of his officers. [11] He said to Bagoas, the eunuch who had charge of his personal affairs, "Go and persuade the Hebrew woman who is in your care to join us and to eat and drink with us. [12] For it would be a disgrace if we let such a woman go without having intercourse with her. If we do not seduce her, she will laugh at us."

[13] So Bagoas left the presence of Holofernes, and approached her and said, "Let this pretty girl not hesitate to come to my lord to be honored in his presence, and to enjoy drinking wine with us, and to become today like one of the Assyrian women who serve in the palace of Nebuchadnezzar." [14] Judith replied, "Who am I to refuse my lord? Whatever pleases him I will do at once, and it will be a joy to me until the day of my death." [15] So she proceeded to dress herself in all her woman's finery. Her maid went ahead and spread for her on the ground before Holofernes the lambskins she had received from Bagoas for her daily use in reclining.

[16] Then Judith came in and lay down. Holofernes' heart was ravished with her and his passion was aroused, for he had been waiting for an opportunity to seduce her from the day he first saw her. [17] So Holofernes said to her, "Have a drink and be merry with us!" [18] Judith said, "I will gladly drink, my lord, because today is the greatest day in my whole life." [19] Then she took what her maid had prepared and ate and drank before him. [20] Holofernes was greatly pleased with her, and drank a great quantity of wine, much more than he had ever drunk in any one day since he was born.

13 [1] When evening came, his slaves quickly withdrew. Bagoas closed the tent from outside and shut out the attendants from his master's presence. They went to bed, for they all were weary because the banquet had lasted so long. [2] But Judith was left alone in the tent, with Holofernes stretched out on his bed, for he was dead drunk.

[3] Now Judith had told her maid to stand outside the bedchamber and to wait for her to come out, as she did on the other days; for she said she would be going out for her prayers. She had said the same thing to Bagoas. [4] So everyone went out, and no one, either small or great, was left in the bedchamber. Then Judith, standing beside his bed, said in her heart, "O Lord God of all might, look in this hour

on the work of my hands for the exaltation of Jerusalem. [5] Now indeed is the time to help your heritage and to carry out my design to destroy the enemies who have risen up against us."

[6] She went up to the bedpost near Holofernes' head, and took down his sword that hung there. [7] She came close to his bed, took hold of the hair of his head, and said, "Give me strength today, O Lord God of Israel!" [8] Then she struck his neck twice with all her might, and cut off his head. [9] Next she rolled his body off the bed and pulled down the canopy from the posts. Soon afterward she went out and gave Holofernes' head to her maid, [10] who placed it in her food bag.

Then the two of them went out together, as they were accustomed to do for prayer. They passed through the camp, circled around the valley, and went up the mountain to Bethulia, and came to its gates.

Discussion questions

1. What are some of the ways in which Judith tries to gain favor with Holofernes in chapter 11?

2. What reason does Judith give Holofernes for why his attack on Bethulia will be successful?

3. Where do you see examples of irony or double meanings in the words of Judith and Holofernes? What role do they play in the development of the plot?

4. Do you think Judith's deception of Holofernes is at odds with her pious prayers in chapter 13? Why or why not?

5. How do Judith's actions compare with those of Jael (Judges 4–5) and Esther? To what extent do these heroines play a similar role in their respective stories?

27

Daniel, 1–2 Maccabees

Key Points

Written in the Hellenistic period, the book of Daniel is the latest composition in the Hebrew Bible. In the Christian Old Testament it is placed among the Prophets, although Daniel rarely engages in traditional prophetic activity. In the Jewish canon, Daniel is included in the Writings, perhaps due to the affinity between the court tales (Dan. 1–6) and other Hebrew short stories. Like Ezra, Daniel is composed partly in Aramaic (Dan. 2:4b–7:28). Like Esther, the Greek text of Daniel includes additional material not found in the Hebrew version.

Daniel consists of two distinct parts. The court tales in Daniel 1–6 feature stories about Daniel and his companions set during the exilic and early postexilic periods. Replete with miracles and mysterious dreams, these chapters are best understood as legends meant to inspire awe about the Most High God. Through memorable stories about abstaining from the king's food (chapter 1), refusing to bow down before a massive statue (chapter 3), or violating an edict prohibiting prayer to God (chapter 6), Daniel 1–6 emphasizes the importance of maintaining one's religious integrity at all cost. These chapters also highlight Daniel's mantic wisdom and the ability of God to reveal mysteries through the interpretation of dreams (chapters 2 and 4) and the "writing on the wall" (chapter 5). Overtly religious in tone, the court tales affirm that it is possible to participate in Gentile life, but success in the Diaspora is still directly tied to allegiance to YHWH and his laws.

Chapters 7–12 represent the only example in the Hebrew Bible of an apocalypse. This literary genre, which becomes prominent in later Jewish writings and early Christianity, typically features angelic revelations, future judgment, heavenly journeys, and a periodization of history leading up to the end times. These chapters are filled with fantastic imagery (chapters 7–8), a reinterpretation of Jeremiah's prophecy about the length of the exile (chapter 9), and a dramatization of King Antiochus IV Ephiphanes's violent persecution of the Jews (chapters 10–12). One of the principal messages of these visions is that conflicts on earth are ultimately resolved by actions of the gods and patron angels, not earthly figures. In the midst of persecution and conflict, hope is found in the everlasting punishment of the wicked and the glorious afterlife, or resurrection, of the faithful.

First and Second Maccabees give different perspectives concerning the infamous reign of the Seleucid ruler Antiochus IV and the subsequent Jewish rebellion. As the official chronicle of the Hasmonean family, 1 Maccabees describes the achievements of Mattathias and his sons in ideal terms. This book also recounts the rededication of the temple (celebrated today through the festival of Hanukkah) and the rise of the Hasmoneans to power as high priests. In slight contrast, Second Maccabees focuses more on Judas Maccabeus, highlights stories about martyrs, and emphasizes the role of divine assistance in the liberation of the Jews and the downfall of Antiochus. Taken together, 1 and 2 Maccabees draws attention not only to the conflict between Hellenism and Judaism but also to the freedom of Jews to practice their religion under Hellenistic and Roman rule.

Key Terms

The Greek text of Daniel   The Greek text (Septuagint or LXX) of Daniel includes several additional passages that do not appear in the Mesoretic Text. Two poetic compositions, "The Prayer of Azariah" and "The Hymn of the Three Young Men" are inserted into chapter 3 while Daniel's three friends are in the fiery furnace. Prose stories about Susanna and Bel and the Dragon appear after chapter 12, both of which show how a faithful Jew is delivered from danger through divine intervention. These additions are included among the Apocryphal or Deuterocanonical books in the Christian canon.

Seventy years   This refers to the number of years Jerusalem was supposed to lie desolate according to the prophecy of Jeremiah (Jer. 25:11-12; 29:10-14). However, in Daniel 9 an angel explains that the seventy years are actually seventy weeks of years, or 490 years. The exile ends after seven weeks and the final week is associated with Antiochus IV's persecution. While it is hard to reconcile these calculations with what we know from history, Jeremiah's prophecy plays a significant role in apocalyptic speculation about the timing of the end.

The resurrection   The resurrection refers to a person being brought back from death and to a state of everlasting life. The only clear reference in the Hebrew Bible to the resurrection is found in Daniel 12:2. However, Daniel does not say that everyone will be raised and makes no mention of a bodily resurrection. In both 2 Maccabees and many examples of apocalyptic literature, belief in the resurrection is a profound source of hope for those facing persecution and life-threatening trials.

"One like a son of man"   In his vision of the heavenly throne room (Dan. 7:13), Daniel sees "one like a son of man (or human being)" coming with the clouds of heaven to the Ancient One and being given dominion, glory, and kingship. The identity of this figure is widely debated. Though traditionally understood as the messiah, it is more likely that this figure is either a collective symbol for the faithful Jewish community or is the archangel Michael, the representative of the Jewish people on a heavenly level.

Martyr The transliteration of a Greek term meaning "witness" or "testimony," martyr refers to a person who is willing to suffer or die for his or her faith. The resolution of a martyr is often rooted in the belief in a heavenly reward, such as a glorious afterlife. Stories about martyrs feature prominently in 2 Maccabees, where certain faithful Jews suffer death instead of violating their religion during the crisis with Antiochus IV Epiphanes. In this context, much of the success of the Maccabean rebellion is attributed to martyrdom.

Key Personalities

Antiochus IV Epiphanes

King Antiochus IV Epiphanes was the most infamous Seleucid ruler. The events surrounding his reign (175–164 BCE) form the backdrop of the visions of Daniel and are described—though in slightly different ways—in 1 and 2 Maccabees. For somewhat unknown reasons, Antiochus attacked Jerusalem and plundered the temple after being defeated in a battle against Egypt in 168 BCE. With the support of a certain portion of the Jewish population, he established Greek institutions, destroyed copies of the Torah, put Jews to death for having their sons circumcised, and profaned the temple by setting up "an abomination that desolates" (Dan. 11:31; 12:11) or "desolating sacrifice" (1 Macc. 1:54), both of which refer to a pagan altar associated with "the Lord of heaven" (that is, Baal Shamin). Antiochus is the first Hellenistic king to be designated as *theōs* ("god") on

his coinage, a fact which is perhaps hinted at in Daniel 7:25. Antiochus's persecution prompted a valiant Jewish revolt led by the Maccabean family, beginning with Mattathias and continuing with his sons Judas, Jonathan, and Simon. Conflicting reports are given of Antiochus's death, though it seems that he died in Persia in 164 BCE due to wounds received from an attempt to rob a temple. Daniel's vision in chapter 7 dramatizes the Jewish conflict with Antiochus, referring to him as the offensive "little horn" on the fourth beast. While the interpretation predicts that the Jews will be given into his power "for a time, two times, and half a time" (that is, three and a half years), his dominion will be taken away and the Most High will ultimately prevail. Likewise, Daniel 8 looks to divine intervention as an answer to Antiochus's persecution.

Nebuchadnezzar, Belshazzar, and Darius the Mede

The court tales in Daniel 1–6 are ostensibly set during the reigns of Nebuchadnezzar, Belshazzar, and Darius the Mede. The information provided about these foreign kings in Daniel is historically problematic. For instance, Nebuchadnezzar's siege on Jerusalem is set during the third year of Jehoiakim (606 BCE) rather than 598–7 BCE and the story about his madness (chapter 4) probably was originally about Nabonidus. Belshazzar is said to reign after his father Nebuchadnezzar (Dan. 5:2) while in fact he was the son of Nabonidus and never officially was king (though he did govern in place of his father for a period of time). Darius the Mede is said to be the successor to Belshazzar (Dan. 5:30-31), but no such figure is known to history. Nevertheless, these three kings are important stock characters within the court tales. Nebuchadnezzar is prone to fits of rage (Dan. 2:12; 3:13) and violence (Dan. 3:19-27), but he also is capable of being momentarily transformed: he expresses admiration for Daniel's God (Dan. 2:46-49), issues a decree that forbids blasphemy against YHWH (Dan. 3:29), and praises the Most High (Dan. 4:34-35). Darius the Mede is likewise presented as a sympathetic figure (chapter 6). While he is duped into issuing the decree that results in Daniel being thrown into the lion's den, he is troubled by these circumstances and rejoices when Daniel survives the ordeal. Belshazzar, on the other hand, is portrayed in a purely negative light (chapter 5). The destruction of Babylon is interpreted as due punishment for Belshazzar's idolatry and sacrilegious use of the temple vessels. The overall message of the court tales is that while it is appropriate for Jews in the Diaspora to be loyal to foreign kings, their ultimate success depends on fidelity to YHWH and his law.

Questions for Study and Discussion

1. As was the case with Esther, Judith, and the other Hebrew short stories, Daniel and 1 and 2 Maccabees reflect the struggle to maintain Jewish identity in the context of external, often imperial, pressures. How do these books depict the struggle? What sorts of issues do they focus on? Are there modern communities that are currently experiencing similar conflicts?

2. Related to the previous question, both Daniel and 1 and 2 Maccabees depict various strategies of resistance, that is, ways of objecting to the demands of rulers. How would you describe those strategies? Are there modern day "resistance movements" that utilize similar strategies?

3. The book of Daniel is divided into two parts. The first six chapters contain court tales about Daniel and his friends and their interactions with various Near Eastern kings. Chapters 7–12 relate a number of visions, which are interpreted by an angelic mediatory. From the perspective of theology, how are these two sections similar or different?

4. Heroes say a lot about an author's values, hopes, and ideals. Who are the heroes in these stories? What are their dominant characteristics? What might these characteristics say about the authors that wrote these stories and the communities that treasured them?

Primary Text

Bel and the Dragon

CLOSE READING TIPS

▶ Bel and the Dragon appears as chapter 14 in the Greek version of Daniel.

▶ Bel is an epithet of Marduk, the chief deity of the Babylonian pantheon. It was customary in ancient Near Eastern religions to treat idols, or cult statues, as living things that were routinely feed, washed, clothed, and crowned.

- ▶ The notion that idols are "made with (human) hands" (verse 5) is a common retort in idol parodies in Second Isaiah and Jeremiah.
- ▶ Note that Daniel laughs derisively at several points in this story (verses 7 and 19). This detail highlights the fact that Bel and the Dragon is primarily intended to mock Babylonian idolatry.
- ▶ Dragons and snakes could symbolize deities in the ancient Near East but there is no specific evidence for Babylonian snake worship.
- ▶ Note that verse 24 clarifies that the dragon is a living god, unlike Bel's idol.
- ▶ Note the irony in verse 27: the dragon is proven to be a false god because it eats something and dies. Bel's idol is proven to be a false god because it is not able to eat.
- ▶ The king's reluctance to hand Daniel over is similar to that of Darius the Mede in Daniel 6.
- ▶ The prophet referred to as Habakkuk elsewhere in the Hebrew Bible was active between 612–597 BCE, well before the time period described in this story.
- ▶ Note that "with the speed of the wind" in verse 36 might also be interpreted as meaning "by the power of the spirit."

[1] When King Astyages was laid to rest with his ancestors, Cyrus the Persian succeeded to his kingdom. [2] Daniel was a companion of the king, and was the most honored of all his Friends.

[3] Now the Babylonians had an idol called Bel, and every day they provided for it twelve bushels of choice flour and forty sheep and six measures of wine. [4] The king revered it and went every day to worship it. But Daniel worshiped his own God.

So the king said to him, "Why do you not worship Bel?" [5] He answered, "Because I do not revere idols made with hands, but the living God, who created heaven and earth and has dominion over all living creatures."

[6] The king said to him, "Do you not think that Bel is a living god? Do you not see how much he eats and drinks every day?" [7] And Daniel laughed, and said, "Do not be deceived, O king, for this thing is only clay inside and bronze outside, and it never ate or drank anything."

[8] Then the king was angry and called the priests of Bel and said to them, "If you do not tell me who is eating these provisions, you shall die. [9] But if you prove that Bel is eating them, Daniel shall die, because he has spoken blasphemy against Bel." Daniel said to the king, "Let it be done as you have said."

[10] Now there were seventy priests of Bel, besides their wives and children. So the king went with Daniel into the temple of Bel. [11] The priests of Bel said, "See, we are now going outside; you yourself, O king, set out the food and prepare the wine, and shut the door and seal it with your signet. [12] When you return in the morning, if you do not find that Bel has eaten it all, we will die; otherwise Daniel will, who is telling lies about us." [13] They were unconcerned, for beneath the table they had made a hidden entrance, through which they used to go in regularly and consume the provisions. [14] After they had gone out, the king set out the food for Bel. Then Daniel ordered his servants to bring ashes, and they scattered them throughout the whole temple in the presence of the king alone. Then

they went out, shut the door and sealed it with the king's signet, and departed. ¹⁵ During the night the priests came as usual, with their wives and children, and they ate and drank everything.

¹⁶ Early in the morning the king rose and came, and Daniel with him. ¹⁷ The king said, "Are the seals unbroken, Daniel?" He answered, "They are unbroken, O king." ¹⁸ As soon as the doors were opened, the king looked at the table, and shouted in a loud voice, "You are great, O Bel, and in you there is no deceit at all!"

¹⁹ But Daniel laughed and restrained the king from going in. "Look at the floor," he said, "and notice whose footprints these are." ²⁰ The king said, "I see the footprints of men and women and children."

²¹ Then the king was enraged, and he arrested the priests and their wives and children. They showed him the secret doors through which they used to enter to consume what was on the table. ²² Therefore the king put them to death, and gave Bel over to Daniel, who destroyed it and its temple.

²³ Now in that place there was a great dragon, which the Babylonians revered. ²⁴ The king said to Daniel, "You cannot deny that this is a living god; so worship him." ²⁵ Daniel said, "I worship the Lord my God, for he is the living God. ²⁶ But give me permission, O king, and I will kill the dragon without sword or club." The king said, "I give you permission."

²⁷ Then Daniel took pitch, fat, and hair, and boiled them together and made cakes, which he fed to the dragon. The dragon ate them, and burst open. Then Daniel said, "See what you have been worshiping!"

²⁸ When the Babylonians heard about it, they were very indignant and conspired against the king, saying, "The king has become a Jew; he has destroyed Bel, and killed the dragon, and slaughtered the priests." ²⁹ Going to the king, they said, "Hand Daniel over to us, or else we will kill you and your household." ³⁰ The king saw that they were pressing him hard, and under compulsion he handed Daniel over to them.

³¹ They threw Daniel into the lions' den, and he was there for six days. ³² There were seven lions in the den, and every day they had been given two human bodies and two sheep; but now they were given nothing, so that they would devour Daniel.

³³ Now the prophet Habakkuk was in Judea; he had made a stew and had broken bread into a bowl, and was going into the field to take it to the reapers. ³⁴ But the angel of the Lord said to Habakkuk, "Take the food that you have to Babylon, to Daniel, in the lions' den." ³⁵ Habakkuk said, "Sir, I have never seen Babylon, and I know nothing about the den." ³⁶ Then the angel of the Lord took him by the crown of his head and carried him by his hair; with the speed of the wind he set him down in Babylon, right over the den.

³⁷ Then Habakkuk shouted, "Daniel, Daniel! Take the food that God has sent you." ³⁸ Daniel said, "You have remembered me, O God, and have not forsaken those who love you." ³⁹ So Daniel got up and ate. And the angel of God immediately returned Habakkuk to his own place.

⁴⁰ On the seventh day the king came to mourn for Daniel. When he came to the den he looked in, and there sat Daniel! ⁴¹ The king shouted with a loud voice, "You are great, O Lord, the God of Daniel, and there is no other besides you!" ⁴² Then he pulled Daniel out, and threw into the den those who had attempted his destruction, and they were instantly eaten before his eyes.

Discussion questions

1. What do Bel's priests do in order to make it seem like the idol has consumed food? How does Daniel expose this trickery?

2. Compare the characterization of the king (Cyrus of Persia) in verses 21-22 with that of Nebuchadnezzar in Daniel 1–5. What similarities do you see?

3. How do the events surrounding Daniel being in a lion's den differ from what happens in Daniel's other "lion's den" experience (chapter 6)?

4. In what ways does the king's response to Daniel's accusers in verses 40-42 parallel the actions of Darius the Mede in Daniel 6?

5. What role does eating (or not eating) play in Bel and the Dragon? Where does the theme of food or eating occur elsewhere in the book of Daniel?

2 Maccabees 7:1-23; 8:1-7

Close reading tips

▶ The entirety of this chapter 7 (verses 1-42) is the main subject of a text known as 4 Maccabees and may be inspired by Jeremiah 15:9 or an independent source.

▶ The king mentioned in 2 Maccabees 7:1 is Antiochus IV. Eleazar also refuses to eat swine's flesh and is killed (2 Macc 6:18-31).

▶ The emphasis on martyrdom is a prominent theme in 2 Maccabees. The woman's seventh son is martyred by the end of the chapter (see 2 Macc. 7:39-40).

▶ The appeal to God's compassion in 2 Maccabees 7:7 draws on the language of Deuteronomy 32.

▶ The second brother expresses hope in the resurrection (2 Macc. 7:9). In offering a similar hope, the third brother implies that the resurrection will be bodily (2 Macc. 7:11).

▶ Note that in 2 Maccabees 7:18, the sixth brother suggests that their suffering is a result of sin.

▶ In the mother's speech (2 Macc. 7:20-23), the resurrection is portrayed as being a divine mystery on par with the creation of the world.

▶ Note that Maccabeus means "the hammer" (2 Macc. 8:1). Judas replaces his father Mattathias, who dies at the end of chapter 2.

▶ The prayer in 2 Maccabees 8:2-4 summarizes the events described in the book thus far.

▶ The beginning of the Jewish revolt is also described in 1 Maccabees 3:1-41.

7 ¹ It happened also that seven brothers and their mother were arrested and were being compelled by the king, under torture with whips and thongs, to partake of unlawful swine's flesh. ² One of them, acting as their spokesman, said, "What do you intend to ask and learn from us? For we are ready to die rather than transgress the laws of our ancestors." ³ The king fell into a rage, and gave orders to have pans and caldrons heated. 4 These were heated immediately, and he commanded that the tongue

of their spokesman be cut out and that they scalp him and cut off his hands and feet, while the rest of the brothers and the mother looked on. [5] When he was utterly helpless, the king ordered them to take him to the fire, still breathing, and to fry him in a pan. The smoke from the pan spread widely, but the brothers and their mother encouraged one another to die nobly, saying, [6] "The Lord God is watching over us and in truth has compassion on us, as Moses declared in his song that bore witness against the people to their faces, when he said, 'And he will have compassion on his servants.'"

[7] After the first brother had died in this way, they brought forward the second for their sport. They tore off the skin of his head with the hair, and asked him, "Will you eat rather than have your body punished limb by limb?" [8] He replied in the language of his ancestors and said to them, "No." Therefore he in turn underwent tortures as the first brother had done. [9] And when he was at his last breath, he said, "You accursed wretch, you dismiss us from this present life, but the King of the universe will raise us up to an everlasting renewal of life, because we have died for his laws."

[10] After him, the third was the victim of their sport. When it was demanded, he quickly put out his tongue and courageously stretched forth his hands, [11] and said nobly, "I got these from Heaven, and because of his laws I disdain them, and from him I hope to get them back again." [12] As a result the king himself and those with him were astonished at the young man's spirit, for he regarded his sufferings as nothing.

[13] After he too had died, they maltreated and tortured the fourth in the same way. [14] When he was near death, he said, "One cannot but choose to die at the hands of mortals and to cherish the hope God gives of being raised again by him. But for you there will be no resurrection to life!"

[15] Next they brought forward the fifth and maltreated him. [16] But he looked at the king, and said, "Because you have authority among mortals, though you also are mortal, you do what you please. But do not think that God has forsaken our people. [17] Keep on, and see how his mighty power will torture you and your descendants!"

[18] After him they brought forward the sixth. And when he was about to die, he said, "Do not deceive yourself in vain. For we are suffering these things on our own account, because of our sins against our own God. Therefore astounding things have happened. [19] But do not think that you will go unpunished for having tried to fight against God!"

[20] The mother was especially admirable and worthy of honorable memory. Although she saw her seven sons perish within a single day, she bore it with good courage because of her hope in the Lord. [21] She encouraged each of them in the language of their ancestors. Filled with a noble spirit, she reinforced her woman's reasoning with a man's courage, and said to them, [22] "I do not know how you came into being in my womb. It was not I who gave you life and breath, nor I who set in order the elements within each of you. [23] Therefore the Creator of the world, who shaped the beginning of humankind and devised the origin of all things, will in his mercy give life and breath back to you again, since you now forget yourselves for the sake of his laws."

8 [1] Meanwhile Judas, who was also called Maccabeus, and his companions secretly entered the villages and summoned their kindred and enlisted those who had continued in the Jewish faith, and so they gathered about six thousand. [2] They implored the Lord to look upon the people who were oppressed by all; and to have pity on the temple that had been

profaned by the godless; [3] to have mercy on the city that was being destroyed and about to be leveled to the ground; to hearken to the blood that cried out to him; [4] to remember also the lawless destruction of the innocent babies and the blasphemies committed against his name; and to show his hatred of evil.

[5] As soon as Maccabeus got his army organized, the Gentiles could not withstand him, for the wrath of the Lord had turned to mercy. [6] Coming without warning, he would set fire to towns and villages. He captured strategic positions and put to flight not a few of the enemy. [7] He found the nights most advantageous for such attacks. And talk of his valor spread everywhere.

DISCUSSION QUESTIONS

1. Examine the mini-speeches given by each of the brothers just prior to their deaths. What themes do you notice and how do they give the brothers the courage to face martyrdom?
2. Where do you see references to the resurrection in 2 Maccabees 7:1-23?
3. What role does divine intervention play in each of these excerpts?
4. Does the revolt seem unduly harsh or violent? In what sense is this response proportional to Antiochus's actions?

Daniel 3

CLOSE READING TIPS

▶ This chapter is written in Aramaic, as is the rest of the material between Daniel 2:4b—7:28.

▶ Note the size of the statue—sixty cubits is equivalent to ninety feet. These exaggerated dimensions are typical of a folktale.

▶ The repetition of the officials suggests the wide scope of acceptance of Nebuchadnezzar's rule.

▶ Chaldeans is typically used as a synonym for Babylonians, but in the Hellenistic period it is also used to describe a class of diviners and astrologers.

▶ Note that the king's question ("who is the god. . .") in verse 15 might imply that this story did not originally follow chapter 2, where the identity of the friends' god is made clear.

▶ Note that "The Prayer of Azariah" and "The Hymn of the Three Young Men" is inserted immediately after verse 23 in the Greek translation (LXX).

▶ Note that "having the appearance of a god" implies an angel or watcher.

▶ In verse 26, the king essentially answers his own questions from verse 15.

[1] King Nebuchadnezzar made a golden statue whose height was sixty cubits and whose width was six cubits; he set it up on the plain of Dura in the province of Babylon. [2] Then King Nebuchadnezzar sent for the satraps, the prefects, and the governors, the counselors, the treasurers, the justices, the magistrates, and all the officials of the provinces to assemble and come to the dedication of the statue that King Nebuchadnezzar had set up. [3] So the satraps, the prefects, and the governors, the counselors, the treasurers, the justices, the magistrates, and all the officials of the provinces, assembled for the dedication of the statue that King Nebuchadnezzar had set up. When they were standing before the statue that Nebuchadnezzar had set up, [4] the herald proclaimed aloud, "You are commanded, O peoples, nations, and languages, [5] that when you hear the sound of the horn, pipe, lyre, trigon, harp, drum, and entire musical ensemble, you are to fall down and worship the golden statue that King Nebuchadnezzar has set up. [6] Whoever does not fall down and worship shall immediately be thrown into a furnace of blazing fire." [7] Therefore, as soon as all the peoples heard the sound of the horn, pipe, lyre, trigon, harp, drum, and entire musical ensemble, all the peoples, nations, and languages fell down and worshiped the golden statue that King Nebuchadnezzar had set up.

[8] Accordingly, at this time certain Chaldeans came forward and denounced the Jews. [9] They said to King Nebuchadnezzar, "O king, live forever! [10] You, O king, have made a decree, that everyone who hears the sound of the horn, pipe, lyre, trigon, harp, drum, and entire musical ensemble, shall fall down and worship the golden statue, [11] and whoever does not fall down and worship shall be thrown into a furnace of blazing fire. [12] There are certain Jews whom you have appointed over the affairs of the province of Babylon: Shadrach, Meshach, and Abednego.

These pay no heed to you, O King. They do not serve your gods and they do not worship the golden statue that you have set up."

[13] Then Nebuchadnezzar in furious rage commanded that Shadrach, Meshach, and Abednego be brought in; so they brought those men before the king. 14 Nebuchadnezzar said to them, "Is it true, O Shadrach, Meshach, and Abednego, that you do not serve my gods and you do not worship the golden statue that I have set up? [15] Now if you are ready when you hear the sound of the horn, pipe, lyre, trigon, harp, drum, and entire musical ensemble to fall down and worship the statue that I have made, well and good. But if you do not worship, you shall immediately be thrown into a furnace of blazing fire, and who is the god that will deliver you out of my hands?"

[16] Shadrach, Meshach, and Abednego answered the king, "O Nebuchadnezzar, we have no need to present a defense to you in this matter. [17] If our God whom we serve is able to deliver us from the furnace of blazing fire and out of your hand, O king, let him deliver us. [18] But if not, be it known to you, O king, that we will not serve your gods and we will not worship the golden statue that you have set up."

[19] Then Nebuchadnezzar was so filled with rage against Shadrach, Meshach, and Abednego that his face was distorted. He ordered the furnace heated up seven times more than was customary, [20] and ordered some of the strongest guards in his army to bind Shadrach, Meshach, and Abednego and to throw them into the furnace of blazing fire. [21] So the men were bound, still wearing their tunics, their trousers, their hats, and their other garments, and they were thrown into the furnace of blazing fire. [22] Because the king's command was urgent and the furnace was so overheated, the raging flames killed the men who lifted Shadrach, Meshach, and Abednego. [23] But the

three men, Shadrach, Meshach, and Abednego, fell down, bound, into the furnace of blazing fire.

²⁴ Then King Nebuchadnezzar was astonished and rose up quickly. He said to his counselors, "Was it not three men that we threw bound into the fire?" They answered the king, "True, O king." ²⁵ He replied, "But I see four men unbound, walking in the middle of the fire, and they are not hurt; and the fourth has the appearance of a god." ²⁶ Nebuchadnezzar then approached the door of the furnace of blazing fire and said, "Shadrach, Meshach, and Abednego, servants of the Most High God, come out! Come here!" So Shadrach, Meshach, and Abednego came out from the fire. ²⁷ And the satraps, the prefects, the governors, and the king's counselors gathered together and saw that the fire had not had any power over the bodies of those men; the hair of their heads was not singed, their tunics were not harmed, and not even the smell of fire came from them. ²⁸ Nebuchadnezzar said, "Blessed be the God of Shadrach, Meshach, and Abednego, who has sent his angel and delivered his servants who trusted in him. They disobeyed the king's command and yielded up their bodies rather than serve and worship any god except their own God. ²⁹ Therefore I make a decree: Any people, nation, or language that utters blasphemy against the God of Shadrach, Meshach, and Abednego shall be torn limb from limb, and their houses laid in ruins; for there is no other god who is able to deliver in this way." ³⁰ Then the king promoted Shadrach, Meshach, and Abednego in the province of Babylon.

DISCUSSION QUESTIONS

1. What role does exaggeration and repetition play in building the drama of this story?
2. This story begins and ends with a decree from the king. How does the content of these decrees express a pattern of ironic reversal in fortunes?
3. Compare the speech of the three friends in verse 16-18 with the speeches of the brothers in 2 Maccabees 7:1-19. What is similar about their attitudes and the rationale behind their decisions?
4. Where else in the court tales does the foreign king react favorably to the God of Daniel and his friends?
5. What does this story teach about Jewish life in the Diaspora?

28

The Deuterocanonical Wisdom Books: Ben Sira, Wisdom of Solomon, Baruch

Key Points

In the previous chapters, we have encountered the topic of wisdom in a variety of places: Proverbs, Qoheleth, and Job as well as portions of other canonical books, including Daniel and the Psalms. Three additional books—Baruch, the Wisdom of Solomon, and Ben Sira—further develop Jewish understandings of wisdom. Dating to the Hellenistic and early Roman periods, these texts show contact with aspects of Greek philosophy and anticipate concepts that are more fully developed in the New Testament (for example, the *Logos* and the immortality of the soul). Although not included in the Jewish canon, these three books are valuable to the study of the Hebrew Bible not only because they provide a window into the intellectual and theological background of Hellenistic Judaism but also because they revisit—and at times, reinterpret—biblical ideas surrounding creation, the Torah, righteousness, idolatry, and the exile.

Ben Sira, which is also known as Sirach (for the Greek version) or Ecclesiasticus (for the Latin text), was written in Jerusalem during the first quarter of the second century BCE. The original Hebrew is only partly preserved, and according to the preface of the book was translated into Greek by Ben Sira's grandson. Ben Sira's rather troubling view of women should be understood against the backdrop of a social world that was hierarchical and deeply rooted in a system of honor and shame. In the remarkable poem on Wisdom in chapter 24, Ben Sira personifies Wisdom as a female intermediary between God and the world. He also identifies the Torah as an important source of wisdom. Ben Sira is perhaps most well known for its lengthy praise of famous Israelite leaders (chapters 44–50) and its high view of the profession of a scribe (Sir. 38:24—39:11).

In contrast to Ben Sira, the Wisdom of Solomon was composed in Greek and addresses the situation of Jews living in Alexandria, Egypt in the first century CE. It consists of three sections: the "book of eschatology" (Wisd. of Sol. 1:1—6:21), the "book of wisdom" (Wisd. of Sol. 6:22—10:21), and the "book of history" (Wisd. of Sol. 11–19). Major themes in the book include the contrasting fates of the righteous and the wicked, the knowability of God through the created order (that is, "natural theology"), the immortality of the soul, and the pivotal role of Wisdom throughout history. Much of the final section of the book consists of a series of antitheses that contrasts the worship of God with the worship of idols. On the whole, while the Wisdom of Solomon reflects ethnic tensions between Jewish and non-Jewish communities at Alexandria, it maintains a relatively positive view of the Gentile world, including Hellenistic philosophy.

Though purported to be the writing of the sixth century scribe of Jeremiah, the book of Baruch is typically dated to the second century BCE. The first half of the book (Bar. 1:1—3:8) consists of communal prayers in a style reminiscent of Deuteronomy. The second section includes a lengthy hymn in praise of Wisdom (Bar. 3:9—4:4) as well as a message of consolation (Bar. 4:5—5:9). Baruch, like Ben Sira, draws a close connection between Wisdom and the Torah, though it does not suggest that wisdom had a role in creation.

Key Terms

House of instruction   House of instruction (Heb.: *bt midrash*) refers to a school in Jewish tradition. The earliest reference to this term is found in the final poem of Ben Sira, when the scribe calls on the uneducated to come to him "and lodge in my house of instruction" (Sir. 51:23). Ben Sira's school was probably more like a tutorial system in which a student became attached to a wise teacher. In Ben Sira's perspective, this instruction would have combined the teaching of Torah with traditional wisdom.

Immortality of the soul   This concept, which is derived from Platonic philosophy, affirms that while the body is perishable, there will be continued life for the soul. According to the Wisdom of Solomon, the soul is immortal because it is made in the image of God. The soul's immorality is maintained through righteousness, and conversely, can be lost through unrighteousness. Wisdom of Solomon 3:1 affirms that "the souls of the righteous are in the hand of God," an expression which is used in Roman Catholic burial liturgies.

Natural theology   This type of theology assumes that the study of the created order can lead to knowledge about God and his attributes. As such, natural theology is based on reason and experience, not supernatural revelation. This type of reasoning is evident in Ben Sira and the Wisdom of Solomon, especially in their notion that wisdom is infused throughout creation. Arguments crucial for natural theology are already present in Stoic philosophy and have been influential in Christian theological traditions, particularly in the Middle Ages.

Stoicism   Stoicism is a form of Hellenistic philosophy first developed in the third century BCE. It affirms that the material universe is infused with the divine spirit and that everything is created for a purpose. Stoics also assert that good cannot exist without evil and they seek happiness through the cultivation of wisdom and virtue.

A blending of Stoicism and Platonism (known as Middle Platonism) forms an important philosophical backdrop to the Wisdom of Solomon.

Logos   *Logos* (Word or Reason) is an important concept in Hellenistic philosophy. The *Logos* was a vital force or rational principle that pervades the whole universe and is associated with the spirit or mind of God. This concept of *Logos* likely influenced Wisdom of Solomon 7:22—8:1, which describes wisdom not only as the power of God and an emanation of his glory but also as a substance that can transform individuals. The concept of the *Logos* is further developed in the New Testament, where it is specifically identified with Jesus (John 1:1-14).

Key Personalities

The Jewish community in Alexandria

Alexandria, a seaport located on the western Delta of the Nile River, flourished as the capital of Egypt under the Ptolemies. Though Jews had migrated to Egypt as early as the sixth century BCE, a larger Jewish community was established in Alexandria not long after the Greeks conquered Egypt near the end of the third century. Alexandria was the center of intellectual life for Jews over the next two or three centuries, as is especially evident in the work of Philo. In addition, the Hebrew Bible was translated into Greek by Hellenistic Jews in Alexandria sometime between 150–50 BCE. Though likely exaggerating, Philo claims that by the mid-first century CE, there were a million Jews living in Egypt, many of whom would have been located in Alexandria. On the whole, Jews at Alexandria prospered under the reign of the Ptolemies. However, things would change drastically with the advent of Roman rule around 30 BCE. During this period, most Jews were not considered citizens and

tensions with the non-Jewish population in Alexandria ran high. After a series of violent eruptions, the Jewish community in Alexandria was virtually wiped out by the Romans in 115–117 CE. Certain aspects of the Wisdom of Solomon, which was written in Alexandria in the early first century CE, refer to the difficulties Jews faced under Roman rule. Nevertheless, the Wisdom of Solomon maintains a mostly positive attitude toward the Gentile world, drawing on key concepts from Hellenistic philosophy.

The "famous men" of Ben Sira

A long poem in Ben Sira (chapters 44–50) praises a series of "famous men" from Israel's past. Rather than recounting specific events in biblical history, this poem eulogizes specific individuals and their character. Ben Sira begins with Enoch and proceeds to address a number of other key figures, including certain prophets (Elijah, Elisha, Isaiah, Ezekiel), kings (David, Samuel, Hezekiah, Josiah), and leaders (Noah, Moses, Joshua, Caleb). Brief mention is also made of Adam, Job, Zerubbabel, Jeshua, Nehemiah, and the Twelve Prophets. However, his list gives greatest attention to priests. Three times the amount of space is given to Aaron in comparison to Moses and the hymn concludes with a celebration of the high priest Simon (219–196 BCE), a contemporary of Ben Sira. The fact that only men are included in this list is not surprising in light of Ben Sira's negative view of women. This hymn is patterned on the model of Hellenistic *encomia*, which praised famous leaders in commemoration of local shrines and cities. However, in contrast to the *encomium*, Ben Sira emphasizes a person's election to office over his genealogy and his personal piety and religious duties over heroic achievements. The reward received by these famous men consists of the honor confirmed on them by both God and other people.

Questions for Study Discussion

1. Ben Sira clearly reflects negative views of women, even claiming that it is because of women that humanity must face death. As you scan the breadth of biblical literature, do you see other biblical books that reflect similar views? Alternatively, are there biblical texts that offer alternative, more positive views of women?

2. How is Ben Sira different from earlier, biblical wisdom books like Proverbs, Job, and Qoheleth? What might these differences suggest about the development of Judaism in the Hellenistic period?

3. Many books in the Bible wrestle with the problem of evil in the world. Why does humanity perpetually do harm to itself and the world in which it lives? Why do disasters strike without any apparent connection to wrongdoing? How might Ben Sira and the Wisdom of Solomon respond to these questions? Are you convinced by his answer? If not, why? How would you respond to the problem of evil?

4. Ben Sira clearly has a lot to say about his career as a scribe. Analyze Ben Sira from the perspective of class, society, and economics? Whom does he perceive to be "above" and "below" him on the ladder of society? How do your answers to these questions affect how you understand Ben Sira and his emphasis on Torah—a document written and read by the literate elite—as wisdom?

5. Compare "Wisdom," in Ben Sira, Wisdom of Solomon, and The Book of Baruch. What are the similarities and differences? How do they describe wisdom and its sources differently or similarly? What fundamental assumptions drive their thinking on wisdom? Are their views of God and the world fundamentally different or the same?

Primary Text

Ben Sira 24

> **CLOSE READING TIPS**
>
> ▶ The poem in verses 1-22 is often called "The Praise of Wisdom." It begins with Wisdom praising herself in the assembly of the Most High (verses 1-2), a features which shares much in common with a genre of poem associated with the Egyptian goddess Isis (known as an aretalogy).
>
> ▶ Note that the pillar of cloud (verse 4) is associated with God's presence in the book of Exodus; here, God's presence on earth is manifested through Wisdom.
>
> ▶ Not unlike the description of Wisdom holding sway over the earth (verse 6), the goddess Isis is said to rule as a queen over the land.
>
> ▶ Note that the reference to Wisdom seeking a resting place (verses 7-8) suggests that humans could have access to Wisdom in the earthy realm of creation.

▶ Note that in verse 10, Wisdom is portrayed as a priest-like figure, ministering before YHWH in the temple.

▶ In contrast to verses 8-12, the pseudepigraphical book of 1 Enoch suggests that Wisdom finds no place to dwell among humans and so returns to heaven (1 Enoch 42).

▶ Some ancient manuscripts include verse 18, which talks about Wisdom as a mother who is given to all her children.

▶ Note that the Torah is described as a valid source of Wisdom (verses 23-24). This view differs markedly from Proverbs, Qoheleth, and Job, which rarely mention the Torah.

▶ The imagery of pouring out (verse 33) is common in Ben Sira, where it is used in reference to Wisdom (Sir. 1:9), the scribe (Sir. 39:6), God's blessing (Sir. 39:22), Solomon's wisdom (Sir. 47:14-15), and Ben Sira's instruction (here and Sir. 50:27).

¹ Wisdom praises herself,
   and tells of her glory in the midst of her
      people.
² In the assembly of the Most High she opens
      her mouth,
   and in the presence of his hosts she tells of
      her glory:
³ "I came forth from the mouth of the Most
      High,
   and covered the earth like a mist.
⁴ I dwelt in the highest heavens,
   and my throne was in a pillar of cloud.
⁵ Alone I compassed the vault of heaven
   and traversed the depths of the abyss.
⁶ Over waves of the sea, over all the earth,
   and over every people and nation I have
      held sway.
⁷ Among all these I sought a resting place;
   in whose territory should I abide?

⁸ "Then the Creator of all things gave me a
      command,
   and my Creator chose the place for my tent.
He said, 'Make your dwelling in Jacob,
   and in Israel receive your inheritance.'

⁹ Before the ages, in the beginning, he created
      me,
   and for all the ages I shall not cease to be.
¹⁰ In the holy tent I ministered before him,
   and so I was established in Zion
¹¹ Thus in the beloved city he gave me a resting
      place,
   and in Jerusalem was my domain.
¹² I took root in an honored people,
   in the portion of the Lord, his heritage.

¹³ "I grew tall like a cedar in Lebanon,
   and like a cypress on the heights of
      Hermon.
¹⁴ I grew tall like a palm tree in En-gedi,
   and like rosebushes in Jericho;
like a fair olive tree in the field,
   and like a plane tree beside water I grew
      tall.
¹⁵ Like cassia and camel's thorn I gave forth
      perfume,
   and like choice myrrh I spread my
      fragrance,
like galbanum, onycha, and stacte,
   and like the odor of incense in the tent.

[16] Like a terebinth I spread out my branches,
    and my branches are glorious and graceful.
[17] Like the vine I bud forth delights,
    and my blossoms become glorious and
        abundant fruit.

[19] "Come to me, you who desire me,
    and eat your fill of my fruits.
[20] For the memory of me is sweeter than honey,
    and the possession of me sweeter than the
        honeycomb.
[21] Those who eat of me will hunger for more,
    and those who drink of me will thirst for
        more.
[22] Whoever obeys me will not be put to shame,
    and those who work with me will not sin."

[23] All this is the book of the covenant of the
    Most High God,
    the law that Moses commanded us
    as an inheritance for the congregations of
        Jacob.
[25] It overflows, like the Pishon, with wisdom,
    and like the Tigris at the time of the first
        fruits.
[26] It runs over, like the Euphrates, with
    understanding,
    and like the Jordan at harvest time.
[27] It pours forth instruction like the Nile,
    like the Gihon at the time of vintage.
[28] The first man did not know wisdom fully,
    nor will the last one fathom her.
[29] For her thoughts are more abundant than the
    sea,
    and her counsel deeper than the great
        abyss.

[30] As for me, I was like a canal from a river,
    like a water channel into a garden.
[31] I said, "I will water my garden
    and drench my flower-beds."
And lo, my canal became a river,
    and my river a sea.
[32] I will again make instruction shine forth like
    the dawn,
    and I will make it clear from far away.
[33] I will again pour out teaching like prophecy,
    and leave it to all future generations.
[34] Observe that I have not labored for myself
    alone,
    but for all who seek wisdom.

DISCUSSION QUESTIONS

1. What do you learn about the origins of wisdom in the first stanza (verses 3-7)? How does the language here recall imagery or ideas from Genesis 1?

2. In the second stanza (verses 8-12), where specifically does Wisdom find a resting place? What does this suggest about the accessibility of Wisdom?

3. In what ways are trees and fruit apt metaphors (verses 13-17) for describing the value of Wisdom according to Ben Sira?

4. In verses 23-24, Wisdom is identified with the Torah of Moses. How might this change how you understand both the purpose of the Torah and the nature of Wisdom?

5. What are several ways in which Ben Sira's understanding of Wisdom in this passage differ from that which is found in the book of Proverbs?

Wisdom of Solomon 7:22b—8:21

CLOSE READING TIPS

▶ Note that Wisdom of Solomon 7:22b-23 includes twenty-one characteristics of Wisdom. Simlar lists are found in Stoic philosophy in relation to the *Logos*.

▶ The notion that Wisdom "pervades and penetrates all things" is closely related to how the Stoics conceived of the spirit (*pneuma*).

▶ A connection between Wisdom and sun and light (Wisd. of Sol. 7:29-30) is also evident in the work of Philo.

▶ The extended metaphor in Wisdom of Solomon 8:2-16 describes how Solomon made Wisdom his bride.

▶ Note that Wisdom of Solomon 8:5-8 juxtapose four successive clauses beginning with "if." In each case, the "if" statement is assumed to be true.

▶ Wisdom of Solomon 8:7 enumerates the four cardinal virtues of Wisdom in Greek thought: self-control, prudence, justice, and courage.

▶ Note that the reference to "immortality" in Wisdom of Solomon 8:13 does not suggest the idea of a resurrection but rather the hope for the continued life of the soul. This immortality is maintained through a righteous life. See also Wisdom of Solomon 8:17 and 2:23.

▶ Note that Solomon is described as being "naturally gifted" with Wisdom.

▶ The passage ends with an introduction to Solomon's prayer for Wisdom, which is an expanded version of the prayer found in 1 Kings 3:6-9 and 2 Chronicles 1:8-10.

22b There is in her a spirit that is intelligent, holy,
unique, manifold, subtle,
mobile, clear, unpolluted,
distinct, invulnerable, loving the good, keen,
irresistible, 23 beneficent, humane,
steadfast, sure, free from anxiety,
all-powerful, overseeing all,
and penetrating through all spirits
that are intelligent, pure, and altogether subtle.
24 For wisdom is more mobile than any motion;
because of her pureness she pervades and penetrates all things.
25 For she is a breath of the power of God,
and a pure emanation of the glory of the Almighty;
therefore nothing defiled gains entrance into her.
26 For she is a reflection of eternal light,
a spotless mirror of the working of God,
and an image of his goodness.
27 Although she is but one, she can do all things,
and while remaining in herself, she renews all things;
in every generation she passes into holy souls
and makes them friends of God, and prophets;
28 for God loves nothing so much as the person who lives with wisdom.

[29] She is more beautiful than the sun,
and excels every constellation of the stars.
Compared with the light she is found to be
    superior,
[30] for it is succeeded by the night,
but against wisdom evil does not prevail.
8 [1] She reaches mightily from one end of the
    earth to the other,
and she orders all things well.
[2] I loved her and sought her from my youth;
I desired to take her for my bride,
and became enamored of her beauty.
[3] She glorifies her noble birth by living with
    God,
and the Lord of all loves her.
[4] For she is an initiate in the knowledge of God,
and an associate in his works.
[5] If riches are a desirable possession in life,
what is richer than wisdom, the active cause of
    all things?
[6] And if understanding is effective,
who more than she is fashioner of what exists?
[7] And if anyone loves righteousness,
her labors are virtues;
for she teaches self-control and prudence,
justice and courage;
nothing in life is more profitable for mortals
    than these.
[8] And if anyone longs for wide experience,
she knows the things of old, and infers the
    things to come;
she understands turns of speech and the solu-
    tions of riddles;
she has foreknowledge of signs and wonders
and of the outcome of seasons and times.
[9] Therefore I determined to take her to live
    with me,
knowing that she would give me good counsel

and encouragement in cares and grief.
[10] Because of her I shall have glory among the
    multitudes
and honor in the presence of the elders, though
    I am young.
[11] I shall be found keen in judgment,
and in the sight of rulers I shall be admired.
[12] When I am silent they will wait for me,
and when I speak they will give heed;
if I speak at greater length,
they will put their hands on their mouths.
[13] Because of her I shall have immortality,
and leave an everlasting remembrance to those
    who come after me.
[14] I shall govern peoples,
and nations will be subject to me;
[15] dread monarchs will be afraid of me when
    they hear of me;
among the people I shall show myself capable,
    and courageous in war.
[16] When I enter my house, I shall find rest with
    her;
for companionship with her has no bitterness,
and life with her has no pain, but gladness and
    joy.
[17] When I considered these things inwardly,
and pondered in my heart
that in kinship with wisdom there is
    immortality,
[18] and in friendship with her, pure delight,
and in the labors of her hands, unfailing
    wealth,
and in the experience of her company,
    understanding,
and renown in sharing her words,
I went about seeking how to get her for myself.
[19] As a child I was naturally gifted,
and a good soul fell to my lot;

[20] or rather, being good, I entered an undefiled
body.

[21] But I perceived that I would not possess wisdom unless God gave her to me—

and it was a mark of insight to know whose gift
she was—

so I appealed to the Lord and implored him,
and with my whole heart I said:

DISCUSSION QUESTIONS

1. How would you characterize the relationship between Wisdom and God in Wisdom of Solomon
   7:22b—8:1?

2. What do you learn about the nature of Wisdom from the five metaphors in Wisdom of Solomon 7:25-26?

3. What effect does Wisdom have on individuals in Wisdom of Solomon 7:27-8:1?

4. From what you know about Solomon from 1 Kings, to what extent was the king "faithful" to his bride
   Wisdom?

5. According to Wisdom of Solomon 8:9-21, what benefits does Wisdom offer to rulers? How is such
   wisdom obtained?

Baruch 3:9—4:4

CLOSE READING TIPS

▸ Note that "commandments of life" (Bar. 3:9) refers to the Torah (see Deut. 30:15-20).

▸ Note that "growing old" (Bar. 3:10) suggests that the exile had been going on for a long time.
   However, this date is not easily reconciled with the reference to the "fifth year" (either 592 or 581
   BCE) mentioned in Baruch 1:2.

▸ In Baruch 3:17-19, those who seek riches face certain death (Hades). In contrast, those seek the
   Torah find life (see Bar. 4:1).

▸ Teman is the capital of Edom. Merran may refer to Midian. Canaan is likely a reference to
   Phoenicia, whose cities Tyre and Sidon were traditionally associated with wisdom and trade.

▸ In this context, "the house of God" (Bar. 3:24) refers to all of creation not just the temple.

▸ Note that the accessibility of Wisdom in Baruch 3:29-30 is described in a similar way as the
   accessibility of the divine commandments in Deuteronomy 30:12-13.

▸ The notion that Wisdom appears on earth (Bar. 3:37) is also found in Proverbs 8 and Sirach 24:6-
   12; a contrasting perspective is found in 1 Enoch 42, where Wisdom does not find a suitable
   dwelling on earth and thus returns to heaven.

▸ The possession of Wisdom, like the keeping of the Torah, is a matter of life and death (Bar. 4:1).

[9] Hear the commandments of life, O Israel;
    give ear, and learn wisdom!
[10] Why is it, O Israel, why is it that you are in
    the land of your enemies,
      that you are growing old in a foreign
        country,
that you are defiled with the dead,
    [11] that you are counted among those in
      Hades?
[12] You have forsaken the fountain of wisdom.
[13] If you had walked in the way of God,
    you would be living in peace forever.
[14] Learn where there is wisdom,
    where there is strength,
    where there is understanding,
so that you may at the same time discern
    where there is length of days, and life,
    where there is light for the eyes, and peace.

[15] Who has found her place?
    And who has entered her storehouses?
[16] Where are the rulers of the nations,
    and those who lorded it over the animals
      on earth;
[17] those who made sport of the birds of the air,
    and who hoarded up silver and gold
in which people trust,
    and there is no end to their getting;
[18] those who schemed to get silver, and were
    anxious,
    but there is no trace of their works?
[19] They have vanished and gone down to
    Hades,
    and others have arisen in their place.

[20] Later generations have seen the light of day,
    and have lived upon the earth;
but they have not learned the way to
    knowledge,

    nor understood her paths,
    nor laid hold of her.
[21] Their descendants have strayed far from her
    way.
[22] She has not been heard of in Canaan,
    or seen in Teman;
[23] the descendants of Hagar, who seek for
    understanding on the earth,
    the merchants of Merran and Teman,
    the story-tellers and the seekers for
      understanding,
have not learned the way to wisdom,
    or given thought to her paths.

[24] O Israel, how great is the house of God,
    how vast the territory that he possesses!
[25] It is great and has no bounds;
    it is high and immeasurable.
[26] The giants were born there, who were famous
    of old,
    great in stature, expert in war.
[27] God did not choose them,
    or give them the way to knowledge;
[28] so they perished because they had no
    wisdom,
    they perished through their folly.

[29] Who has gone up into heaven, and taken her,
    and brought her down from the clouds?
[30] Who has gone over the sea, and found her,
    and will buy her for pure gold?
[31] No one knows the way to her,
    or is concerned about the path to her.
[32] But the one who knows all things knows her,
    he found her by his understanding.
The one who prepared the earth for all time
    filled it with four-footed creatures;
[33] the one who sends forth the light, and it goes;
    he called it, and it obeyed him, trembling;

³⁴ the stars shone in their watches, and were
     glad;
   he called them, and they said, "Here we
     are!"
   They shone with gladness for him who
     made them.
³⁵ This is our God;
   no other can be compared to him.
   36 He found the whole way to knowledge,
   and gave her to his servant Jacob
   and to Israel, whom he loved.
³⁷ Afterward she appeared on earth
   and lived with humankind.

4 ¹ She is the book of the commandments of
     God,
   the law that endures forever.
   All who hold her fast will live,
     and those who forsake her will die.
² Turn, O Jacob, and take her;
   walk toward the shining of her light.
³ Do not give your glory to another,
   or your advantages to an alien people.
⁴ Happy are we, O Israel,
   for we know what is pleasing to God.

DISCUSSION QUESTIONS

1. In what sense is Israel's experience of exile used as an object lesson in this passage?
2. According to this passage, to what extent is wisdom accessible to Gentile nations? The wealthy and powerful? Israel? All of humanity?
3. God is said to "find" Wisdom in Baruch 3:32, 36. How does this statement compare with God's relationship with Wisdom in Ben Sira (see especially Sir. 24:4, 9)?
4. Where in this passage is Wisdom explicitly identified with the Torah?
5. Where do you see a more subtle or implicit connection between Wisdom and the Torah?

29

From Tradition to Canon

Key Points

For many Jews and Christians over the centuries, the Hebrew Bible (or Old Testament) has been thought of as more than just a collection of documents about the history of ancient Israel or an anthology of stories about prophets, priest, kings, and sages. Rather, these texts have functioned as sacred scripture—an authoritative source for how people live and what they believe. This understanding is often tied to claims about inspiration and revelation, or in other words, the relationship between the biblical text and divine truth. While some version of these beliefs play a fundamental role in a variety of religious traditions, from an academic perspective it is essential to keep in mind several caveats about the nature of the Hebrew Bible as a sacred, inspired, and authoritative text.

First, as we have seen in many of the preceding chapters, the Hebrew Bible was composed, copied, and revised over several hundred years and preserves a diversity of voices and perspectives. The Hebrew Bible is a crucial resource for theological reflection, yet it does not provide us with tightly coherent systematic theology. As such, it is not always possible to impose uniform principles on this text. This observation does not by any means diminish the authority or "sacredness" of the Hebrew Bible. Rather, it highlights the fact that this text is adaptable to life, capable of speaking to the ever-changing circumstances of religious communities, both past and present.

Second, claims about inspiration and authority have important implications for how the Hebrew Bible is interpreted. In some conservative circles, it is assumed that an authoritative text must be historically accurate and morally edifying. Certainly, some parts of the Hebrew Bible fit both criteria. Yet on the whole, this viewpoint tends to impose interpretive (or theological) presuppositions on these texts that would have been foreign to their original authors and readers. Instead of relying on literal or allegorical interpretations, it is best to engage the Hebrew Bible on its own terms, paying close attention to questions about a given text's genre, intention, historical context, and social location. These considerations can give us a clearer sense of the meaning of the Hebrew Bible—a point which ultimately enhances our ability to engage and use these texts as sacred scripture.

Finally, to speak of the Hebrew Bible as a canon implies that this text is a standard for faith and practice. However, a list of canonical texts did not float down from heaven one day. Rather, the canon is the product of a broad consensus over time. Further, the way in which the Bible functions as a canon varies widely among different religious traditions. Neither does the canon include all the writings that were important to ancient Judaism or early Christianity. It also must be kept in mind that the canonical status of the Hebrew Bible is only one factor that contributes to its importance in Judaism and Christianity. Whether due to its teaching about social justice and idolatry or its enduring characters and stories, the Hebrew Bible has had—and will continue to have—a lasting influence on western culture.

Key Terms

Sacred scripture   This term refers to the authoritative status of the Hebrew Bible in Jewish and Christian traditions. It acknowledges that these texts are more than just a collection of documents about ancient Israel and its religion. As a crucial source of knowledge about God, creation, history, ethics, and so forth, sacred scripture guides communities of faith in how they live and what they believe. The notion of sacred scripture is closely tied to how the Bible is interpreted, and thus intersects with doctrines about inspiration, revelation, and biblical authority.

Inspiration   Derived from a Latin term meaning "to breathe into," inspiration suggests that the Bible originated with or was prompted by the Spirit of God. Only certain parts of the Hebrew Bible, such as the law of Moses and the words of the prophets, make the claim of divine inspiration. However, this concept is eventually applied to the whole canon. Even still, the doctrine of inspiration does not preclude the fact that human authors and editors were chiefly responsible—even if urged on by the Spirit—for the shape and shaping of biblical texts.

Allegorical interpretation   Allegorical interpretation brings to light symbolic meanings that lie behind the literal words of a text. This method was first applied by Greek scholars to Homeric stories. Later, it was widely adopted by Hellenistic Jewish scholars and many early Church Fathers. Allegorical interpretation is often used as a way of explaining biblical meaning in light of philosophical or theological presuppositions, ethical concerns, or historical problems. Examples of allegorical interpretation include reading the Songs of Songs as a poem about Christ's love for the church or explaining the command to wipe out the Canaanites in Joshua in terms of one's battle against personal vice and sin.

Pseudepigrapha   This term is used to describe a variety of noncanonical Jewish writings from the Hellenistic and Roman periods (c. 250 BCE–200 CE). The term Pseudepigrapha (lit: "falsely ascribed writings") reflects the fact that many of these texts are associated with a figure from the Hebrew Bible such as Enoch, Ezra, Adam,

Abraham, and Baruch. These writings often fill in gaps or rewrite biblical stories, smooth over theological problems, or imitate biblical and Greek epic poetry. The Pseudepigrapha are essential for understanding the religious, political, and social world of early Judaism.

Idolatry One of the most persistent themes throughout the Hebrew Bible is the critique of idolatry. Typically, idolatry refers either to improper objects of worship (that is, foreign deities and their idols) or to an improper manner of worshiping Yahweh (that is, by means of images or carved statues). However, idolatry can also function as a theological evaluation of any action or belief that leads an individual to honor some entity (money, power, success, and so on) above or in place of God.

Key Personalities

Philo of Alexandria

Philo of Alexandra (c. 20 BCE–50 CE) was one of the most prolific Jewish writers of antiquity. His writing provides a window into Hellenistic Judaism at the turn of the era. He produced a great number of commentaries, most of which employ an allegorical interpretation of scripture. His writings are sophisticated, showing not only profound knowledge of Judaism but also Greek philosophy. In fact, his allegorical interpretations often have the goal of showing a high level of consistency between the Hebrew Bible and Middle Platonism. For instance, in *Special Laws* Philo allegorizes the Jewish practice of circumcision, describing it as a symbolic act by which an individual excises undue pleasures in life. In a similar fashion, he reinterprets other major facets of Jewish life, including the temple, scripture, and ritual laws, as symbolic categories that apply equally well to Jews and gentiles in Alexandria. Further, Philo's treatment of Moses and the patriarchs emphasizes how their virtues are compatible with the values of Hellenistic Stoic philosophy. Philo blends together elements of Hellenistic philosophy (namely Stoicism and Neoplatonism) with the figures and beliefs of historic Judaism. Philo's writings were not only highly influential in Jewish circles but they also were read and adapted by Christian thinkers such as Clement of Alexandria, Origen, Ambrose, and Augustine. Some New Testament books (for example, Hebrews) may have been influenced by Hellenistic Jewish traditions that are also evident in Philo's work.

Brevard Childs

Brevard Childs was one of the most prominent biblical scholars of the second half of the twentieth century. He is especially known for developing an approach to biblical interpretation known as canonical criticism or the "canonical approach." By focusing on the final form of a biblical text, his approach signaled a significant departure from historical-critical methods, which concentrate on the complex processes behind the composition and editing of biblical books. Without denying the existence of literary or pre-literary layers in the text, Childs attempted to assess how and why these earlier traditions were put together from a canonical perspective. In this sense, the present shape of the text serves as evidence of how a certain community of faith had organized past traditions as sacred scripture. Childs's canonical approach tends to draw attention to the unity of individual books, the presence of intertextuality, the conscious shaping of the canon, and the interpretation of the Old Testament as Christian Scripture. While insightful in many respects, the validity of Childs's approach is debated and faces several lines of critique. For instance, reading the book of Amos in light of its final form would potentially give greater weight to the theological and ideological concerns of its latest editors, who affirm the Davidic covenant and soften the critique of the eighth-century prophet. By privileging their perspective, a canonical approach runs the risk of minimizing the biting critique of the prophet Amos on Israel and the sacrificial cult.

Questions for Study and Discussion

1. Interpreters have often tried to find a theological center in the Hebrew Bible. Yet many have claimed that this is an ill-fated task, whose results typically say more about the interpreter than they do about the Hebrew Bible itself. Do you agree with this assessment? Is it in fact the case that the Hebrew Bible has no center?
2. This chapter draws attention to problematic assumptions that religious communities make about "Scripture" and what it can do. What are some of those assumptions? Can you think of others? Do you think religious communities are correct in making such assumptions?
3. Claiming that a particular canon of texts is "Scripture" raises problems for faith communities. Explore and evaluate some of these.
4. How would you evaluate the Bible's legacy in Western culture? Has it been largely beneficial or harmful? Or perhaps a bit of both? Are there "biblical" notions that, in your view, inform admirable aspects of Western culture? On the flipside, are there "biblical" notions that inform detestable aspects of Western culture?

A Short Guide to Writing Exegetical Research Papers

This guide is meant to help you organize and compose an exegetical research paper. You may also find portions of this sequence and resources helpful in other disciplines.

Short or long, your exegetical paper can be crafted in six steps: 1) choose a text or topic, 2) study the text yourself, 3) study the secondary literature, 4) develop your argument, 5) write the first draft, and 6) refine the final paper.

1. Choose a Text

If your text or topic is not chosen for you, the first step in your writing process involves selecting a text to work with. It is important to remember that the success of your paper does *not* depend on the text you choose. Nevertheless, there are several helpful things to keep in mind:

1. **Select a text that is interesting to you**. The more you like a text, the more likely you will invest quality time in research and writing.
2. **Remember the "Goldilocks principle."** Be careful not to pick a text that is too short or too long, which can either result in not having enough to say or not having enough space to say what you want to say. As a general rule, aim for 12–25 verses, which is the equivalent of a short chapter or portion of a longer chapter.
3. **Let your curiosity lead the way**. The goal of the paper is to develop an argument, supported by specific observations about the text. The best way to start this process is to gravitate toward a text for which you can raise compelling questions about its historical background, social location, rhetorical argument, main characters, plot, theological implications, and so forth.

If you are feeling stuck getting started, try reading back through this Study Companion. Did any chapters interest you more than others? Did any key terms or key personalities pique your curiosity? For which of the primary texts did you most enjoy the discussion questions or close reading tips?

It is occasionally acceptable to choose a certain theme and then study that theme across a number of different texts. For instance, you might choose to study the relationship of wisdom and creation in Job, Proverbs, Baruch, and Wisdom of Solomon, or you could analyze the role of non-Israelite women in Joshua and Judges. You might even focus in on a specific image, such as the ruined vineyard in First Isaiah or the renewed land in Ezekiel 40–48. Before moving in this direction, check with your professor to make sure that this option fits within the parameters of your assignment.

2. Study the Text Yourself

After selecting a text, many beginning students come down with a severe case of "expert anxiety." Aware that they are not experts, students immediately rush to commentaries and journals to unlock the meaning of their text. While books and articles are invaluable resources, the best place to start your paper is actually *not* in the library. Remember, the goal of an exegesis paper is to present *your* argument (albeit supported by scholarship) about a specific aspect of the text at hand. Thus, it is best to begin with your own observations about the text, including its language, structure, argument, imagery, etc. You may try some of the following strategies:

1. **Read the text several times**. Go slowly and try not to assume you know what the meaning of the text is. What details, imagery, or terms jump out to you? What questions do you have about the historical background of this text? Its social location? Its audience? Its language? Keep track for your questions and observations.
2. **Try reading the text in several different translations**. What differences stand out to you? Do any of the translation choices make you think differently about the meaning of specific terms? If you have training in Biblical Hebrew, you might also read the text in its original language.
3. **Develop a structural outline of the text**. The goal of a structure outline is to briefly summarize and organize the content of a passage in your own words. Using Roman numerals, a multi-layered list of bullet points, or another graphic format, how would you display the flow of the passage? Do you notice any patterns or repetitions? Is the argument or plot linear? Is a certain theme developed throughout the text?

At this stage, it would also be helpful to consider the different sorts of questions that are raised by various methods of biblical exegesis. You might not be able to answer some of these questions on your own, but identifying these issues now will help direct your use of secondary sources later in the research process.

Composition History

Is there a named author of the text? What do we know about him, her, or them? Is the attributed author the actual author, or is the work pseudepigraphic? When, where, and under what circumstances was the text written? Who seem to be the text's recipients?

Redaction Criticism

How has the author used the source or sources in shaping this text? Are there any parallel texts and how is this text similar or different? What particular views or theological emphases does the author show? How did the author's life circumstances (if they are known) affect the shaping of the text?

Literary Criticism

What words are used, and what range of meanings do they have? What images and symbols are used? What characters appear in the story? What are we told and what can you surmise about these characters? How are the characters related to one another in the story?

Source Criticism

Does the text have any underlying source or sources? Does it quote from elsewhere in scripture? Which version of a source was used, in case there is more than one? What do the sources actually say and mean in their original contexts? How are the sources used (quoted, paraphrased, adapted, and so on) in your text?

RELATED BIBLICAL OR ANCIENT TEXTS

In addition to looking for the quotation of other biblical texts, you may detect some thematic similarity between your chosen text and other passages in the bible. Does your text seem to be an allusion to another text? What passages surround your text? From where has the reader just come, and where will the reader go next?

Form Criticism

What is the literary form of "genre" of the text? Does the text follow or diverge from the typical expectations and style of this genre? What is the customary purpose or goal of this genre? In what social context would texts of this genre been used?

Socio-Historical Criticism

If the story claims to be historical, what really happened? What social, historical, or cultural information can be gleaned from the text? What background information is necessary to better understand the text? What was life like for people living in this time?

History of Interpretation

How has this text been interpreted over time? What are the most common questions raised and theses posed about this text? Has opinion or interpretation changed? What events or discoveries led to such change?

Of course, these comprise just some of the many available strategies for interpreting biblical material. You'll likely draw from several strategies as you work toward your own conclusions. Placing your interpretation in conversation with the work of other scholars will help clarify and strengthen your thinking.

3. Study the Secondary Literature

After completing this initial stage of research on your own, it is now time to turn to the secondary literature. This can be overwhelming. There is probably no shortage of articles, books, and commentaries that address your text or topic. You simply will not have enough time to consult all of this material. Equally challenging is the fact that you might well come across conflicting opinions about certain aspects of the text. In light of these challenges, your goal is twofold: to narrow your research to those resources that are most relevant to your analysis, and to adjudicate between different interpretive conclusions, being able to explain *why* you agree with one view over another.

In your research, take care not to allow your expanding knowledge of what others think about your text or topic to drown your own curiosities, sensibilities, and insights. Instead, as your initial questions expand and then diminish with increased knowledge from your research, your own deeper concerns, insights, and point of view should emerge and grow.

Encyclopedia articles, scholarly books, commentaries, journal articles, and other standard reference tools contain a wealth of material and helpful bibliographies to orient you to your text and its interpretation. Look for the most authoritative and up-to-date sources. Checking cross-references will deepen your knowledge. In addition, be sure to consult with a reference librarian (if available) or someone else who can help you maximize your use of print and online resources.

It is wise to start listing the sources you have consulted right away in standard bibliographical format (see section 6, below, for examples of usual formats). You will want to assign a number or code to each one so you'll be able to reference them easily when you're writing the paper.

Reference Resources

Concordances

R. E. Whitaker and J. R. Kohlenberger III, *The Analytical Concordance to the New Revised Standard Version of the Bible.* Oxford: Oxford University Press, 2000.

Bible Dictionaries

W. R. F. Browning, ed., *A Dictionary of the Bible,* 2nd ed. Oxford: Oxford University Press, 2009
M. A. Powell, ed., *HarperCollins Bible Dictionary,* rev. and updated. San Francisco: HarperOne, 2011
D. N. Freedman, ed., *The Anchor Bible Dictionary,* 6 vols. New York: Doubleday, 1992

Commentaries

One- and two-volume:
J. L. Mays, *The HarperCollins Bible Commentary,* rev. ed. San Francisco: HarperOne, 2000
R. E. Brown, J. A. Fitzmyer, and R. E. Murphy, eds., *The New Jerome Biblical Commentary,* 3d ed. Upper Saddle River, N.J.: Prentice Hall, 1999
J. Barton and J. Muddiman, eds., *The Oxford Bible Commentary.* Oxford: Oxford University Press, 2001

G. A. Yee, H. R. Page Jr., and M. J. M. Coomber, eds., *Fortress Commentary on the Bible: The Old Testament and Apocrypha*. Minneapolis: Fortress Press, 2014

M. Aymer, C. B. Kittredge, and D. A. Sánchez, eds., *Fortress Commentary on the Bible: The New Testament*. Minneapolis: Fortress Press, 2014

Online Resources

A list of resources for research in biblical studies is available at the homepage of the Society of Biblical Literature, here: http://www.sbl-site.org/educational/researchtools.aspx

Periodical Literature

Even though your own interpretation should drive your exegesis, you'll be able to better place your interpretation in contemporary context by referring to what other scholars are saying. Their work is largely published in academic journals and periodicals. In consulting the chief articles dealing with your topic, you'll learn where agreements, disagreements, and open questions stand; how older treatments have fared; and the latest relevant tools and insights. Since you cannot consult them all, work back from the latest, looking for the best and most directly relevant articles from the last five, ten, or twenty years, as ambition and time allow.

A good place to start is the ATLA Religion Database (www.atla.com), which indexes articles, essays, book reviews, dissertations, theses, and even essays in collections. You can search by keywords, subjects, persons, or scripture references. Below are other standard indexes to periodical literature. Check with your institution's library to learn which ones it subscribes to.

▶ Guide to Social Science and Religion in Periodical Literature (http://www.nplguide.com)
▶ Readers' Guide to Periodical Literature
▶ Dissertation Abstracts International
▶ ATLA Catholic Periodical and Literature Index
▶ Humanities International Index

Identify the Most Important Secondary Sources

By now you can identify the most important sources for your text or topic, both primary and secondary. Apart from books and journal articles you've identified, you can find the chief works on any topic readily listed in your college or seminary library's catalog, the Library of Congress subject index (http://catalog2.loc.gov), and other online library catalog sites. Many theological libraries and archives are linked at the "Religious Studies Web Guide": http://www.ucalgary.ca/~lipton/catalogues.html.

Take Notes

Now review each source, noting down its most important or relevant facts, observations, or opinions. Be sure to keep your notes organized consistently. You may choose to create a separate document for the notes on each source you consult, for example. As you take notes, you should identify the subtopic, the source information (including page numbers), and the main idea or direct quotation.

While most of the notes you take will simply summarize points made in primary or secondary sources, direct quotes are used for 1) word-for-word transcriptions, 2) key words or phrases coined by the author, or 3) especially clear or summary formulations of an author's point of view. Remember, re-presenting another's insight or formulation without attribution is plagiarism. You should also be sure to keep separate notes about your own ideas or insights into the text or topic as they evolve.

When Can I Stop?

As you research your text in books, articles, or reference works, you will find it coalescing into a unified body of knowledge or at least into a set of interrelated questions. Your topic will become more and more focused, partly because that is where the open question, key insight, or most illuminating instance resides, and partly for sheer manageability. The vast range of scholarly methods and opinions and sharply differing points of view about most biblical texts (especially in the contemporary period) may force you to narrow your topic further. While the sources may never dry up, your increased knowledge will gradually give you confidence that you have the most informed, authoritative, and critical sources covered in your notes.

4. Developing Your Argument

On the basis of your research findings and your own interpretation of the text, in this crucial step you refine or reformulate your general interpretation into a specific question about the text answered by a defensible thesis. You then arrange or rework your supporting materials into a clear outline that will coherently and convincingly present your thesis to your reader.

First, review your research notes carefully. Some of what you initially read may now seem obvious or irrelevant, or perhaps the whole topic is simply too massive. As your reading and note taking progressed, however, you might also have found a piece of your topic, from which a key question or problem has emerged and around which your research has jelled. Ask yourself:

▶ What is the subtopic or subquestion presented by this text that is most interesting, enlightening, and manageable?

▶ Which other biblical or ancient texts surround this text, are related to it, or raise similar questions?

▶ What have been the most clarifying and illuminating insights I have found in my research?

▶ In what ways have my findings contradicted my initial expectations? Can this serve as a clue to a new and different approach to the text?

▶ Can I frame a question about this text in a clear way, and, in light of my research, do I have something specific to say and defend (that is, a thesis) that will answer my question and clarify my materials?

What is a thesis?

Most exegesis papers are *thesis-driven* papers, which is to say they are designed to articulate and defend a particular interpretive argument. In its most basic definition, a thesis is a statement or theory that is put forward as a premise to be maintained or proved. A thesis essentially answers the question: What is the focus of this essay?

In other words, a thesis-driven paper has a clear purpose and advances a specific idea. It is not a "museum tour" in which a series of interesting observations and research insights are linked together.

There is no one-size-fits-all method for writing a good thesis statement. Even still, it will be helpful to keep the following principles in mind. First, a thesis does not simply state a fact. Rather, it makes an argument. "Genesis 1 is a biblical creation account"only states a fact whereas "Genesis 1 reinterprets Babylonian creation myths in order to highlight the sovereignty of YHWH" is the beginning of an argument that could be developed and supported by evidence.

Second, your thesis should try to answer two questions: "what?" and "so what?" The answer to the first question is your interpretive observation. The answer to the second question suggests why this observations matters to the meaning of the text. For instance, the following statement primarily answers the "what?" question: "Amos 5 reinterprets the concept of the Day of the LORD as a time of judgment, not deliverance, for Israel." This is an adequate thesis, but it does not yet develop an answer to the "so what?" question. The following statement begins to bring both questions together: "By reinterpreting the Day of the LORD as a time of judgment, not deliverance, for Israel, Amos 5 heightens its critique of the sacrificial cult at Bethel during the eighth century."

Finally, a good thesis should be focused enough to be adequately supported within the parameters of your paper. The thesis statement "First Isaiah uses a variety of metaphors in order to depict the threat of the Assyrian invasion" would be too broad for most exegesis papers. You could further narrow your thesis by focusing on metaphors that involve agricultural imagery, but even this would probably be too broad. Instead, it would be better to focus on an even more specific image or text. A thesis that explored the metaphor of the ruined vineyard in Isaiah 5 would allow you to develop a more detailed and in-depth argument within the parameters of a relatively short paper.

Outlining your paper

After coming up with an appropriate thesis, your next step is to outline how you will present evidence to support your interpretive argument. Suppose your research focuses on the role of women in the book of Judges. Through reading primary and secondary sources, you might find that women are portrayed in this biblical text as tricksters who use creative means to achieve their goals, even while marginalized. You might then advance a thesis that biblical heroines such as Deborah were able to subvert their typically marginalized role in society and achieve their desired ends through innovative and even revolutionary means. So you have:

Topic: Women in the book of Judges
Specific topic: Women as tricksters in the book of Judges
Specific question: How did Deborah achieve her goals as a marginalized person in a patriarchal society?
Thesis: Deborah serves one example of the trickster type in the Bible, displaying the subversive potential of biblical women to achieve their goals.

You can then outline a presentation of your thesis that organizes your research materials into an orderly and convincing argument. Functionally, your outline might look like this:

Introduction: Raise the key question and announce your thesis.

Background: Summarize your text and present the necessary textual or historical or theological context of the question. Note the "state of the question" or the main agreements and disagreements about it.

Development: Present your own insight in a clear and logical way. Present evidence to support your thesis, and develop it further by:

- ▶ offering examples from the text itself
- ▶ pointing to related biblical or ancient texts
- ▶ citing or discussing authorities to bolster your argument
- ▶ contrasting your thesis with other treatments, either historical or contemporary
    - ▶ confirming it by showing how it makes good sense of the text, answers related questions, or solves previous puzzles.

Conclusion: Restate the thesis in a way that recapitulates your argument and its consequences for the field or the contemporary religious horizon.

The more detailed your outline, the easier your writing will be. Go through your notes, reorganizing them according to your outline. Fill in the outline with the specifics from your research, right down to the topic sentences of your paragraphs. Don't hesitate to set aside any materials that now seem off-point, extraneous, or superfluous to the development of your argument.

5. Write the First Draft

You are now ready to draft your paper, essentially by putting your outline into sentence form while incorporating specifics from your research notes.

Your main task, initially, is just to set your ideas down in as straightforward a way as possible. Assume your reader is intelligent but knows little or nothing about your particular topic or the text being discussed. You can follow your outline closely, but you may find that logical presentation of your argument requires making some adjustments to the outline. As you write, weave in quotes judiciously from primary and secondary literature to clarify or add specificity to your points. Add brief, strong headings at major junctures. Add footnotes to acknowledge ideas, attribute quotations, reinforce your key points through authorities, or refer the reader to further discussion or resources. Your draft footnotes will refer to your sources as abbreviated in your notes (be sure to include page numbers). You can add full publishing data once your text is firm.

6. Refine the Final Paper

Any accomplished writer and researcher knows that the first draft of a paper should *never* be the last draft of a paper. Arguably the most important step in writing and research comes in the revision process. Your first draft puts you within sight of your goal, but your project's real strength emerges from reworking your initial text in a series of revisions and refinements.

In this final phase, make frequent use of one of the many excellent style manuals available for help with grammar, punctuation, footnote form, abbreviations, and so forth:

▶ Alexander, Patrick H. *et al.*, eds. *The SBL Handbook of Style: For Ancient Near Eastern, Biblical, and Early Christian Studies.* Peabody, Mass.: Hendrickson, 1999.
▶ *The Chicago Manual of Style.* 15th ed. Chicago: University of Chicago Press, 2003.
▶ Turabian, Kate L. *A Manual for Writers of Term Papers, Theses, and Dissertations,* 7th ed. Rev. by Wayne C. Booth, Gregory G. Colomb, Joseph M. Williams, and the University of Chicago Press Editorial Staff. Chicago: University of Chicago Press, 2007.

Online, see the searchable website Guide to Grammar and Writing: http://grammar.ccc.commnet.edu/grammar/

Polishing the Prose

To check spelling and meaning of words or to help vary your prose, try Merriam-Webster Online, which contains both the Collegiate Dictionary and the Thesaurus: http://www.m-w.com.

Closely examine your work several times, paying attention to:

▶ Structure and Argument. Ask yourself these questions: Do I state my question and thesis accurately? Does my paper do what my introduction promised? (If not, adjust one or the other.) Do I argue my thesis well? Do the headings clearly guide the reader through my outline and argument? Does this sequence of topics orchestrate the insights my reader needs to understand my thesis?
▶ Style. "Style" here refers to writing patterns that enliven prose and engage the reader. Three simple ways to strengthen your academic prose are:

    a. Topic sentences: Be sure each paragraph clearly states its main assertion.
    b. Transition words: Be sure that your argument "flows" throughout the paper through the use of important transition words at the beginning of paragraphs.
    c. Active verbs: As much as possible, avoid using the linking verb "to be," and instead rephrase using active verbs.
    d. Sentence flow: Above all, look for awkward sentences in your draft. Disentangle and rework them into smooth, clear sequences. To avoid boring the reader, vary the length and form of your sentences. Check to see if your paragraphs unfold with questions and simple declarative sentences, in addition to longer descriptive phrases.

Likewise, tackle some stylistic quirks that frequently invade academic prose:

a. Repetition: Unless you need the word count, this can go.

b. Unnecessary words: Such filler phrases as "the fact that," "in order to," "there is," and "there are" numb your reader. Similarly, such qualifiers as "somewhat," "fairly," and "very" should be avoided unless they are part of a clearly defined comparison.

c. Jargon. Avoid technical terms when possible. Explain all technical terms that you do use. Avoid or translate foreign-language terms.

d. Overly complex sentences. Short sentences are best. Beware of run-on sentences. Avoid "etc."

e. The passive voice. It's okay (and stylistically preferable) to use "I" to express an argument or thesis rather than the passive voice or the ambiguous "we" (unless the paper is actually co-written).

Along with typographical errors, look for stealth errors—the common but overlooked grammatical gaffes: subject-verb disagreement, dangling participles, mixed verb tenses, overuse and underuse of commas, misuse of semicolons, easily confused words, and inconsistency in capitalization, hyphenation, italicization, and treatment of numbers.

Footnotes

Your footnotes credit your sources for every direct quotation and for other people's ideas you have used. Below are samples of typical citation formats following the Chicago Manual of Style. (For a basic summary of Chicago Manual of Style, visit http://www.chicagomanualofstyle.org/tools_citationguide.html)

Basic order

Author's full name, *Book Title,* ed., trans., series, edition, vol. number (Place: Publisher, year), pages.

Book

Amy Kalmanofsky, *Dangerous Sisters of the Hebrew Bible* (Minneapolis: Fortress Press, 2014), 101–118.

Book in a series

Marcus J. Borg, *Conflict, Holiness, and Politics in the Teaching of Jesus*, Studies in the Bible and Early Christianity 5 (Toronto: Edwin Mellen, 1984), 1–2.

Essay or chapter in an edited book

Yak-Hwee Tan, "The Johannine Community," in *Soundings in Cultural Criticism*, ed. Francisco Lozada Jr. and Greg Carey (Minneapolis: Fortress Press, 2013), 84–85.

Multivolume work

Karl Rahner, "On the Theology of Hope," *Theological Investigations*, vol. 10 (New York: Herder and Herder, 1973), 250.

JOURNAL ARTICLE

Joan B. Burton, "Women's Commensality in the Ancient Greek World," *Greece and Rome* 45, no. 2 (October 1998): 144.

ENCYCLOPEDIA ARTICLE

Hans-Josef Klauck, "Lord's Supper," *The Anchor Bible Dictionary,* ed. David Noel Freedman, vol. 2 (New York: Doubleday, 1992), 275.

ONLINE JOURNAL ARTICLE

Pamela Sue Anderson, "The Case for a Feminist Philosophy of Religion: Transforming Philosophy's Imagery and Myths," *Ars Disputandi* 1 (2000/2001); http://www.arsdisputandi.org.

CITING THE BIBLE

Cite in your text (not in your footnotes) by book, chapter, and verse: Gen. 1:1-2; Exod. 7:13; Rom. 5:1-8. In your Bibliography list the version of the Bible you have used.

If a footnote cites the immediately preceding source, use "Ibid." (from the Latin *ibidem*, meaning "there"). For example: 61. Ibid., 39.

Sources cited earlier can be referred to by author or editor's last name (or last names), a shorter title, and page number. For example: Burton, "Women's Commensality," 145.

Bibliography

Your bibliography can be any of several types:

▶ Works Cited: just the works—books, articles, and so forth—that appear in your footnotes
▶ Works Consulted: all the works you checked in your research, whether they were cited or not in the final draft
▶ Select Bibliography: primary and secondary works that, in your judgment, are the most important source materials on this topic, whether cited or not in your footnotes

Some teachers might ask for your bibliographic entries to be annotated, that is, with a comment from you on the content, import, approach, and helpfulness of each work.

Bibliographic style differs somewhat from footnote style. Here are samples of typical bibliographic formats following CMS:

BASIC ORDER

Author's last name, first name and initial. *Book Title.* Ed. Trans. Series. Edition. Vol. Place: Publisher, Year.

Book

Kalmanofsky, Amy. *Dangerous Sisters of the Hebrew Bible*. Minneapolis: Fortress Press, 2014.

Book in a series

Borg, Marcus J. *Conflict, Holiness, and Politics in the Teaching of Jesus*. Studies in the Bible and Early Christianity 5. Toronto: Edwin Mellen, 1984.

Essay or chapter in an edited book

Tan, Yak-Hwee. "The Johannine Community." In *Soundings in Cultural Criticism*. Ed. Francisco Lozada Jr. and Greg Carey. Minneapolis: Fortress Press, 2013.

Multivolume work

Rahner, Karl. "On the Theology of Hope." In Theological Investigations, vol. 10. New York: Herder and Herder, 1973.

Journal article

Burton, Joan B. "Women's Commensality in the Ancient Greek World." *Greece and Rome* 45, no. 2 (October 1998): 143–65.

Encyclopedia article

Klauck, Hans-Josef. "Lord's Supper." *The Anchor Bible Dictionary*. Ed. David Noel Freedman. Vol. 2. New York: Doubleday, 1992.

Online journal article

Anderson, Pamela Sue. "The Case for a Feminist Philosophy of Religion: Transforming Philosophy's Imagery and Myths." *Ars Disputandi* 1 (2000/2001); http://www.arsdisputandi.org.

Citing the Bible

The Holy Bible: Revised Standard Version. New York: Oxford University Press, 1973.

Final Steps

After incorporating the revisions and refinements into your paper, print out a fresh copy, proofread it carefully, make your last corrections to the electronic file, format it to your teacher's or school's specifications, and print your final paper.